T0355191

The Last Kings of Macedonia and the Triumph of Rome

The Last Kings of Macedonia and the Triumph of Rome

IAN WORTHINGTON

OXFORD

UNIVERSITY PRESS

OXFORD
UNIVERSITY PRESS

Oxford University Press is a department of the University of Oxford. It furthers
the University's objective of excellence in research, scholarship, and education
by publishing worldwide. Oxford is a registered trade mark of Oxford University
Press in the UK and certain other countries.

Published in the United States of America by Oxford University Press
198 Madison Avenue, New York, NY 10016, United States of America.

© Oxford University Press 2023

CIP data is on file at the Library of Congress

ISBN 978–0–19–752005–5

DOI: 10.1093/oso/9780197520055.001.0001

Printed by Sheridan Books, Inc., United States of America

in memoriam
Tim (T.T.B.) Ryder
who first introduced me to Greek history
and who was the proverbial scholar and gentleman

Contents

List of Figures

List of Maps

Preface

THIS BOOK IS a history and reassessment of the last three kings of ancient Macedonia: Philip V (r. 221–179), his son Perseus (r. 179–168), and the pretender Andriscus, also called Philip VI (r. 149–148). Their names are not as immediately recognizable as predecessors like Philip II (r. 359–336) and Alexander the Great (r. 336–323), and by the time Philip V came to the throne the heyday of Macedonia as an imperial power under Alexander was long over. Yet their reigns underpin one of the more important periods in antiquity: the rise of Roman dominion in the east. All three kings were at war with Rome, for which ancient writers denounced them for flawed policies, disreputable personal qualities, and rashness, so that their reigns are seen as postscripts to Macedonian history and subsumed within the history of Roman expansion.

Certainly, these three kings are not the household names that their illustrious predecessors are, nor did they forge or maintain a vast, overseas empire, as had Alexander. But they were far from being a postscript to Macedonia's Classical greatness or merely collateral damage in Rome's rise in the east. Philip and Perseus deserve credit as they often had the upper hand in their wars against Rome and had to contend with hostile eastern powers and Greeks south of Mount Olympus.

Rather than appraising each king individually, this book—the first full-scale treatment of Philip V in eighty years and the first in English of Perseus and Andriscus in over fifty—discusses them together to argue that they and the period deserve to be rated more highly. They fought to preserve their kingdom's independence and standing in the Greek world, no matter the odds against them, and so deserve to be center stage in Macedonia's, not just Rome's, history.

It is my pleasure to thank once again Stefan Vranka for his support and feedback and all the admirable staff at Oxford University Press who saw the book through production.

I am indebted to Monica D'Agostini, Joseph Roisman, and Robin Waterfield for generously agreeing to read an earlier draft of the book: their sharp and precise comments improved greatly what they had to read.

My thanks also go to the anonymous Oxford University Press referees for equally excellent remarks and for thinking the book has merit.

I am grateful to Monica D'Agostini for sending me a copy of her book on Philip V when access to libraries was impossible; my excellent colleague Danijel Dzino for chats about Illyria; Yuri Kuzmin for setting me straight about Philip's mother; Robin Waterfield for some needed personal photos of the Aous Gorge, Cynoscephalae, and Pydna sites; and Albert Nguyen for graciously granting his permission to reuse his drawing of the frieze on the Paullus monument at Delphi. As well, I thank Angela Abberton for the thankless task of checking many ancient references and Sarah Plant for the equally herculean task of compiling the index.

I am obliged to Macquarie University for granting me OSP leave in the second semester 2020, which allowed me to finish a second draft of the book and make substantial progress on another.

My deep regret is that the dedicatee of this book did not live to see it. I knew Tim Ryder, who died in October 2021, for forty-five years since my undergraduate days at Hull (1976–1979), and we kept in good contact since I left there. He inspired in me a love for Greek history, which shows no sign of abating, and for that I thank him.

Last but certainly not least, I thank my family for being there.

Ian Worthington
Macquarie University
October 2022

List of Abbreviations

BNJ   *Brill's New Jacoby* (*Jacoby Online*), numerous ancient writers prepared by modern scholars, editor-in-chief Ian Worthington (Leiden: 2003–)

IG   *Inscriptiones Graecae*, many volumes with different editors (Berlin: 1873–)

ISE   *Iscrizioni storiche ellenistiche*, 2 vols., editor L. Moretti (Florence: 1967–75)

SEG   *Supplementum Epigraphicum Graecum*, many volumes, various editors (Leiden: 1923–)

SIG³   *Sylloge Inscriptionum Graecarum*, 4 vols., editor W. Dittenberger (Leipizg: 1915–24)

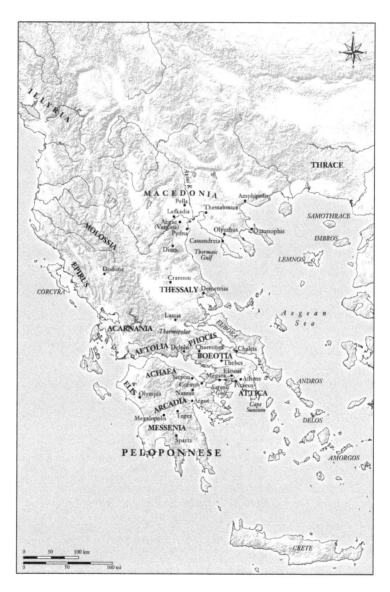

MAP 1. Overview: Greece and the Balkans. Reproduced from Ian Worthington, *Ptolemy I: King and Pharaoh of Egypt*, Oxford University Press, 2016.

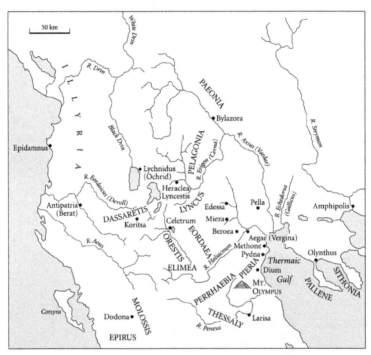

MAP 2. Macedonia. Reproduced from Ian Worthington, *Athens After Empire: A History from Alexander the Great to the Emperor Hadrian*, Oxford University Press, 2021.

MAP 3. Macedonia and Illyria. Reproduced from N.G.L. Hammond and F.W. Walbank, *A History of Macedonia*, vol. 3, Oxford University Press, 1988.

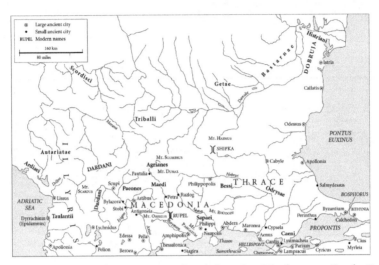

MAP 4. Macedonia and Thrace. Reproduced from Ian Worthington, *By the Spear: Philip II, Alexander the Great, and the Rise and Fall of the Macedonian Empire*, Oxford University Press, 2014.

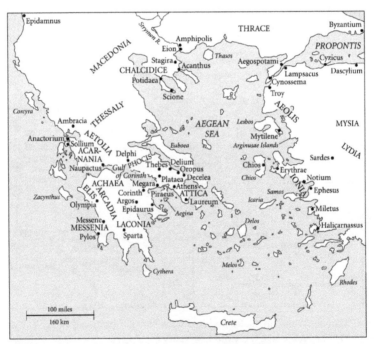

MAP 5. Greece and the Aegean. Reproduced from Ian Worthington, *Athens After Empire: A History from Alexander the Great to the Emperor Hadrian*, Oxford University Press, 2021.

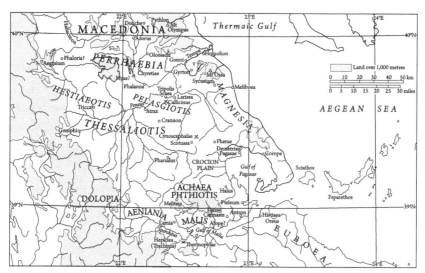

MAP 6. Thessaly. Reproduced from P.J. Burton, *Rome and the Third Macedonian War*, Cambridge University Press, 2017. Reproduced with permission of The Licensor through PLSclear.

MAP 7. The Peloponnese. Reproduced from N.G.L. Hammond and F.W. Walbank, *A History of Macedonia*, vol. 3, Oxford University Press, 1988.

Introduction

WE THREE KINGS

THIS BOOK IS a study of the last three kings of ancient Macedonia, north of Mount Olympus in Greece: Philip V (r. 221–179), his son Perseus (r. 179–168), and the pretender Andriscus, also called Philip VI (r. 149–148). They are not the household names that their distinguished predecessors Philip II (r. 359–336) and Alexander the Great (r. 336–323) are, in both antiquity and today.[1] Philip II laid the foundations of a Macedonian empire that, thanks to Alexander, stretched from Greece to India. By the time Philip V came to the throne in 221, a little over a century after Alexander's death, Macedonia no longer had an empire, and a new power in the Mediterranean was emerging: Rome. And by the end of Andriscus' reign the Macedonian monarchy was no more, and Greece was part of the Roman Empire.

Still, the reigns of the last three kings underpin an important period in antiquity: the rise of Roman dominion in the east. Yet they are routinely denounced for self-serving ambitions, flawed policies, unsavory personal qualities, and even foolhardiness that led to their defeats at Roman hands and the eventual absorption of Greece into the Roman Empire. They are viewed as postscripts to the kingdom's heyday and even folded into the history of Roman expansion in the east. These views are far from true as I show in this book, at the same time placing these kings more center stage in Macedonia's, not just Rome's, history.

Philip V was one of the more colorful characters of the period. He seems to have striven the most to emulate Philip II, Alexander the Great, Demetrius

---

1. On them, see, for example, Worthington 2014.

The Last Kings of Macedonia and the Triumph of Rome. Ian Worthington, Oxford University Press.
© Oxford University Press 2023. DOI: 10.1093/oso/9780197520055.003.0001

I Poliorcetes ("the besieger"), and Pyrrhus of Epirus, all dynamic rulers, always to be found in the thick of battle, and demonstrating strategic skills, decisiveness, speed of execution, and daring. Perseus also showed similar qualities and did well for his kingdom, though his entanglement with Rome dominated his reign too much. Andriscus, king for only one year, was not on the throne long enough to achieve anything substantial, but his reign bookends what Philip II had begun in the 350s.

All three kings were at war with Rome. Yet despite Roman manpower and resources always putting them at a disadvantage, Philip and Perseus many times had the upper hand in their conflicts and won victories over Roman troops. In the end, they were routed by Roman armies, with the Senate imposing settlements on Macedonia and finally turning it into a province after Andriscus' downfall in 147. If the Macedonians under Philip II and Alexander enjoyed being an imperial power, those under the later monarchs must surely have had heavy hearts at their situation.[2]

When Philip V became king, the Antigonid dynasty—starting with Antigonus I Monophthalmus ("the one-eyed") at the tail end of the fourth century—was well established. But Antigonid kings faced a different world from rulers of the previous dynasty, the Argead (which had ruled since the early eighth century), especially Philip II and Alexander. Philip had turned the kingdom from a backwater on the periphery of the Greek world into a formidable military and economic power, in the process establishing Macedonian hegemony over the Greeks. Alexander had inherited his father's plan to invade Asia and in a spectacular decade-long campaign toppled the Persian Empire and extended Macedonian sway—albeit briefly—as far east as what the Greeks called India (present-day Pakistan).

On Alexander's death in 323, however, his senior staff divided up his empire and then waged war against each other for forty years for greater slices of territory, eventually (in 306) calling themselves kings. When the "Wars of the Successors" were over in 280, the Hellenistic-era kingdoms of Seleucid Syria and Ptolemaic Egypt had formed, and Antigonid Macedonia and Greece were not far behind.

But Macedonia's hold on Greece was never as strong as under Philip II and Alexander. The reasons are several. Those two monarchs never had to deal with two powerful leagues, the Achaean (in the northern Peloponnese) and Aetolian (in central Greece), which defied Macedonian power. In addition,

---

2. Macedonians under Philip II and Alexander: Worthington 2014, pp. 105–109.

there were the defiance and eventual independence of Athens in 229. In the Hellenistic period (323–30) Athens was no longer the military, economic, or even cultural powerhouse it had been in the Classical age (478–323), yet it was still a force with which to be reckoned and coveted by Antigonid and other Hellenistic rulers.[3] Finally, from the early third century onward Rome played a role in Greek affairs, among other things encouraging cities to fight Macedonia and waging war on the kingdom no fewer than four times.

Some Antigonid kings worked to promote Macedonia's standing in Greece but were plagued by the belligerent activities of the Aetolian League and issues with border security, especially on the northwestern border with Illyria. In contrast to the days of the Argead dynasty, Rome had a "protectorate" of cities in a part of Illyria called Illyris, abutting western Macedonia, in what is now Albania and Dalmatia. On top of that, the Dardanians, an aggressive Illyrian tribe to Macedonia's north, were a frequent menace to the kingdom and invaded parts of it. Thus, Antigonid kings had to contend with a Roman presence in Illyria, the need to protect their borders, and a severely compromised relationship with the Greeks. We trace all these issues and how they were dealt with in more detail in later chapters.

Philip V therefore faced many threats when he assumed the throne and decided to do something about them once and for all. Unfortunately, our ancient literary writers are openly hostile to Philip and Perseus, as noted throughout this book and in the appendix. Besides denigrating their characters and moral worth, ancient literary writers accuse Philip of the grandiose intentions of invading Italy to attack Rome and eventually achieve world dominion. They see a treaty he made with the Carthaginian general Hannibal in 215, when the Romans were embroiled in the Second Punic War against Carthage (218–201), as evidence of an anti-Roman offensive. They also claim that toward the end of his reign Philip was planning a war against Rome, which his son Perseus inherited, thereby showing the latter's animosity to Rome. Their view is echoed by some modern scholars when writing of these kings and the period.

Those views are wrong. Philip was never able to invade Italy because he lacked a strong war fleet. More than that, his focus was on safeguarding his borders, with Perseus following suit. To this end, both kings aimed at reversing Macedonia's weak position in Greece, and Philip was especially intent on confronting the Romans' involvement in Illyria.

---

3. See Worthington 2021a.

Philip II had overcome the Illyrians in 358, even integrating them into the organization of Macedonia and deploying them in his army. Even so, he was constantly worried by the security of his northwest border. In the 350s he founded a series of cities along it, populated by people he moved from other parts of his kingdom, to maintain its strength and defend it if need be. Later, when some cities in Illyria came under Rome's protection, and Roman troops began to operate there, Macedonia was placed in a perilous position. The Illyrian factor, to call it that, explains Philip's alliance with Hannibal. Only after Philip was defeated at the battle of Cynoscephalae in 197 was he forced to abandon attempts to regain Illyria.

Likewise, all kings were always concerned about their southern border with Thessaly, through which an invading army had easy access into Macedonia. Philip and Perseus went to great lengths to ensure good relations with Thessaly, and even control of it. They worked to restore confidence in them among the Greeks, and also to offset any danger from enemy armies landing on the mainland and joining forces with hostile Greek cities. Again, their reasoning was all to do with keeping their borders safe. After Cynoscephalae, Philip conducted a series of campaigns in Thrace. These were not to try to establish some sort of Balkan empire but this time to protect his eastern border, something in which Perseus also put great stock. And it was for border protection that Philip was planning another operation against the troublesome Dardanians when he died: this operation was what Perseus inherited, not a war against Rome as our ancient writers would have it. Thus, castigated like his father for daring to defy Rome, Perseus also deserves rehabilitation. No matter what he did or did not do, he was in the Senate's crosshairs from the moment he became king.

The time is ripe for this book. All three kings feature in numerous general histories and more focused treatments of the Hellenistic period and Romano-Greek affairs. Principal among these are E. Gruen, *The Hellenistic World and the Coming of Rome* (1984); A.M. Eckstein, *Rome Enters the Greek East: From Anarchy to Hierarchy in the Hellenistic Mediterranean, 230–170 BC* (2008); and F. Camia, *Roma e le poleis. L'intervento di Roma nelle controversie territoriali tra le communità greche di Grecia e di Asia minore nell II secolo c. C.* (2009). To these we can add M.B. Hatzopoulos, *Macedonian Institutions under the Kings*, 2 vols. (1996), which as the title shows is vital for any study of Macedonian history and organization. And then there is the third volume of the monumental *History of Macedonia* by N.G.L. Hammond and F.W. Walbank (1988), with their brilliant accounts of Philip on pp. 367–487 and Perseus on pp. 488–558. I have more to say about these two scholars below.

Actual biographies can be counted on one hand and are well out of date. In the case of Philip, we have only F.W. Walbank's *Philip V of Macedon*, which was published in 1940 but is still indispensable. More recently, M. D'Agostini's *The Rise of Philip V: Kingship and Rule in the Hellenistic World* (2019), though not a biography, uses Philip's earlier years (229–212) as a model to study Hellenistic kingship and contains many incisive comments on Philip and his relations with his inner circle.

Perseus enjoys two biographies: P. Meloni's magisterial *Perseo e la Fine della Monarchia Macedonia*, published in 1953, and P.G. Gyioka's *Perseus, ho teleutaios basileus ton Makedonon* of 1975 (in Greek), both of which are inaccessible to an English-only reading audience. More recently, there is P.J. Burton's excellent *Rome and the Third Macedonian War* (Cambridge: 2017). Although written from the Roman viewpoint, Burton treats Perseus' reign in some detail as well as addressing the last years of Philip V.

I am indebted to everyone from whose works I have learned so much in writing this book. But two influential figures stand out, both deceased: Nick Hammond and Frank Walbank. Rereading their work (and in some cases reading several things for the first time) brought home again their total mastery of the source material, history, and topography, especially Hammond, who personally walked so much of Greece in his life. These great scholars will never be equaled, and my debt to their work is evident on every page of this book.

Now, a word of warning, so to speak. My book is not a historiographical study of the sources on Philip and Perseus, especially Polybius' literary study, on which much has already been written (especially by Walbank). Those who find my treatment of the bias of Polybius and Livy or the survey of our sources in the appendix unsophisticated are directed to the works cited in the notes. Nor is this a book about Roman politics or the reasons for the growth of Roman imperialism in the east: I bring these aspects into my narrative only when they pertain to Macedonia. Again, readers wishing to know more about Roman history should consult the works cited in the notes.

All translations are from the Loeb Classical Library except where indicated. All dates and references to centuries are BC except where indicated.

I

The Kingdom of Macedonia

PHILIP AND PERSEUS were members of the Antigonid dynasty, taking its name from Antigonus I Monophthalmus (the "one-eyed"), one of Alexander the Great's Successors, who shot to power in the aftermath of Alexander's death in 323. In antiquity the area called Macedonia lay north of Mount Olympus, the home of the Olympian gods and at 9,461 feet (2,883 meters) Greece's tallest mountain. Because of this geography, the "Macedonians," who were almost certainly Greeks and Greek-speaking, as we discuss below, lived independently of their Greek neighbors south of Olympus. Throughout this book, when I speak of "Macedonians" I mean the people living north of the mountain and "Greeks" as those living south of it, as well as on the islands and coast of Asia Minor.

Land and People

Macedonia was never a static region in the sense of having clearly defined borders that seldom changed over time. Rather like Rome, the Macedonian kingdom grew from relatively small beginnings to an imperial power under Alexander the Great, and then declined dramatically in size after his death in 323 until finally, in 168, Rome turned Macedonia into a province.[1]

---

1. On ancient Macedonia, its history, and people, see the essays in Roisman and Worthington 2010 and Lane Fox 2011a, with Cloché 1960; Daskalakis 1965; Hammond 1972; Hammond and Griffith 1979; Hammond and Walbank 1988; Kalléris 1988; Hammond 1992; Hatzopoulos 1996; Hatzopoulos 2020.

Macedonia was a rugged mountainous region, which made travel and communications within it difficult (maps 1 and 2).[2] There were only a few passes through its mountains, and the Pindus range effectively split the kingdom into two parts: Upper Macedonia to the west and Lower Macedonia to the east (map 2).[3] Lower Macedonia—with its original centers of Olympus; Pieria; the plain of Emathia and Bottiaea; and the areas of Amphaxitis, Crestonia, Mygdonia, Bisaltia, Crousis, and Anthemus—reached to the Thermaic Gulf and the Strymon River. Its temperate climate and rich soil (in contrast to Upper Macedonia) enabled the people to grow cereal crops, vegetables, grapes, and fruits and graze sheep, goats, cattle, and horses.

Upper Macedonia was made up of the originally semi-autonomous kingdoms of Elimiotis in the south, Orestis to the west, and Lyncestis to the northwest, by Lake Lychnitis, together with cantons such as Tymphaea, Eordaea, Lyncus, Pelagonia, and Derriopus.[4] For much of their earlier history they comprised mostly nomadic peoples, who moved their flocks and herds to Lower Macedonia for pasturage. They were ruled by individual chieftains, who felt little allegiance to the king. Yet archaeology has shown the region had major urban settlements, as at Aiani in Elimiotis. By Philip V's time most of its people were likely farmers and had a high standard of living and culture as the remains of large public buildings and elaborate grave goods reveal.[5]

Macedonia was surrounded by different tribal regions, of which the most threatening was Illyria to its north and west (maps 1–3).[6] Illyria did not have static borders, and its people were divided into several tribes, of which the Dardanians to the far north posed the biggest danger to Macedonian kings.[7] Philip II (whom we discuss in the next chapter) had defeated the Illyrians in 358, but they continued to give him trouble, forcing him in the mid-350s to build a series of military outposts along his northwest frontier for protection. As a result, all subsequent kings strove to ensure that their borders were secure

---

2. Geographical description: Hammond 1972, pp. 3–211; Borza 1990, pp. 28–50; Hatzopoulos 1996, vol. 1, pp. 167–216; Thomas 2010; Hatzopoulos 2011a; Hatzopoulos 2020, pp. 4–48; see also Edson 1970; Sivignon 1983.

3. Herodotus 7.173.4 and 8.137–139; Thucydides 2.99.1.

4. See Xydopoulos 2012.

5. See the chapters on cities in Lane Fox 2011a for archaeological finds.

6. On the Illyrians: Wilkes 1995; Ceka 2013; Dzino 2010; see too Hammond 1966a; Hammond 1968; Dell 1970; Dell 1977; Cabanes 1993; Greenwalt 2010.

7. On the different Illyrian tribes, their locales, and their organizations, see Papazoglou 1978; Dzino 2010; cf. Wilkes 1995, pp. 94–104; Hammond 1966a, pp. 239–245; Greenwalt 2010.

from Illyrian invasions; on the domestic front, Illyria would be the biggest worry for Philip and Perseus, especially as there was considerable Roman influence in it by their time.

East of Illyria were the Paeonians of the Axius Valley, conquered by Philip in 358, but who still posed a danger if they decided to march south.[8] To the east of the kingdom was Thrace, which Philip II had absorbed into Macedonia's growing empire in the 340s (maps 4 and 5).[9] To the southwest was the wealthy and largely independent kingdom of Epirus, home to the Oracle of Zeus at Dodona. Philip II had forged strong ties with the ruling dynasty, but these fluctuated under the Antigonid kings (maps 1 and 2).[10] Philip V and Perseus always maintained good contacts with the Epirotes in case of Illyrian attacks. Still, the Macedonians' stance toward these and other peoples was that they were "of dubious loyalty and unstable character."[11]

South of Mount Olympus lay Greece (maps 1 and 5). There, cities like Athens and Thebes had a long history of hostility with the Argead and Antigonid dynasties, though by the latter's time the Greeks' military capabilities were a shadow of what they had been in the Classical era. Directly bordering on Macedonia was Thessaly, which afforded easy access into the southernmost cantons of the kingdom and beyond (maps 1, 5 and 6).[12] There had been diplomatic contacts between Macedonia and Thessaly for some centuries, but it had become part of Philip II's growing empire when he had conquered all Greece in 338 at the battle of Chaeronea.[13] Over the years Thessaly had worked to regain its independence but given its strategic location—access to Macedonia for any invading army from the south—the Antigonid kings were always careful to maintain good relations with, if not control, this important buffer region.[14]

The Macedonians were tough people. All boys, including those of the royal family, were subjected to the same training regimen from an early age of fighting, riding, and hunting, and a focus on excelling continued even in

---

8. Paeonians: Merker 1965.

9. Thrace: Archibald 1998; cf. Archibald 2010.

10. Hammond 1967 is still the standard work; cf. Cabanes 1993; Greenwalt 2010.

11. Justin 11.1.1–6.

12. Graninger 2010.

13. Battle: Worthington 2008, pp. 147–151; Worthington 2014, pp. 85–90.

14. Two letters of Philip V to Larissa (dated 217) show the control that kings had over Thessaly: Austin 2006, no. 75, pp. 157–159. I neglect to mention the Chalcidice, which was more of a threat for earlier Argead kings: see, for example, Psoma 2011.

adulthood—no man, for example, could recline at a banquet until he had killed a ferocious wild boar without using a net to trap it, and a soldier had to wear a rope or sash around his waist until he had killed his first man in battle. While Macedonia was not as militaristic a society as Sparta, its army was the backbone of the state, as we shall see—the Spartan mother who famously told her son as he set off to battle to come back carrying his shield or on it could just as easily have been a Macedonian mother.[15]

The Greeks called the Macedonians "barbarians," which had nothing to do with a lack of culture, as we might assume, but was a term they used of people speaking a different language. Yet even though aspects of social customs, beliefs, and political systems made the Macedonians seem worlds apart from the Greeks at times, they were surely Greek-speaking.[16] Among other things, archaeological evidence such as inscriptions and coins is all in Greek; Macedonian proper names are Greek; and the correct term for the people— "Makedones"—is a Greek word and may have meant "highlanders." Equally telling is the similarity between Macedonian and Greek religion, for the Macedonians were polytheistic, revering in particular Zeus, Dionysus, and Heracles, to whom kings traced their lineage.[17] Most likely, given the various tribes on their borders, the Macedonians spoke a dialect of Greek, but it was different enough to make it seem like another language, which the Greeks could not understand.[18]

There were also social and religious differences between the Macedonians and Greeks. These included the Macedonians drinking their wine neat (*akratos*) rather than watering it down, as did the Greeks.[19] As a result at symposia (drinking parties) they were often drunk "while they were still being served the first course and could not enjoy their food," and alcohol-fueled boasting at boisterous parties led to actual fights.[20] Also, the people or at least their kings were polygamists. Kings often married for political and military reasons as well as to continue their dynasty, despite succession issues arising

---

15. For this and other "sayings of Spartan women," see Plutarch, *Moralia* 240c–242d.

16. Ethnicity: Hatzopoulos 1996, vol. 1, pp. 167–209; Engels 2010; Hatzopoulos 2011a; Hatzopoulos 2011b; Hatzopoulos 2020, pp. 49–124.

17. See for example Christesen and Murray 2010; Mari 2011; see too Hatzopoulos 1994a; Hatzopoulos 2020, pp. 79–88. On Greek religion, see Mikalson 2005.

18. See now Hatzopoulos 2020, pp. 63–69.

19. Social customs: Sawada 2010.

20. Ephippus, *BNJ* 126 F 1 = Athenaeus 3.120e.

from multiple heirs.[21] Philip II, for example, married seven times without ever divorcing a wife and was said to have "made war by marriage."[22] Their queens appear to have had equal status and lived with the king in the palace at Pella (figure 1.1a–b). Evidently not every wife was willing to share her husband or perhaps to coexist amicably with another wife: when Philip V's father Demetrius II married Phthia of Epirus his current wife Stratonice of Syria soon went back home (p. 27).

Kingship and Organization

Macedonia's original capital was Aegae (modern Vergina). However, King Archelaus (413–399) established a new one at Pella, northwest of the Thermaic Gulf on a branch of the Loudias River. His reasons were mostly strategic and economic: the site of Pella commanded a panoramic view over the plain and Lake Loudias in case of an enemy strike, and the mountains behind it were a natural obstacle.[23] It also had easy access to the Thermaic Gulf as in antiquity Pella was coastal; nowadays, because of silting sea over the centuries, it is about 22 miles (35 kilometers) inland. Aegae did not fall into ruin, however; it was an important secondary royal residence with a large and splendid palace and a theater for cultural life as well as being the venue for royal weddings and funerals.[24]

The military and economic nuclei of the kingdom were the cities, many of which were originally independent and Greek, such as Pydna and Amphipolis, and which were integrated into the kingdom under Philip II and changed into Macedonian ones.[25] Archaeology shows cities were of varying sizes, carefully laid out, often located on overland routes such as Dium and Pella, and had fortification walls.[26] The various city officials charged with the day-to-day administration were appointed by the people and were headed by the *epistates*

---

21. See Greenwalt 1989, for example.

22. Satyrus, quoted in Athenaeus 13.557b–e; cf. 13.560c.

23. See, further, Borza 1990, pp. 166–171; Greenwalt 1999.

24. See Drougou 2011 and Kottaridi 2011.

25. On the organization of Macedonia and cities see the succinct discussion of Hammond and Walbank 1988, pp. 474–485, with Kahrstedt 1953, especially Papazoglou 1988; Hatzopoulos 1996, e.g., vol. 1, pp. 51–123 (locations, populations, nature) and 129–165 (political and civic institutions); cf. Hatzopoulos 2015 and the chapters on various cities in Lane Fox 2011a.

26. Papazoglou 1988; Hatzopoulos, 1996, e.g., vol. 1, pp. 51–104; cf. Hammond and Walbank 1988, pp. 477–482.

FIGURE 1.1 a–b. Pella. Photo credit: Ian Worthington.

(overseer). Although this person had some freedom in local affairs he was ultimately under the authority of the king, especially when it came to matters of religion, warfare, and foreign policy.[27]

---

27. Autonomy of cities and local communities: Hatzopoulos, 1996, vol. 1, pp. 365–460. On various local officials: Hatzopoulos, 1996, vol. 1, pp. 149–165 (with pp. 372–424 on the *epistates*),

The cities in Lower Macedonia had populations engaged in agriculture and cattle, and Philip V, as we shall see, added Thracian and other workers to them to help strengthen the economy. Those on the coast engaged in maritime trade, which increased greatly in Philip's reign, as did the three largest ports of Pella, Thessalonica, and Amphipolis, which even issued their own coinage.[28] In Upper Macedonia the cities (many being new foundations with a mix of Macedonians and non-Macedonians) also played a valuable role in the economy, stimulating agriculture and trade as well as reinforcing defenses.

For three centuries Macedonia was ruled by kings of the Argead dynasty, founded most likely by Perdiccas I in the early eighth century. Although a king had great powers, it was really his personal authority that enabled him to rule and make policy. The Antigonid kings, with whom we are concerned, had more checks and balances on their power, while still having the final say in most matters.

Argead kings may have been one-half of what we might call a constitution.[29] The monarch was often simply referred to by name by those addressing him and on official documents, but at times our sources put *basileus* (king) before a name.[30] An autocrat, he oversaw domestic and foreign policy, was chief priest in the kingdom, and had the right to make treaties and declare war, during which time he was commander of the army.[31] He also owned all his kingdom's natural resources, but these were not properly exploited until Philip II's reign.[32] Kings often had little liquid capital, and practiced a "rolling economy," funding the next campaign from the proceeds of the previous one.[33] It is also possible that Macedonian kings were worshipped after death, possibly even in their lifetime, as part of a ruler cult.[34]

---

and more wider ranging see vol. 1, pp. 47–216, 259–269, 372–429; Hatzopoulos 2015. The king communicated directly with his officials by, for example, royal letter or the more impersonal order or resolution (*diagramma*); Hatzopoulos 1996, vol. 1, pp. 396–429; cf. Welles 1938, pp. 255–260.

28. Hammond and Walbank 1988, p. 476, with n. 6.

29. Hammond 1992, pp. 391–395; Hatzopoulos 1996, vol. 1, pp. 219–260; King 2010. But against this, see on the monarchy Anson 1985a; Anson 1991.

30. On nomenclature see Errington 1974a; Papazoglou 1983.

31. Hatzopoulos 1996, vol. 2, nos. 23–35 (cf. nos. 64–81 for dedications by city and other officials, sometimes linking king to a god).

32. Natural resources: Borza 1982; cf. Hammond 1992, pp. 177–187.

33. See, further, Millett 2010.

34. Mari 2008; Mari 2011, p. 458.

Powerful noble Macedonians did lead factions at court, but while the king was careful in his cultivation of relations with his nobles they needed his goodwill, and everyone knew that. In the Hellenistic period the kings' advisers were known as "friends" or *philoi* (an official title even with subdivisions, such as "first friends"), who replaced the factionalism of individual nobles.[35] A king could turn to these men for advice, but he need not heed it.

It has often been assumed that an Assembly of male citizens existed, which could make decisions and provide advice to the king though he was free to ignore it. Among other things, this Assembly judged treason cases (in which the king was the final judge), decided a regent if the heir was a minor, and acclaimed the next king.[36] But it is unlikely that a king shared any of his powers with the Assembly, and even its existence has been queried.[37] Certainly, Philip V did not turn to such a body, and he even discussed the trials of his advisers with his friends (*philoi*), though since these guardians were influential he may have felt the need to ensure the loyalty of all his *philoi*.[38]

The king and his subjects enjoyed a close social relationship. Both attended symposia and hunted together, turning both into quasi-political events.[39] Religious festivals, with athletic, theatrical, and musical competitions, took on a political slant as they were also opportunities for king and people to come together. Like his subjects the king preferred a simple style of clothing, such as a purple cloak and the distinctive, wide-brimmed felt hat known as the *kausia*, and he ate plain meals. One of the reasons why Alexander the Great's troops grew discontented with him was because he dressed lavishly, enjoyed perfumes and scented oils, and so became less of a warrior king. Philip and Perseus were careful never to fall into that trap.

Artistic and Cultural Life

Macedonian kings were intellectuals, and some had courts that were cultural centers of sorts. Archelaus (r. 413–399), for example, invited Socrates and the

---

35. Hatzopoulos 1996, vol. 1, pp. 334–336.

36. Hatzopoulos 1996, vol. 1, pp. 260–322; see too King 2010. Judicial: Anson 2008. Regency and age: Hatzopoulos 1986, but see LeBohec 1993 that the age for kings was twenty.

37. Anson 1985a; Anson 1991.

38. I thank Monica D'Agostini for pointing out to me the importance of Philip discussing his trials with his friends.

39. Cf. Anson 1991; Carney 2002.

Athenian tragic playwrights Agathon and Euripides to Pella, where Euripides wrote the *Bacchae* and the (now fragmentary) *Archelaus*, and he may have died there in 406. Perdiccas III (r. 368–359) was a patron of Plato's Academy, Philip II enjoyed meaningful exchanges with the Athenian orator Isocrates and Speusippus (Plato's successor at the Academy) and hired Aristotle to tutor his son Alexander from age fourteen to sixteen. The latter was a precocious child, by all accounts reading all Greek literature as a young boy and settling on Homer and Euripides as his favorites. When he invaded Asia in 334, he took with him a retinue that included philosophers, artists, and musicians. Antigonus II Gonatas (r. 277–239) studied in Athens in his youth under Zeno, the founder of Stoicism, and invited various intellectuals to his court.[40] We have no reason to think Philip V and Perseus would not have been as intellectually curious as their predecessors, and both were certainly philhellenes or "lovers of all things Greek."

Our knowledge of the cultural and daily lives of the Macedonians derives almost entirely from archaeology, which has revealed impressive theaters, tombs, and large and luxurious palaces. The existence of theaters, some quite large as at Aegae and Pella, show that people enjoyed dramatic entertainment—otherwise Archelaus would hardly have invited Agathon and Euripides to his court. The theaters could also hold processions—it was at one in the summer of 336 in Aegae that Philip II was assassinated.[41] Cities also had agoras or marketplaces of varying sizes. While not for entertainment, they give us another glimpse into a busy and flourishing city life, where people would go to trade and, perhaps as in the Athenian Agora, use them as focal points to gather socially.

Unlike the Greeks, the Macedonians had few monumental temples but opted for smaller sanctuaries. They did build large and elaborate tombs for members of royal and noble families as well as the very wealthy, which were filled with lavish and expensive grave goods, connected to a belief in an active afterlife, with death coming last in a series of rites of passage.[42] The excavations

---

40. Tarn 1913, pp. 21–36; Gabbert 1997, pp. 4–6. Court: Tarn 1913, pp. 223–256; cf. Gabbert 1997, pp. 69–70.

41. Worthington 2008, pp. 181–186; Worthington 2014, pp. 111–115.

42. See Hatzopoulos 1994a; Christesen and Murray 2010, pp. 431–433; Mari 2011, pp. 456–458. Greek attitudes about death and the afterlife: Mikalson 2005, pp. 320–331. This belief in the afterlife explains why chthonic deities such as Hades, Demeter, and Persephone are found on paintings on walls of tombs: Hardiman 2010, pp. 511–514; Paspalas 2011, pp. 192–197. Chthonic deities: Mikalson 2005, pp. 83–86. For another illustration of the diversity of Macedonian religious practice, the belief in magic, see Christesen and Murray 2010, pp. 433–435.

FIGURE 1.2. Mosaic of a lion hunt, Pella. Photo credit: Juliana Lees. Licensed under a CC BY-SA 2.0 License (https://creativecommons.org/licenses/by-sa/2.0/).

at the cemetery at Sindos (a suburb of Thessaloniki) have revealed an abundance of gold and silver goods, including death masks, jewelry, weapons, and everyday items.[43]

Macedonian craftsmen produced artworks of the highest quality in bronze, silver, and gold, not to mention marble sculptures and on buildings, although marble had to be imported. Even more spectacular were tomb paintings and mosaics.[44] The enormous tomb at Amphipolis, for example, boasts a magnificent mosaic of Hades abducting Persephone; a similar painting is on the north wall of Tomb I at Aegae, and there is a splendid hunt frieze sadly in poor condition across the façade of Tomb II, that of Philip II.[45]

Mosaics had a long life in Macedonia. Archelaus attracted Zeuxis, the foremost fresco painter, from Italy to set up a school in Pella that pioneered mosaic painting.[46] The superb mosaics include ones from Pella depicting a lion hunt (showing Alexander and one of his friends, perhaps Craterus), and a stag hunt (figures 1.2 and 1.3).

---

43. Vokotopoulou, Despinis, Misailidou, and Tiverios 1985. On tombs, see too Saatsoglou-Paliadeli 2011, pp. 288–290.

44. Andronikos 1983; Hardiman 2010; Paspalas 2011; cf. Saatsoglou-Paliadeli 2011; see too Hatzopoulos 1994b, pp. 116–219, with many lavish illustrations, e.g., mosaics: pp. 116–136; pottery: pp. 138–143; tombs: pp. 145–191 (at Vergina, pp. 154–177); dedications outside Macedonia: pp. 193–219.

45. Hardiman 2010, pp. 505–521; Saatsoglou-Paliadeli 2011, pp. 282–286.

46. On patronage, cf. Hardiman 2010, pp. 506–511.

FIGURE 1.3. Mosaic of a stag hunt, Pella. Public Domain.

Artistic life was starting to change by Philip V's time as Rome began to make its presence known more forcefully. By 146, when Rome absorbed Greece into its empire, statues of the gods in sanctuaries and temples, theaters, and gymnasia were all in line with Classical and early Hellenistic precedents, but artistic output was declining.[47] Yet Macedonian art and architecture had a great impact on Roman visual culture, such as Antigonid palaces being something of a blueprint for Late Republican villas.[48] Perhaps most obvious are the mosaics found in numerous houses and villas in the Bay of Naples. Most famous is the Alexander Mosaic showing Alexander and Darius at the battle of Issus in 333, from the House of the Fawn at Pompeii, which may have been modeled on a contemporary painting (figure 1.4).

Victory monuments likewise affected the Romans, who set up substantial numbers throughout their empire. At Delphi, Perseus had intended a propaganda monument recording his various benefactions, together with a gilded statue of himself by the temple of Apollo (pp. 185–186). After Lucius Aemilius Paullus defeated him at Pydna in 167, Paullus traveled to Delphi, where he commandeered the column-bases Perseus had intended for his

---

47. Touratsoglou 1983; Kousser 2010, with judicious comments on the decline and a definition of "Macedonian" art on pp. 522–525; Palagia 2011.

48. Kousser 2010, p. 531, citing references.

FIGURE 1.4. Alexander mosaic. Photo credit: Berthold Werner. Licensed under a CC BY-SA 2.0 License (https://creativecommons.org/licenses/by-sa/2.0/).

statue and ordered a frieze depicting his victory at Pydna (see figures 11.4 and 11.5).[49]

The Army

The Macedonian army's success and fearsome reputation thanks to Philip II (figure 2.2) were eclipsed in antiquity only by the Roman army. Philip created a professional fighting force, with new tactics, equipment, promotion pathways, and pay, which was still used to great effect by the Antigonid kings long after him.[50] More than that, the army became the backbone of the Macedonian state and enjoyed a close relationship with the king as its commander.[51]

Before Philip came to the throne in 359, the army's strength lay in its cavalry of noblemen as only the wealthy could afford their own horses and

49. Kähler 1965; Jacquemin and Laroche 1982; Hammond and Walbank 1988, pp. 613–617; Jacquemin, Laroche, and Lefèvre 1995; Kousser 2010, pp. 528–531; Taylor 2016.

50. Hatzopoulos 1996, vol. 1, pp. 443–460; Sekunda 2010; cf. Milns 1976; English 2009a; Karunanithy 2013; King 2018, pp. 107–130; Taylor 2020. Antigonid army: Hatzopoulos 2001; Sekunda and Dennis 2012; Sekunda 2013; cf. Walbank 1940, pp. 289–294; LeBohec 1993, pp. 289–320.

51. Errington 1990, pp. 229–249; Hatzopoulos 1996, vol. 1, pp. 443–460; cf. Errington 1978; Heckel 2009.

equipment. Their social status is shown by them being known simply as *hetairoi* or the king's companions as they socialized with him at symposia and when hunting.[52] The infantry seemed to be mostly conscript farmers, poorly trained and equipped, and probably called up with little advance warning.[53] They would not have been able to hold their own against incursions from fierce bordering tribes or in fighting trained hoplite Greek armies, which might explain Thucydides' comment that the only fighting wing of the army was the cavalry, and infantry was not needed against invaders.[54] Kings could use mercenaries, who would be properly trained and equipped, but they were costly, and their loyalty not always guaranteed.

When he was thirteen Philip was sent as a hostage to Thebes under the terms of a pact between that city and his brother Alexander II.[55] He spent two years there, during which time he encountered two of the period's more distinguished generals, Epaminondas and Pelopidas, and got to watch the daily training of the famous Sacred Band, the crack infantry corps. His experiences there may have helped shape his military reforms and realization that, with the right military and diplomatic mixture, any city could dominate affairs regardless of its size or the strength of its opponents—and from 371 to 362 Thebes exercised hegemony over Greece.[56]

Once he was king, Diodorus claims he enacted his military reforms.[57] He revolutionized the army and added significantly to its manpower.[58] By the time he died in 336 the army had mushroomed from about 10,000 infantry and 600 cavalry to 24,000 infantry and 3,000 cavalry.[59] In a dramatic reversal of standard Greek fighting, he trained his cavalry to charge the opposite line first, followed by the infantry, a shock-and-awe tactic that devastated their

52. English 2009a, pp. 36–59 (pp. 43–44 on the companions); cf. Sekunda 2013, pp. 67–77.

53. See especially Kalléris 1987 and Nogueira Borell 2007; cf. Sekunda 2010, pp. 446–449; King 2018, pp. 107–110.

54. Thucydides 2.100.5–6. Hoplites: see for example, Hanson 1991; cf. Wiseman 1989.

55. Between 369–367: Aymard 1954, pp. 23–26; Hatzopoulos 1996, vol. 1 p. 178.

56. Hammond 1997; cf. Worthington 2008, pp. 17–19.

57. Diodorus 16.3.1–2.

58. Fuller 1960, pp. 39–54; Griffith in Hammond and Griffith 1979, pp. 405–449; Lloyd 1996; Worthington 2008, pp. 26–32; Gabriel 2010, pp. 62–92; Sekunda 2010, pp. 449–452; Worthington 2014, pp. 32–38; King 2018, pp. 107–114.

59. Diodorus 16.4.3, 17.7.5.

foes and deliberately demoralized them. The Greeks never seemed to have caught onto the change, with disastrous consequences as at Chaeonea in 338.

Philip organized his infantry into a phalanx line composed of different units and of varying depths from eight to thirty-two men, depending on the other side's numbers. The phalanx was supported by lighter armed troops called peltasts, who had a crescent-shaped shield or *pelte*, hence their name, whose job was to prevent the phalanx's sides or rear from attack. The phalanx infantrymen were known as phalangites, who were recruited from the different regions of Macedonia.[60] Some units had different functions, such as the *hetairoi* or foot companions, who were lighter-armed and marched at faster speeds, but all were united under a complex command structure.[61] Another unit was the hypaspists or "shield bearers"; they were akin to "special forces" and remained a crucial component of the phalanx well into the Antigonid period.[62] They also formed a 1,000-strong royal bodyguard (*agema*), flanking the king when he fought on foot.[63]

All infantrymen were given new equipment and weaponry. The "heavy" infantry received lighter armor—a cuirass; greaves; a small wooden shield with a layer of metal on top, which was carried over one shoulder; a short sword; and a lighter iron, hoplite-style helmet, providing more vision than the Greek-style one as it was open.[64] The most formidable weapon these infantrymen were given was a sarissa (a Macedonian dialect word meaning "hafted weapon") made of cornel wood. Polybius tells us that it was originally 16 cubits (24 feet or 7.4 meters) long, but by his time (second century) it was 14 cubits (21 feet or 6.45 meters).[65] It projected about 10 cubits (c. 5.6 meters) in front of each soldier and weighed about 14 pounds (6 kilograms). At one end was a narrow, sharp blade and at the other a sharpened butt spike for finishing off enemy combatants lying underfoot.

---

60. Hammond and Walbank 1988, p. 477; cf. Hatzopoulos 2001, pp. 73–84 and 133–140.

61. Milns 1976, pp. 101–106; English 2009a, pp. 10–16 and 110–120; Sekunda 2010, pp. 456–458; Taylor 2020.

62. Milns 1967; Hammond and Griffith 1979, pp. 705–709; Anson 1985b; English 2009a, pp. 28–35; Sekunda 2010, pp. 454–456; cf. Hatzopoulos 2001, pp. 56–66.

63. Arrian 3.11.9, with English 2009a, pp. 115–117; cf. Hatzopoulos 2001, pp. 66–73; Sekunda 2013, pp. 52–56.

64. Infantry equipment: English 2009a, pp. 16–25; cf. Hatzopoulos 2001, pp. 61–66, 80–84; Sekunda 2013, pp. 78–87; Karunanithy 2013, pp. 100–115.

65. Polybius 18.29.1–5. See further, Sekunda 2001; Anson 2010; Sekunda 2013, pp. 78–81; see too Hammond 1980.

The sarissa's length and weight required both hands to wield it, hence the need for the over-the-shoulder shield. The long weapon was carried in two parts when the men were marching and then joined in the middle before battle. At that time the infantrymen held their weapons upright so as not to impede any turning maneuvers. Then the first three ranks lowered their sarissas to charge, while their comrades in the fourth and fifth lines brought theirs down but not dead straight, and the remaining ranks kept theirs upright until needed and to deflect missiles (figure 1.5).

This formidable "hedge" of sarissas was an intimidating sight. Some years after the battle of Pydna, Lucius Aemilius Paullus made the comment that "he had never seen so frightening a sight" as when he confronted Perseus' massed Macedonian phalanx.[66] But there was a weakness: for the phalanx to operate with maximum efficiency and deadly effect, its long line needed space and level ground. As Polybius remarked, it was difficult to find a large, flat battlefield free of ditches, ravines, depressions, ridges, and riverbeds (the full passage is quoted on pp. 138–139).[67] Once the phalanx line was thrown into disorder by rocky or steep terrain, movement became limited and the long sarissas were a hindrance. Philip V and Perseus discovered too late that a disrupted phalanx was a sitting duck for Roman legionaries, who proved superior in hand-to-hand fighting. We discuss the demise of the phalanx before the Roman legion in chapter 7.

The cavalry was also revamped, with Philip arranging it in squadrons (*ilai*) of about 200 men, also based on the regions from which they came. He trained the cavalry to attack in a new wedge formation like the Thracians and Scythians, with the riders brandishing spears and short swords, slashing and stabbing from on high. The "heavy" cavalrymen wore armor (a metal helmet, cuirass, and greaves), carried a round shield, spear, and sword, while the "light" cavalry had lighter armor, fought in an open formation, and threw javelins or shot arrows at their foes before fighting at close quarters with swords.[68]

It was all well and good to introduce these measures, but the men needed to be properly trained and could not be farmers at the same time. Philip therefore abolished conscription and created a professional army, making it a career and a home. He introduced regular pay, a promotion pathway, and provided

---

66. Plutarch, *Paullus* 19.2.

67. Polybius 18.28–32 (= Austin 2006, no. 83, pp. 170–172 abridged).

68. Hammond and Walbank 1988, p. 541, with n. 1, citing references for the light cavalry; see further Hatzopoulos 2001, pp. 32–54; Sekunda 2013, pp. 67–77. Cavalrymen's outfits: Karunanithy 2013, pp. 81–99.

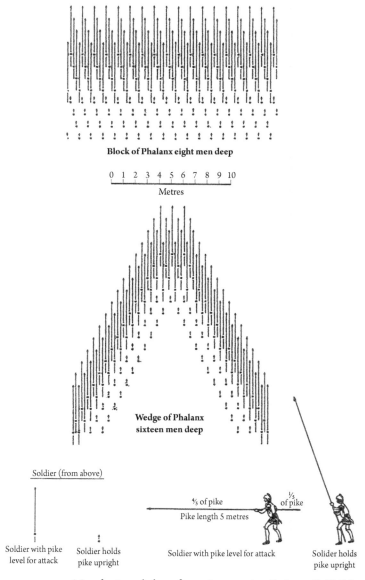

Block of Phalanx eight men deep

0 1 2 3 4 5 6 7 8 9 10

Metres

**Wedge of Phalanx
sixteen men deep**

Soldier (from above)

⁴⁄₅ of pike

¹⁄₅ of pike

Pike length 5 metres

Soldier with pike
level for attack

Soldier holds
pike upright

Soldier with pike level for attack

Solider holds
pike upright

FIGURE 1.5. Macedonian phalanx formation carrying Sarissas. © N.G.L. Hammond, 1989, *Alexander the Great: King, Commander, and Statesman* and Bristol Classical Press, an imprint of Bloomsbury Publishing Plc.

arms and armor for the troops (although cavalrymen still had to provide their own horses). Training now became full-time, and it was arduous: the men were taken on forced marches of 300 stades, roughly 30 miles (48 kilometers), perhaps lasting for forty days, over all manner of terrain. They had to carry all equipment and rations and learn to look after themselves.[69] To support self-sufficiency, Philip included in his army trained personnel, such as surveyors, road builders, rivercraft builders, doctors, siegecraft technicians, and repairers of arms and armor, and some soldiers even had this technical expertise.[70]

Philip's military reforms continued throughout his reign. In perhaps 350 he founded an engineering corps, which designed siege machinery.[71] Among this technology was the torsion catapult, a spring-loaded crossbow that fired arrows farther and faster than the traditional mechanically drawn catapult.[72] The king probably also founded the School of the Royal Pages (*basilikoi paides*).[73] These were teenagers, possibly as many as 200, from prominent families who lived at court from fourteen to eighteen years of age, received a military training, and served in their final year with the king on campaign. While they were being trained as the next generation of military commanders, the system was a form of hostage taking as the boys' well-being depended on the loyalty of their fathers.

The kings who followed Philip did little to change the fighting capabilities of the army, though the soldiers received daily training throwing javelins and in archery.[74] Interestingly, the literary sources do not refer to hypaspists in the armies of Philip V and Perseus except on one occasion: after his defeat at Cynoscephalae in 197, Philip sent a hypaspist to Pella to burn his state papers.[75] Philip's hypaspists are cited in the epigraphic evidence, as we shall see. The cavalry remained organized in *ilia*, but the elite unit was renamed the "sacred squadron"; Philip V had 800 cavalry in 219, of which 400 probably constituted this sacred squadron.[76]

---

69. Polyaenus 4.2.10. Training: Karunanithy 2013, pp. 19–39 and 174–175 (marching with weapons). Demosthenes 18.157 tells us that the troops carried forty days' worth of food, which may not be an exaggeration.

70. Karunanithy 2013, pp. 164–170 and 209–223.

71. Garlan 1974, pp. 202–244; Marsden 1977, with p. 212, for the date. On siegecraft, see too English 2009b, pp. 17–32.

72. Marsden 1977; Keyser 1994; English 2009a, pp. 100–109; Gabriel 2010, pp. 88–92.

73. Arrian 4.13.1 (who says the institution went back to Philip's time); Curtius 8.6.2, with Carney 2008; Hammond 1990.

74. Recruitment and training: Hatzopoulos 2001, pp. 87–127; Sekunda 2013, pp. 101–104; cf. Hatzopoulos 1996, vol. 1, pp. 451–452. Two sizes of shield seem to have been used, depending on the combat: Sekunda 2013, pp. 81–87.

75. Polybius 18.33.1–7, with Walbank 1940, pp. 290–291.

76. Sekunda 2010, p. 460, citing sources.

Philip also added to his army's organizational and command structure. We have an important albeit fragmentary inscription from Amphipolis, which is a royal *diagramma* (edict) about infantry organization and management of war booty, likely issued in 218.[77] We learn, among other things, that at nighttime a tetrarch (lieutenant) had to check on all the men posted on guard duties to ensure no one was sitting or sleeping—anyone doing so was fined one drachma. If the tetrarchs did not report any guards derelict in their duties they too were fined, with the money going to the hypaspists.

We also learn that the king's quarters in a camp were to be built first, then the barracks of the hypaspists, and then those of the regular soldiers, while those foraging in enemy territory or destroying crops, presumably without permission, were to be punished, with a reward to those who named then. The distribution of booty, all of which is to be shared, was carefully regulated, which perhaps gives us a context for this edict as in 218 Philip faced rebellious troops over unfair distribution of booty (p. 61).[78]

In the same inscription the various units of the phalanx are named from larger (a *strategia*, which was subdivided into a *speira*, perhaps of 256 men) to smaller (a *tetrarchia* composed of four unis called *lochoi*, each of fifteen or sixteen men), along with the titles of their commanding officers, beginning with the *strategoi* (generals), *speirarchai*, and *tetrarchai*, and including *grammateis* (secretaries). The various subdivisions and offices show an elaborate military hierarchy, yet they were all connected and under the king's overall authority.

Philip V also involved himself in the lives of his men on individual levels, as a letter to Archippus, the *epistates* of the city of Gria, shows. It granted land that used to belong to a metic (resident alien) named Corrhagus to some soldiers if they performed sacrifices in a certain month (Apellaios).[79] The petitioning group is referred to as "the men with Nicanor the tetrarch"

---

77. *ISE*, no. 114, pp. 108–114 = Hatzopoulos 1996, vol. 2, no. 12, pp. 32–36 = Austin 2006, no. 90, pp. 180–182; Walbank 1940, pp. 291 and 293; Loreto 1990; Hatzopoulos 1996, vol. 1, pp. 453–455; Hatzopoulos 2001, pp. 15–26, 143–145; Juhel 2002; Hatzopoulos 2016; D'Agostini 2019, pp. 49–57; see too English 2009a, pp. 110–120; Sekunda 2013, pp. 88–98.

78. Hatzopoulos 2016 suggests that the stipulations may not have been introduced by Philip at any one time but were the product of both Philip and Perseus.

79. *SEG* 13, no. 403 = *ISE*, no. 110, pp. 97–100 = Hatzopoulos 1996, vol. 2, no. 17, pp. 41–42, with Welles 1938, pp. 246–249; Walbank 1940, p. 291; Hatzopoulos 1996, vol. 1, pp. 95–102 (preferring Euia, not Greia) and 419–422; Hatzopoulos 2001, p. 167; Sekunda 2013, pp. 89–90 and 100–101.

and as "the soldiers of the *protolochia*," and are probably members of a *lochos*.[80]

The army created by Philip II was used with devastating effect by his successors, especially his son Alexander the Great in Asia. It remained almost unbeatable for two centuries until, under Philip V, it fell to a new fighting machine—the Roman legion.

80. Welles 1938, pp. 248–249; Hatzopoulos 1996, vol. 1, pp. 453–454.

2

Introducing Philip V

PHILIP V WAS a member of the Antigonid ruling dynasty, which we discuss below. He was king from 221 to 179, a long reign of forty-two years that saw plenty of drama, including war with Rome.[1] Philip is one of the more colorful characters in Greek history—a warrior king, a careful diplomat, a skilled administrator and strategist, a hard-drinking and hard-living individual who often saw red. All these characteristics were reminiscent of earlier kings such as Philip II and Alexander the Great (of the previous Argead dynasty), his great-grandfather Demetrius I Poliorcetes, and the energetic and bellicose Pyrrhus of Epirus, from where Philip's mother hailed.[2] Yet our two principal sources, Polybius and Livy, portray Philip in an unsympathetic light; they mock and criticize him for intending to overpower Rome and seek world dominion, attributing his downfall to *Tyche*, "Chance" or "Fortune" (see appendix). His kingship becomes one of failure, and even a postscript to the reigns of his predecessors. Nothing could be further from the truth.

Certainly, he did not lay the foundations of an empire as did Philip II or conquer on the scale of Alexander the Great a century before our Philip came to be king. But he did not over-extend himself like Alexander or some of the earlier Antigonids with unrealistic foreign ventures. Instead, he strove to

---

1. Walbank 1940; Hammond and Walbank 1988, pp. 367–487; Errington 1990, pp. 184–212; Hammond 1992, pp. 330–362; cf. Walbank 1984a, pp. 473–481; King 2018, pp. 246–256. Philip is constantly discussed in Gruen 1984; Hatzopoulos 1996; Eckstein 2008; Camia 2009; Waterfield 2014. D'Agostini 2019 uses Philip's accession and the first few years of his reign from 222 to 217 as a study of Hellenistic kingship; see too Walbank 1984b.

2. Pyrrhus launched an abortive conquest of southern Italy and Sicily in the 280s. He defeated Roman armies in several battles—most famously at the battle of Asculum (in Apulia) in 279, where he lost so many men that his victory gave rise to the term "Pyrrhic victory." On Pyrrhus see Lévèque 1957; Garoufalias 1979; Champion 2012.

The Last Kings of Macedonia and the Triumph of Rome. Ian Worthington, Oxford University Press.
© Oxford University Press 2023. DOI: 10.1093/oso/9780197520055.003.0003

reassert his kingdom's standing in Greece and Illyria and keep Rome at arm's length. That Philip was able to hold Rome at bay for so long while struggling against hostile Greek states and foreign powers, suffer a massive defeat at the hands of the Roman legion at Cynoscephalae in 197, and yet leave his son and successor Perseus a united and prosperous kingdom with a rebuilt army are all testament to Philip's prowess and resilience. He hardly deserves to be scorned.

Background and Youth

Philip was born most likely in the late summer of 238, the son of Demetrius II (r. 239–229).[3] His mother was Phthia, the daughter of Alexander II of Epirus, whose marriage to Demetrius had been arranged by Phthia's mother, Olympias, to procure military help against Aetolian threats on the death of Alexander.[4] The marriage took place perhaps not long after Demetrius became king.[5]

Although Phthia's name (and calling her queen) is found on inscriptions, some sources claim that Philip's mother was named Chryseis.[6] Macedonian queens did change their names when they married, but suggestions for the two names have been made.[7] One is that Phthia died after giving birth and Demetrius then married a lady named Chryseis, who adopted the young boy. Another has it that Chryseis was Philip's mother but she was only the concubine of his father Demetrius, who was formally married to Phthia.[8] Another

---

3. Walbank 1940, p. 295, drawing on Polybius 4.5.3 and 4.24.1 that he was seventeen in fall-winter 221 and late summer 220; cf. Walbank 1957, pp. 290–291, on Polybius 2.70.8.

4. Walbank 1940, pp. 9–10; cf. Scherberich 2009, pp. 49–57; D'Agostini 2019, pp. 13–14.

5. I thank Yuri Kuzmin for the following about when Demetrius married. *IG* ii³ 1023, an Athenian decree to honor grain protectors of 239/38, refers to King Demetrius and Queen Phila; the decree was reissued and expanded the following year (238/37) but this time the reference is to King Demetrius and Queen Phthia. Kuzmin suggests that Phila was the mother of Demetrius and widow of Gonatas, showing Demetrius was not married at the start of his kingship; at some later point he married Phthia, with the Athenians recognizing her as queen in their reissued decree. Of course, as Kuzmin admits, the name Phila in the first decree could have been a mistake. See now Kuzmin 2022.

6. *Inscriptions de Délos*, ed. École Française d'Athènes (Paris: 1926–1972), no. 407, line 20; *IG* ii² 1299 = *SIG* 485. Polybius 5.89.7; Porphyry, *BNJ* 260 F 3; Eusebius 1.237, 238; see too Hammond and Walbank 1988, p. 338 n. 1; King 2018, p. 242; D'Agostini 2019, pp. 18–22; and especially LeBohec 1981, discussing all sources. Older studies: Tarn 1924 (cf. Walbank 1940, p. 10 with n. 3); Fine 1934; Dow and Edson 1937.

7. J. Roisman commented to me about them changing their maiden names.

8. LeBohec 1981.

theory is that when Antigonus III Doson was required to marry Demetrius' widow and become regent of the young Philip, as we shall see, Doson was already married to Chryseis and stayed married to her after he took Phthia as his wife.[9] Rather than bowing to these sophisticated hypotheses, in my opinion it is more sensible to accept that the issue of the two names cannot be currently solved but that the simple explanation is best: Chryseis became a popular nickname for Phthia, which the literary sources thought was her actual name, hence the two women were one and the same person.[10]

Demetrius already had a wife, his cousin Stratonice, the sister of Antiochus II of Syria. He married her in 253, but for some reason she returned home when Demetrius took Phthia as his wife. Stratonice may have felt that because she had not produced a son for the king she was being replaced.[11] She cannot have been confounded by her husband's new nuptials as Macedonian kings were polygamists, nor were queens cast aside if they did not have sons. Philip II, we know, had seven wives, yet only two bore him sons and we do not hear of his other wives taking umbrage or being set aside. More plausibly the two queens did not get along or Demetrius simply liked Phthia more, in which case he sent Stratonice home, causing tension between him and Antiochus.[12]

For a description of Philip, we must rely on his coinage and to a lesser extent on a series of herms—small quadrangular pillars with the carved head of usually Hermes on top and male genitalia below—from Roman times.[13] His gold and silver coins carry the full title of the king (*basileos Philippou*) and the bronze ones the same or abbreviations such as *Ba Phi*.

Philip's silver tetradrachms of the late third century depict him as a mature man, with large eyes, a prominent nose, curly medium-length hair (typical of monarchs after Alexander the Great), and wearing a diadem, the symbol of Hellenistic kingship.[14] He also has a beard, which is uncommon on the portraits of over fifty Hellenistic rulers that we have, and was therefore

---

9. D'Agostini 2019, pp. 18–22.

10. Walbank 1940, p. 49 n. 3; Walbank 1957, p. 621; Hammond and Walbank 1988, p. 338 n. 1; cf. Porphyry, *BNJ* 260 F 3, with the commentary of Toye, *ad loc.*

11. Waterfield 2021, p. 198.

12. Justin 28.1.1–4; cf. Agatharchides, *BNJ* 86 F. 20; see further D'Agostini 2019, pp. 14–16.

13. Hammond and Walbank 1988, pp. 461–468, citing bibliography on all numismatic issues to do with Philip V.

14. The coin also seems to have been a model for those of Flamininus after defeating Philip at Cynoscephalae in 197: Kousser 2010, pp. 527–528, on the depiction.

FIGURE 2.1. Silver tetradrachm of Philip V. © Classical Numismatic Group, LLC, https://cngcoins.com/.

making a conscious break with his predecessors, presenting "a more aggressive, charismatic image of himself."[15]

A Romanized rather than naturalistic likeness of Philip is found on several herms from the Roman period, possibly the result of his friendship with various influential Romans.[16] On these herms, the figure is wearing an iron or bronze cuirass with a leather top and a *kausia* with cheek pieces, a nape protector, and ram's horns at the top. Philip was the only Macedonian monarch to wear ram's horns on his helmet.[17] They made his helmet so distinctive that during a campaign in the Peloponnese he was thrown from his horse and broke off one of the two horns on a tree branch. It was taken to Scerdilaidas of the Illyrians, who recognized it and presumed the king was dead.[18]

Why Philip wore this distinctive helmet is unknown. He may have wanted to highlight his association with Epirus, from where Phthia came, or even to emulate his great-grandfather Pyrrhus of Epirus, who wore goat's horns and a "towering crest" on his helmet, which enabled him to be recognized by Macedonian troops in 286 when they were deserting Poliorcetes (see below).[19] The horns and the beard may indicate that Philip wanted to be seen as different from his predecessors and keen to usher in a new era of Macedonian rule on the mainland.

---

15. Kousser 2010, p. 526, and see pp. 526–527, on the coin.

16. See for discussion Sekunda 2013, pp. 29–33.

17. Sekunda 2013, pp. 30, and see pp. 29–33 generally.

18. Livy 27.33.3.

19. Plutarch, *Pyrrhus* 11.5.

Nothing is known of Philip's early childhood. He must have been reared in the same tough tradition as all Macedonian boys, and most likely would have been enrolled in the School of the Royal Pages at age fourteen. He would have been exposed to Greek culture and literature like his predecessors. After all, a disdain or ignorance of things Greek would have worked against him when he was making conscious efforts to endear himself to members of the Greek league of which he was hegemon. His contacts with Athens, unlike previous kings such as Philip II or his grandfather Antigonus II Gonatas, may not have been close. The city went to war against him in 200 and even cursed him and all the Antigonid kings when he despoiled their sanctuaries (chapter 6). Then again, Gonatas maintained intellectual and cultural contacts with the Athenians, even though during his reign they were at war with him (see below).

Like all kings Philip was pious and took his role as chief priest seriously, sacrificing to the gods on behalf of himself and his kingdom. His outlook on religion is best summed up by his defiant response to the Roman general Flamininus in 198 that he was "afraid of no one but the gods."[20] He put the head of Athena Archidemus, the Macedonian goddess of war, on his first coinage and symbols of Heracles and Zeus on later coinage and supported traditional cults elsewhere in the Greek world such as Asclepius at Cos and Apollo at Delos. But like the people, he was open to other religions, including Isis and Serapis, who had sanctuaries throughout Macedonia.[21] He took an interest in the cult of Serapis, for we have an order from him sent to a certain Andronicus, probably the *epistates* (overseer) of Thessalonica, responding to complaints from priests for switching jurisdiction of the funds of the Serapeum (temple of Serapis) from the city to the *epistates* and judges.[22]

At the same time, when it was necessary to punish or demoralize his enemies, he did not hesitate to commit sacrilegious acts. Thus, he destroyed the Aetolians' religious center Thermum in part for their raids on Dodona and Dium and sacked sanctuaries in Attica. Realpolitik trumped religion.

---

20. Polybius 18.1.7.

21. Their worship was prevalent throughout the Mediterranean: Mikalson 2005, pp. 337–342. For a dedication to Sarapis and Isis by Perseus' sons, see Hatzopoulos 1996, vol. 2, no. 31, p. 51, and see too Witt 1970.

22. *ISE* 2, no. 111, pp. 100–102 = Burstein 1985, no. 72, pp. 97–98 = Hatzopoulos 1996, vol. 2, no. 15, pp. 39–40; see too Hammond and Walbank 1988, p. 487 with n. 2; Hatzopoulos 1996, vol. 1, pp. 406–410, against Welles 1938, pp. 249–251.

As a man, he had a sense of humor, was courageous, and like all Macedonians enjoyed his wine.[23] He did have a short temper, which, if we can believe the sources, led those close to him to be fearful of speaking their minds.[24] He was much influenced by his predecessors, and if the ram's horns on his helmet are anything to go by, he may even have modeled himself to an extent after Pyrrhus of Epirus. But there was one king who stood out for him: Philip II. Our Philip even excerpted passages about his namesake from Theopompus' monumental history of Philip II, the *Philippika*:[25]

> Thus, with a large number of digressions on miscellaneous historical (topics) Theopompus extends his historical narratives. For this reason, Philip (V), who fought the Romans, extracted Philip's deeds that appear in Theopompos and arranged them into only 16 books. He himself added and left out nothing except, as it is said, the digressions, all of which he excised.

It was this Philip who had elevated Macedonia's presence in the Greek world and who was responsible for its rise to imperial power. He did this by a dazzling display of diplomacy, deceit, and military action. However, it was his use of deception that caused the ancient writer Pausanias, for example, to claim that was why Philip V admired him, among other things because he flattered those willing to betray their country.[26]

One thing Philip II had shown—as indeed had Argead kings before him—was the need to secure borders for the well-being of the kingdom. By Philip V's time Rome was master of the Adriatic and had a "protectorate" in a part of Illyria called Illyris, an area roughly 120 miles (193 kilometers) long and 20 to 40 miles (32 to 64 kilometers) wide bordering western Macedonia at Antipatrea (Berat), in what is today Dalmatia and Croatia.[27] The Roman presence in Illyria put great pressure on Philip's border, something he was not prepared to allow.

---

23. Livy 37.7.12 (love of drinking); cf. Plutarch, *Flamininus* 9.2–3 (Philip's bold spirit and poking fun mocked).

24. Diodorus 28.2.

25. Theopompus, *BNJ* 115 T 31 (trans. Morison), and see the commentary of Morison *ad loc.* Polybius 9–11 is highly critical of Theopompus' adverse presentation of Philip II: see Walbank 1967, pp. 79–87, with references.

26. Pausanias 7.7.5–6.

27. See Hammond 1968, based on firsthand knowledge of the geography.

From Philip II to Philip V

For most of the Classical period (478–323) Greece had been a land of autonomous city states (*poleis*), with those of Athens, Sparta, and Thebes dominating affairs, especially in the fourth century because of their military capabilities. All that changed in 338 when Philip II defeated a coalition Greek army headed by Athens and Thebes at Chaeronea in Boeotia and imposed Macedonian hegemony over Greece.[28]

No one could have predicted that outcome, for at the time of Philip's accession in 359 Macedonia was in a perilous state. It was disunited; there was no centralization of the capital at Pella; its economy was poorly developed; it was prone to incursions by various tribes on its borders as well as interference in its domestic politics by cities such as Athens and Thebes; and its king Perdiccas III and 4,000 troops had just been killed in battle against plundering Illyrians. On top of that, the Athenians and the king of western Thrace were backing separate pretenders to the throne, the Paeonians were mustering an invasion army, and the legitimate heir, Perdiccas' son Amyntas, was only a minor. The Assembly did not appoint a regent but acclaimed his uncle Philip, the dead king's brother, king.[29]

Against the odds, Philip saved the kingdom from these threats and went on to turn Macedonia into a superpower (figure 2.2).[30] By the time he died in 336, after a reign of only twenty-three years, he had united both parts of the kingdom and centralized the capital at Pella, secured his borders, and embarked on a rapid and successful expansionist policy that more than doubled Macedonia's size and population to include Greece to his south and as far east as the Hellespont. Additionally, he forged a new, professional army, as we saw in chapter 1, and put into place an ambitious economic policy, which included developing natural resources, especially mines, and introducing a solid and stable coinage. Macedonia prospered as never before.

Throughout his reign, Philip slowly but steadily expanded his sway in Greece, which brought him into conflict with several states, especially Athens. After Chaeronea, he used the Greeks' distrust of each other, one of the downsides of their *polis* system, as a deterrent to insurrection. At the

---

28. Worthington 2008, pp. 147–163; cf. Worthington 2014, pp. 85–90 and 97–101.

29. Worthington 2008, pp. 20–21.

30. Philip's reign: Worthington 2008 and Worthington 2014 (comparing and contrasting him to Alexander), citing bibliography; Müller 2010; Lane Fox 2011b; King 2018, pp. 70–106. Focusing on Philip as general and tactician: Gabriel 2010.

FIGURE 2.2. Philip II facial reconstruction. Licensed under a CC0 1.0 Universal License (https://creative commons.org/publicdomain/zero/1.0/deed.en).

strategically important city of Corinth on the isthmus, he proclaimed a Common Peace, whereby every Greek city swore a separate oath of allegiance to one another and to Macedonia to have the same friends and enemies and not engage in subversive activities.[31] If any city contravened these terms, then the other members could go to war against it.[32] Philip had stated that the cities would be free, meeting together in a council to discuss policy, but appearance was far from reality; the call to freedom was a mere slogan even in

---

31. Rhodes and Osborne 2003, no. 76, with commentary (pp. 376–379).

32. Background: Worthington 2008, pp. 158–171, to which add Ager 1996, pp. 39–43; Dmitriev 2011, pp. 67–90.

the Roman era.[33] And so was created what modern scholars call the League of Corinth, the ancestor of the Hellenic League that Philip V headed, as we shall see.

Philip II was assassinated in 336 and buried in Aegae (modern Vergina).[34] His unplundered tomb, containing his skeletal remains and exceptional and beautiful grave goods, was discovered and excavated in 1977 by the Greek archaeologist Manolis Andronikos.[35] The skull fragments were reassembled by a British forensic team, which also reconstructed his face (figure 2.2). Noticeable is the closed right eye, which is in keeping with a wound he suffered at the siege of Methone on the Thermaic Gulf during the winter of 355–354 when he was struck and blinded by an arrow or javelin from the ramparts. His battle scars show the sort of life he led: always the warrior king in the thick of fighting.

Philip never got to launch his next grand plan, announced at a meeting of the League of Corinth in 337: an invasion of Asia. Instead, it was his son Alexander III ("the Great") who led an army onto Asian soil in 334 (figure 2.3). He left behind one of Philip's senior generals, Antipater, to oversee Macedonia and Greece in his absence. By 330 the young king (he was only twenty-six in that year) had toppled the Persian Empire and ended the Achaemenid dynasty. He followed those accomplishments by invading Bactria, Sogdiana, and India, creating a vast empire that was without parallel for a time.[36] But in June 323, on the eve of invading Arabia, he died in Babylon a little shy of his thirty-third birthday. He had his failures as a man and as a king, not least his paranoia, pretensions to personal divinity, and inattention to his dynastic line, but he was without doubt a strategic genius and heroic warrior. It is easy to understand why his generalship and audacity in the face of superior odds made him a role model for his successors, including Philip V.

Alexander's death in 323 led to a new age in world history, the Hellenistic (323–30). During this period Greek language and culture spread far and wide

33. Dmitriev 2011, with a very succinct discussion on pp. 351–379; see too Gruen 1984, pp. 132–157.

34. Worthington 2008, pp. 181–186; Worthington 2014a, pp. 112–115, citing bibliography, to which add Heckel, Howe, and Müller 2017.

35. Andronikos 2004; see too Andronikos 1980, pp. 188–231; Saatsoglou-Paliadeli 2011, pp. 282–286, citing bibliography. Some controversy remains over the occupant of the main chamber of Tomb II, but it is surely Philip: Worthington 2008, pp. 233–240, and especially Lane Fox 2011c.

36. See Worthington 2014, citing further bibliography, to which add King 2018, pp. 114–177; succinct survey: Gilley and Worthington 2010.

FIGURE 2.3. Head of Alexander the Great. Photo credit: Yair Haklai. Licensed under a CC BY-SA 3.0 Unported License (https://creativecommons.org/licenses/by-sa/3.0/).

in the east, and the Greeks of the Mediterranean grasped they were part of a bigger world. In Egypt, thanks to Ptolemy I, Alexandria with its great Library and Museum eclipsed Athens as the preeminent intellectual and scientific center, though Athens never lost its reputation for philosophy and attracted many Romans to study and even live there.[37] It was also during this period that Rome established itself as the dominant power of the Mediterranean.

The Macedonian Empire did not survive Alexander's death. He had not produced an heir to succeed him as his wife Roxane of Bactria was pregnant when he died, so his senior staff met in Babylon to divide up his lands among themselves. Ptolemy, for example, took over Egypt, Antigonus

37. On the Hellenistic era, see as starting points Tarn and Griffith 1952; Green 1990; the essays in Erskine 2003 and Bugh 2007; and the multi-edited *Cambridge Ancient History*[2], vols. 7–9 (1984–1994).

Monophthalmus ("the one-eyed") much of Asia, Lysimachus Thrace, while Greece was shared by Antipater and another general, Craterus. After the second-in-command Perdiccas appointed himself guardian of Roxane's baby, the rank and file of the army compelled him to declare Alexander's half-brother Arrhidaeus king as Philip III; when Roxane subsequently gave birth to a boy, Alexander IV, a dual monarchy came into being.[38]

What had been decided in Babylon in 323 was soon wrecked because of the protagonists' personal dislike of each other and ambitions for a greater slice of empire. Backed by their own armies, four decades of warfare with minor interruptions from equally ephemeral settlements began, commonly referred to as the "Wars of the Successors."[39] During them Philip III was put to death in 317, as were Alexander IV and his mother, Roxane, in 310, ending the Argead dynasty. And in 306 the Successors began calling themselves kings; the era of Hellenistic kingship had formally arrived.[40] When the wars finally ended the kingdoms of the Hellenistic age were coming of age: Ptolemaic Egypt, Seleucid Syria—and Antigonid Macedonia. But like Alexander in the east, the rulers' positions were not anchored in constitutionality but military conquest; the dynasties that the Successors founded were military monarchies.

The Antigonid dynasty did not abruptly establish itself after Alexander IV's murder. Nine years earlier in 319, Antipater had died, and his son Cassander seized the throne—the man who ordered the execution of Alexander IV and Roxane.[41] He was continually opposed by Alexander's former general Antigonus Monophthalmus (who gave his name to the dynasty) and his son Demetrius Poliorcetes.[42] In 307 Poliorcetes liberated the Greek cities from Cassander's rule, including Athens, which voted him and his father excessive

---

38. Background and settlement at Babylon: Errington 1970; Bosworth 2002; Meeus 2008; Worthington 2016a, pp. 71–83.

39. Will 1984a (to 301); Will 1984b (301–276); Hammond and Walbank 1988, pp. 117–244; Green 1990, pp. 5–134; Hammond 1992, pp. 237–294; Adams 1997; Bosworth 2002; Braund 2003; Bosworth 2007; Adams 2010; Waterfield 2011; Roisman 2012; King 2018, pp. 205–234.

40. Austin 2006, no. 44, pp. 94–96. On kingship, see Ma 2003; Ma 2011; Walbank 1984b, pp. 62–100; Grainger 2017; D'Agostini 2019.

41. Diodorus 19.105.2; see too Justin 15.2.5; Pausanias 9.7.2, with Hammond and Walbank 1988, pp. 164–167; King 2018, pp. 211–216.

42. On the former, see Billows 1990; Champion 2014; on the latter, Manni 1951; Wheatley and Dunn 2020. Poliorcetes received that epithet after his famous year-long siege of Rhodes in 305/4, even though the Rhodians successfully resisted him: Austin 2006, no. 47, pp. 98–99, with Champion 2014, pp. 124–129; Worthington 2016a, pp. 165–166.

honors and called them savior gods.[43] In 302 Poliorcetes announced his father's intention of reconstituting the earlier League of Corinth (abandoned on Alexander's death)—or rather, a Hellenic League, which both would head. But then came a major military defeat of Monophthalmus and Poliorcetes at Ipsus in central Phrygia in spring 301 against a coalition army of Cassander, Lysimachus, and Seleucus, with additional troops supplied by Ptolemy.[44] Monophthalmus was killed, and Poliorcetes escaped with 5,000 infantry and 4,000 cavalry to Ephesus.

Cassander died from tuberculosis in 297 and was succeeded by his eldest son, Philip IV, who died of tuberculosis four months later. A dual kingship was then established of Cassander's other sons, Antipater I and Alexander V, with their mother, Thessalonice, as regent. But in 295 Antipater murdered her and ousted his brother. The resulting chaos in Macedonia and a call for help from the Athenians, who were enduring the brutal tyranny of a certain Lachares, gave Poliorcetes the opportunity to return to Greece.[45] He took control of Athens, and in the fall of 294 turned to Macedonia, where Pyrrhus of Epirus had expelled Antipater I and made Alexander V king. Poliorcetes lulled the latter into a trap, murdered him, and became king as Demetrius I.[46] But in 288 he faced a dual invasion of the kingdom by Pyrrhus from the west and Lysimachus from the east. Leaving behind his son Antigonus Gonatas in Greece, Poliorcetes marched to meet them, but his troops deserted him, and he fled. After a vain attempt to take Asia he went to the court of Seleucus and drank himself to death four years later. Seleucus sent his ashes to Gonatas, who buried them at Demetrias, a town in Thessaly that his father had founded.[47]

Although for the next several years Macedonia was under the sway of Lysimachus and Pyrrhus, and after them Ptolemy Ceraunus (the eldest son of Ptolemy I of Egypt), Gonatas had always regarded himself as Macedonia's king after his father's death. His chance to assume the kingship came in 279. In that year Galatians from central Europe went on several brutal marauding expeditions through Macedonia, Greece, and Asia Minor, during which

---

43. Diodorus 20.46.1–2; Plutarch, *Demetrius* 10.2–11.1 (cf. Austin 2006, no. 42, pp. 91–93), with Worthington 2021a, pp. 71–75.

44. Battle: Diodorus 21.1.2–4; Plutarch, *Demetrius* 28.3–29; Polyaenus 4.7.4, 12.1, with Billows 1990, pp. 181–184; Champion 2014, pp. 158–161.

45. Background: Worthington 2021a, pp. 84–85 and 93–94.

46. Poliorcetes as king: Hammond and Walbank 1988, pp. 219–229; Waterfield 2011, pp. 186–190 and 193–196; Worthington 2021a, pp. 94–100.

47. Plutarch, *Demetrius* 53.1–3.

Ceraunus was killed.[48] In 277 Gonatas defeated a Galatian army of 18,000 at Lysimachia in the Thracian Chersonese, which had the ripple effect of forcing the Galatians in Macedonia to leave.[49] Gonatas then marched to Macedonia to claim the throne as Antigonus II, though he faced opposition from Pyrrhus until the latter's death in 272.

Antigonus II Gonatas' long reign from 277 to 239 was the starting point of the ongoing Antigonid dynasty, even though Monophthalmus and Poliorcetes had declared themselves kings in 306.[50] Gonatas revitalized the economy; built fortresses and roads in Upper Macedonia, enhancing border security against the Illyrians and creating jobs; rebuilt military power; introduced dynastic stability; and followed a careful and strategic foreign policy. He was conscious about the need to thwart Ptolemaic ascendancy at sea, and to this end built up his navy and scored a significant naval victory over Ptolemy II that give him naval dominance of the Aegean.[51]

Gonatas was also careful to maintain control of Greece, holding onto his father's possessions, including the strategic naval strongholds of Corinth, Chalcis on Euboea, and Demetrias in Thessaly—known as the "fetters of Greece."[52] But the Athenians allied with Sparta and Egypt against him in 268 in hopes of recovering their freedom. The resulting Chremonidean War—named after the Athenian politician Chremonides, who persuaded the Athenians to go to war—ended in 261 with Gonatas' victory and Athens subject to a series of punitive measures.[53]

---

48. Memnon, *BNJ* 434 F 11.1–7 (= Burstein 1985, no. 16, pp. 21–22); Diodorus 22.3–4, 5, 9; Justin 24.3.10–5.11; Pausanias 1.4.1–4, 10.19.5–23. Invasion: Tarn 1913, pp. 139–166; Nachtergael 1977, pp. 126–205; Hammond and Walbank 1988, pp. 251–258; Hammond 1992, pp. 298–302; Mitchell 2003, pp. 280–284 (pp. 280–293 on Galatians in general).

49. Diogenes Laertius 2.141–142; Justin 25.1.2–10, with Tarn 1913, p. 165; Hammond and Walbank 1988, p. 256.

50. Tarn 1913; Hammond and Walbank 1988, pp. 259–316; Errington 1990, pp. 163–173; Green 1990, pp. 138–154; Hammond 1992, pp. 307–315; Gabbert 1997; Waterfield 2021; cf. Waterfield 2011, pp. 197–212; Lane Fox 2011d; King 2018, pp. 237–241; cf. Briscoe 1978.

51. See Walbank 1982 on Antigonid naval policy and sea power from Poliorcetes to Perseus (pp. 216–223 on Gonatas). Comments on Antigonus' fleet: Tarn 1913, pp. 340–346.

52. Memnon, *BNJ* 434 F 8.8; Justin 24.1, 25.2.2.

53. War: Tarn 1913, pp. 295–310; Walbank 1984c, pp. 236–243; Hammond and Walbank 1988, pp. 276–289; Gabbert 1997, pp. 45–53; Habicht 1997, pp. 142–149; Scholten 2003, pp. 145–148; O'Neil 2008; Worthington 2021a, pp. 117–122. Chremonides' decree calling for the alliance survives: *IG* ii³ 1, 912, *SIG* 434/5 (= Burstein 1985, no. 56, pp. 77–80; Austin 2006, no. 61, pp. 130–133 as ii² 687+686).

By now two ambitious federal states were on the rise, destined to play a major role in our story of Philip V. The first was the Aetolian League located in central Greece (map 5). The Aetolians were fierce people, guerrilla fighters rather than the sort of troops found in a phalanx, and they became a force with which to be reckoned in the third century.[54] They had their own assembly and army led by an appointed general and they held the strategic port of Naupactus. After helping to defeat the Galatians in battle in 279, the Aetolians began to spread westward into Acarnania and took charge of the Delphic Amphictyony—a religious league of about two dozen Greek states charged with administering and safeguarding the oracle of Apollo at Delphi. Although neutral, the Amphictyonic League viewed Gonatas with hostility.

Then there was the Achaean League of a dozen northern and central Peloponnesian cities, also with its own council and army led by a single elected general (maps 5 and 7).[55] The Achaean League had combined against more dominant cities such as Sparta, Corinth, and Argos, and its energetic general Aratus of Sicyon was not enamored about Macedonia extending its presence in the Peloponnese. In 243 Aratus had wrested Acrocorinth (the citadel of Corinth and one of the "fetters" of Greece) from Macedonian control. Aratus had a considerable impact on Philip V, though the latter's advisers were wary of Aratus' attitude to Macedonia's presence in the Peloponnese.

In either late 240 or early 239, aged eighty, Gonatas died—remarkably for that period in his sleep.[56] His reign had benefitted Macedonia and its status in Greece, although in his final half-dozen years he faced increasing problems, especially from the Aetolians. Gonatas' son Demetrius II, father of Philip V, succeeded him, and ruled from 239 to 229.[57] The new king was at war for most of his short reign with the Aetolian League, which may have earned him the nickname *Aetolicus* ("he who keeps fighting the Aetolian" or "he who spends

54. Aetolian League: Antonetti 1990; Grainger 1999; Scholten 2000. Fighters: cf. Polybius 4.8.10 and 4.11.8, with Hammond and Walbank 1988, pp. 377–378.

55. Rise of the league: Austin 2006, no. 67, pp. 141–145; see too Walbank 1957, pp. 215–291; Walbank 2000.

56. Date: Walbank 1940, p. 9; Hammond and Walbank 1988, p. 313 n. 6. Evaluation of his kingship: Tarn 1913, pp. 394–409; Hammond and Walbank 1988, pp. 313–316; Gabbert 1997, pp. 59–72.

57. Walbank 1984a, pp. 446–453; Hammond and Walbank 1988, pp. 317–336; Errington 1990, pp. 173–175; Hammond 1992, pp. 315–318; Scholten 2003, pp. 150–153, and see now the reappraisal by Kuzmin 2019.

all his time in Aetolia").[58] In the spring of 229 the Dardanians (an Illyrian tribe) raided Macedonia, and in battle against them Demetrius was killed.[59]

Demetrius' son Philip (the future Philip V) was only about eight years old, so too young to succeed in his own right. That prompted the hostile Aetolian League to seize the important buffer state of Thessaly, plunging Macedonia into sudden turmoil.[60] At this crucial time we turn more fully to our Philip.

Becoming King

The young Philip was proclaimed king, but leading Macedonians organized a regent for him, who was to marry his father's widow.[61] These circumstances must have been even more exceptional than in 359 when Perdiccas III was killed, and the Assembly bypassed his young son Amyntas to acclaim his uncle Philip II king. Now, in 229, the Assembly turned to Antigonus Doson, a cousin of Demetrius II.

According to Polybius, Doson was ruler or regent and general (*strategos*) of the army, but in reality, and as Polybius also says, "he was the undisputed master of Macedonia."[62] Yet an inscription from Demetrias was addressed to "King Antigonus and Philip," and another from Priene of about 227 refers to "King Antigonus" as "heir to the kingdom of Philip."[63] This type of evidence tells us that Doson accepted Philip as his successor and even an equal, and on Doson's death in 221 the young Philip succeeded to the throne without opposition.[64]

---

58. Hammond and Walbank 1988, pp. 317–336; Scholten 2000, pp. 144–157. Nickname *Aetolicus*: Ehrhardt 1978.

59. Dardanians: Hammond 1966a, pp. 249–253.

60. Scholten 2000, pp. 165–170. Philip's age: Hammond and Walbank 1988, p. 336 n. 3.

61. Polybius 2.45.2 (Philip "still a child"); Plutarch, *Paullus* 8.2–3; Pausanias 7.7.4, with Hammond and Walbank 1988, p. 368; D'Agostini 2019, pp. 16–18. There is no mention of the Assembly doing this.

62. Polybius 2.45.2; Porphyry, *BNJ* 260 F 3.16; Justin 28.3.10; Plutarch, *Paullus* 8.3 (later called king); Pausanias 7.7.4. The Assembly would have officially elected him, but he also had the support of various Macedonian nobles who had been friends of Demetrius II and who supported his accession to the kingship (*basileia*): D'Agostini 2019, pp. 22–26.

63. Demetrias: Pouilloux and Verdélis 1950, pp. 42–43. Priene: Hiller von Gaertringen 1906, no. 37, lines 136–137.

64. See Hammond and Walbank 1988, p. 366, with evidence.

Antigonus III Doson had a short but vital reign from 229 to 221.[65] He ended the Dardanian threat—how, we do not know, but it must have been with a significant enough defeat as it was six years before Macedonia faced another Illyrian invasion. He also recovered some towns in Thessaly that the Aetolians had recently seized.[66] Elsewhere there were problems in Boeotia and the Peloponnese, and in 229 Athens reasserted its independence and expelled the Macedonian garrison that Antipater had originally installed in its port, the Piraeus, and the one established by Poliorcetes on the Museum Hill, a short distance from the Acropolis.[67] But for now Macedonia was secure.

After some military involvement in Caria in 227, perhaps part of a strategy against Egyptian possessions in Asia Minor, Doson addressed the deteriorating situation in the Peloponnese. Since 229 Sparta, under its dynamic king Cleomenes III, had been reestablishing its influence at the Achaeans' expense, forcing Aratus to seek help from the Macedonian king in the winter of 227–226. Doson abandoned his campaign in Caria and disbanded his navy as he intended to restore Macedonian influence in the Peloponnese and recover Acrocorinth, lost to the Achaeans during Gonatas' reign. In 224 Doson defeated Cleomenes, forcing him back to Sparta, and recovered Acrocorinth, where he installed a garrison, along with several other towns (map 7).

Doson and Aratus developed a friendship, and the king kept Aratus close, although he was always careful to ensure that Macedonia did not suffer because of it.[68] He had also sent the young Philip to stay with Aratus so that he could "attach himself to Aratus above all others, and through him to deal with the cities and make the acquaintance of the Achaeans," and Aratus took him under his wing.[69] Philip turned to the older and politically savvy Aratus

65. Walbank 1940, pp. 10–23; Hammond and Walbank 1988, pp. 337–364; Errington 1990, pp. 175–186; Hammond 1992, pp. 318–329; LeBohec 1993; see too King 2018, pp. 242–245.

66. Hammond and Walbank 1988, pp. 337–364.

67. Worthington 2021a, pp. 132–134.

68. Plutarch, *Aratus* 43.2–3, with Errington 1967, pp. 20–21.

69. Plutarch, *Aratus* 46.1–2 and 48.3, refers to Aratus as the *paidagogos* of Philip, someone who had tutoring responsibilities; *contra* Errington 1967, p. 21, that Doson sent Philip to the Peloponnese where he encountered Aratus, not that going to Aratus was the primary aim. Yet given the importance of the Achaean League and Macedonia's position in the Peloponnese it would make sense for Philip to go to Aratus and earn his support for when he became king.

a number of times for advice, something that did not always sit well with the guardians whom Doson had arranged for him, as we shall see.[70]

That winter Doson fashioned his own Hellenic League, a variant of those of Philip II and the earlier Antigonids since its members were not cities but leagues—the Achaeans, Macedonians, Thessalians, Epirotes, Acarnanians, Boeotians, Phocians, Euboeans, and perhaps the Opuntian Locrians.[71] They all remained autonomous, but there was a league council (*synedrion*) presided over by the king, who was also commander-in-chief, although all decisions had to be ratified by the individual leagues when their assemblies met.[72]

In 222 Doson defeated the Spartans in battle at Sellasia, after which Cleomenes fled to Egypt.[73] Unfortunately, the Macedonian king stayed too long in Greece, for in 221 the Illyrians seized on his absence to invade Macedonia. He rushed home and defeated them, but he died soon afterward from a burst blood vessel, "by the very shout that he raised on the field of battle."[74] Although the Aetolian League was still a powerful entity and held towns in Thessaly, and Athens (still the most prominent city in Greece) remained independent, Doson's reign had stabilized Macedonia as well as restored its position in southern Greece. The Macedonia he left Philip was certainly a better one than what he had inherited a decade earlier.

Philip, now about sixteen or seventeen years old, succeeded to the throne in the summer of 221. He was still one or two years shy of the age of majority (eighteen) and perhaps even needed to be twenty before ruling in his own right.[75] Doson, conceivably knowing he was ailing, had drawn up a list of several older guardians to advise Philip on military and foreign affairs until he came of age.[76] He may have wanted no discontent at court or to ensure that

---

70. Plutarch, *Aratus* 48.2–3, on Aratus' influence over Philip (the king "was wholly his"), with D'Agostini 2019, pp. 29–37, calling it "unprecedented" in Antigonid Macedonia, for ordinarily only the king's Friends had this influence (pp. 36–37).

71. Polybius 4.9.5, 7.11.7, and 11.4–6.

72. On the league, see Scherberich 2009.

73. Hammond and Walbank 1988, pp. 354–361.

74. Plutarch, *Cleomenes* 30.2 (from Phylarchus); cf. Polybius 2.70.6, with Walbank 1957, p. 290.

75. Walbank 1940, pp. 295–299. Eighteen is commonly accepted as the age of majority: Hatzopoulos 1986, p. 285 n. 35; Hammond and Walbank 1988, p. 371 n. 2. But see LeBohec 1993—that for kings it was twenty (pp. 780–781 and 785–786 on Philip's age at his accession).

76. Errington 1990, p. 184. See too D'Agostini 2019, pp. 39–41, on Doson's will and its intention, and pp. 41–46 on the "council"; cf. Hatzopoulos 1996, vol. 1, p. 347, though inadvertently claiming that Philip chose his own advisers.

Philip did not undo his achievements either foolishly or ignorantly because of his age.[77] The Assembly confirmed this arrangement when it acclaimed Philip king, who made it clear he would continue Doson's policies, which by implication meant deferring to his guardians.[78]

These men included Leontius, commander of the peltasts; Alexander, commander of the bodyguard and the royal pages; Megaleas, who was in charge of the secretariat; Taurion, who was made general of the Peloponnese (including oversight of the garrisons there); and a man named Apelles.[79] Whether Doson assigned these posts to them is unknown; he may have intended them to look after the kingdom as equals but the Assembly gave them more specific duties, making Apelles, who did not have a particular task, the actual guardian of the young king.[80] Certainly, Apelles comes to have an important advisory role, which led to clashes with Aratus, who was said by Polybius to speak for the king at times as a boy of seventeen could not be expected to speak about affairs of state.[81] Indeed, bitter rivalry soon emerged among the advisers, who split into separate groups, and which led to Philip ridding himself of some of them, including Apelles, as we will see in the next chapter.

Meanwhile there was upheaval throughout Greece. The Dardanians pounced on Philip's borders "because they despised his youth," and the Aetolians attacked the coast of Epirus as well as cities in the Peloponnese.[82] Their actions are a reflection on how they viewed Philip, at least until he came to rule in his own name and was shedding his guardians' influence (chapter 3).[83] Under a brutal commander named Dorimachus they turned first on Messenia in the southwest Peloponnese, which was friendly to the Achaean League, while their allied fleet pillaged the coast of Epirus and

---

77. Walbank 1940, p. 20.

78. Hatzopoulos 2014. Philip's youth and his dealings with his guardians also influenced Polybius' presentation of him: McGing 2013.

79. Polybius 4.87.8; Justin 29.1.8, 10.

80. Several guardians including Apelles, but the other men were not guardians as they had different duties: Hammond and Walbank 1988, pp. 368–369 with n. 8; Hammond 1992, p. 331; *contra* Walbank 1957, p. 356, that all were guardians. On the history of Philip and his guardians, see D'Agostini 2019.

81. Polybius 4.24.1–8 (Aratus' speaking for Philip at 4.24.3), with D'Agostini 2019, pp. 44–46.

82. Dardanians: Justin 29.1.10. Aetolians: Polybius 4.6.1–3.

83. LeBohec 1993.

seized and sold the cargo and crew of a Macedonian merchant ship off Cythera.

Apelles was anxious that if the Aetolians split Achaea's Peloponnesian allies from its league, as was their intention, then Macedonia would be compromised in the Peloponnese. Messenia was also requesting membership of the Hellenic League, which was proving ineffectual. Macedonia was too consumed in the Dardanian menace to intervene properly in Greece, but by spring 220, as complaints against Aetolian behavior and requests for Achaean help intensified, something had to be done.

At a meeting of the Achaean League, Aratus was elected general for the following year and referred Messenia's request formally to the Hellenic League. Until then the Achaeans were to make their own alliance with Messenia to help defend it, though Aratus insisted on its surrendering hostages to ensure loyalty.[84] At this point, in the summer of 220, Philip was old enough to rule in his own right. He had until then been following the policies of Doson and his guardians; now he could deal personally with Macedonia and the issues in Greece, for he had no intention of letting events run their course there. Potentially weighing on his mind was that Egypt, Syria, or even Rome might interfere in Greece, and that if one or more of them supported the Aetolian League against him, he would face a greater threat to his position and kingdom's security.

He could not allow any loss of influence in Greece, especially as the Hellenic League had not been pulling its weight there, probably because it was being led by his advisers who were far from showing a united front.[85] Among other things, Apelles had tried to have Taurion replaced as general in the Peloponnese, which had set Apelles, Leontius, and Megaleas against Taurion and Alexander. The dissension and upheaval would eventually be too much for Philip.[86]

---

84. Walbank 1940, pp. 25–26.

85. Hammond and Walbank 1988, p. 369.

86. Errington 1967, p. 26.

3

The Social War

THE ROMANS HAD already established themselves in Italy and the western Mediterranean before they turned to the eastern Mediterranean.[1] Whether they were consciously imperialistic from the outset or were drawn into the Greek world because of events there continues to divide scholars.[2] Since, however, they already had a "protectorate" of cities in Illyria (Illyris) abutting western Macedonia, it was probably only a matter of time before they turned more fully eastward (map 3).

Rome Arrives in Greece

Philip quickly defeated the Dardanians and turned to the Hellenic League. Its Achaean members were sending out missions to various states urging action against the Aetolians for their incursions into Achaean territory over the years and to admit Messenia as members.[3] The Aetolians, who would prove to be the bane of Philip's life, had suffered losses to the Achaeans but

---

1. For some discussions, see Errington 1971a, pp. 12–34; Derow 1979; Harris 1979, pp. 182–194; Scullard 1989; cf. Eckstein 2006, pp. 158–176. Roman expansion eastward: Errington 1971a; Gruen 1984; Derow 2003; Eckstein 2006; Eckstein 2008; Burton 2011; Rosenstein 2012; Waterfield 2014; cf. Walbank 1963; Green 1990, pp. 414–432; Hoyos 2007. Eckstein's drawing on modern international relations theory to explain Rome's aggressive expansion has met with criticism: see Burton 2011, for example.

2. Cf. Badian 1968; Harris 1979; Gruen 1984; Sherwin-White 1984; Ferrary 1988; Errington 1971a; Kallet-Marx 1995 (from 148 to 162); Eckstein 2006; Eckstein 2008; Camia 2009; Rosenstein 2012; Waterfield 2014. Eckstein 2008, pp. 3–28, has a discussion of both sides.

3. Polybius 4.15.1, with Scholten 2000, pp. 59–95 and 131–163. Achaean relations with Philip after Doson's death: Scherberich 2009, pp. 103–156.

The Last Kings of Macedonia and the Triumph of Rome. Ian Worthington, Oxford University Press.
© Oxford University Press 2023. DOI: 10.1093/oso/9780197520055.003.0004

were still powerful.[4] They had recently defeated Aratus near Caphyae, which concerned Philip greatly as Taurion (his general of the Peloponnese) had supported Aratus and his army against them.[5] An Achaean League assembly held after Aratus' defeat was highly critical of him, and even levied troops.[6] At this time the Aetolians held their own assembly and passed a resolution that they would be at peace with everyone, including Achaea, but only if the latter abandoned its alliance with Messenia.[7] In doing so they neatly avoided wider-ranging hostilities by making it clear that their discontent lay not with Philip or the Hellenic League but only the Achaeans.[8]

The theater of conflict suddenly widened in the summer of 220 when an Illyrian pirate fleet of ninety vessels commanded by Scerdilaidas (a brother of the Illyrian king Agron) and Demetrius of Pharos sailed past Lissus (Lezhë) in Illyria (map 3).[9] It joined the Aetolians in plundering raids in the Peloponnese. But in sailing past Lissus the commanders broke a treaty between Illyria and Rome, to which we now turn to trace Rome's involvement in Greece.

In 229 (the year Demetrius II died and was succeeded by Antigonus III Doson), the Romans sent two envoys to Teuta, queen of the Illyrian tribe of the Ardiaea. Italian traders had complained to the Senate about Illyrian pirates preying on their vessels and hampering the trade route from South Italy to the eastern Adriatic, forcing the Senate to action.[10] Teuta was continuing the policy of her recently deceased husband and Illyrian king Agron.[11] In the 230s Agron had captured the rich city of Phoenice in northwestern Epirus, located on a key route between Illyria and Epirus to Illyria's south. He had, however, died from over-drinking after a victory over the Aetolians that put Acarnania (the area to his west and part of Epirus) under his control. Teuta went on to raid towns along the Adriatic coast and had her eyes set

---

4. Scholten 2000, pp. 198–204.

5. Polybius 4.10–12.14.

6. Polybius 4.14–15.7, with Scholten 2000, pp. 59–95 and 131–163.

7. Polybius 4.15.8–11.

8. Walbank 1940, pp. 27–28.

9. Polybius 4.16.6–11.

10. Polybius 2.8; Appian, *Illyrian Wars* 7, with Gruen 1984, pp. 359–364; Errington 1989a, pp. 85–90; Derow 2003, pp. 51–53. On the dynasty, cf. Hammond 1966a, pp. 242–243; on the tribe, see his pp. 249–250.

11. Polybius 2.2–6, 8–10, with Walbank 1957, pp. 153–167, and see Hammond 1968, pp. 4–7 and 20–21; Gruen 1984, pp. 359–368; Waterfield 2014, pp. 6–10; D'Agostini 2019, pp. 64–67.

on Epidamnus and Corcyra (map 2). These were strategic ports for Adriatic trade, but probably more worrying for the Romans was that she would hold the coast facing Italy and the southern port of Brundisium (Brindisi), the departure point for their fleets across the Adriatic.

When the Roman envoys came into Teuta's presence, she contemptuously killed one of them and imprisoned the other. Rome thus declared war on Illyria in 229, and this First Illyrian War (the name is a modern one) lasted only one year.[12] Teuta acted first; she almost succeeding in taking Epidamnus to thwart a Roman landing there, but the Epidamnians resisted her, forcing her to Corcyra. She overcame a largely Achaean navy, making Demetrius, ruler of the Illyrian island of Pharos (modern Hvar—not to be confused with Pharos at Alexandria), commander of a garrison there. Teuta went back to Epidamnus, but when a Roman army put in at Corcyra, Demetrius surrendered. The Romans then sailed north to the strategic port of Apollonia in southern Illyria on the right bank of the Aous (Aoös) River, only six miles (ten kilometers) from the Adriatic. From there they went to Epidamnus and Issa, which they saved from Teuta; realizing all was lost, she surrendered.

Corcyra, Apollonia, and Epidamnus, all strategic ports, placed themselves under Rome's protection, and the Romans went on to conclude friendship treaties (*amicitia*) with various other Illyrian peoples, such as the Parthini and the peoples of Atintania and Issa.[13] Teuta was spared, but had to live at Rhizon, abandon all her territory, and—what Polybius says "mostly concerned the Greeks"—agree to no more than two unarmed Illyrian ships sailing south of Lissus.[14] The First Illyrian War expanded Rome's presence in Illyria; the limits of its protectorate now ran from north of Epidamnus to the south of Apollonia, bringing it closer to Epirus and Macedonia.[15]

Now, in the summer of 220, the activities of the Illyrian pirates created a new dynamic in the escalating tensions in Greece. After their raids, the two Illyrian commanders split up, with Scerdilaidas agreeing to support the

---

12. Polybius 2.11–12, and see Gruen 1984, pp. 364–368, 438–439; Hammond and Walbank 1988, pp. 334–335; Errington 1989a, pp. 86–90; Eckstein 2008, pp. 30–41; Matyszak 2009, pp. 20–22; Waterfield 2014, pp. 21–25; Burton 2017, pp. 19–22.

13. Polybius 2.11.5–11—these were not actual treaties of alliance or *foedera*. On the settlement, see Hammond 1968, pp. 7–9 (especially important for the geography); see too Derow 1991, especially pp. 267–270. Nomenclature of treaties: Gruen 1984, pp. 13–17, 55–69, 95; especially Burton 2011.

14. Polybius 2.12.3.

15. Borders of protectorate: Hammond 1967, p. 599.

Aetolians against Achaea.[16] Aratus, pressed harder by Aetolian attacks, sent out a call for help to Philip, which may have prompted the king to order Taurion to solicit Demetrius of Pharos' help for the Achaeans.[17] Philip likely saw Demetrius as a useful ally because of his connections in Illyria, and if we accept Polybius' views, Demetrius came to exert no small influence over the king.[18]

Philip and his army in the meantime marched to Corinth, where he ordered all member states of the Hellenic League to send representatives to a council meeting.[19] He campaigned briefly in the Peloponnese to counteract a group in Sparta that had made a pact with Aetolia, leading to violence in the city and the deaths of some pro-Macedonian leaders.[20] Although he was urged to destroy Sparta, he refused to do so as he had accepted the reasons given by an embassy of ten Spartans that also emphasized Spartan loyalty to Macedonia.

His reasoning is not seen as his own by Polybius, who writes that "it is scarcely probable that a boy of seventeen should be able to decide about such grave matters."[21] Whether Philip was influenced by someone else, say Aratus, is unknown, but a young age does not exclude maturity of opinions.[22] He may well have realized that moderation would endear him more to the members of the Hellenic League, given he needed their support in any war against the Aetolians.[23]

Back at Corinth, the allied council aired various grievances against the Aetolians and unanimously voted to declare war on them, resolving to liberate cities captured by the Aetolians after the death of Demetrius II and coerced

---

16. Polybius 4.29.5–6, with Walbank 1940, pp. 29–30.

17. Aratus: Polybius 4.19.1. Taurion: Polybius 4.19.78 (Taurion acting independently). On Aetolian affairs, see Scholten 2000, pp. 194–214.

18. Scherberich 2009, pp. 132–134; Kleu 2015, pp. 24–25. On Demetrius, see Coppola 1993, with Derow 1991; Eckstein 1994. See too Errington 1971a, pp. 102–109, noting that Demetrius probably did not think the piratical voyage violated the terms of the treaty as it was between Rome and Teuta (p. 106); *contra* Eckstein 1994, p. 58.

19. Polybius 4.22.2.

20. Polybius 4.22.3–24.9.

21. Polybius 4.24.1.

22. But see D'Agostini 2019, pp. 32–37.

23. Hammond and Walbank 1988, p. 373 with n. 1. Generally, see Briscoe 1978 (pp. 153–157 on Philip).

into their league, including Delphi.[24] These resolves have been described as a "ringing declaration" for the restoration of those states' ancestral laws and constitutions, echoing the slogan of "the freedom of the Greeks" from earlier times, and have ominous similarities to Rome's settlement of Greece in 196 (pp. 144–146).[25]

Philip returned to Pella in the fall to prepare for war, which included persuading Scerdilaidas, who was aggrieved that the Aetolians had not given him any spoils, to attack them with thirty boats—but for a payment of twenty talents per year.[26] This retainer meant that Philip was encouraging an Illyrian fleet to operate south of Lissus, which broke the terms of the alliance between Rome and Illyria.[27] He must have been aware of this, so why was he willing to risk conflict with Rome?

Perhaps his action stemmed from the snub Antigonus III Doson suffered at the end of the First Illyrian War in 228. Philip was only about eight at the time, but he had a long memory. After negotiating the peace terms in that year, one of the Roman army commanders, Lucius Postumius Albinus, sent embassies on probably courtesy visits to the Aetolian and Achaean Leagues, which had also been fighting the Illyrians, and then Corinth and Athens.[28] Curiously, no embassy went to Macedonia, despite its enmity with Illyria and its influence in the Greek world.

Rome's disregard of Macedonia, along with the Epirote League and Acarnania—the states most affected by Rome's intervention in Illyria—was not an oversight: the Romans knew Macedonia's history. Even Livy admits that the Second Macedonian War, which we discuss in chapters 6 and 7, "was almost more noteworthy [than the Second Punic War] because of the fame of Macedonian kings of old [Philip II and Alexander the Great], the ancient glory of its people, and the extent of its empire, within which the Macedonians had earlier held much of Europe and most of Asia."[29] As Hammond sagely notes, it is significant that Roman embassies went to Macedonia's enemies,

24. Polybius 4.25–26.2 = Austin 2006, no. 72, pp. 152–153, with Fine 1940; Walbank 1940, p. 32; Scherberich 2009, pp. 81–102.

25. Gruen 1984, p. 141. On the concept, see Gruen 1984, pp. 132–157, and especially Dmitriev 2011.

26. Polybius 4.27.9–10, 4.29.1–7; Justin 29.1.10–11.

27. Hammond and Walbank 1988, p. 274.

28. Polybius 2.12.4–8.

29. Livy 31.1.6–7.

showing that in the event of warfare Rome's sympathies in the first instance lay not with Macedonia.[30] Nor would the Romans' feelings about Macedonia have been lost on the Greeks.[31]

What lay at the heart of Philip's thinking was the reduction of the Roman presence in Illyria. In 220 an opportunity presented itself to Philip when relations between Rome and Carthage were deteriorating to the extent that war between them loomed. Unfortunately for Philip at this time, in the spring of 219 the Senate deployed a large naval and military force under the consul Lucius Aemilius Paullus to Illyria to counter the ambitious Demetrius, who had been attacking cities allied to Rome in Illyria. Thus began the Second Illyrian War.[32]

This second war did not last long. Paullus, with 20,000 infantry and 2,000 cavalry, besieged Dimale (sometimes called Dimallum, inland from Apollonia), which Demetrius had garrisoned. When Dimale fell a week later, Paullus besieged Pharos, which soon capitulated. With his troops deserting him, Demetrius fled for refuge to Philip, leaving Rome even more vested in Illyria. That outcome left Philip with little choice but to return to the so-called Social War or War of the Allies against the Aetolians.

The First Phase of the Social War

The Social War lasted from 220 to 217 and turned Greece into a war zone.[33] It may be divided into two broad phases. The first was from its outset to the winter of 219/18, when Philip had gone to Argos after some hard-fought engagements and disaffection on the part of his army. The second, which included a naval offensive, was from late winter or spring 218 to the war's conclusion in 217. In the following account of the war the focus is on actions involving Philip rather than all details of the many clashes between Achaeans and Aetolians.

---

30. Hammond 1968, p. 9.

31. Waterfield 2014, pp. 25–26.

32. Polybius 3.16, 3.18–19; Appian, *Illyrian Wars* 2.8, with Walbank 1957, pp. 324–327 and 330–331. War: Hammond 1968, pp. 11–15; Errington 1971a, pp. 102–109; Gruen 1984, pp. 369–373; Errington 1989a, pp. 90–94; Eckstein 1994, pp. 46–59; Eckstein 2008, pp. 60–73; Matyszak 2009, pp. 24–27; Waterfield 2014, pp. 30–33.

33. Walbank 1940, pp. 24–67; Walbank 1957, pp. 451–487, 513–562, and 622–630; Walbank 1984a, pp. 474–481; Hammond and Walbank 1988, pp. 371–391; Scholten 2000, pp. 200–228; Matyszak 2009, pp. 28–32.

The Social War allowed Philip to continue Doson's policy of strengthening Macedonia's hold in Greece and forging closer ties with the strategic areas of Epirus and Acarnania.[34] But Philip was not going to act impulsively even with the Achaean League on his side. One crucial aspect of his foresight and planning that we see time and again is the maintenance of his communication and supply lines, even opening new ones where needed. That was why he decided that committing troops into central Greece and the Peloponnese needed a new line of communication down the west coast through friendly Epirus and Acarnania.

In the summer of 219 Philip set off from Pella with 15,000 infantry and 800 cavalry.[35] On paper, so to speak, his resources looked strong, but in reality, Macedonia "had been punching above its weight" for over a century.[36] He did not have abundant manpower and he was faced by more than his fair share of adversaries, to which we can soon add Rome. Not that these factors were going to stop him. He traveled through Thessaly, and then over the Zygos Pass into Epirus, where he received the entire Epirote military levy, 300 infantry (slingers) from Acarnania, and 500 Cretan infantry. Then he made his way to the fortified town of Ambracus (Arta), the port of Ambracia, to try to sever the alliance between that state and the Aetolian League.[37]

Polybius claims that if Philip had marched directly into Aetolia he would have ended the Social War there and then; instead the Epirotes persuaded him to besiege Ambracus, a city they were eager to recover.[38] However, Philip needed to take the city to lay claim to the Ambracian Gulf and so be in a better position to march on Aetolia.[39] His detour, though, allowed the Aetolian general Scopas to muster an army and march via Thessaly into Macedonia, destroying crops and collecting booty, before turning back to storm Dium, the religious center of the kingdom and home to the sanctuary of the chief god Zeus Olympius, Macedonia's protector. He burned and destroyed many of Dium's houses and monuments and toppled the royal statues, though the

---

34. Errington 1990, p. 186. On the Epirote League, see Hammond 1967, pp. 595–635 and 648–657 (in Philip's reign, see pp. 602–621).

35. Polybius 4.37.7.

36. Matyszak 2009, p. 27.

37. Polybius 5.61.1–2, with Hammond 1967, p. 603. Chronology: Walbank 1957, p. 515; Errington 1990, p. 186.

38. Polybius 4.61.3–7.

39. Walbank 1940, pp. 38–39.

population was able to escape into the hills.[40] After that Scopas returned to Aetolia to a hero's welcome.

The Aetolians' despoiling the shrine of Zeus may also have had a political element to it—"an explicit attack on the Antigonid dynastic charisma, and specifically on Philip's leadership claim: it was designed to show the ineptitude of the heir and his unsuitability to rule."[41] If that is so, it did not work as Philip's leadership was never questioned even though he did not abandon the siege of Ambracus when news reached him of the attack. After forty days the Aetolian forces at Ambracus surrendered, and Philip handed the city to the Epirotes. He next ferried his army over to Actium, the port of Acarnania, where many years later in 31 Antony and Cleopatra were famously defeated by Agrippa and Octavian.[42]

At Actium Philip took on 2,000 Acarnanian infantry and 200 cavalry and marched to Phoetiae, which was in Aetolian hands. Phoetiae fell after a two-day siege, after which he marched and set up a camp close to Stratus. There he received calls from Aratus for help (a sign that the destruction at Dium had not affected his standing) since the Achaeans had suffered setbacks in the Peloponnese, but for the moment Philip did not respond to the pleas.[43] He was intent on establishing his communications line and securing a base from which to carry out operations against Aetolia. In this, we see his resolve to adhere to his original strategy, despite the disheartening psychological effect of the Aetolians' destruction at Dium.

Philip continued moving south in Acarnania, destroying Aetolian forts along the way.[44] He reached the fortified town of Oeniadae, on the west bank of the Achelous River, which afforded access to the whole of the south of Acarnania and was the chief port at the entrance to the Corinthian Gulf. After taking other towns in the area, he reinforced Oeniadae's citadel and built a protecting wall to shield its harbor and dockyards with a view to turning it into a naval base. Most important, he had his desired supply line for future inroads in the Peloponnese.[45]

---

40. Polybius 4.62.1–3, with Walbank 1957, pp. 516–517; Grainger 1999, p. 14; Scholten 2000, pp. 214–220; D'Agostini 2019, pp. 69–70.

41. D'Agostini 2019, p. 69.

42. Polybius 4.63.1–4.

43. Polybius 4.63.7–64.3.

44. Polybius 4.64.4–11.

45. Polybius 4.65; cf. Walbank 1957, pp. 519–521; Walbank 1940, p. 41.

The news now reached him of an impending Dardanian invasion of his kingdom, something he could not ignore. He told the Achaean envoys he could not give them military support after all and prepared to cross the Gulf of Ambracia from Acarnania to Epirus just as Demetrius of Pharos arrived at his camp, having been defeated by Rome in the Second Illyrian War (see above).[46] Philip sent Demetrius to Corinth, and thence to Macedonia at his own pace. The Romans had taken no further action against Demetrius, presumably because the Second Punic War pitting Rome against Carthage had just begun (218–201), but they would have taken note that Philip had welcomed him.[47]

The Dardanians abandoned their invasion because of Philip's sudden return to his kingdom, allowing the king to move to Larissa in Thessaly for the summer to block any Aetolian inroads into Macedonia.[48] The Aetolians were indeed on the offensive, for in late fall under their new general Dorimachus they overwhelmed parts of Epirus and sacked the oracular sanctuary of Dodona, destroying the temple of Zeus.[49] This raid was meant to have a demoralizing effect on the people, though whether it was also intended to show Philip's failings as king, this time in the eyes of the Epirotes, is another matter.[50] On the other hand, Philip may have felt he needed to restore some faith in himself as he mounted a sudden winter offensive, relying on his new western coast route for his provisions, into Arcadia and Elis. Armies did not usually campaign in winter and those on the move were hard to keep secret, but Philip did both. With 5,000 infantry and 400 cavalry he stormed fortresses, collected booty, and captured prisoners, in revenge for the destruction at Dodona.[51] A fast march now followed to Corinth, where he arrived unannounced in December 219.[52]

From Corinth Philip sent orders to the Achaean troops to muster at the Arcadian city of Caphyae. On his way there, he encamped at Phlius, where he

46. Polybius 4.66.1–5; Hammond 1968, p. 11; LeBohec 1987, pp. 203–208; Coppola 1993, p. 41; Scherberich 2009, pp. 215–216.

47. On this war, see for example Errington 1971a, pp. 49–101; Lazenby 1978; Briscoe 1989.

48. Polybius 4.66.6–7.

49. Polybius 4.67.1–4 (with Walbank 1957, p. 522); Diodorus 26.4.7, with Hammond 1967, pp. 576, 604; Scholten 2000, pp. 222–224.

50. D'Agostini 2019, p. 73.

51. Polybius 4.75.2–7. Campaigns at this time: Walbank 1940, pp. 40–43.

52. Polybius 4.67.7–8.

came upon a force of 2,000 Aetolian men under Euripidas, soundly defeating them. Eight hundred of the enemy were killed and the rest were taken prisoner, though Euripidas escaped and spread the news that the Macedonians were in the Peloponnese, robbing Philip of his element of surprise. At Caphyae, Aratus' son, also named Aratus, brought him 4,000 reinforcements. Philip allowed his men two days of rest before besieging the seemingly impregnable fortress of Psophis in northwest Arcadia where Euripidas had taken refuge. Philip's men eventually scaled the walls and overcame a sudden sally by the defenders, leaving Euripidas no option but to surrender. After giving the city to the Achaeans, Philip continued south, arriving at Olympia five days later, where he sacrificed to Zeus and gave his men a well-deserved three-day rest.[53]

Philip was certainly enjoying military successes, but he was coming into increasing conflict with his guardians, especially Apelles. They resented that he had been handing over key towns to the Achaeans and they mistrusted Aratus; if we believe Polybius, Apelles had a "base project" of reducing the Achaeans to the status of the Thessalians, who had to obey Macedonian orders.[54] Philip knew that Macedonia needed the Achaeans as allies, but matters came to a head at Olympia.[55] There, Aratus angrily denounced Apelles to the king for his handling of the Achaean troops, which included roughly ejecting them from their quarters and taking them over, refusing to share booty, and even flogging them for petty crimes. Philip cautioned Apelles to treat the Achaeans properly but did no more.[56]

Given the conflict and to try to prevent similar animosity in the future, Philip may now have issued an edict to do with military organization and management, given its stipulations about sharing booty, stationing quarters, and punishments, which we mentioned in chapter 2.[57] It has been suggested that Philip's edict was the start of an estrangement between Apelles and the king, by now twenty years old and eager to become his own man.[58]

---

53. Polybius 4.67.8–73.4. The campaign into Elis that Polybius goes on to describe likely took place earlier, following Walbank: see above.

54. Polybius 4.76.1–2. The view that Apelles worked to discredit Aratus by supporting a group wanting socioeconomic change in the league (put forward by Walbank 1940, pp. 48–50) is erroneous: Mendels 1977, pp. 157–158.

55. Walbank 1940, pp. 30–31 and 44–67; Errington 1967; D'Agostini 2019, pp. 41–49.

56. Polybius 4.76.3–9.

57. Juhel 2002.

58. D'Agostini 2019, pp. 55–57. On the age of majority for kings being twenty, see LeBohec 1993.

This may be so. But it is well to remember that Philip did nothing more than admonish Apelles, leaving Aratus still resentful. We return to Apelles below.

Philip next conducted a six-day maneuver in Triphylia, an area of Elis with Messenia to its south of great strategic value.[59] The Aetolians were now led by Euripidas' successor Phillidas, who headed into Triphylia and divided his men among its three major fortresses: Lepreum, Alipheira, and Typaneae. In doing so he played into Philip's hands. The king stormed Alipheira first; he scaled the walls at sunrise, and the defenders could do nothing but surrender. Phillidas then evacuated his men from Typaneae and rushed to Lepreum, at which point Typaneae and other fortresses capitulated.

His successes spurred the people of another fortress town, Phigalia, to expel their Aetolian garrison and ally to Philip, who sent Taurion and some troops to defend them. In the meantime, the king marched against Lepreum, which soon surrendered. Phillidas fled, but later gave himself up and was allowed to withdraw to Elis. Philip then handed over all fortresses bar Lepreum (in which he installed a Macedonian garrison) to the Achaean League; if Apelles had been against his decision, he was evidently overruled.[60]

Philip's campaign checked any further Aetolian forays in the Peloponnese, and as Sparta was effectively isolated there its defiance was inconsequential. Afterward, and ending the first phase of the Social War, Philip decided to winter in Argos, said to be the original home of the Argeads and Antigonids.[61] His speed and successes put him on a par with a young Alexander the Great, who in a single year (335) battled tribes in Thrace and Illyria and besieged and razed Thebes—the Thebans at first did not believe it was him as he covered the 250 miles (402 kilometers) from Illyria to Thebes (with only one day's rest in Thessaly) in a mere thirteen days.[62] And like Alexander, Philip led from the front and exhorted his men, even when that meant putting his life in danger, as was expected of a Macedonian warrior king.

But a weakness for Philip—and for all Macedonian kings—was his need of money. The Macedonians, as we mentioned earlier, practiced a rolling economy, using the proceeds of one campaign to finance the next. Philip had installed garrisons at Heraea, Lepreum, Phigalia, Orchomenus, and

---

59. Polybius 4.77.5–80.16, with Walbank 1957, pp. 528–531, on the location. Details: Walbank 1940, pp. 46–47; Scholten 2000, pp. 218–220; Scherberich 2009, pp. 139–142.

60. Cf. D'Agostini 2019, pp. 72–75.

61. Polybius 4.82.1.

62. Worthington 2014, pp. 128–135.

Acrocorinth, and he probably relied on mercenaries for garrison duty elsewhere and to help guard Thessaly and his supply depot at Chalcis on Euboea.
The drain on his resources must have been severe. We see this in an order he
issued to the *epistates* (overseer) of Thessalonica to switch oversight of the
considerable funds in the Serapeum and perhaps all sanctuaries throughout
Macedonia from the city to his *epistates*.[63] His measure may have been to
safeguard these funds if people impoverished from years of warfare had been
appropriating them—or it could have been a cynical attempt to raise revenue.

The Second Phase of the Social War

At Argos, Philip decided on a divide-and-conquer naval operation against
the Aetolian League in tandem with his land army severing the communication lines of Sparta, Elis, and Aetolia, and attacking each one individually.[64]
Macedonian naval ascendancy had been eroded after Antigonus Doson's
Carian expedition of 227, so in 218 Philip set to work to restore some sem-
blance of it.[65] For this he needed Achaean support, which is why he attended
the February 218 meeting of the Achaean Assembly at Sicyon.[66] Despite
Aratus' coolness toward him because of the continuing intrigues of Apelles,
the league provided the king fifty talents, together with three months' pay for
the troops, seventeen talents a month for his costs in the Peloponnese, 10,000
bushels of grain, and several warships.

Philip's joint land and sea venture was a new strategy in the war. It may
have been on the advice of Demetrius of Pharos, who had recently joined the
king at Larisa, for Justin credits Demetrius with turning Philip's attention to
the northwest.[67] Possibly Taurion also had the ear of the king, who was much
less worried about what Philip might do with a navy than, say, some of his
guardians like Apelles.[68] The king of course was not building a war fleet. He

---

63. *ISE* 2, no. 111, pp. 100–102 = Burstein 1985, no. 72, pp. 97–98 = Hatzopoulos 1996, vol. 2, no. 15, pp. 39–40; see too Welles 1938, pp. 249–251 (p. 250 for Philip protecting the money).

64. Walbank 1940, pp. 50–51. On Philp's dealings with Elis, see D'Agostini 2019, pp. 60–62.

65. Walbank 1982, pp. 224–225 (Antigonus III) and pp. 225–229 (Philip's naval policy); in detail on Philip: Kleu 2015.

66. Polybius 5.1.6–12, with Walbank 1957, pp. 538–539; D'Agostini 2019, pp. 74–75. On
Achaean assemblies, see Walbank 1957, pp. 219–220; especially Walbank 1979, pp. 406–414.

67. Justin 29.2.1–6, with D'Agostini 2019, pp. 75–77.

68. D'Agostini 2019, pp. 75–80. See too Walbank 1940, pp. 50–51; Kleu 2015, pp. 31–42; cf.
Coppola 1993, pp. 132–136.

had no more than twelve warships and forty light craft, which he intended as transport vessels for his troops to obstruct the Aetolians, Spartans, and Eleans from uniting with each other while putting pressure on their supply lines.[69]

After moving to Corinth, Philip trained his infantrymen and mercenaries as oarsmen and sent Apelles to Chalcis on Euboea to manage his important supply depot there.[70] Then in May 218 he embarked on a dual campaign against the Aetolians and to protect Epirus and Acarnania.[71] He sent his fleet with 6,000 Macedonians and 1,200 mercenaries from Corinth's port of Lechaeum to invest the strategically important island of Cephallenia (Cephalonia); lying off western Greece in the Ionian Sea, it was the Aetolian naval base for plundering the coasts of Epirus, Acarnania, and the Peloponnese. Philip's fleet was joined by contingents from Messenia and the Acarnanian and Epirote Leagues, and he paid for fifteen *lembi* (fast smaller craft with a complement of fifty, favored by Illyrian pirates) from Scerdilaidas.[72]

In response, half the Aetolian levy led by Dorimachus invaded Thessaly and Epirus to try to halt Philip and even threaten Macedonia; the other half remained in western Aetolia. Philip by now had arrived at Cephallenia and laid siege to the town of Pale (perhaps modern Lixouri). Despite damaging its walls, his men suffered heavy casualties, especially when Leontius the peltast commander tried to break into the city, forcing Philip to cut his losses.[73] He was said to have thought Leontius acted cowardly—yet it was Philip who ordered the retreat probably because of the casualty rate, and Leontius kept the loyalty of the peltasts until he was executed (see below).[74]

The Acarnanians urged Philip to sail to Aetolia, taking advantage of half of the Aetolian army's absence, but the Messenians, facing hostile Aetolians, needed him in the Peloponnese on their behalf. Leontius supported the latter, seeing it as a means of restoring Macedonian domination in the Peloponnese. Apelles and Megaleas may have been of the same mind, as all three had been

---

69. D'Agostini 2019, pp. 75–80. See too Walbank 1940, pp. 50–51; Kleu 2015, pp. 31–42; cf. Coppola 1993, pp. 132–136.

70. Polybius 5.2.7–11.

71. Polybius 5.2.11–6.6. On the campaign in detail, see Walbank 1940, pp. 50–53; Hammond and Walbank 1988, pp. 378–379; Coppola 1993, pp. 136–139; Scherberich 2009, pp. 143–144; D'Agostini 2019, pp. 83–93.

72. Polybius 5.95.1–3, with Kleu 2015, pp. 33–36. Messenia was now involved in the war after the capture of Phigaleia: Walbank 1940, p. 53 n. 1.

73. Polybius 5.4.9–13.

74. Errington 1967, pp. 30–31.

against Philip's campaign the previous spring and believed operations in the Peloponnese would counteract the Aetolians and Aratus' influence there.[75] Aratus naturally was against this and urged the king to conquer Aetolia.[76]

Philip, perhaps eager to follow up on his previous successes, decided on Aetolia, hence siding with Aratus, though he did send the Achaean general Eperatus to support Messenia against the Aetolians there.[77] He sailed quickly from Cephallenia to the Ionian island of Leucas, entered the Ambracian Gulf by night, and landed by dawn in the Acarnanian town of Limnaea in the southeast Ambracian Gulf. He was close to the northeast border with Aetolia, where Acarnanian and Epirote soldiers were waiting. Since he had cannily brought provisions with him from Pale, he had no need to waste time foraging.

He left Limnaea one afternoon and with 10,000 troops embarked on a series of forced marches over 50 miles (80 kilometers) in only twenty-eight hours to Thermum, the religious center of the Aetolian League and the location of its assembly meetings.[78] But tensions between Aratus and Leontius were rising. Aratus had wanted the army to reach Thermum as soon as possible and not risk a pitched battle with the Aetolians who were rushing to its defense. Leontius had advised the king to rest the men after their night march, perhaps worried by his experience at Pale of over-tired troops battling an army on its own soil. Philip again sided with Aratus, though he cautiously kept his army in a battle formation in case he was ambushed.

Philip gave orders to devastate Thermum—for the first time in its history—and the surrounding villages, perhaps bowing here to Demetrius of Pharos and Aratus, who hated the Aetolians.[79] The men destroyed and burned temples and other buildings, sparing only statues of the gods out of respect, as Philip got his revenge for the Aetolians' despoiling of Dium and Dodona. Likewise, he approved of his men who scribbled a graffito on the walls of the temple of Apollo that the sacking of Thermum was the vengeance of Zeus: "Do you see how far the thunderbolt of Zeus has stretched?" The verse was a

75. Errington 1967, pp. 31–32; D'Agostini 2019, p. 83.

76. Polybius 5.5.5–9.

77. Walbank 1940, pp. 53–54; cf. D'Agostini 2019, p. 83.

78. Polybius 5.7.7–8.4, with Walbank 1957, pp. 543–545, on his route; Walbank 1940, p. 54; cf. Scholten 2000, pp. 294–295. Importance of Thermum: Antonetti 1990, pp. 151–209; Scholten 2000, pp. 220–223; cf. Walbank 1957, p. 546.

79. Polybius 5.8.3–9.7, with Scholten 2000, pp. 223–224, 284–286; cf. Kleu 2015, pp. 36 and 186. On the influences on Philip, see Eckstein 1994, pp. 53–54 and 55; D'Agostini 2019, pp. 85–87.

parody by Samus (one of the king's Friends) of a line from Euripides to evoke
the sacking of Zeus' sanctuaries at Dium and Dodona, hence connecting Zeus
to Philip as the avenger of his people.[80] That association continued in com-
memorative coinage that he now struck, including a bronze coin with Zeus'
head and oak wreath on the obverse and *Basileos Philippou* ("King Philip")
with Pan on the reverse.[81]

Polybius, our only author to record Philip's actions at Thermum, has a
long excursus condemning him for the destruction.[82] He called it irrational
and illegal; compared him to Philip II and Alexander, who never resorted
to such terrible acts; and lectured that Philip should have had the same high
principles as them. Yet invasion and devastation of lands and towns in war
were expected, even when they were religious sites; Alexander in Asia was
certainly guilty of this, and more recently the Aetolians had committed similar sacrilegious acts at Dium and Dodona.[83] Again we see Polybius' bias, especially as he deliberately gives his account of the destruction a moral twist
by referring to "the laws of war" to discredit Philip's action while applying the
same term to Achaean actions with no similar criticism.[84]

The attack on Thermum was also intended to break the spirit of the
Aetolians and force them to terms, though they did not do so.[85] After stocking
up on fodder and grain, Philip returned to Limnaea. He expected an Aetolian
strike, so he sent the booty and phalangites first, then the Acarnanians and
mercenaries, and finally he laid an ambush with handpicked peltasts and some
Illyrians concealed in undergrowth by a hill.[86] Leontius was put in charge
of the operation. As soon as Philip left, 3,000 Aetolians entered Thermum
and then rushed to charge what they thought was his rear, but they were

---

80. Polybius 5.8.46; line: Euripides, *Suppliants* 860. D'Agostini 2019, pp. 86–87, sees Philip's
action at Thermum as a turning point in his kingship: by it, he had shown to all and sundry
that he was the protector of his people and had Zeus on his side confirming the legitimacy of
his kingship (*basileia*). But no one was doubting his kingship, and in acclaiming him king the
Assembly had confirmed his legitimate kingship.

81. D'Agostini 2019, pp. 90–91, for illustrations.

82. Polybius 5.10–12.8.

83. But see D'Agostini 2019, pp. 91–93.

84. On the phrasing and implications for Polybius, cf. Nicholson 2018a.

85. Psychology of destruction: Walbank 1940, pp. 54–55.

86. Polybius 5.13.1–14.8. Walbank 1957, p. 510, suspects the Illyrians were mercenaries, but they
may have been sent earlier by Scerdilaidas to Cephallenia on the fifteen *lembi* (D'Agostini 2019,
p. 96).

trapped by the ambush and fled with losses. Later, not far from Stratus, 4,000 Aetolian and Cretan troops tried to block Philip at the Achelous River. Philip crossed the river and in fierce fighting, with the Illyrians proving their mettle, defeated them. When he reached Limnaea he made a sacrifice of thanksgiving followed by a celebratory banquet for his campaign and safe return.

Conspiracy or Purge?

The friction between Aratus and the guardians now exploded. As Aratus was leaving the banquet, Leontius, Megaleas, and an unknown man named Crinon verbally abused him and pelted him with stones, which grew into an all-out brawl when supporters of all the men rushed to their aid.[87] Philip demanded to know what had happened before responding in a "new and autocratic light."[88] He fined Megaleas and Crinon the huge sum of twenty talents each—far beyond any prescribed penalties for transgressions in his military edict of 218 (see p. 53). But these were exceptional circumstances, and he may have wanted to make a point.[89]

Curiously, after he embarked on his next campaign and put in to Leucas, Philip called his Friends (*philoi*) together to hear the protests of the accused men and approve their fine, perhaps because he wanted to test his advisers' loyalty as Leontius had defended Megaleas.[90] They reaffirmed his decision even though Crinon and Megaleas did not speak, despite Aratus condemning them. Neither man could afford the fine, so Crinon was imprisoned and Leontius stood bail for Megaleas.

The confrontation at Limnaea had clearly grown out of hand. But it is going too far to speculate that Leontius, Megaleas, and Crinon were out to murder Aratus as part of a conspiracy organized by Apelles because he felt he could no longer control Philip.[91] It is striking that the hostile Polybius would not take the opportunity to tell us about a plot as that would paint

---

87. Polybius 5.15.1–5; Plutarch, *Aratus* 48.4 (see 48.1–4 on relations with the guardians).

88. Walbank 1940, p. 56.

89. Polybius 5.15.7–9, with Walbank 1957, pp. 550–552. D'Agostini 2019, pp. 98–99, makes too much in this instance of Philip's penalty departing from the code.

90. Polybius 5.16.1–8, with D'Agostini 2019, pp. 99–10.

91. D'Agostini 2019, pp. 98–101; cf. Hammond and Walbank 1988, p. 381, against Walbank 1940 pp. 56–57. Cf. Polybius 5.26.3–5 (Apelles intended more power though this was not an accusation against him). Polybius added Aratus to the mix when he had him speak at the meeting of the Friends and denounce Megaleas and Crinon.

Philip in an unfavorable light. In fact, there is little to support the idea of a conspiracy.[92] Polybius is biased against Apelles because of his attitude to Aratus, whose character Polybius regarded with the utmost favor. Polybius' pro-Achaean stance underpins his version of events.[93] Possibly even Philip implicated Apelles and the others in a conspiracy to end the dissension among the guardians, sever all ties to Doson's reign, and assert his kingship (*basileia*) once and for all.[94] We should therefore not rule out that some of Philip's other advisers, even at the instigation of Aratus, denounced Apelles and his friends, causing Philip to conduct a purge of opponents, which became confused with a conspiracy.[95]

It was inevitable that a young king would butt heads with older advisers inherited from a predecessor. He was not alone. When Alexander the Great became king at age twenty in 336 he ignored the urging of the "Old Guard" generals Antipater and Parmenion to marry and have an heir before he embarked for Asia in 334. The standoffs with Parmenion, and with his son Philotas, continued during the campaign and led to their executions, even engineered by Alexander, in 330.[96]

D'Agostini argues that the whole affair of Philip's guardians shows the existence of factionalism at court, with Apelles, Leontius, and Megaleas representing traditional barons against Philip's new ventures like his ambitious naval program, while others like Taurion supported them. True, factionalism existed at any court, but in 218 Philip had not been king for very long; he had to enforce his authority and ensure the stability of his kingship.[97] Despite the setback at Pale, Macedonia had the edge in the Social War, especially after the destruction of Thermum, hence he now felt he could shed himself of his advisers.

Philip set sail to meet up with the full levy of the Achaean League at Tegea (map 7). They laid waste the Laconian plain near Amyclae and as far south

---

92. Cf. Walbank 1940, pp. 48–52 and 56–61; Errington 1967, pp. 19–36; Hammond and Walbank 1988, pp. 382–383; especially D'Agostini 2019, pp. 95–115, arguing that the episode is more to do with Aratus' moves than Apelles.

93. Haegemans and Kosmetatou 2005; cf. Gruen 1972. See Polybius 4.8 on Aratus.

94. Errington 1967, pp. 29–35; D'Agostini 2019, for example, pp. 79–80 and 95–115.

95. Errington 1967, pp. 35–36; cf. Walbank 1940, p. 52.

96. Worthington 2014, pp. 216–220.

97. D'Agostini 2019, pp. 77–80.

as Taenarum and Malea and even defeated a Spartan army under its king Lycurgus.[98] The king amassed considerable booty, which he sold at Tegea, where envoys from Rhodes and Chios met him and offered to negotiate peace with the Aetolians. This is an example of the common practice of third-party mediation in warfare. Philip was receptive to them, but Polybius says this was simply to mask his intentions to continue the war.

Polybius tells us that at this time the Royal Guard (*agema*) and the peltasts, commanded by Leontius, Megaleas, and Ptolemy (the guard commander), suddenly rioted over their treatment and especially that they were being deprived of booty, probably because Philip had to divert all his liquid money to his running costs, one of the downsides to a rolling economy.[99] The men went on a rampage, plundering from the tents of the king's Friends and the royal apartments. Their anger was probably legitimate, for they had put their lives on the line for their king. The edict introduced by Philip in 218 made it clear what bonuses the men were to receive, but their grievances may have gone beyond merely a fair share of loot.

Philip rushed to Corinth, where he summoned his army in what was probably a formal assembly. He was clearly out to reestablish his authority as the men had openly defied him; as was his right, he addressed them all equally, protesters and supporters alike, a sign in many respects of his leadership even in the face of such opposition.[100] He deliberately did not punish the commanding officers to help diffuse the situation, but the days of Leontius, Megaleas, and Ptolemy were numbered. He also recalled Apelles, who cannot have had anything to do with the soldiers' riot, from Chalcis to Corinth.

Why Apelles was recalled is not known. Polybius claims that he had overstepped his authority in Chalcis and that governors in Macedonia and Thessaly were appealing to him, hence Philip viewed him suspiciously, but all that could be bias on Polybius' part.[101] Apelles, in all ignorance, arrived to a tumultuous welcome from Leontius, Megaleas, Ptolemy, and the soldiers in general, but then as he made his way to Philip he was suddenly prevented from visiting him and sent to his lodgings alone.[102] Although he was invited to banquets and the like, he was no longer consulted on any matters of importance.

---

98. Polybius 5.17.2–24.12, with Walbank 1957, pp. 553–557; cf. D'Agostini 2019, pp. 101–103.

99. Polybius 5.25.1–3. On the riot: Errington 1967, p. 34; D'Agostini 2019, pp. 103–106.

100. Polybius 5.25.4–7. Philip's power: Roisman 2015, pp. 79–81.

101. Polybius 5.26.1–6.

102. Polybius 5.26.1–11.

The argument has been made that Philip recalled Apelles to help him plan a campaign in Phocis, given Apelles' expertise in central Greek affairs and that the king took him on that venture.[103] Yet Apelles' duties at Chalcis were crucial. Philip was always attentive to his supply routes, as is shown by an undated military order (*diagramma*) ordering his royal "managers" (*oikonomoi*) to ensure there was always a ready supply of grain, wood, wine, and military supplies for wherever his army was deployed.[104] Chalcis was one of the principal depots; hence, recalling Apelles from his important position there to draw up an invasion plan of Phocis does not make sense unless the king was suspicious of him and decided that the time had come for a purge of his inner circle. Supporting that argument is that after the campaign Philip appointed Alexander of the hypaspists, and not the "expert" Apelles, to govern Phocis.[105]

When Philip was returning from his Phocian campaign he stopped off at Sicyon to stay with Aratus, from where he ordered Apelles back to Corinth, perhaps to prevent friction between the two men.[106] News reached the king now that Megaleas, taking heed of Apelles' decline in influence, had fled to Athens, which refused to take him in; his flight exposed Leontius, who had stood bail for him, to legal redress.[107] Philip now decided to remove the popular Leontius and ordered his peltasts to march under Taurion to Triphylia on an unknown mission to get them out of the way.[108] As soon as they left, Leontius was arrested. When they heard the news his troops sent an envoy requesting to be present at his trial and offering to pay off his twenty-talent fine, but Leontius had already been executed.[109] Philip as king wielded judicial power in the state, so Leontius may not have had a trial.[110] Despite the

---

103. Walbank 1940, pp. 59–60; Hammond and Walbank 1988, p. 382; Scherberich 2009, pp. 146–148; D'Agostini 2019, pp. 106–109; cf. Scholten 2000, pp. 215–217.

104. Hatzopoulos 1996, vol. 2, no. 13, pp. 36–38, with Welles 1938, pp. 251–254.

105. Polybius 5.96.4.

106. Polybius 5.27.3.

107. Polybius 5.26.13–14, 5.27.1, 5.27.4, with Hammond and Walbank 1988, p. 382. On the Athenians' reasoning, see Worthington 2021a, p. 139.

108. Polybius 5.27.4; see too Errington 1967, p. 34; D'Agostini 2019, pp. 109–112.

109. Polybius 5.27.4–8.

110. Diodorus 28.3 might refer to Leontius when he claims that Philip "had his friends put to death without benefit of trial." See Hatzopoulos 1996, vol. 1, pp. 301–302, that there was a trial. See too Roisman 2012, pp. 136–139, on the king's power and how it was not to be contested.

earlier reaction of Leontius' men there was no further outcry against the general's fate.

The envoys from Rhodes and Chios trying to broker peace now returned to the king, bringing word that the Aetolians were willing to discuss terms and had agreed to a truce of thirty days. Both sides were to meet at Rhium, and while traveling there Philip made his final moves against his guardians. Alexander the governor of Phocis sent him letters from Megaleas to the Aetolians in which he encouraged them to continue the war and denigrated the king's authority.[111] Philip sent Alexander to arrest Megaleas, who had gone to Thebes when the Athenians refused to allow him into their city, but he committed suicide rather than be captured. Philip also arrested Apelles and his family and sent them to Taurion at Corinth, believing that Megaleas' treasonable letters included him, but Apelles and his son also killed themselves.

Unfortunately, the deaths of these men, and the earlier riot by some of Philip's army, gave the Aetolians hope they could still overcome the king, hence they postponed peace negotiations. Philip turned his back on them anyway. Since the end of the campaigning season was approaching, he sent his army home to Macedonia and set up his court at Demetrias.[112] There he put the last of the so-called conspirators or friends of Leontius, Ptolemy, on trial "before the Macedonians" on a charge of treason and had him executed. Crinon's fate is not known, but Philip would surely have had him removed—permanently or imprisoned—to end the purge.

The whole controversial affair shows us Philip's ruthlessness and quick actions. Taurion and Alexander, who had always cooperated with him and who were sympathetic to Aratus, now came to the fore as his advisers. But their relationship to Aratus raises the likelihood of his involvement in a conspiracy, given Aratus' hatred of Apelles and our sources attributing the men's "outrageous conduct to Aratus that brought them to ruin."[113] If there was a conspiracy, perhaps it was one engineered by Aratus, Taurion, and Alexander, whose discovery of the treacherous letters was opportune, to

---

111. Polybius 5.28.4–9, and see Walbank 1940, p. 61; D'Agostini 2019, pp. 113–114, citing bibliography.

112. Polybius 5.29.1–6.

113. Polybius 5.28.9; cf. Plutarch, *Aratus* 48.1 and 4.

remove the conservative Old Guard of Doson's circle and promote them-selves at court.[114]

Whatever the truth, we can agree with Errington that Philip had "severed his future from Doson's past by destroying the inconvenient traditionalists."[115] He would have the same attitude in his dealings with Rome.

---

114. Coppola 1993, pp. 146–147; D'Agostini 2019, pp. 113–115.

115. Errington 1967, p. 35.

4

Taking on Rome and the First Macedonian War

PHILIP RETURNED NORTH for the winter of 218–217. He left behind Taurion at Corinth to work in tandem with Aratus—again elected general of the Achaean League—against Aetolian aggression and protect Achaean interests in the Peloponnese.[1] Philip also left troops in Phocis under Alexander to keep the Aetolians at bay there. Alexander and the commander of the garrison at Phanoteus, a man named Jason, tricked the Aetolian general Agetas into thinking that Jason was betraying Phanoteus to him. When Agetas arrived with troops one night, Jason and Alexander captured 100 while Agetas beat a hasty retreat.[2] These moves brought Phocis more fully into the Social War, which was perhaps the king's intention.[3]

The End of the Social War

In the meantime, Philip was facing problems from the Dardanians. They had attacked their southern neighbors the Paeonians, who lay on the path of any Dardanian advance in that direction and were threatening Lower Macedonia (maps 2 and 3).[4] The king decided to increase the number of his garrisons at key points to shore up his northern frontier against the Dardanians. He

---

1. Polybius 5.90–96.

2. Polybius 5.96.

3. Cf. Scherberich 2009, pp. 150–151.

4. Paeonia as part of Macedonia: Hammond and Griffith 1979, p. 656; Hammond and Walbank 1988, p. 237 n. 5.

The Last Kings of Macedonia and the Triumph of Rome. Ian Worthington, Oxford University Press.
© Oxford University Press 2023. DOI: 10.1093/oso/9780197520055.003.0005

already had two garrisons in the Axius valley, one at Manastir at the north end of the Demir Kapu defile and the other at Antigonea, which was farther upstream near Banja. Now he seized Bylazora (Titov Veles), the largest city in Paeonia, which commanded the passes from Dardania into Macedonia.[5]

Thessaly remained crucial for Macedonia's southern security. Philip marched via Edessa to Larissa, about 125 miles (200 kilometers) away, covering the distance in only six days.[6] His plan was to drive a wedge between Phthiotic Achaea (which took its name from its location in Phthiotis in southeastern Thessaly not far from Larissa) and Aetolia and invest Phthiotic Thebes in the northeastern part of Phthiotis. This Thebes was the chief Aetolian base for invading eastern Thessaly; it would give him the key to all Phthiotic Achaea and a new harbor for troop movements from Thessaly to Taurion in the Peloponnese.[7]

A night march of 43 miles (70 kilometers) brought him to Melitaea, close to the River Enipeus, so still in Phthiotis. Control of that town would sever the Aetolians' line of communication with Phthiotic Thebes, so he besieged it.[8] Melitaea's walls were too high for his scaling ladders, forcing him to abandon the siege. Undaunted, he turned to invest Phthiotic Thebes, which was protected all around by a long fortification wall.[9] There may well have been a sense of urgency on his part to be successful as he had failed to take Pale and Melitaea and needed to project a winning image to his enemy and his own men.[10] He set up three fortified camps, linked them to each other by a trench and a double palisade, and built towers at intervals of 100 feet (30 meters).[11] The walls of the besieged city were bombarded by 150 catapults and 25 stone throwers while sappers dug under a section of the fortification wall for twelve days—including throughout the nights for the last three days—until 230 feet (70 meters) of it collapsed.

---

5. Polybius 5.97.1–2, with Hammond and Walbank 1988, pp. 385–386.

6. Polybius 5.97.3–4, with Walbank 1940, p. 63.

7. Walbank 1940, pp. 62–64.

8. Polybius 5.97.5–98.11 (with some differences and an excursus on siege warfare): see Walbank 1957, p. 626; Hammond and Walbank 1988, p. 385).

9. Polybius 5.99–100.8.

10. Cf. D'Agostini 2019, pp. 122–123.

11. On what a fortified camp entailed and how to establish one, see Karunanithy 2013, pp. 186–202.

The garrison and citizens surrendered, though it did them little good.[12] Philip called the people traitors for joining the Aetolians and sold them as slaves. Then to send out a message that all Phthiotic Achaea was under his rule he turned the city into a Macedonian colony named Philippopolis (or Philippi). In doing so he showed an affinity to Philip II, who had refounded the Thracian township of Crenides as Philippopolis in the 350s.[13] Possibly now our Philip was called *soter* (savior) of Macedonia and Thessaly for saving them from Aetolian and perhaps also Dardanian aggression.[14] The savior image is consistent with Hellenistic kingship, as Philip would have known, going back to Antigonus I Monophthalmus and Demetrius I Poliorcetes, whom the Athenians had called savior gods, and Ptolemy I of Egypt, who was called savior by his people.[15]

Then came news that Scerdilaidas had broken his earlier agreement with Philip and seized four of the ships Taurion had with him at Leucas.[16] At about the same time, envoys from Chios, Rhodes, Byzantium, and Ptolemy II arrived to try to persuade him to discuss peace terms with the Aetolians; as before, he sent them to his enemy to find out their stance prior to committing himself.[17] In any case Scerdilaidas' action opened the door to a possible strike at Macedonia; hence, peace was the last thing on Philip's mind at that moment.

The king immediately headed south, but Scerdilaidas stayed away from Macedonia, allowing Philip to move to Cenchreae, the eastern harbor of Corinth on the isthmus, where he had some of his vessels dragged across the isthmus to Lechaeum. From there he revisited Argos in July to watch the Nemean Games in honor of Zeus. It was here that a messenger from Pella brought news that is sometimes thought to have made him end the Social

---

12. Polybius 5.100.8.

13. Worthington 2008, pp. 45–46.

14. See also D'Agostini 2019, pp. 87–89, with bibliography, citing an epigram by Alcaeus of Messene (*Anth. Pal.* 9.518), in which Philip scales the walls of Mount Olympus and conquers the home of the gods (perhaps dated to 218–214 or even 202–200) and five dedications to the king as savior, and pp. 124–126 (after Philip took Phthiotic Thebes in 217). Possibly this was part of a Hellenistic pattern of ruler cult: Mari 2008; cf. Suk Fong Jim 2017. But see Eckstein 2010, p. 230, that the poem should be taken as evidence of Philip's ambition for world power—it shows that his "vast ambitions were well-known and taken seriously at the time" (in other words, if he could capture the home of the gods, he could defeat anyone).

15. Antigonids: Worthington 2021a, pp. 72–75; Ptolemy: Worthington 2016b (revising Worthington 2016a, pp. 168–169).

16. Polybius 5.101.1.

17. Polybius 5.100.9–11, with Walbank 1940, p. 64.

War and even contemplate an invasion of Italy. This was the victory of the Carthaginian general Hannibal (who the previous year had famously led his elephants over the Alps) over a Roman army at Lake Trasimene in Etruria.[18]

According to Polybius, Philip told this news only to Demetrius of Pharos, who seized on this opportunity and grandly advised the king to settle with the Aetolians, win over all Illyria, and invade Italy as a precursor to conquering the world. Demetrius went on to say, so Polybius claims, that Greece was subservient to Philip, the Aetolians were cowed, and a campaign to Italy would be a stepping-stone to world conquest, "an enterprise which belonged to none more properly than to himself."[19]

The veracity of the exchange is suspect, and it may have been shaped by Polybius to portray both Philip's ambition and the continued influence of Demetrius over him, despite the presence of Aratus at Argos.[20] Certainly, news of Hannibal's victory did reach Philip and he would soon bring the Social War to an abrupt end. But Polybius is almost certainly wrong on the effect of Hannibal's victory on the course of the Social War or on Philip's aim of descending on Italy as we shall see.[21]

In the summer of 217, after Philip first consulted Demetrius and Aratus for advice, he and the Aetolians held negotiations to end the war at Naupactus on the north coast of the Gulf of Corinth so in Aetolian territory.[22] While waiting for the Aetolians to arrive he seized the island of Zacynthus from Elis, which allowed him access to the Adriatic, as had Pyrrhus before him.[23] Negotiations to end the war were successful and led in August to the Peace of Naupactus, which had favorable terms for both the Hellenic League and the Aetolian League.[24] The latter was not disbanded; each state was to keep the

---

18. Polybius 5.101.5–6.

19. Polybius 5.101.8–10. Livy 23.33.2–3 speaks of Philip hearing of Hannibal crossing the Alps and being pleased that Rome and Hannibal were at war but not yet sure who he wanted to win! Justin 29.2.1–6 has Demetrius warning the king that the Romans would come after him but Philip thinking that they would be easy prey as Hannibal had already defeated them.

20. D'Agostini 2019, pp. 129–131.

21. Walbank 1940, pp. 64–65; Walbank 1983; Gruen 1984, pp. 374–375; Hammond and Walbank 1988, pp. 387–388 and 389–390; Hammond 1992, p. 337; Derow 2003, p. 54; cf. Waterfield 2014, pp. 38–40.

22. Polybius 5.102.2–105.2. On the veracity of the speeches, see below.

23. Polybius 5.102.10. See too Walbank 1940, p. 66; Kleu 2015, p. 42; D'Agostini 2019, p. 132.

24. Austin 2006, no. 73, pp. 154–156 (abridged); Justin 29.2–3; Ager 1996, pp. 145–146, with Walbank 1940, pp. 66–67; Hammond and Walbank 1988, pp. 388–389; Scholten 2000, pp. 224–228; Scherberich 2009, pp. 153–154; D'Agostini 2019, pp. 133–134.

possessions it then held (which meant that the Aetolians continued to have a say in the Amphictyonic League, despite the opposition of the Achaeans); Philip's rule over Phthiotic Achaea, Epirus, Acarnania, and Zacynthus was recognized; Macedonian garrisons were to remain in the Peloponnese; and the Achaeans enjoyed a greater role in the Peloponnese at the expense of Elis and Sparta.

The Social War had been Philip's coming of age as a military leader and king. He had rid himself of his guardians and rebuilt Macedonia's standing in the Hellenic League. The war's conclusion in 217 brought six years of peace to the mainland and even the chance of prosperity, especially in the ravaged Peloponnese. For Philip, however, there now seemed the lure of Italy, for after relating the supposed conversation between Demetrius and Philip over the news of Hannibal's victory at Cannae, Polybius added that Demetrius turned the king's head to a campaign in the west.[25] But was Philip really finessing, as Waterfield puts it, "grander plans than mere resistance"?[26]

Invading Italy?

True, Philip was young, daring, and ambitious. But a war against Rome is likely the fabrication of Polybius and Justin, who set the negotiations that led to the ending of the war against the background not of a settlement in Greece but of Philip's ambition to make inroads into Italy.[27] The differences in their accounts alert us to their unreliability, especially when it comes to a single speech they provide of the peace debate at Naupactus.

In Justin Philip is the speaker, warning of the danger from the Romans, which he referred to as the "cloud in the west," and urging Greece to unite under him to resist Rome.[28] Yet in Polybius the same arguments—and the same metaphor of the cloud—are attributed to a speech at the start of the conference by the prominent Aetolian Agelaus, a colleague of Dorimachus and Scopas. According to Polybius, Agelaus pleaded with Philip to put aside

---

25. Polybius 5.102.1. See too Walbank 1940, pp. 64–65; Walbank 1983; Eckstein 1994, pp. 54–55; D'Agostini 2015.

26. Waterfield 2014, p. 38, and see pp. 38–40 on Philip's ambitions; cf. Scherberich 2009, pp. 153–154; D'Agostini 2019, pp. 131–132.

27. Scherberich 2009, pp. 152–161; D'Agostini 2019, p. 134.

28. Justin 29.2.8–3.5.

any remaining differences he had with the Greeks, unite them under him against Rome, and lay a claim to worldwide rule.[29]

The same speech presented by two different speakers, one a king and the other a relatively unknown individual, on different sides of the war is clearly problematic.[30] In any case, Philip was hardly able to launch a naval offensive across the Adriatic. There was the ever-present pressure on his border from the Dardanians, the activities of the Aetolian League, the struggles of the Hellenic League, and his lack of war fleet compared to Rome's navy with its enormous quadriremes and quinquiremes—even Polybius had to admit that Philip's fleet was no match for the Roman.[31] In fact, as we discuss below, when he was about to invest Apollonia and heard that a Roman war fleet was bearing down on him, he promptly fled as he felt so vulnerable. On top of all that, he could not gauge the inclination of the Italian cities to him, whose support was essential if he took on Rome.

Still, previous kings of Epirus like Pyrrhus and Alexander did not let their naval inferiority stop them from invading Italy.[32] But Philip would have been aware of their lack of success and would have had no wish to follow suit. Moreover, he needed to persuade the members of the Hellenic League to wage war on Rome at a time when Greece was only starting to recover from the ravages of the Social War.

Philip was not planning any takeover of Italy now or in 215 when he actually made an alliance with Hannibal (see below).[33] But Philip did have an interest in Hannibal, which led to an abandonment of the cautious consolidation of Antigonus III Doson and a "new activism" in his thinking.[34] That "new activism" was to turn to Carthage as part of a long-term plan to combat Rome's presence in Illyria before his own kingdom was compromised. If Hannibal defeated Rome in the Second Punic War, Philip would then be

29. Polybius 5.103.9–104.1; cf. Walbank 1957, p. 629: "he was evidently leader of the peace party in Aetolia."

30. See Mørkholm 1970; Mørkholm 1974; Deininger 1973; Champion 1997; D'Agostini 2019, pp. 134–138.

31. Polybius 5.109.1–4.

32. Pointed out to me by J. Roisman in his comments on an earlier draft of this text.

33. Livy 23.33.10 (with a fleet of 200 ships, "it was thought," would sail to Italy and ravage the coast).

34. Errington 1990, pp. 189–190.

free to take Illyria and its ports.[35] Good arguments have been made for Philip championing Macedonia and Greece not against Rome but against a much greater Illyrian presence.[36] The key therefore to understanding Philip at this time revolves not around any grand design to invade Italy but around Illyria and, like his predecessors, protecting his realm. That was why he had to leave Greece quickly to save his kingdom.[37]

The timing of the news about Hannibal's victory and the ending of the Social War is coincidental. Indeed, Polybius states on more than one occasion that the Aetolians were eager to make peace, especially as the loss of Phthiotic Thebes had been a major blow to them.[38] Just as the armies of Philip and Aratus were more than a match for the Aetolians in pitched battle, Philip and Aratus had no chance of combating the Aetolians in guerrilla warfare. Further, Scerdilaidas had all too recently changed sides and was intent on reducing Macedonia's sway in the Balkans.[39] The war had deteriorated into a costly stalemate, and a solution to offset time and costs was needed.

Philip, Rome, and Hannibal

In the summer of 217 Roman envoys visited Philip. As a young boy he had experienced Rome's affront to Antigonus III Doson when Albinus sent diplomatic embassies to various Greek states but not to Macedonia (pp. 48–49). Now, in 217, the Romans were not trying to make up for their earlier behavior by paying Philip a social visit: they were demanding he hand over their enemy Demetrius of Pharos, who had fled to the Macedonian court at the end of the Second Illyrian War. Rome of course had no right to expect Philip to obey such a high-handed order, and he refused. Demetrius, like Hannibal, was a valuable part of his strategy to counter Rome's stake in Illyria and protect his kingdom's security. Understandably, Rome was not prepared for Philip to back Demetrius' return to Illyria; relations between Philip and Rome were thus strained further.[40]

---

35. Errington 1990, pp. 191–192; King 2018, p. 249.

36. See Walbank 1983; Coppola 1993, p. 154; D'Agostini 2015; D'Agostini 2019, pp. 134–138.

37. Cf. Hammond 1967, pp. 606–607; Hammond 1968, pp. 15–16.

38. Polybius 5.29.1 and 5.103.1–3. See too Scholten 2000, pp. 226–227.

39. Gruen 1984, p. 375. Philip may even have been following Demetrius' advice to wage war on Scerdilaidas: Polybius 5.108.4–5, with Coppola 1993, pp. 149–150 and 164–165.

40. Rich 1984, p. 126. On the role of Demetrius, see Eckstein 2008, pp. 58–73.

Over the winter of 217–216 Philip ordered the construction of 100 Illyrian *lembi* at Demetrias using Illyrian designers and trained more of his own men to row them as he did not have the financial resources to construct huge war vessels.[41] The *lembi* were useless against the quadriremes and quinqueremes of the Roman navy, but their speed, size, and the fact that the oarsmen were also fighters made them perfect for surprise raids and taking on other *lembi*. The latter included those of Scerdilaidas, against whom Philip had recently and successfully campaigned in Pelagonia and Illyria.[42]

In the spring or early summer of 216, taking advantage of Rome's distraction with Hannibal's campaign in Italy, Philip decided to capture the prime southern Illyrian port of Apollonia.[43] He set off from Demetrias and drove his men hard the entire day; after resting them the following day, he sailed up the Aous River that night to besiege Apollonia. But then he received word that a fleet of Roman quinqueremes was en route from Lilybaeum in western Sicily to prop up Scerdilaidas, who must have summoned help when he heard of Philip's shipbuilding program and suspected he was coming after him. Although Philip did not know the size of the Roman fleet, he abandoned his plan to take Apollonia, knowing he faced defeat if caught between Rome and Scerdilaidas, and fled.[44] Two days later he was 180 miles (290 kilometers) away at Cephallenia in the Ionian Sea and safe.

The Roman fleet turned out to be only ten ships, however, with probably 4,000 men on board, but by the time Philip learned this he was already at Cephallenia. His whole campaign had been costly and had no tangible gains, but now he suffered the ignominy of fleeing before inferior numbers. Predictably, Polybius scorned him, accusing him of panicking and losing his "prestige" as a result, but Polybius does not mention Scerdilaidas' ships that could have assisted the Roman fleet and had every chance of defeating him in battle.[45] In addition, Philip may have retreated from Apollonia because he heard the news of Hannibal's resounding victory over a Roman army at

---

41. Polybius 1.109.1–4, and see Walbank 1982, p. 226.

42. Polybius 5.108.1–8. We should disregard Polybius' claim that Demetrius was tempting him with ideas of invading Italy after settling affairs in Illyria.

43. Polybius 5.109.6–110.1.

44. Polybius 5.110.2–11, with Walbank 1940, p. 40; Hammond 1968, pp. 16–18; Gruen 1984, p. 375; Hammond 1992, p. 337.

45. Polybius 5.110.9–10, with Hammond 1968, pp. 17–18.

Cannae in Apulia, south-east Italy, in August 216.[46] If he had any hope of winning over Illyria, he needed a formidable ally like Hannibal. That was surely the reason for his withdrawal rather than the opportunity to "redouble his efforts to invade Italy, to become a second Pyrrhus," not least because his recent vulnerability against a Roman war fleet underscored the impossibility of invading Italy.[47]

That winter, Philip sent an envoy, Xenophanes, to Hannibal and eventually in the summer of 215 he concluded a treaty with Carthage, which earned him Rome's hatred.[48] He must have done so in tandem with the members of the Hellenic League, which shows his influence and reputation in Greece.[49] Then again, the league was probably acting not from fear of Rome but because the latter's control of Corcyra and Epidamnus was affecting their economic interests, given these were vital ports for trade across the Adriatic.[50]

The Romans intercepted Xenophanes on his way back to Philip from Carthage and discovered the correspondence between the king and Hannibal. They probably copied it so the Senate had a record of it.[51] We have only the Carthaginian version of the treaty, but presumably the Greek version said much the same thing.[52] The terms were that Macedonia and Carthage were to be friends, with the former supporting the latter in its war with Rome. Carthage agreed to include Macedonia and Illyria in a peace treaty if it defeated Rome in the war. Rome was not allowed to make war on Philip, nor was it to have Corcyra, Apollonia, Epidamnus, Pharos, Dimale (home of the Parthini tribe), and Atintania (bordering Illyria and Epirus), thus relinquishing its presence in those areas and cities (map 3). Rome also had to give back to Demetrius either all prisoners or his former areas it had seized. Finally, Carthage would stand behind Philip if Rome declared war

---

46. Timing: Burton 2017, pp. 22–23.

47. Quote: Burton 2017, p. 23.

48. Polybius 7.9 (= Austin 2006, no. 76, pp. 159–161); Livy 23.33.9–34.1, with Walbank 1967, pp. 42–56; Walbank 1940, pp. 70–72 and 299; Errington 1971a, pp. 111–112; Gruen 1984, pp. 375–376; Rich 1984, pp. 126–127; Hammond and Walbank 1988, pp. 393–394; Longaretti 1989; Brizzi 2003; Eckstein 2008, pp. 78–84; Matyszak 2009, pp. 33–36; D'Agostini 2019, pp. 142–144.

49. Hammond 1992, p. 338.

50. Cf. Hammond 1968, pp. 3–4.

51. Livy 23.34; cf. 23.38.4 and 39.1–3.

52. Hammond and Walbank 1988 p. 394 n. 3; *contra* Walbank 1967, pp. 55–56.

on him—but it is important to note that there was no stipulation that Philip would campaign in Italy.[53]

Both sides benefitted from the treaty. Carthage now had Macedonia and Greece standing with it against Rome, even though Rome's oversight of Corcyra and the Illyrian ports would impede Philip sending help to Hannibal. Philip saw it as a stepping-stone to combating Roman presence in Illyria and to taking over northern Epirus. The latter would rid him of the treacherous Scerdilaidas and secure the coastline and its ports, and he could then reinstate Demetrius as a vassal of sorts.

In late 215 Philip attacked Corcyra. Since there is no mention of Roman vessels there in the following year, he was probably successful.[54] Despite the Romans' dire straits in the war with Hannibal, the Senate ordered Marcus Valerius Laevinus to prepare to sail a fleet from Tarentum to Macedonia "to keep Philip within his kingdom."[55] At this stage, the Senate did not seem to see Philip as a risk to Rome, but it was angry at his refusal to surrender Demetrius and exploitation of Roman weaknesses in the conflict with Hannibal. Thus, we have the background to what modern scholars call the First Macedonian War between Rome and Philip (214–205).[56]

Control of Corcyra gave Philip an excellent base from which to overrun Illyria. In the summer of 214 he prepared to launch another assault on Apollonia and one on the northern Epirote city of Oricum. He had a fleet of 120 *lembi* (perhaps with a full complement of 6,000 troops if each *lembus* held fifty men) from Corcyra and counted on the military deployment of the Hellenic League to boost his own army numbers. However, Aratus held the Achaean fleet back, although in 218 he had readily supported the king against Apollonia.[57]

Aratus' stance stemmed from a dispute with Philip over the city of Messene in Messenia (map 7). Both Philip as hegemon of the Hellenic League and

---

53. Walbank 1940, p. 71; Gruen 1984, p. 324; Hatzopoulos 2014.

54. Appian, *Macedonian Wars* 1; Zonaras 9.4, with Hammond and Walbank 1988, p. 395 n. 2; Coppola 1993, pp. 188–189, but note Walbank 1940, p. 299.

55. Livy 23.38.11.

56. Walbank 1940, pp. 76–105; Errington 1971a, pp. 109–118; Harris 1979, pp. 205–208; Gruen 1984, pp. 375–381; Rich 1984; Hammond and Walbank 1988, pp. 391–410; Errington 1989a, pp. 94–106; Eckstein 2002, especially pp. 273–295; Eckstein 2008, pp. 85–116; Matyszak 2009, pp. 33–52; Eckstein 2010, pp. 229–234; Waterfield 2014, pp. 41–57; Burton 2017, pp. 24–27. Cf. Walbank 1940, pp. 299–301, for some chronological notes.

57. Cf. Livy 24.40.1–3.

Aratus as general of the Achaean League had marched there when internal strife (*stasis*) broke out between two factions of the population: aristocrats and "populists" (or democrats).[58] Philip could not afford any issues to destabilize the Peloponnese and cause warfare between the Achaean and Aetolian Leagues, therefore disturbing his plans for Illyria. He arrived at Messene one day before Aratus and was said to have secretly urged each side to act against the other, which led to the massacre of two hundred citizens before the democrats prevailed.[59]

It has been thought that Philip's encouragement of the populists at Messene meant he had a policy of sorts to champion the lower social stratum against the upper in Greek cities and so gain popularity.[60] That is not so, for he also propped up aristocratic factions in Greece, and not even the hostile Polybius accuses him of populism.[61] When he did interfere in domestic politics it was often to benefit a city, as in 217 and 215 when he wrote to Larissa, which had suffered depopulation from Aetolian invasions, urging the people to grant citizenship to other Thessalians and Greeks and so benefit the city economically.[62] His son Perseus was also believed to champion the masses for popularity, but both kings simply used whomever they could to their advantage—by siding with both factions in Messene, Philip would earn the goodwill of whichever won.[63]

Aratus was unhappy when he arrived at Messene, but willing to discuss what had happened there with Philip. They held a summit, literally, at the top of Mount Ithome in Messenia, with Aratus accompanied by his son and Philip with the bellicose Demetrius. The latter had urged Philip to intervene in Messene's dispute, using the phrase "take the bull by both horns"

---

58. Polybius 7.12.9; Plutarch, *Aratus* 49.2–50.2, with Walbank 1940, pp. 73–75; Mendels 1980.

59. Cf. Walbank 1967, p. 57, on Polybius 7.10.1, probably referring "to the situation in Messene after Philip had egged on the democrats to destroy their opponents," which view Walbank repeats on pp. 59–60 on Polybius 7.12.1. Coppola 1993, pp. 187–193, argues that the reason why Philip did not engage the Roman fleet but retreated the previous year was because of *stasis* in Messene, but this does not follow as Illyria was more important to his immediate interests than the Peloponnese: see, though, Kleu 2015, pp. 48–50 and 195–200.

60. Support: Walbank 1967, pp. 57 and 59–60; Walbank 1940, pp. 72–73, and see Mendels 1977, p. 15 n. 3, for more bibliography.

61. Mendels 1977; Gruen 1981.

62. Full discussion of his actions: D'Agostini 2019, pp. 147–155, with references (especially n. 38). Devastation in Thessaly from Aetolian attacks: Scholten 2000, p. 216.

63. Mendels 1977, pp. 159–161 (noting Philip's "cunning" on pp. 159–160).

to signify garrisoning both Messene and Acrocorinth.[64] Philip intended to hold onto Messene, but Aratus advised against this and for him to act in a moral manner, which apparently shamed Philip into changing his mind.[65] He allowed Messene to introduce a radical democracy and ally to Macedonia before leaving.[66] Still, relations between Philip and the Achaeans were now at a low, which is why in the summer of 214 Philip did not have their support against Apollonia.

"Darling of the Greeks"?

Polybius viewed the massacre at Messene as "the beginning of the revolution in Philip's character," and that "after his attack on Messene all underwent a total change."[67] Thus, his presentation of Philip in his history changes significantly here after a glowing account of Philip's first years, though at the same time he criticized the influence of Demetrius over the king.[68] Polybius attributed the king's cynical action at Messene to a moral deterioration (*metabole*) in his character: from a good king he became a tyrant.[69] Polybius' stance is not surprising as he must have thought more favorably of Philip when he was close to Aratus and supporting the Achaean cause in the Social War, but after the clash with Aratus over Messene, Philip's attitude to him and the league cooled. Polybius, who was an influential member of the Achaean League and very much biased toward it and Aratus, allowed his feeling to come into play in his account of Philip, as discussed further in this book's appendix.

There is a particular phrase that Polybius used here about Philip: he called him a "universal darling of the Greeks."[70] Scholars have tended to interpret it as a positive one, that Philip was well liked by all the Greeks because of his actions and good deeds. That interpretation is still very likely. After all, the king was going to some lengths to rebuild Macedonia's popularity in Greece,

64. Polybius 7.12.1–3; Plutarch, *Aratus* 50.4, but see Eckstein 1994, pp. 55–56, on how this is part of Polybius' warped presentation of Demetrius; cf. Walbank 1967, pp. 60–61.

65. Polybius 7.12.5–7, 7.14.1–3; Plutarch, *Aratus* 50.5–6.

66. *Contra* Walbank 1967, p. 57, that this recognition was later.

67. Polybius 7.11–14 (quotes at 11.1 and 11.10); cf. 8.8.

68. Polybius 7.12.1–3, 7.13.6, and 7.14.5; cf. Plutarch, *Aratus* 51.2–3.

69. Walbank 1940, pp. 74–75; Walbank 1967, pp. 59–60; Gruen 1981, pp. 171–173; Hammond and Walbank 1988, pp. 472–474.

70. Polybius 7.11.8.

and his Hellenic League had waged war on the Aetolians on behalf of the Achaeans and other Greek states. The Greeks later renounced Philip, as we shall see, but at least in this earlier part of his reign the phrase indicates they liked him.

Recently, there has been a different take on "darling of the Greeks" based on its Greek wording: *erômenos tôn Ellênôn*.[71] The word *erômenos* ("darling") was what a passive lover in a Greek homoerotic relationship was called; the active lover was known as an *erastês*, who was usually older and had a pedagogical role in his lover's life. Polybius was therefore assigning the passive role but in a nonsexual sense to Philip in his relations with the Greeks.[72] In other words, Philip was a young man, needing to be guided in politics and other aspects of his life, including moral behavior, by his more worldly and knowledgeable elders.

The Greeks and especially Aratus thus become the *erastês* in an instructive sense to Philip the *erômenos*.[73] But all their good work and guidance were undone in the aftermath of the Social War, especially evident in Philip's behavior at Messene. Philip, according to Polybius, had shown his best until then and even the promise of being a good king. After Messene, he cast off the guiding hands of the Greeks; his character deteriorated to the extent that his Greek allies turned their back on him, and eventually it led to his defeat by Rome.

Polybius, then, has used *erômenos tôn Ellênôn* of Philip as a metaphor to show a different relationship between him and the Greeks in the early years of his reign, one that he ended up contaminating. There may be truth to this complicated argument. However, equating an *erastês* with the Greeks en masse is questionable, and we can hardly ask Polybius himself why he used the phrase. The reason though may be much simpler.[74] It is important to note that Polybius claims Philip was called this title because of his good deeds.[75] In other words, in the early years of his reign Philip promoted Greek interests and was a powerful ally against the Aetolians—and for that he was liked and admired, just as an *erastês* liked his *erômenos* for the person he was. But then

---

71. Nicholson 2018b—she suggests that it might even be a title that Polybius himself linked to the king: pp. 247–248.

72. On the use of the word in Polybius, see Nicholson 2018b, pp. 242–243; on the *erômenos* and pederasty, see Nicholson 2018b, pp. 244–247.

73. Nicholson 2018b, p. 249.

74. As J. Roisman pointed out to me.

75. Polybius 7.11.8: *dia to tês aireseôs euergetikon*.

Philip changed for the worse as Polybius sees it, especially after he rid himself of his guardians and disrespected Aratus, after which the Greeks came to disparage him.

What we can say with certainty is that we must be on our guard for Polybius' shaping of Philip the king and the man as we move forward in our narrative.

The First Macedonian War

Philip's initial assault on Apollonia failed. He therefore changed tack and captured Oricum, with its large and secure inner harbor before leaving to try his luck again at Apollonia.[76] That allowed Laevinus to take possession of Oricum from Philip and blockade the mouth of the Aous, neatly trapping the Macedonians up-river.[77] Laevinus sent at least 2,000 Roman troops under Quintus Naevius Crista to sneak into Apollonia by night—possibly Philip mistook them for Illyrian reinforcements and relaxed his guard.[78]

Together with some of the defenders, Crista's men one night made a stealthy sortie and infiltrated Philip's camp.[79] The king's men awoke to find the enemy literally in their midst; still half asleep, they were easily overcome by the ferocity of the Roman soldiers. At least 3,000 were killed or captured while the rest, including Philip, had no choice but to flee. The next day the people of Apollonia seized Philip's siege engines and displayed them triumphantly on their walls. Laevinus' position on the Aous forced Philip to burn some of his vessels to prevent them from falling into Roman hands, after which he led his men home over the mountains.[80]

Plutarch mocked Philip, speaking of his "most shameful" defeat and loss of ships.[81] His criticism is justified. Philip had framed a good plan to capture Apollonia and, given his treaty with the Carthaginians, probably expected

---

76. Livy 24.40.3–4, with Hammond 1968, pp. 18–19.

77. Livy 24.40.5–8, with Walbank 1940, pp. 75–76.

78. Matyszak 2009, p. 38.

79. Livy 24.40.9–16.

80. Livy 24.40.17. Plutarch, *Aratus* 51.1, has Philip taking his men straight to the Peloponnese, but this would have been foolhardy: Walbank 1940, p. 76 n. 2. D'Agostini 2019, p. 145, is right that Philip made a reasonable retreat as he knew his forces could not match those of the Romans, but the morale of his men had suffered.

81. Plutarch, *Aratus* 51.2.

Carthage would send him support against Laevinus' fleet. But he went on to make some costly mistakes, especially not setting up a proper guard around his camp and underestimating Laevinus. His defeat put an end to his current naval policy, for Rome now placed a permanent fleet in Illyria.[82]

Philip's reputation took a further hit later in 214 when Messene revolted from him. He sent Demetrius to retake it and presumably install a new regime, despite assuring Aratus the previous year that he would leave the city untouched. Demetrius, however, was killed in the siege, sending Philip into a fury. In a terror campaign he invaded and ravaged the countryside, but rather than surrender to him the Messenians joined the Aetolian League.[83] On top of that, any remaining slivers of friendship between Philip and the now ailing Aratus were severed when Philip took Polycratea (the wife of Aratus' son) back to Pella with him after enjoying a long affair with her—he married her after the death of Aratus the son in 213.[84]

The year 214 was undoubtedly one of Philip's worst to date, with the loss of his fleet, the death of Demetrius, growing resentment of him among the Greeks, and a Roman fleet under Laevinus stationed in Illyria, which ominously opened the door to further Roman operations against him. Yet one of Philip's enduring characteristics was his resilience. At this time he was merely down but not out: reminiscent of his predecessors Philip II, Alexander the Great, and Demetrius I Poliorcetes, he acted quickly to establish his reputation and influence.

In 213, exploiting the Romans' occupation with the siege of Syracuse to give them control of Sicily, their war in Spain, and their conflict with Hannibal, Philip marched into Illyria.[85] Keeping away from the coast in case Laevinus suddenly returned, he waged a vigorous and swift advance, first annexing Dassaretis, a gateway from southern Illyria into Macedonia, and therefore a danger point. From there he captured three border strongholds, including Dimale, before moving north to win over the tribes of the Parthini and the Atinantes in Atintania. In doing so, he had effectively isolated Apollonia

---

82. Walbank 1940, p. 77.

83. Walbank 1940, pp. 77–79. Eckstein 1994, p. 56, calls it a reckless attack by Demetrius.

84. Plutarch, *Aratus* 49.1; cf. Livy 27.31.8. Monica D'Agostini suggested to me that his action was a sign of friendship toward this family; how friendly that family may have been afterward is suspect!

85. Polybius 8.13.1–14.11 (Lissus), with Walbank 1940, pp. 80–81; Hammond and Walbank 1988, pp. 398–399.

and Epidamnus and reduced the Roman foothold in Illyria to Dyrrachium, Apollonia, and Oricum.

Next Philip dealt with Scerdilaidas. He targeted the main fortified Illyrian town of Lissus, which had a harbor near the mouth of the Drilon (Drin) River, allowing him access to the Adriatic Sea should he ever need it.[86] Capture of Lissus would also effectively cut off Scerdilaidas from the Romans in the south of Illyria and vice versa.[87] On his arrival he rested his men for one day and then gave an exhortatory address to them. That night he posted a contingent of light-armed troops in some wooded ravines on the north side of its citadel Acrolissus at the summit of the 1,340-foot (410-meter) high Mount Shelbuemit. The following morning, he led the rest of the army around the west and north sides of Lissus until he reached the ridge of level ground between the Acropolis and the lowest slope of Acrolissus.

The Illyrians from Lissus rushed his position, and he sent his light-armed troops to engage them. They were driven back to the level ground, but as the Illyrians pursued them and garrison troops ran out from Lissus thinking they were gaining the upper hand, Philip called on the troops he had hidden the previous night in the ravines to attack. They cut the troops off from the citadel and chased away the other Illyrians into Lissus. After several assaults the next day the city surrendered, and the surrounding Illyrian cities followed suit.

By early 212 Philip controlled the region around the city of Scodra (or Scutari) to its northern point and the Ostrog Pass, thus jeopardizing Rome's oversight of Dyrrhacium. His gains brought him decidedly closer to the Roman protectorate and were also at the expense of Scerdilaidas. Now in control of the harbor at Lissus he decided to use Illyrian shipwrights and timber floated down the Drilon to build a new fleet of 100 vessels, paying the people of Lissus enough to issue their first coinage, the "Lissitae," with the Macedonian goat and thunderbolt emblems on it.[88] His fleet was not intended for any Italian campaign, however—even the Senate did not think of him as a potential invader, and Laevinus took no steps to secure allies in Greece against him.[89]

---

86. Polybius 8.13.1–14.11. Walbank 1940, p. 300, dates it to summer 213 or 212; cf. Walbank 1967, p. 90 ("probably" 213, but given the evidence 212 "cannot be excluded as a possibility").

87. Walbank 1940, pp. 80–81; Walbank 1967, pp. 90–93; Hammond 1968, p. 18; Dell 1977, p. 307; Waterfield 2014, p. 48.

88. Hammond and Walbank 1988, p. 399 n. 3, with further references, to which add Kleu 2017.

89. Walbank 1940, p. 82.

The year 213 had been a better one for Philip, and it was also marked by the birth of his son Perseus. Since Philip identified closely with his divine ancestor Perseus, his choice of his son's name was expected. In the same year, the aged and sickly Aratus died, perhaps of consumption, as did his namesake son. There is a story, which began with Polybius, that Philip secretly had them poisoned.[90] Perhaps we should be skeptical about the accusation, though Philip did have cause to remove them: he had become increasingly estranged from Aratus senior, and Aratus junior's death allowed him to marry his widow.

90. Polybius 8.12.2–6; Plutarch, *Aratus* 51.1–2; probably the allegation had its origins in Polybius and should be doubted: Walbank 1967, pp. 87–88.

5

Keeping Calm and Carrying On

THE SENATE HAD to respond to Philip's worrying gains in Illyria at the expense of Scerdilaidas. In probably the summer of 212 Laevinus made secret overtures to the Aetolians, knowing that if he coaxed them to Rome's side, Philip would be compelled to deal with them.[1] The Aetolians by now had regrouped after their setbacks in the Social War, and their allies included Attalus I of Pergamum, a growing power in Asia Minor, who saw Philip as jeopardizing his expansion in the west. They were unresponsive to Laevinus, perhaps because of the Peace of Naupactus or that Rome's fluctuating fortunes in the Second Punic War might prevent it from sending troops to them.[2] At the same time, they were focused on invading Acarnania and may not have wanted another distraction.[3]

But Laevinus persisted, addressing a special assembly of the Aetolian League in the summer of 211.[4] This time he was successful. In probably the fall of 211, the Aetolians made a treaty of friendship and alliance with Rome against Philip and the Hellenic League. It took the Senate two years to swear to it, however, perhaps due to the current challenges from Carthage and wanting to wait until Laevinus was consul the following year (210).[5]

---

1. Livy 26.24.1. Timing: Walbank 1940, pp. 301–304.

2. Walbank 1940, p. 83.

3. Polybius 9.40; cf. 9.28–39.

4. Livy 26.24.

5. Two-year gap before both parties set up their sworn texts to the alliance: Livy 26.24.14. See further, Walbank 1967, pp. 162–163; Walbank 1940, pp. 301–304.

The Last Kings of Macedonia and the Triumph of Rome. Ian Worthington, Oxford University Press.
© Oxford University Press 2023. DOI: 10.1093/oso/9780197520055.003.0006

The Aetolians Hit Back

The alliance with the Aetolian League showed the Senate's desperation to curb Philip's successes and keep him in areas that had seen the most conflict in the Social War, so away from Illyria, despite the pressure Hannibal was putting on Rome.[6] The city even offered alliance to Elis, Sparta, Attalus of Pergamum, and Scerdilaidas and his son Pleuratus, expecting they would take part in a war against the king, and so help keep Roman troops at home to fight Hannibal.[7]

We have fragments of the Greek version of the Roman-Aetolian alliance.[8] Polybius may have seen both Greek and Latin copies since the terms he uses in his narrative, followed by Livy, echo the inscription.[9] The terms were that neither Rome or Aetolia was to make a separate peace with either Philip or the Hellenic League. Aetolia was to be in command of land operations and Rome naval ones, with the Aetolians contributing five quinquiremes. In joint operations, any city that the latter captured would be an Aetolian possession, but any city voluntarily aligning with Rome would be a dependent and granted "friendship and autonomy." Rome was to help its Aetolian allies capture Acarnania, and was to receive only transportable booty, including captives.

This was "a treaty of expediency between unscrupulous partners. No principles of liberty or morality were proclaimed."[10] It was clear that both parties were simply out to get what they could at the expense of Philip and his allies and to divert his attention from the Roman protectorate in Illyria. But by guaranteeing the Aetolian League Roman support the Senate was trying to drive a wedge between Philip and Hannibal, given that the Carthaginians in their treaty with Philip had not pledged to sail to Macedonia's aid.

---

6. Cf. Walbank 1940, pp. 83–84; Gruen 1984, pp. 17–19 and 377–379; Errington 1990, p. 194. See too Rich 1984, pp. 131–136, on the treaty and Roman activities with the Greek allies, and pp. 155–157 on the date of 211.

7. Dell 1977.

8. *SEG* 13.382 (part of the treaty); see too Livy 26.24.8–14 (= Sherk 1984, no. 2, pp. 1–2 = Austin 2006, no. 77, pp. 161–163); Justin 29.4.5, with Walbank 1940, pp. 82–84; Walbank 1967, pp. 162–163; Errington 1971a, pp. 113–115; Gruen 1984, pp. 17–25; Hammond and Walbank 1988, pp. 400–405 and 602–603; Eckstein 2008, pp. 88–91 (only formally sworn to by Rome in summer 209); Waterfield 2014, pp. 49–51. Treaty: Gruen 1984, pp. 25–33, 377–378, and 440–441; Hammond and Walbank 1988, pp. 602–603; Eckstein 2002, pp. 271–272; Derow 2003, pp. 55–56.

9. Hammond and Walbank 1988, pp. 602–603.

10. Hammond and Walbank 1988, p. 401.

Philip was at Pella when news reached him of the Roman-Aetolian alliance.[11] He may have pondered sending an embassy to Rome but was astute enough to realize it would have been pointless. He was likely more worried about Roman fleets in the Corinthian Gulf and the Aegean, bolstered by Attalus of Pergamum and his vessels. In fact, shortly after the Senate ratified the treaty with the Aetolians (in fall 211), Laevinus and a fleet of quinquiremes, each with a complement of 4,000 troops, captured Zacynthus and then, to hinder Philip's entry into the Corinthian Gulf, took Oeniadae, his naval base off the mouth of the gulf.

Philip did not panic or abandon hope: he kept calm and carried on on all fronts. As a show of strength and to safeguard his borders, he conducted an offensive against Oricum and Apollonia and devasted parts of Illyria perhaps in the upper Black Drin region.[12] Then he continued north-east via Pelagonia into Dardania, where he plundered the territories of Scerdilaidas in the upper valley of the Black Drin and seized the frontier town of Sintia, hindering the Dardanians' route into Macedonia.[13] From there he went south along the coast to Tempe, a strategic pass in Thessaly from Larissa to the coast, and reinforced the Tempe garrison with 4,000 men. Finally, he headed northeast into Thrace to besiege Iamphorynna, the capital of the Maedi tribe of the middle Strymon valley (map 4).[14]

Around the same time as the siege of Iamphorynna, the Aetolian general Scopas marched and attacked Philip's ally Acarnania west of Aetolia, forcing the Acarnanians to send the women, children, and men over sixty into Epirus for safety and call up all males from fifteen to sixty.[15] They were expected to fight to the death; anyone who survived a battle was exiled, and if the Epirotes took in any fugitives they were to be cursed. The Acarnanians called on Philip for help, who at once left the Strymon region. When the Aetolians heard he had marched against them and was already at Dium, they returned home—as did Philip to Pella.

11. Walbank 1940, p. 303, dates the news to August.

12. Livy 26.25.1–2. Chronology: Hammond and Walbank 1988, p. 401 n. 3, with references. See too Hammond 1968, pp. 18–19; Dell 1977, p. 307.

13. Livy 26.25.3.

14. Livy 26.25.4–8 and 15, with Walbank 1940, p. 86 n. 3, on the name Iamphorynna.

15. Polybius 9.40.4–6; cf. 16.32.3; Livy 26.25.9–17. On the status of Epirus, see Walbank 1940, p. 86 n. 6.

To commemorate his victories and giving us an insight into how he thought of himself, Philip dedicated ten pikes, ten shields, and ten helmets to Athena of Lindus on Rhodes.[16] Her temple was of great importance to her cult, but Philip likely dedicated these spoils for symbolic and historical reasons, given that Alexander the Great and several successors had done the same thing after their victories. He was therefore sending a signal to his various allies—the Achaeans, Epirotes, Boeotians, Phocians, and those of the Thessalians who had not fallen to Rome—that he was not a lost cause. What might also have been running through his mind was that he was a king and warrior like Alexander—certainly Philip's speed, cunning, audacity, and strategic planning evoked the great Alexander. In response, Rome focused attention on the Peloponnese; in 210 it persuaded Sparta, Messenia, and Elis to leave the Hellenic League and join the Aetolian, despite Acarnanian urging to the contrary.[17]

Philip's strategy was to keep his enemy at bay at the passes and avoid a pitched battle, not just because he lacked manpower but because his phalanx could not effectively deploy on mountainous terrain. In the same year another foe came onto his radar when Attalus I of Pergamum was elected general of the Aetolian League for 209. Attalus' election showed his determination to secure allies against his adversaries, including Egypt, Syria, and Bithynia (a kingdom in northwest Asia Minor along the southern coast of the Black Sea). That election also heralded the start of an enmity between Pergamum and Macedonia that lasted throughout the reigns of Philip and his son Perseus.[18]

Laevinus continued his plan of drawing Philip's allies to his side. He set off from Corcyra in the spring to Naupactus, from where he sent word to Scopas to join him with an Aetolian force at Anticyra in Phocis (map 1). They began the siege of Anticyra two days later, and when the city fell not long after, they killed many of its people indiscriminately, enslaved the rest, and left for all to see "dogs cut in two and limbs hacked off animals" to terrorize Philip's Greek allies and hamper his moves south.[19] Laevinus handed Anticyra over to the Aetolians while he took the booty according to the terms of the treaty with Aetolia. Shortly after the atrocity at Anticyra, he was told he had been elected

---

16. *Lindian Chronicle*, *BNJ* 532 F 42 (= Burstein 1985, no. 46, pp. 60–63).

17. Walbank 1940, pp. 87–88.

18. Kertész 1993, pp. 669–672, on Attalus, and pp. 669–670 n. 3, on the views of other scholars for why Attalus joined the war. Pergamum and the Attalid dynasty: Hansen 1971.

19. Polybius 10.15.5; cf. 9.42.5; Livy 26.26.1–4 (who is wrong to speak of Anticyra in Locris).

consul and was required in Rome. His successor in Greece was the proconsul Publius Sulpicius Galba, whose aggressive actions sparked great unpopularity among the Greeks.[20]

By spring 209 Aetolian, Roman, and Pergamene troops held the approaches to Thermopylae. This strategic pass, affording the best route from northern into central Greece, was the site of the famous battle in 480 when 300 Spartans under Leonidas were said to have held out for three days against Xerxes' Persian army. As well, Galba and the Aetolian general Dorimachus sailed into the Saronic Gulf to seize Aegina from Athens, which Galba gave to the Aetolians. Not knowing what to do with it, they sold it to Attalus for a mere thirty talents, thereby giving him a base in that gulf. Well aware of the growing threat from Attalus, Philip reached out to his relative by marriage— and Attalus' neighbor and rival—Prusias I of Bithynia, who offered Philip some of his ships to use against the Pergamene king.

The seizure of Anticyra did not stop Philip. Throughout the summer of 209 he fared well in Greece. With Achaean help he overcame the Aetolians and Romans at the Thessalian town of Echinus, which he captured after a siege, and advanced farther west to take over Phalara, the port of Lamia (map 6).[21] That protected his coast route and allowed him to maintain contact with Euboea and even to carry out an assault on Thermopylae. But then the Achaeans urgently sent for his help when they were overcome by a Spartan army and an Aetolian navy.[22] The king defeated an Aetolian force that included Pergamene and Roman troops under Pyrrhias in two brief battles and then returned to Phalara.[23] There a further attempt was made to mediate between Philip and Aetolia by several states: neutral Athens (which had stayed friendly to Rome since the First Illyrian War), Rhodes, Egypt, and the northern Aegean island of Chios, whose commercial interests were suffering in the war; Amynander of Athamania (a small kingdom in southeast Epirus), who was an ally of the Aetolians, represented them.[24] Philip and the Aetolians

20. See, for example, Eckstein 1976, pp. 126–127; cf. Walbank 1940, p. 141, on Galba's diplomatic strategy.

21. Polybius 9.41.1–42.4, with Walbank 1967, pp. 183–185. Campaign: Walbank 1940, pp. 88–89.

22. Polybius 10.41.2; Livy 27.29.9.

23. Livy 27.30.1–3.

24. Livy 27.30.4–7. They had attempted as early as 209 but usually were blocked by Philip, Aetolia, or Rome: Eckstein 2002, pp. 268–297. See too Eckstein 2008, pp. 91–116; Gruen 1984, pp. 101–119, for the first war. Note Briscoe 1973, p. 127, that Amynander is called a king in literary sources (cf. Walbank 1957, p. 463), but no epigraphic or numismatic evidence says so.

were persuaded to agree to a 30-day ceasefire and hold talks at Aegium, west of the Selinus River in Achaea.

Philip was probably keen for peace because of Attalus' danger to him in the Aegean and the realization that help from Carthage was not coming as Hannibal was now tied down in Italy—very recently a Carthaginian fleet had sailed to help him but turned back at Corcyra.[25] The king went to Chalcis to prevent Attalus from making any attempt on strategic Euboea, vital for his supplies, and garrisoned it before moving to Argos.[26] There he presided over the Nemean Games and was said to have acted disgracefully by ditching his regal clothing for ordinary people's dress and "lowering himself to the level of a private citizen" while enjoying multiple dalliances with married and unmarried women.[27] As Walbank notes, there was "probably a hostile tradition behind this, exaggerating the extent of Philip's debauchery."[28]

Peace talks at Aegium were wrecked when Attalus arrived at Aegina and Galba left Naupactus for Corinth to help stiffen the resolve of the southern Greeks.[29] The Aetolians latched onto Galba's presence to demand that Philip return territory to themselves as well as Illyria and Rome, to which Philip responded angrily and returned to Argos. Galba now decided to embark on a more aggressive policy, landing troops in Sicyon between Corinth and Achaea in the northern Peloponnese and ravaging the countryside. In retaliation, Philip marched at speed from Argos; he overcame the Romans, who dropped their loot as they fled back to the ships to escape to Naupactus.[30] Satisfied, he went back to Argos—and his alleged debauchery.[31] Later, he decided to expel the Aetolian garrison from Elis (the main Aetolian base against Achaea) but was unaware that Galba had reinforced it with 4,000

25. Livy 27.30.16; cf. 27.15.7, Appian, *Macedonian Wars* 3, with Walbank 1940, pp. 90–91; Habicht 1982, pp. 135–137.

26. Polybius 10.26.1 (here Philip "returned" to Argos, so Polybius may be confusing this visit with one shortly after, as we shall see); Livy 27.30.7–8.

27. Polybius 10.26.1–6; Livy 27.31.3–6; cf. 27.31.9, with Walbank 1940, p. 91; Walbank 1967, pp. 230–231. But this mention of rough clothing may again be Polybius' denigration and should not be seen as Philip identifying with one sector of society: Mendels 1977, pp. 169–173.

28. Walbank 1967, p. 230. But Walbank 1940, p. 92, suggests that his behavior stemmed from the setbacks he had suffered that year.

29. Livy 27.30.11–15.

30. Livy 27.31.2–3.

31. See the Polybius references in nn. 26–27 above, which might refer to Philip's behavior in Argos at this time.

legionaries.[32] Philip came upon an opposing army as he neared Elis and easily defeated it in a cavalry battle, but was then faced by Elean, Aetolian, and Roman troops. He began the assault nevertheless, but in bitter fighting his horse was run through by a javelin and threw him over its head. He had no choice but to retreat, helped onto another horse by his men.

The following day Philip rebounded by capturing the nearby fortress of Phyricus, netting himself 4,000 men and 20,000 cattle as booty.[33] At this point news reached him that back home a certain Aeropus had embarked on a campaign in Dassaretis, the gateway from southern Illyria into Macedonia which Philip had annexed in 213, and was inciting the Dardanians to raid the kingdom.[34] Philip hurried north through Achaea, Boeotia, and Euboea to Demetrias, arriving there only ten days later to learn that the Dardanians had invaded Orestis, believing a rumor circulated by Scerdilaidas that Philip was dead.[35] Philip's arrival sent them scattering back to their homes, although he was said to have taken 20,000 of their number as prisoners.[36]

Judging by his name, Aeropus may have been a pretender to the throne—three sons of Aeropus at the time of Philip II's assassination in 336 had been traitors; two had been put to death by Alexander the Great on his accession that year, and the third executed two years later.[37] The family may not have stopped meddling in dynastic affairs even a century later, for at some point before 209 Philip V executed five noble Macedonians, possible supporters of Aeropus.[38] On the other hand, it does not follow that Aeropus was a pretender: with the combination of Rome and Aetolia massing against Macedonia and the near-constant Dardanian menace, why would anyone want the throne at this perilous time?[39]

Galba in the interim had the Roman fleet of twenty-five quinquiremes join Attalus' thirty-five quinquiremes at Aegina for the winter of 209–208. In the spring of 208, Philip was pushed to his limits of endurance and

32. Livy 27.31.9–32.5–6.

33. Livy 27.32.7–9 (who has Pyrgus, but see Walbank 1940, p. 92 n. 1, on the name).

34. Livy 27.32.9–11.

35. Livy 27.33.1–3, with Walbank 1940, p. 92 n. 2. On the rumor, see my p. 28.

36. Justin 29.4.6.

37. Hammond and Walbank 1988, p. 404 with n. 1.

38. Diodorus 28.2.

39. See my p. 137 for another possible pretender, Philip of Megalopolis, in 173–172.

resilience. He went to Demetrias to meet with representatives of the Achaeans, Acarnanians, Epirotes, Boeotians, and Euboeans, who were seeking his help against the Aetolians. His own frontiers were at risk from the Illyrians under Pleuratus (Scerdilaidas having died by now) and by the Maedi of Thrace, who had been seeking revenge since 211 when he seized their capital Iamphorynna. Further, the Aetolians, taking heart from Roman and Pergamene naval reinforcements, had added a palisade, trench, and a garrison to the fortifications at Thermopylae to block Philip from operating along the Malian Gulf. Despite his own problems, Philip promised to help his allies.[40]

He began by marching to the Thessalian town of Scotussa in Pelasgiotis between Pherae and Pharsalus. When he heard that the Aetolian leaders were meeting at Heraclea, he went there to intimidate them. Arriving too late to catch them, he devastated crops in the region and returned to Scotussa.[41] In retaliation, the fleet of Attalus and Galba sailed to Euboea, capturing Oreus in the north, and then attacking Chalcis, one of the "fetters" of Greece and one of Philip's principal grain depots.[42]

Philip could not allow Chalcis to fall into enemy hands even though its inhabitants were putting up stout resistance. Gathering all his men, he went to relieve the city, forcing his way through Thermopylae, where the Aetolians offered no resistance. Fortunately for him the siege of Chalcis proved too much for the attackers, who abandoned it. At Cynus, the main port of the Opuntian Locrians on the northern tip of the Opuntian Gulf, he discovered Attalus organizing supplies and almost captured him, but Attalus fled back to Oreus in the nick of time.[43] He was not there for long: Prusias took advantage of his absence to invade Pergamum, forcing Attaus to leave at once to defend his kingdom.

The king could now head south against the Aetolians, and between the middle of June and early July 208 he restored his southern communications.[44] On his approach, the Spartans and Aetolians, who had been threatening Achaea, decided it was in their better interests to leave, giving Philip a secure route to the Peloponnese. Thus, within only a few months Philip had

---

40. Polybius 10.41; Livy 28.5.7–11; Justin 29.4.7–10. Campaign: Walbank 1940, pp. 94–95. See too Walbank 1967, pp. 255–261.

41. Polybius 10.42; Livy 28.5.14–16.

42. Livy 28.5.18–7.5.

43. Livy 28.7.5–7.

44. Walbank 1940, pp. 95–96.

reversed his vulnerable position. He then withdrew his troops from Heraea and Triphylia and gave them back to the Achaean League while transferring Alipheira from Triphylia to Megalopolis—in fact, at this time he probably only promised to give it back as he still held it a decade later and only then fulfilled his promise (p. 117).[45] Regardless, his treatment of these places shows the diminishing role of the Aetolian League in the Peloponnese and Rome's lack of zeal in helping them. Nor did he need to occupy himself in Peloponnesian affairs as much thanks to the rise of the highly competent and energetic Philopoemen as general of the Achaean League.[46]

Philip deserved some self-congratulation after a bumpy start to the year. The Aetolians were now cowed; he had regained a presence in Illyria and in Greece (especially Thessaly) at Aetolian expense; Achaea, Epirus, and Acarnania were firmly pro-Macedonian; and Rome was preoccupied with the Second Punic War and wavering in Illyria. His successes and the allure of Carthaginian naval support led him in the winter of 208/7 to order the construction of one hundred *lembi*, at Cassandrea, the former Potidaea, renamed by Cassander.[47] But then the Romans all but withdrew from the Aegean, so Philip abandoned the shipbuilding project as only the keels had been built. We cannot rule out the cost savings for his decision, but more likely Rome's withdrawal changed his thinking, for he had enough ships to ferry his troops where he needed or for smaller expeditions.[48]

The End of the First Macedonian War

The paucity of our evidence makes a precise narrative of the years 207 and 206 uncertain. What follows is based on reconstructions by Walbank and Hammond.[49]

---

45. Walbank 1940, pp. 96–97; Hammond and Walbank 1988, p. 405 with n. 2.

46. Who unsurprisingly received a highly favorable assessment from Polybius: see 10.21–24, 11.8–10.6, and 23.12.

47. Livy 28.8.18.

48. Walbank 1982, p. 227.

49. Walbank 1940, pp. 98–103; Hammond and Walbank 1988, pp. 405–407. Chronology is a controversial issue because Polybius had to use the different reckoning systems of the Greek Calendar, Roman Calendar (as did Livy), and Olympiad years. The last is what he largely followed for his treatment of Greek affairs.
    An Olympiad was a four-year period anchored in the four panhellenic festivals to various gods, each one held in the summer (late July or early August) of a particular year. The

In the spring of 207 Philip sought Amynander's permission to march through Athamania into northern Aetolia. Amynander's price was the island of Zacynthus, which Laevinus had taken from Philip in 211. We do not know the details of Philip's campaign, but he recovered Zacynthus and gave it to Amynander.[50] He then ravaged much territory in northern Aetolia, seizing livestock and other booty. It is unlikely that in this offensive he again raided Thermum but did so a little later (see below).[51] The Aetolians unsurprisingly asked for Roman help, but none was forthcoming because of Hasdrubal joining his brother Hannibal in Apulia, threats from the Gauls in the alpine provinces, and social and economic distress in Italy. The Aetolians were no match for Philip's army by themselves, so in the early fall of 207 they had to consider proposals for peace put forward by neutral Egypt, Rhodes, Byzantium, Chios, Mytilene, and perhaps Athens.[52]

The Senate insisted that the Aetolians stay true to their treaty with Rome, but the days of the Aetolian-Roman alliance were numbered, thanks to Rome's lack of military support for the league. The final nail in the coffin came in the early summer of 206 when Philip retook Ambracia and continued south

---

period began with the Olympic Games in honor of Zeus at Olympia; the following year the Nemean Games (honoring Zeus at Nemea in the northeast Peloponnese) were held; the year after that came the Pythian Games (to Apollo at Delphi); finally, the next year the Isthmian Games to Poseidon were celebrated at the isthmus of Corinth. Then the cycle began again with the Games at Olympia, followed by the others. In the Hellenistic period the Olympiad began to be used as a calendar. Since the first Olympic Games were traditionally held in 776, the first Olympiad was therefore summer 776 to summer 772. In the latter summer, the Olympic Games were held again, so the second Olympiad began (thus Olympiad 2 would be the period 772–768, and so on). Each four-year block was subdivided into separate years because of the other festivals, which thus had their own years. For example, Olympiad 3 was 768–764, divided into Olympiad 3.1 (Olympic Games), 3.2 (Nemea Games), 3.3 (Pythian Games), and 3.4 (Isthmian Games). Then we move to Olympiad 4 (764–760) with the next Olympic Games. Olympiad 3.2 was thus 767/66. Olympiad chronology was far from ideal because it did not correspond to the military campaigning season. In other words, if a campaign was conducted from spring to the approach of winter, it thus stretched over two separate Olympiad years (for example 142.1 and 142.2), given that the summer in between was the start of a new year.

Polybius, as Walbank explains, therefore modified the Olympiad year to align with the campaigning season, ending his Olympiad years in tandem with the army moving into winter quarters. While it appears logical to treat a campaigning season as one block, it also forces him to place certain events at the start or end of another Olympiad year even if they occurred prior to or after that season. Thus, as Walbank notes, Polybius has no consistent or rigid chronological scheme. See further Walbank 1957, pp. 35–37, and Walbank 1940, pp. 295–335, for some specific chronological issues. See also below with n. 89.

50. Livy 36.31.11, with Walbank 1940, p. 98.

51. *Contra* Walbank 1940, p. 98; cf. Walbank 1967, pp. 278–279.

52. Eckstein 2002, pp. 284–292.

to Thermum, where he destroyed whatever was left standing from his earlier attack.[53] By now the king had recaptured almost every place the Aetolians had taken in 211 and 210. The Aetolians were further hampered because in the Peloponnese Philopoemen had defeated the Spartans at Mantinea in June 207, isolating Aetolia's other allies there, Elis and Messenia. Philip's second wave of destruction at Thermum was meant to dishearten the Aetolians completely, and it worked.

The Aetolians held an assembly to debate peace, heckling a Roman delegation that tried to persuade them to stay loyal to Rome. They and their allies Sparta, Elis, and Messenia concluded a peace with Philip and the Hellenic League, which must have included surrendering those towns in Thessaly in Aetolian hands.[54] The Aetolians' decision to renege on their treaty with Rome would come back to haunt them in 197, as we shall see. The Senate was furious that they had not continued the war alone—that Rome had ignored *their* pleas was inconsequential.[55]

In an effort to endear himself to the Greeks, especially the Achaeans, Philip bought the freedom of the people of the Achaean town of Dyme, whom the Romans had earlier enslaved and sold, and restored them to their city.[56] There is no record of him campaigning in 206, though that does not mean he did not do so.[57] But history comes alive again in the spring of 205 when Rome, fresh off victories in Spain, sent Publius Sempronius Tuditanus with 10,000 infantry and 1,000 cavalry on thirty-five warships to Dyrrhachium in Illyria (map 3). Upon arrival, Tuditanus sent fifteen warships and some of his troops to Aetolia to try to entice the league back into the war on Rome's side. He also engineered revolts among the Parthini and laid siege to Dimale, which had been in Philip's hands since 213, to keep open the land route between Epidamnus and Apollonia. But a series of forced marches brought Philip onto the scene. He blocked all the inland routes, forcing Tuditanus to withdraw to Apollonia and wait for a response from the Aetolian League.

The Aetolians rejected any Roman overtures as they still felt abandoned and treated badly by the Senate and had no desire to fight in Illyria for Rome.

---

53. Polybius 11.7.1–3; cf. Livy 36.3.11 (raid of 207). Rich 1984, p. 139, doubted a second raid but we should prefer two: Hammond and Walbank 1988, p. 407 n. 2.

54. Walbank 1940, pp. 99–102; Eckstein 2002.

55. Rich 1984, pp. 136–137; Burton 2011, pp. 270–278.

56. Livy 32.22.10.

57. Walbank 1940, p. 102 with n. 2.

Tuditanus was put in a difficult position, which shows how vital the Aetolians were for Rome, at least during the Second Punic War.[58] He could not be re-inforced from Rome because of the war with Carthage, whereas Philip, even though he had no hope of defeating a Roman fleet with his *lembi*, may have gambled on still taking Apollonia. Given his quick changes of mind and daring, his gamble was not fanciful.

At this point came a diplomatic initiative from the Epirote League, which had suffered badly over the years, not least from losing its usual trade outlets of Oricum and Ambracia, and may even have thought itself a target of Roman expansion.[59] The Epirotes diplomatically sought the permission of Tuditanus to invite Philip to a conference in the city of Phoenice in north-western Epirus that summer. Philip was quick to accept as the costly war was wearing down his kingdom and he had problems with the Dardanians and the troublesome Attalus of Pergamum. Therefore, Philip and Tuditanus discussed the terms of the proposed peace before Amynander and represent-atives of the Epirote League and Acarnania.[60] All of this meant that Philip was thus breaking the terms of his alliance of 215 with Carthage. Then again, the Carthaginians had never come to his rescue, so he felt no obligation to honor the terms.

The Peace of Phoenice was concluded most likely in spring 205 between Philip, the Hellenic League, and Prusias on one side, and Rome, Attalus, and Pleuratus on the other, showing that the war had covered a wide geo-graphical area.[61] Rome retained its authority around Apollonia and received back Dimale as well as two border towns guarding the land route between Epidamnus and Apollonia.[62] Philip was granted Atintania, formerly within the Roman protectorate, to give him control of Lissus and the Scodra basin—a hoard of copper coins dated to this time was found north-east of Lake Scodra and bore on the obverse a Macedonian shield and on the

---

58. Rich 1984, pp. 148–150.

59. Livy 29.12.8–9, with Hammond 1967, p. 612.

60. Livy 29.12.11–16 (= Austin 2006, no. 80, pp. 166–167); Appian, *Macedonian Wars* 3; Justin 29.4.11, with Walbank 1940, pp. 103–105; Hammond and Walbank 1988, pp. 408–410; Errington 1989a, pp. 104–106; Errington 1990, pp. 195–196; Eckstein 2002, pp. 293–295; Derow 2003, pp. 57–58; Matyszak 2009, pp. 52–55; Waterfield 2014, pp. 55–57.

61. For an earlier dating, see Rich 1984, pp. 136–143. See too Walbank 1940, p. 103 n. 6; Rich 1984, p. 150; Hammond and Walbank 1988, p. 409 with n. 1.

62. Hammond and Walbank 1988, p. 409 n.1.

reverse a Macedonian helmet.[63] He now held northern Illyria, Dassaretis, and Atintania, thereby ensuring the safety of his border with Illyria, but that made him an immediate neighbor of Rome with no buffer in between them, and Pleuratus was also concerned that Philip might come after him.[64] Walbank claims that the peace was "a triumph for Philip," but there was still a substantial Roman presence in Illyria, and not even the most optimistic person must have thought that Rome and Philip would be friendly neighbors.[65]

Indeed, the Romans believed Philip had won more favorable terms than he deserved, and further, that they had been backed into a corner to make these concessions because of the exhaustion of the people in the war against Hannibal.[66] Five years later warfare again broke out between Rome and Philip (the Second Macedonian War), making the Peace of Phoenice a mere breathing space in hostilities.

The Uneasy Peace

After swearing to the peace Philip remained active. A scattered mention in Polybius speaks of him campaigning in Thrace. Few details are known but perhaps this was an attempt to reassert Macedonian influence at least in parts of the region, which had last been controlled by Macedonia in the reign of Philip II.[67] Our Philip's campaign did worry Attalus, who was expanding there, and Rhodes, which had an extensive trading network with the area and the Black Sea.

Philip was also busy in the Aegean. By now, he was reputedly falling under the influence of a certain Heracleides of Tarentum, whom Diodorus claimed "transformed Philip from a virtuous king into a harsh and godless tyrant and had thereby incurred the deep hatred of all Macedonians and Greeks."[68] Heracleides had gone to Philip at some point before 209 after

---

63. Hammond and Walbank 1988, pp. 409–410, citing the numismatic evidence (and n. 1 on p. 409), as our sources do not cite Lissus and Scodra in the terms of the treaty. Errington 1990, p. 195, for the view that Philip did not hold Lissus.

64. Hammond 1968, pp. 19–20; cf. Dell 1977, pp. 307–308.

65. Walbank 1940, p. 104.

66. Eckstein 2010, p. 233; *contra* Walbank 1940, p. 105, that the Romans were ready for peace and made it in good faith.

67. Polybius 13.10, with Errington 1990, p. 196.

68. Diodorus 28.9; cf. Polybius 13.4–5 on Heracleides' baseness.

allegedly betraying Tarentum to Rome and then the Romans to Hannibal. He was considered a disreputable character by Polybius, who even says he was a prostitute in his youth, which Greeks would have found abhorrent.[69] Philip was said to have asked Heracleides for a plan to damage the Rhodian navy and incite the Cretans (as the king was president of their league) to war against Rhodes. Heracleides went to Rhodes, where he burned thirteen ship-sheds, and persuaded Philip to give twenty ships to an Aetolian named Dicaearchus to plunder the Troad and the Cyclades, again to undermine Rhodes' naval presence.[70]

Was Philip really swayed by Heracleides' advice, and what was he hoping to accomplish? Polybius, our ultimate source for these expeditions, may again be seizing the chance to denigrate Philip by showing how easily he succumbed to venal and ignoble men. More likely is that Philip wanted to keep Attalus, Rhodes, and Egypt at bay, given that the recent activities of the Rhodian and Pergamene fleets off the Aegean coast of Greece posed a threat to him and could even disrupt the grain route from the Black Sea to Greece, causing a shortage of supplies. He certainly did not have the ships or men to mount anything major against these states, so he decided to protect his kingdom by nullifying any threat from the Aegean.[71]

Likewise, his alliance in the winter of 203/2 with Antiochus III "the Great" of Syria against the new Egyptian king Ptolemy V was for Macedonia's security.[72] Ptolemy was only a boy at this time, but his advisers proposed a marriage alliance to Philip, who responded politely enough but was more attracted to Antiochus' significant manpower reserves and resources that could be used against Attalus and Rhodes.[73] Antiochus had recently waged a major campaign from 212 to 205 against the eastern satrapies of the Seleucid Empire, which went no small way toward resurrecting the Asian empire of Alexander the Great.[74] He was now eager to exploit Ptolemy's young age and

69. Polybius 13.4–5.1.

70. Diodorus 28.1.

71. Though see Briscoe 1978, p. 155.

72. Polybius 15.20; Livy 31.14.5; *Appian, Macedonian Wars* 4.1; Justin 30.2.8; Porphyry, *BNJ* 260 F 45, and see McDonald and Walbank 1937; Walbank 1940, pp. 113 and 128; Walbank 1967, pp. 471–474 (cf. Walbank 1979, p. 785); Gruen 1984, pp. 387–388. See especially Errington 1971b, who thinks it was a pact between Philip and Antiochus' general Zeuxis, but Zeuxis offered little help to Philip; cf. Eckstein 2008, pp. 121–180.

73. Walbank 1940, pp. 108 and 112–113.

74. Errington 1989b, pp. 248–250. Antiochus: Grainger 2002. Seleucids: Grainger 2014.

weak position and take over Coele Syria ("Hollow" Syria, the area between the Lebanon and anti-Lebanon mountain ranges, in what is now Syria and Lebanon), an area disputed since the days of Ptolemy I and Seleucus I.

Our ancient writers give inconsistent details about the terms of Philip's alliance with Antiochus; hence they may not have known what they were.[75] Probably both rulers would use their own troops to seize Egyptian possessions, which for Antiochus included Coele Syria and Phoenicia, and for Philip Samos (the Egyptian naval base in the eastern Aegean) and Caria in southwestern Anatolia. It is sometimes thought that the alliance was made in secret so that the Senate would be unaware of it, and that when Attalus and the Rhodians later brought it to the senators' attention it was a factor in the outbreak of the Second Macedonian War. This is unlikely and is better treated in discussion of the factors leading to that war in the next chapter.

Antiochus invaded Coele Syria in the spring of 202, sparking the Fifth Syrian War (202–195). But Philip's plan to take Ptolemaic possessions depended on his Greek allies' support, which was unknown as the Achaeans had been embroiled in a war against Sparta since 204 and were increasingly suspicious of the Aetolians. Philip therefore decided to sideline any activity in the Aegean for the moment; he set off for the Hellespont and Bosporus regions to put pressure on the trade route, and by extension, pressure the Aetolians.[76] He won over several cities, including Perinthus from Byzantium, and Lysimachia and Chalcedon from the Aetolian League, expelling their garrisons and governors and forcing them to make treaties with Macedonia.[77]

Philip next met up with his ally and relative by marriage Prusias of Bithynia. They besieged the strategic city of Cius, an inland city of Bithynia at the head of a gulf in the Propontis (Sea of Marmara) and member of the Aetolian League. It was suffering internal strife, which Philip supposedly saw as an opportunity, though we are not told which side the king fancied.[78] Perhaps it was the exiled wealthy faction, which appealed for help to Prusias

75. Polybius 15.20, 16.1.9; Livy 31.14.5; Appian, *Macedonian Wars* 4.1; Justin 30.2.8. See further Errington 1971b.

76. Walbank 1940, p. 114.

77. Polybius 15.23.9.

78. Polybius 15.21–23, with Walbank 1940, p. 115; Walbank 1967, pp. 474–475. On Prusias, cf. Walbank 1967, 475–476.

and who brought in Philip, with both rulers out to deprive the Aetolians of this useful ally.[79]

Envoys from Rhodes and perhaps some other states tried to organize a settlement but to no avail. Cius fell and was razed, its population enslaved. Its neighbor, Myrlea, suffered the same fate, with Prusias building new cities on both sites. He renamed Cius Prusa and his son renamed Myrlea Apamea after Prusias' wife.[80] Worse was to come. On his way home Philip stopped off on the northern Aegean island of Thasos, wrangling his way into the city by promising to respect its liberty (map 5). Thasos was independent at the time, but he treacherously seized and garrisoned it and sold the people into slavery.[81]

Philip had weakened the Aetolians, as was his intention, who had lost valuable Thracian allies. But he may not have anticipated the adverse reaction of the Greeks to the fate of Cius and Myrlea. Members of the Hellenic League may even have condemned him, perhaps a factor in their siding with Rome against Philip, as we trace in the next chapter. Philip's actions were brutal for sure, yet they were no more severe than what often happened in Greek warfare. The claim that Philip "lost his moral superiority" over Rome in his treatment of these places is naive, for morality had no place in this period.[82] By protecting his borders Philip kept the Thracian coast toward the Hellespont and the Bosporus in check, similar in design to Philip II's subduing of Thrace in the later 340s.[83] Thasos was in a strategic position facing the borders of Macedonia and Thrace; it was a likely launching point for enemy troops, so control was vital for Macedonia's security.[84]

In the early fall of 202 the Aetolians made a U-turn in their relations with Rome and sent envoys to the Senate seeking an alliance against Macedonia.[85] The senators, perhaps astonished at the Aetolians' gall, sent them packing with the sharp retort "Why bother coming to us now after negotiating peace with Philip without consulting us?"[86] If Philip was pleased at the

---

79. See Mendels 1977, pp. 166–168, citing sources.

80. Walbank 1940, p. 115 with n. 8, for sources.

81. Polybius 15.24.1–3.

82. Hammond and Walbank 1988, p. 474.

83. Worthington 2008, pp. 122–125.

84. Eckstein 2010, p. 230, believes that Philip did have this ambition.

85. Walbank 1940, pp. 310–311, on the year.

86. Livy 31.29.4; Appian, *Macedonian Wars* 4.2.

Senate's response, that feeling was short-lived: in mid-October of the same year Publius Cornelius Scipio resoundingly defeated Hannibal at Zama near Carthage. That victory led to the formal end of the Second Punic War and was followed by Rome's dispatch of a fleet, commanded once more by Laevinus, to Illyria.

Faced by this new situation Philip had no choice but to turn to the Aegean in case Rome united with Attalus, Rhodes, or even Egypt against him. In the spring of 201 he captured several islands in the Cyclades (Aegean islands southeast of the mainland), and may have established garrisons on them, possibly intending to re-create an earlier League of the Cycladic islands.[87] These islands were technically independent but unofficially under Rhodes' protection, which prompted the Rhodians to set sail against him. By then the king was at Samos, where he seized some Egyptian ships, though he never annexed Samos as he did the Cyclades.[88]

Philip sailed northward to besiege the city of Chios on the island of the same name in the northern Aegean, which was an ally of Rhodes and Pergamum.[89] He could afford to engage in these campaigns as news would have reached him that despite Attalus calling on the Aetolian League against Macedonia, the league stayed loyal to its peace with the king. At Chios he was confronted by a large armada from Pergamum, Rhodes, and other allies prepared to do battle.[90] His own fleet of over 200 vessels, 53 large warships (quadriremes and quinquiremes) and 150 *lembi*, with some 30,000 men, was on a par with the enemy one of 65 large warships, 9 medium-sized ships, and 3 triremes. However, the prowess of the Rhodians at sea was well known, and he had no wish to be shut into the Chios Strait, lying between the island and the mainland shore, given that his enemy was positioned opposite Chios to cut him off from his base at Samos. He decided to make a run for Samos at all costs.[91]

---

87. Cf. Livy 31.15.8, with Walbank 1982, p. 230.

88. Walbank 1940, pp. 117–118.

89. The chronology of Philip's engagements for the remainder of 201—two naval battles, an invasion of Pergamum in between them, and a campaign in Caria—is disputed; I follow the order put forward by Walbank 1967, pp. 497–500 (superseding Walbank 1940, pp. 307–308). On chronology see n. 49 above.

90. Polybius 16.2–9. Battle: Walbank 1940, pp. 122–124; Walbank 1967 pp. 503–511; Hammond and Walbank 1988, pp. 414–415.

91. Polybius 16.2.4.

As he put out to sea, Attalus' fleet charged Philip's eastern wing and the Rhodian fleet his slower western wing, forcing two separate battles on either side of the Chios Strait. Their larger warships smashed into his smaller vessels and wreaked havoc; several of the king's vessels sank, and those that were disabled were attacked by enemy soldiers jumping from their ships and fighting the crews. Philip managed to overcome Attalus, pushing him and two quadriremes ashore; their crews escaped to Erythrae on the mainland, which had the domino effect of sending the rest of Attalus' fleet back to its base and the two Macedonian wings linking up to rush the Rhodians, who retreated to the harbor at Chios.

In all, Philip was said to have lost twenty-eight of his large warships, half of his *lembi*, three other vessels, 3,000 Macedonian soldiers and 6,000 sailors, while two quadriremes and 3,000 men were captured. These numbers may be exaggerated as his opponents were said to have lost only eight warships, one light vessel, 130 men, and had three ships captured.[92] Even so, Philip claimed victory as he had remained in battle and had driven Attalus ashore—yet the Rhodians claimed victory because of Philip's heavy losses. In reality, both sides won and both lost, though Philip's casualty rates were the greatest of any one battle he fought.

The king decided to punish Attalus. He left his fleet and with his army descended on Pergamum, most likely in mid-June.[93] He ravaged the land around the city, sacked temples and shrines, and destroyed statues of gods, for which Polybius accused him of insanity and that he "spent most of his fury not on men but on the gods."[94] Although he defeated some Pergamene troops he failed to capture the city, falling victim for once to insufficient provisions as the people had already gathered in the harvest. Accordingly, he returned to where his fleet was stationed.

When Philip next put to sea, he encountered the Rhodian fleet off Lade (an island off the coast of Asia Minor close to Miletus). We have few details of this battle. Since his approach to Miletus and Caria was blocked, he immediately engaged the Rhodians, completely routing them.[95] Afterward, he

---

92. Polybius 16.7, using Rhodian sources that exaggerated his losses and Rhodian successes: Walbank 1967, pp. 509–510.

93. Polybius 16.1; Diodorus 28.5 (dating: Walbank 1967, p. 500). The Pergamum invasion is placed at the start of this Polybian book and so before the battle of Chios, but as Walbank 1967, pp. 499–500, demonstrates, it needs to go after Chios and before Lade (see below).

94. Polybius 16.1.2.

95. Cf. Polybius 16.14.5, 16.15, and see the comments of Walbank 1967, pp. 511–512.

occupied Miletus, from where he launched an invasion of Caria, investing Cnidus in southern Caria and Prinassus to the east, which soon fell to him.[96] It was probably now August, but his movements for several weeks are obscure until he sailed against Iasus on the Gulf of Bargylia in Caria. The town quickly capitulated to give him control of almost all Caria, much to the Rhodians' dismay.[97]

Why Philip embarked on this Carian venture is not known. We can understand his keenness to reestablish Macedonian influence in Thrace and extend it in the Aegean, as had Poliorcetes before him, but the Carian campaign was perhaps only to combat Rhodes and keep it out of the northern Aegean.[98] In this he was unsuccessful, for the Rhodian fleet was still at large. It soon paired up with that of Attalus to blockade Philip in the Gulf of Bargylia for the late fall and winter of 201. He received some supplies from Zeuxis, the Seleucid governor of Asia Minor; they were not enough, and he was forced to raid coastal cities for food, with Polybius likening him to a wolf.[99]

Philip needed to escape from his precarious position, plus he was aware that Attalus and Rhodes had sent envoys to Rome to complain about him and his alliance with Antiochus.[100] He therefore resorted to a trick.[101] When the spring of 200 arrived he arranged for a pretend Egyptian deserter to be captured and reveal that he intended to do battle the next day.[102] The enemy commanders were debating strategy when Philip unexpectedly slipped past them; though they pursued him, he was able to escape back to Macedonia. He left behind garrisons in the towns he had seized and to keep Rhodes' attention diverted from him.[103]

Further warfare between Philip and Rome was now inevitable. Polybius claimed that having defeated the Carthaginians in the Second Punic War, the

---

96. Polybius 16.11.

97. Polybius 16.12, with Walbank 1940, pp. 125–126.

98. Errington 1990, pp. 198–199.

99. Polybius 16.24.4–6, 16.24.9, with Walbank 1940, pp. 126–127, on Philip's winter foraging.

100. Polybius 16.24.3.

101. Polyaenus 4.18.2.

102. Walbank 1940, p. 309, suggests winter 201–200.

103. Walbank 1940, p. 129 n. 4.

senators were "considering that they had taken the most important and necessary step toward their plan of world conquest, were now emboldened to reach out and seize the rest and to cross with an army to Greece and the continent of Asia."[104] True or not, the Peace of Phoenice was now conveniently disregarded: it was the beginning of the end for Philip.

---

104. Polybius 1.3.6.

6

The Second Macedonian War

THE SECOND MACEDONIAN War lasted from 200 to 197 and was a far
greater commitment for Rome than the first one.[1] Following Philip's defeat
the Senate undertook a major reshuffling of his kingdom and then in the following year a settlement of Greece. In this war Athens, still the foremost city
in Greece, abandoned its careful relationship with Macedonia and declared
war on Philip, taking Rome's side, and formally cursing the Antigonid king
and all his predecessors.

The Lead-up to War

The sequence of events in the outbreak of the war and at what times they
occurred are open to debate.[2] In the fall of 201, envoys from Pergamum,
Egypt, Rhodes, and Athens formally complained to the Senate about Philip's
attacks on Greek cities in Asia Minor, his campaign in Thrace, and his treaty
with Antiochus III of Syria.[3] The presumption is that the senators did not
know of that treaty until now, though it would have been hard to keep a treaty
like this secret. Regardless, the Senate did not seem unduly alarmed; it had its

---

1. War: Walbank 1940, pp. 138–185; Errington 1971a, pp. 131–153; Harris 1979, pp. 212–218;
Hammond and Walbank 1988, pp. 416–446; Errington 1989b, pp. 261–274; Derow 2003, pp.
58–62; Eckstein 2006, pp. 257–289; Eckstein 2008, pp. 273–305; Matyszak 2009, pp. 71–94;
Waterfield 2014, pp. 65–95; cf. Briscoe 1973, pp. 42–47. For the view that the first and the
second wars were one continuous one, see Derow 2003, pp. 58–59.

2. On chronology (in Livy 31) see the careful study of Warrior 1996. Lead-up to war: Walbank
1940, pp. 127–129; Errington 1971a, pp. 131–137; Gruen 1984, pp. 392–396; Hamilton 1993;
Eckstein 2008, pp. 230–270; Matyszak 2009, pp. 57–63; cf. Briscoe 1973, pp. 36–42.

3. Livy 31.2.1–2. Date: Walbank 1940, p. 311; see too Briscoe 1973, pp. 55–56.

The Last Kings of Macedonia and the Triumph of Rome. Ian Worthington, Oxford University Press.
© Oxford University Press 2023. DOI: 10.1093/oso/9780197520055.003.0007

fleet under Laevinus in Illyria, and probably expected Pergamum and Rhodes to unite if Philip threatened them as we saw in the previous chapter.

Nevertheless, the Senate did not want to lose the support of Pergamum in the east. It ordered three commissioners, Gaius Claudius Nero, Marcus Aemilius Lepidus, and Publius Sempronius Tuditanus (the same man who had helped to negotiate the Peace of Phoenice), who were then on a goodwill mission to Ptolemy V of Egypt, to stop off in Greece, hear the accusations against Philip, and gauge how the Greeks might react if Rome declared war on Macedonia.[4] Not everyone agreed with this cautious approach, in particular the consuls for 200, Gaius Aurelius Cotta and Publius Sulpicius Galba (who had fought in Greece during the First Macedonian War). They were more hawkish, perhaps because Galba knew the country and its people better than the senators from his time there.[5]

Galba, backed by the Senate, urged the Comitia Centuriata (the popular assembly that actually declared war) to declare war on "King Philip and the Macedonians under his rule because of his offenses and aggression against allies of the people of Rome"; the Comitia, however, led by the tribune Quintus Baebius, rejected the petition—"the natural reaction of men tired of protracted and relentless warfare—and sick of its dangers and hardships."[6] Baebius was an adherent of the influential Scipio Africanus, who was against war with Philip. But we should not underestimate the exhaustion of nearly two decades of war on several fronts, which at times had cost the Roman state dearly. Even Livy seemed exhausted just from writing about it, as he freely admits: "I too am happy to have reached the end of the Punic War, just as if I had myself shared its hardships and dangers!"[7]

Perhaps also Philip was not viewed as a risk at this time. As Hamilton sagely remarked, "There was more than enough to occupy the Senate's efforts in Italy and the West without becoming involved in a major struggle in the

---

4. Livy 31.2.3–4.

5. Galba: Errington 1971a, pp. 141–143; Harris 1979, pp. 214–215; Gruen 1984, pp. 204–207; Errington 1989b, pp. 253–257; Waterfield 2014, pp. 62–66. On military and diplomatic appointments to those with apparent expertise in Greek affairs and their influence on the Senate's policy toward the east, see Gruen 1984, pp. 203–249 (noting this was not always the case).

6. Livy 31.6.1–6; cf. Appian, *Macedonian Wars* 4.2; Justin 30.3; Walbank 1940, pp. 128–129 and Briscoe 1973, pp. 70–71, see Scipio influencing the vote.

7. Livy 31.1.1.

East."[8] But despite the mood of the Comitia Centuriata the Senate evidently wanted war—Baebius had even accused it of "tacking one war onto another so that the plebeians could ever feel the advantages of peace."[9] We discuss the reasons for war below.

The three commissioners visited several Greek cities and the assemblies of the Aetolian, Achaean, and Epirote Leagues seeking allies. They were met with a largely lukewarm response, perhaps because Philip was currently away from Greece.[10] They fared better in Athens because of souring relations between the city and Philip. Athens' fortunes had declined dramatically from its heady days as an imperial power in the fifth and fourth centuries and had lived like the rest of Greece under Macedonian hegemony since 338. The Athenians had spearheaded an abortive Greek revolt on Alexander the Great's death in 323 known as the Lamian War.[11] But Antipater had ended that in the following year and dealt harshly with Athens: he abolished its radical democracy, installed a garrison in the Piraeus, and introduced a wealth requirement for citizenship that disfranchised several thousand citizens. In the Wars of the Successors, Athens had to endure the personal ten-year rule of Cassander's puppet ruler Demetrius of Phalerum (317–307) and then that of Demetrius Poliorcetes, who had even set up a garrison on the Museum Hill, in the heart of the city by the Acropolis.

The Athenians seized hold of the sudden chaos brought about by the death of Demetrius II (Philip V's father) in 229 to declare their independence and expel the garrisons from the Museum and the Piraeus. Commerce began to pick up again, and the city prospered substantially down to the second half of the next century. The Athenians followed a policy of neutrality in Greek affairs and took care not to antagonize Demetrius' successor Antigonus III Doson or Philip when he became king in 221. Indeed, they stressed their friendship to the latter by turning away his secretary Megaleas who had fled for refuge to the city (p. 63).

Relations declined once Philip and Rome were caught up in the events leading to the outbreak of the Second Macedonian War. One particular incident unexpectedly brought them into conflict. In September 201, the

8. Hamilton 1993, p. 559. See too Gruen 1984, pp. 391–392.

9. Livy 31.6.4. Cf. Hamilton 1993, p. 562, and pp. 562–566 on family factions and the motives of individual senators that collectively led to the Senate's thirst for war against Philip.

10. Gruen 1984, pp. 21–22.

11. On the war and its aftermath, see Worthington 2021a, pp. 24–28, citing bibliography.

Athenians executed two young men from Acarnania who had sacrilegiously gone into the temple of Demeter and Persephone at Eleusis at the time of the Eleusinian Mysteries.[12] The Mysteries were a centuries-old secret religious rite that had fallen under the mantle of the Athenians, and only initiates were allowed to go into the temple to those gods at the time of the festival.

The young men may have become mixed up in a crowd and so made a genuine mistake. However, the Athenians did not give them the benefit of the doubt, and the Acarnanians, allies as we know of Philip, angrily complained to him about the Athenians putting their two citizens to death.[13] Philip had just arrived back in Macedonia after his encounter with the Rhodian and Pergamene fleet at Bargylia the previous winter, but he sent troops to the Acarnanians, who plundered the Attic coast while Macedonian vessels seized four Athenian warships and their crews in the Piraeus.[14] Fortunately, the commander of a Rhodian-Pergamene fleet based at Aegina, which had gone there from Bargylia, recaptured them for Athens, after which Attalus sailed up the Attic coast to protect it against any Macedonian reprisal.

The Athenians' execution of the two young men was indeed heavy-handed, but they had acted within their legal rights, and religious crimes affronting the gods were taken very seriously. They would have feared divine wrath had they not punished these violators of the Mysteries. Philip's response to the Acarnanian appeal is interesting. He could have sent a letter of protest, but his more aggressive stance indicates the value of the Acarnanians to him, and perhaps even an opportunity to reassert Macedonian authority over Athens.

The Athenians cast around for allies. Egypt was still in a state of turmoil and Antiochus was too far away, so they turned to Attalus of Pergamum, then on Aegina. They invited him to their city and welcomed him when he arrived, though instead of formally addressing them, he preferred to communicate by a letter read out in the Assembly, which received an enthusiastic response.[15] The three Roman commissioners sent earlier to Greece were also in the city,

12. Livy 31.14.6–8, with Walbank 1940, p. 311 (August–September 201). Episode: Worthington 2021a, pp. 148–149.

13. Livy 31.14.9. Chronology of the following interactions between Athens and Philip: Warrior 1996, pp. 37–42; cf. Worthington 2021a, pp. 149–152, on the events.

14. Livy 31.14.9–10, 15.5; cf. Polybius 16.26.9–10, with McDonald and Walbank 1937, pp. 188–189.

15. Polybius 16.25–26.8 (= Austin 2006, no. 232, pp. 406–407; trans. Austin); Livy 31.14.12–15.4.

and they encouraged the Athenians to wage war on Philip.[16] Livy, echoing Polybius, thought the circumstances were unworthy of war, but with the likelihood of further Macedonian-Acarnanian strikes, the Athenians had little choice and declared war on Philip.[17]

The Rhodians sailed off to Ceos and captured almost all the Cyclades from Philip while Attalus went back to Aegina. Philip decided to deal with Athens when he heard it was now at war with him. Possibly now he ordered his general Philocles, whom he had previously made governor of Euboea, to take 2,000 infantry and 200 cavalry into Attica and ravage the lands.[18] Philocles unsuccessfully tried to seize Eleusis while Philip attacked Athens. When the king also had no luck, he left for the Hellespont to disrupt the grain route to the city, along the way taking places such as Maronea and Aenus in Thrace before moving to the Chersonese to invest Abydus (map 4).[19]

Philocles, however, may have remained on Euboea and not been sent to Attica until 200. In the present campaign we know that one of Philip's generals, Nicanor, had marched as far as the Academy park, just under a mile (1.5 kilometers) from the Dipylon Gate, the main entrance into Athens on the northwest. Whether Philip committed two of his commanders to operations in Attica at the same time, given the importance of Euboea in his supply line, is debatable. We know that the Romans devastated Philip's supply depot on Chalcis in 200, after which Philocles was deployed to Attica (p. 113), so sending Philocles on a mission outside Euboea while Chalcis was still fully operational does not seem logical.

The Roman envoys were still in Athens and confronted Nicanor at the gate. On behalf of the Senate, they delivered an ultimatum intended for Philip: he was not to assault any Greek city and was to compensate Attalus for injuries done to him, with the amount determined by arbitration; otherwise, he would be at war with Rome.[20] Unsurprisingly, after such a provocative ultimatum, the envoys hurriedly left Athens for Rhodes.

---

16. The Roman embassy was in Athens with the others by spring 200: Walbank 1940, pp. 313–317.

17. Livy 31.14.6, 31.15.6.

18. Livy 31.16.2, but see 31.26, with Walbank 1940, p. 131 n. 3.

19. Livy 31.16.3–17.11.

20. Polybius 16.27 on the episode (27.2–3 for the terms of the ultimatum), with McDonald and Walbank 1937, p. 197; Errington 1971a, pp. 138–139.

The Athenians were all but encircled by enemy forces. Nor was there any military help from Attalus and Rhodes: the Rhodians were busy undoing Philip's gains, and Attalus on Aegina sent only money and much-needed grain as a later decree of 188/87 informs us.[21] Both Attalus and Rhodes seemed to think the job of keeping Athens safe should fall to Rome.[22] The commissioners must have sent word of the situation to the Senate by the very end of 201 or the beginning of 200, by which time they had arrived on Rhodes.[23] Galba took the issue of war back to the Comitia Centuriata, where he delivered an impassioned speech peppered with scare-tactic rhetoric and denunciations of Philip for his alliance with Rome's enemy Hannibal. This time—late spring or early summer 200—the Comitia voted for war.[24]

The Comitia's decision permitted the Senate to initiate a formal demand for reparation, which, if refused, was followed by a "notice of war" (*indictio belli*).[25] Lepidus, the most junior of the three commissioners still on Rhodes, was tasked with delivering an ultimatum personally to Philip. At that time the king was besieging Abydus on the Hellespont, part of an ambitious plan to hold the entire Thracian Chersonese in check.[26] He had already taken Maronea and Aenus and some other Thracian cities—for the most part Egyptian possessions—before besieging Abydus. Its defenders, helped by Pergamene and Rhodian troops, put up fierce resistance, destroying his siege engines and forcing his ships to retreat. Eventually, Philip undermined the walls and the people sued for terms, but the king wanted only unconditional surrender. His stance hardened the resolve of the defenders, who initially were willing to resort to mass suicide, though eventually they sent an envoy to Philip in surrender.[27] Their story would soon take a horrific twist.

At that point Lepidus arrived with the Roman ultimatum, distracting Philip from the situation at Abydus.[28] The message was very similar to what Roman commissioners had delivered to his general Nicanor at Athens, except

---

21. *IG* ii³ 1, 1280, lines 3–4.

22. McDonald and Walbank 1937, pp. 198–199; Walbank 1940, pp. 131–132.

23. Chronology: Walbank 1940, pp. 310–317; Briscoe 1973, pp. 42–45.

24. Livy 31.7–8.1.

25. Procedure: Livy 7.6.7, with McDonald and Walbank 1937, pp. 192–193.

26. Walbank 1967, pp. 541–542.

27. Livy 31.17.

28. Polybius 16.30–34; Livy 31.18.1–4; Diodorus 28.6, with Walbank 1967, pp. 543–544.

that Philip now had to respect the possessions of Egypt (clearly reflecting his current Thracian campaign) and submit to arbitration damages due to Attalus and Rhodes. The Romans had no right to impose this high-handed ultimatum on Philip as he had not broken the Peace of Phoenice, and he correctly pointed out that the Rhodians were more to blame for any injustices than he was. Unfortunately for him, the Senate was not interested in any legal, moral, or just arguments, and backed Philip into a corner.[29]

Lepidus pointed out Philip's aggression at Athens, Cius, and Abydus. Presumably because he realized that Rome was intent on warfare, Philip responded defiantly, asking that the Romans not break the treaty but remain at peace with him; otherwise, "If you attack me, you will realize that the kingdom and name of Macedonia—as noble as those of Rome—give me courage, too."[30] He then dismissed Lepidus, who rejoined his colleagues on Rhodes. All three visited Antiochus and Ptolemy, who were both then at war with each other, and received assurances of their friendship to Rome; they returned to Rome by spring 199.[31]

In many respects, Philip's cutting response to Lepidus was an error, guided more by his personal feelings than strategic considerations, for the king must have been aware of the might of the Roman army.[32] But we can say this in hindsight. At the time, Philip may have been expecting support from his Greek allies and Antiochus and could not show any weakness to his people by giving in to what was unjust demand.

With Lepidus gone, Philip turned on the people of Abydus to such an extent that out of fear the men killed first their wives and children and then started on themselves—a surprised Philip cynically gave them three days to compete the deed.[33] He then installed a garrison there and returned to Macedonia. In the meantime, Galba, to whom Macedonia had fallen as his province, was sent to Apollonia with two legions of about 20,000 men and fifty ships.[34] Philip abandoned his Thracian plans to return home, uncomfortably aware that he was at war with Rome.

---

29. Cf. Walbank 1940, p. 134 with n. 3; Hammond and Walbank 1988, pp. 419–420.

30. Livy 31.18.4; cf. Polybius 16.34.7.

31. Walbank 1940, pp. 316–317.

32. Walbank 1940, p. 137; cf. Eckstein 2008, pp. 277–278, on why the ultimatum failed.

33. Livy 31.18.5–8.

34. Walbank 1940, p. 138 n. 1.

Why War?

Walbank rightly stated that Rome's declaration of war on Philip was a change "from apathy to a passionate concern for eastern affairs," given that the city had taken no hostile action against him since the Peace of Phoenice.[35] The question is why the Senate was now so antagonistic, especially given its rebuff by the Comitia. Here Polybius ought to come to the rescue, but if he did give a reason it is lost because of his work's fragmentary nature (cf. Appendix). That means we must turn to Livy, who surely is out to exculpate Rome when he says that the Athenians were behind the Senate's call to arms.[36]

Many theories have been put forward about why this second war against Philip broke out, though there need not be only one reason.[37] One common one is that the embassies from Attalus and Rhodes accusing Philip of an expansionist policy along with news of his treaty with Antiochus were the tipping points for the Senate: worried about this "coalition of kings" it acted to keep Syrian power out of the Aegean and restrict Philip to Macedonia.[38] But the existence of this treaty has not been universally accepted, and even if there was one we should not forget it was against Ptolemy, not Rome. The Senate may have looked askance at Philip's dealings with the Syrian king, but that does not mean it was its reason for declaring war on him.[39]

Polybius claimed that *Tyche* (Fortune) led Rome to the declaration of war—on Philip and later Perseus.[40] But why did Fortune not work on the Comitia Centuriata, which refused war initially, and only gave way when the Senate continued to push for it? Equally, the Athenians' pleas to Rome have been seen as the catalyst, yet they came *after* the Romans were heading to war.

---

35. Walbank 1940, p. 127.

36. Briscoe 1973, pp. 39–47, for Livy's account.

37. For example, McDonald and Walbank 1937; Errington 1971b; Gruen 1984, pp. 359–398 (with analysis and critique of some modern theories at pp. 382–398); Hamilton 1993; Eckstein 2005. More to do with chronology but still linked to causes is Warrior 1996.

38. McDonald and Walbank 1937, especially pp. 203–207; Eckstein 2005.

39. Errington 1971b; Gruen 1984, pp. 387–388; cf. Walbank 1940, pp. 127–128; Hammond 1992, p. 352.

40. Polybius 3.2.8 on the treaty; Polybius 15.20.6 for *Tyche*, on which see Walbank 1940, pp. 128–129; Walbank 1957, pp. 16–26; Walbank 1972, pp. 58–65; Walbank 1994, pp. 356–337; Eckstein 1995, pp. 254–271; Eckstein 2005, pp. 228–242; Deininger 2013. On Polybius' views of Rome's reason for involvement in the east, see too Walbank 1963.

In any case, it is unlikely Rome would have gone to such lengths for another city, especially one not an ally.[41]

Then there is the role of Attalus. The Senate saw him as an important ally in the east, and he had sent it an embassy protesting Philip's actions. Again, Rome's track record with its allies does not point to a long and costly conflict on the other side of the Adriatic to keep Attalus happy, though his embassy and that of the Rhodians for that matter would have been useful in justifying war.

Another explanation is that Rome needed to thwart a possible alliance between Philip and hostile Celtic tribes in Cisalpine Gaul, who posed a greater danger to Italy's northern frontier than Macedonia.[42] Indeed, Hannibal in 218 had counted on Celtic manpower to boost his own troops. Yet the Celts were far closer than Philip, and the Comitia did not initially accept that war was necessary for defensive purposes.

We can also reject any truth to Galba's scare-tactic rhetoric that Philip had mobilized a vast army and navy, and the Romans had to decide "whether you are to transport your legions to Macedonia or else admit your enemy into Italy."[43] As has been noted a number of times, Philip hardly had the means and resources to mount any full-scale invasion of Italy to topple Roman power there.

A potent motive is revenge for Philip's treaty in 215 with Hannibal. Macedonia was the only state that was still unpunished for its allegiance to Rome's greatest foe to date, hence the decision to move against the king, limit Macedonia's influence in the east, and in the process win over the Greeks.[44] Yet if revenge were a factor, given Roman suffering in the Second Punic War, we would expect all Romans to want it, hence the Comitia embrace the Senate's call for war at the outset.

In fact, the reverse happened, perhaps because the hero of the battle of Zama, the politically ambitious Scipio Africanus, was looking out for the interests of his men after their service in the recent wars and brought pressure

---

41. Livy 31.5.5–6. McDonald and Walbank 1937, especially pp. 187–203; cf. Gruen 1984, pp. 391–398; Hammond and Walbank 1988, pp. 416–418; Hamilton 1993, p. 560; Eckstein 2008, pp. 206–211. The Roman-Athenian *foedus* did not occur until after the end of the war, probably in 191: Worthington 2021b.

42. Twyman 1986.

43. Livy 31.7.2.

44. McDonald and Walbank 1937, p. 206; Gruen 1984, pp. 382–398; Errington 1990, pp. 201–203. Whether Rome had an eye on making all of Greece its subject as early as the First Macedonia War and still had that aim, as Rich argues, is unlikely; as late as the settlement of 196 Rome was not focused on subjugating Greece: Rich 1984, pp. 130–136.

to bear on the original decision of the Comitia.[45] Only when Galba promised Baebius that he would not call on any of Scipio's veterans from the Second Punic War—unless they volunteered to go—did the Comitia change its mind and agree on war. We presume that if Galba had insisted on their deployment the Comitia would have continued to oppose war. Hence, domestic politics played a key role in the declaration of war. In addition, factions such as the Claudian were suspicious of Scipio and suspected that his veterans would support him if he turned to politics. Since many of these men were likely to serve in a war, thus robbing him of their political support, we can see a reason for Scipio's enemies provoking a war.[46] This theory cannot be proved, of course, and many veterans were eager for land in Italy rather than more fighting, but they and Scipio may have been a factor in the Senate's thinking and led Galba to use them as a bargaining chip in his dealing with the Comitia Centuriata.

By extension, the Senate also contained several hawkish senators as well as younger aristocrats eager to establish their own military reputations, given that older commanders had won glory in the recent war against Carthage. To achieve that reputation, these war hawks continued their lobbying, making war inevitable. There were immediate causes for the war, such as Philip's naval policy in the Aegean, his relations with Syria and Egypt, the embassies to Rome urging action against him, and of course his treaty with Hannibal, but the truest explanation for the declaration of war lies with the Senate.[47]

Cursing Philip

The Romans had taken the war to Philip in 200. Their strategy was to stretch the king's resources to the utmost, perhaps drawing on the costs of Macedonia's recent Thracian expedition, and to weaken his army by forcing him to split it up to hold all his borders and garrison some of his allies.[48] To this end, Roman commanders aimed to conduct offensives in Greece and Macedonia, apply pressure on Philip in Illyria, and even organize a Dardanian invasion.

---

45. Walbank 1940, pp. 128–129; cf. Briscoe 1973, pp. 62–64; Hamilton 1993, p. 565.

46. Hamilton 1993, pp. 562–566.

47. On the importance of military victories and a military reputation for political and social advancement, hence the continual need to wage wars, see Harris 1979, pp. 10–41. Also, underpinning all motives was always the attraction of accumulating revenue: see Gruen 1984, pp. 288–315, on the "tangible benefits of empire."

48. Cf. Matyszak 2009, p. 71.

Philip could field perhaps 20,000 men, supplemented by troops from Illyria, Thrace, and Thessaly, but even so he was no match for Roman numbers.[49] Since he did not have the resources to fight on land and sea, he decided on a strategy of wearing down his adversaries by land, even if this meant enabling Rome, Attalus, and Rhodes to rule the waves. As a result, he was always fighting on the defensive.

During the fall of 200 the Romans sent thirty ships to hold Corcyra and blockade Epirus, while twenty under Gaius Claudius Cento went to the Piraeus, the port of Athens, which the Romans were using as their base—not that the Athenians had much choice. With some Rhodian and Athenian vessels Cento made a sudden dawn raid on Chalcis.[50] For some reason it was poorly guarded, and Cento's troops burned its arsenal and storehouses, massacred the men of military age (including the governor Sopater), freed prisoners whom Philip had incarcerated there, and in a major blow to the king's supplies, destroyed the grain stored there before returning to the Piraeus.

Philip left Demetrias at once for Chalcis with 5,000 infantry and 300 cavalry but arrived too late to save it.[51] He marched straightaway to Athens, thinking that he might catch the city unawares and as well as inflicting damage on it might even destroy some of the Roman fleet in the Piraeus. But a scout spotted his army and rushed to warn the Athenians despite it being the middle of night; when Philip arrived at the Dipylon Gate before dawn he found it heavily fortified.[52] He had lost the element of surprise, so he allowed his men a rest period and then attacked the defenders at the Dipylon Gate. In fierce fighting he was beaten back by Athenian contingents, supported by a force of Pergamene troops already in the city.[53]

The king had to content himself with destroying buildings both sacred and secular outside the city walls, and perhaps even the Academy—wanton acts arguably not seen since the days of the Persian Wars.[54] After an unsuccessful attempt on Eleusis, home of the sacred Mysteries, he withdrew to Corinth and thence to Argos. There he attended an Achaean League Assembly discussing war against

---

49. Numbers: Hammond and Walbank 1988, p. 431 with n. 1.

50. Livy 31.23.1–12.

51. Livy 31.24.1–3.

52. Livy 31.24.3–7.

53. Livy 31.24.8–18.

54. Livy 31.25.1–2; cf. Diodorus 28.7.

Nabis of Sparta and offered to march into Laconia in return for Achaean troops helping him to garrison Oreus, Chalcis, and Corinth against Rome.[55]

The league's general Cycliadas, a supporter of Philip, was astute enough, however, to grasp that if the Achaeans agreed to Philip's deal, they would suffer a loss of manpower in the Peloponnese and, even worse, antagonize Rome. Since Nabis was less of a danger than a Roman legion bearing down on them, Cycliadas persuaded the Assembly to reject Philip's request, leaving the king no choice but to return to Corinth.[56]

From there Philip decided on a frontal assault on Athens and the Piraeus. It is more likely that it was now that he ordered Philocles and his troops from Euboea, given the devastation Philip had wreaked on Chalcis, and not earlier, as we have mentioned (p. 106). Now Philip split his troops, taking a contingent of them to the Piraeus and ordering Philocles to invest the city with the others.[57] The defenders at the Piraeus beat Philip back, forcing him to link up with Philocles at the city, where a sudden sally by Athenian infantry and cavalry overcame the attackers. Philip had no choice but to break off the siege and headed north through Boeotia into Macedonia for the winter of 200 to 199— but not before he inflicted further destruction on Athenian lands and shrines.[58]

The Athenians finally had had enough of Philip's sacrilegious acts and in either late 200 or early 199 formally cursed him and all Antigonid rulers:[59]

> They immediately proposed a motion which the people ratified, to remove and destroy all the statues and portraits of Philip and the inscriptions on them, as well as those of all his ancestors, men and women, to cancel all the holidays, ceremonies and priesthoods instituted in honor of him and of his ancestors; even the places where something had been placed or inscribed in his honor were to be put under a curse and it should be wrong in future to decide to place or dedicate anything there that religion allowed to place or dedicate in a holy spot; whenever the priests of the state offered prayers on behalf of the people of Athens, their allies, their armies and fleets, they should at the same time

---

55. Livy 31.25.2–7. Character of Achaean assemblies: Walbank 1979, pp. 406–414.

56. Livy 31.25.8–11.

57. Livy 31.26.

58. Livy 31.26.9–13.

59. Livy 31.44.4–9 (= Austin 2006, no. 82, pp. 169–170; trans. Austin), with Worthington 2021a, pp. 152–153, especially Byrne 2010, with pp. 158–159 and 175–176 on chronology.

curse and execrate Philip, his children and his kingdom, his land and sea forces, and the entire race and name of the Macedonians.

Other measures included executing any Athenian who favored Philip and smashing all statues of the king and his ancestors in the city, including an expensive gold one set up to Antigonus Monophthalmus and Demetrius Poliorcetes in 307 and another to Poliorcetes in 303–302. They also erased mention of any Antigonid kings in many inscriptions detailing their diplomatic and other dealings with them over the years—significantly apart from two inscriptions, which on them honored two Athenian patriots and described the kings as enemies of Athens.[60] Ultimately, these measures were empty gestures as Athens was no longer a military power, yet the Athenians' curse must have resonated with the other Greeks.

Philip Challenged

That winter Pleuratus, Amynander, and the Dardanian Bato visited Galba in his camp on the Apsus (Seman) River. They were encouraged to do so by the successes of Galba's lieutenant Lucius Apustius, who had captured and razed several of Philip's allied towns, including Antipatrea (Berat) and Codrion, killing the men of military age, and defeating a Macedonian force while returning to his main camp.[61] It is not a surprise that Galba urged Amynander, who was popular with the Aetolians, to persuade them to join the war, given how much Rome needed them.[62] But at the Aetolian Assembly, Galba's plan of using them came unstuck when Philip, so the story goes, bribed their leader Damocritus to reject Rome, although they agreed only to be neutral.[63]

Philip expected an invasion of his kingdom, but from which direction? He stationed his fleet at Demetrias and divided his army into two groups, which he posted at key points in Upper Macedonia (map 3). One under his young son Perseus was stationed at the Pelagonian pass and the other near

---

60. Byrne 2010, pp. 161–172. The two were Philippides (in 292) and Callias of Sphettus (in 270/69), on whom see Worthington 2021a, pp. 76–77, 82, 87, and 108 (Philippides), and pp. 97–100 and 104–105 (Callias).

61. Livy 31.27–28.1–3. Berat: Hammond 1966b, p. 42.

62. Walbank 1940, p. 141; Errington 1971a, p. 142.

63. Livy 31.28.6–32—bribery at 31.32.1—with Briscoe 1973, pp. 129–139, especially on the speeches.

Heraclea in Lyncus, which gave him control of all the passes in that region.[64] He thus held the territory lying between the army of Pleuratus and Bato and the Roman army, neatly preventing their two armies from uniting and penetrating his border.[65] In May 199 Galba—with 25,000 to 30,000 troops, Illyrian auxiliaries, and elephants from Carthage—advanced through the valley of the Genusus (the more northerly route from Illyria to Macedonia) and set up camp on a hill named Athaeus in southern Lyncestis.[66]

Philip recalled Perseus' men to boost his own numbers to 22,000 men. He did not have the luxury as Galba had of adding to his manpower or the monetary resources to hire mercenaries, and his men were also not as well trained and disciplined as the Roman legionaries. Philip knew he needed to be careful, which is why he resisted Galba's attempts to bring him to battle. He did not want to suffer heavy casualties or see his men demoralized, as had happened when Roman and Macedonian forces fought in Dassaretis, resulting in the deaths of forty Macedonian infantrymen and thirty-five cavalrymen.[67] Instead, he focused on holding his fortified positions and planned on ambushing the Romans when they were foraging for food and vulnerable.

After some minor skirmishes Galba withdrew into Pelagonia. Philip seized his chance and pounced on the enemy foraging parties; he was gaining the upper hand when Galba and his main army rushed to their aid. A battle ensued, in which Philip was thrown from his horse and almost trampled underfoot; he was only able to escape when one of his own men gave him his horse.[68] Galba then continued to lay waste the lands of Upper Macedonia as he traveled through them, including Eordaea, Elimiotis, and Orestis, where Celetrum (Kastoria) surrendered to him. He crossed the mountains into Dassaretis, where he captured and garrisoned the fortified town of Pelium, between southern Illyria and Macedonia, perhaps intending it to be his base

---

64. Livy 31.5–6, 31.33.1–3. Opening stages of the war (in 199 and 198): Hammond 1966b, pp. 42–45; Hammond and Walbank 1988, pp. 420–430. Perseus: Meloni 1953, pp. 16–23 and 38–40.

65. Hammond 1966b, p. 43. On the following campaign see Walbank 1940, pp. 143–144; Hammond 1966b, pp. 43–45. On the Dardanians, see Hammond 1966a, pp. 249–253.

66. Walbank 1940, pp. 317–319, on chronology of this year's campaign (199); see too Warrior 1996, pp. 82–89.

67. Livy 31.33–34.

68. Livy 31.36.7–37.1–12—referring to Philip as "terror stricken," but we have no way of knowing if this was so).

for an invasion of central Macedonia the following year.[69] In all this, Philip wisely kept his distance, for which even Livy commended him.[70]

The Romans were also busy in the Aegean.[71] Apustius had rendezvoused with Attalus in Athens in May, and then sailed to Andros in the Cyclades, which quickly fell to him. They moved on to Euboea, taking Carystus and Oreus, enslaving the population, and thence to the Pallene peninsula of the Chalcidice. They ended their campaign when a seasonal storm wreaked havoc with their fleet and because they had word that the Aetolian League was reconsidering neutrality, and so left Euboea to meet with a prominent league member named Pyrrhias at Heraclea in Oetaea in southern Thessaly. He agreed to bring their appeal to the Aetolians to join them in a war against Philip to a league meeting at Thermum. Their arguments, together with the Senate's positioning itself as a liberator of the Greeks, its support of Athens, and the lure of booty, enticed the Aetolians to ally with Rome on the same terms as in the previous war.[72]

Philip had overcome the Dardanians and sent them packing without any booty.[73] But he had no time to celebrate as an Aetolian army with troops from Amynander marched into Thessaly (map 6). It ravaged towns in Pelasgiotis, the region from the Vale of Tempe in the north to Pherae in the south, and Perrhaebia in northernmost Thessaly, which at the time was part of Macedonia. But instead of invading southern Macedonia it turned back to besiege the strategic town of Gomphi in the southwest, near the borders of Athamania and Dolopia. Gomphi controlled two passes in central Thessaly, one of which (Portes) afforded entry to Athamania and thence Ambracia.[74] Amynander had long wanted Gomphi for himself and decided to capture it, which saved Macedonia and gave Philip the chance to hit back.[75]

The king took an army into Elimiotis and then south-east, crossing the Haliacmon River into the upper Europus valley. He came upon the Aetolians near Pharcadon and inflicted a heavy defeat on them. Amynander, who had encamped not too far away, did not take part in the battle, and guided the

69. Livy 31.39–41. Route: Livy 31.40.1–6, with Hammond 1966b, p. 45.

70. Livy 31.38.

71. Livy 31.44.1–2, 31.45–47.2.

72. Livy 31.40.9–10.

73. Livy 31.40.8.

74. Livy 31.41.1.

75. Walbank 1940, pp. 145–146.

survivors back to Aetolia.[76] With winter drawing near, Philip decided to go home to Pella.

And so ended 199. Despite his losses, the year had been a positive one for Philip.[77] He had successfully staved off invasions of his kingdom, his borders remained safe, and the Romans' need to forage had shown both a major weakness in their supply route and Philip's advantage over them. Indeed, his guerrilla tactics had earlier led to some 2,000 Roman troops mutinying because of a lack of provisions along with a general tiredness of serving in Greece. Galba's successor, the new consul Publius Villius Tappulus, was forced to make concessions to end the insurrection.[78]

Philip now had to guard against possible attacks from Aetolia as well as Rome. The danger posed by the former was shown when he attempted to take the Phthiotic fortress of Thaumaci (Domokos), on a strategic route into Thessaly, but failed because of topography and Aetolian reinforcements.[79] In an effort to bolster Macedonian spirits, he arrested the lackluster commander of his fleet at Demetrias, Heracleides, because of his unpopularity and who had never put to sea against the enemy.[80] He also built up his troop numbers over the winter of 199–198 by withdrawing his garrisons from Lysimachia in the Thracian Chersonese, Orchomenus in Boeotia, and Heraea, Alipheira, and Triphylia in Arcadia. At this time, and to coax the Achaean League to his side as a counter against the Aetolians, he finally fulfilled the promises he had made in the summer of 208 by giving Orchomenus, Heraea, and Triphylia to the Achaean League and Alipheira to Megalopolis (p. 90).[81] For Philip, military action and diplomacy merged.

Tappulus stayed with the fleet at Corcyra throughout the winter. In the following spring (of 198) a pro-Roman Epirote leader named Charops told him that Philip had sent troops under his commander Athenagoras to the junction of the Aous and Drin Rivers in northern Epirus and then himself marched to them.[82] This location was significant. Philip guessed that an

---

76. Livy 31.41.6–42.4. See Walbank 1940, p. 146 n. 3, on the location of Pharcadon.

77. Cf. the summary of Walbank 1940, pp. 147–148.

78. Livy 32.3.1–7; Dio 18.58.

79. Livy 32.4.

80. Livy 32.5.7. His and his people's mood: Livy 32.5.

81. Livy 32.5.4–6. Walbank 1940, p. 148.

82. Livy 32.6.1; cf. 32.5.9–10.

FIGURE 6.1. Aous River Gorge. Photo credit: Robin Waterfield.

incursion into Macedonia would come not from Illyria but from Epirus, so he established a strong defensive position as far west as he could, while continuing to wear down the Romans.[83] To this end he set up a fortified camp on the north side of the Aous River gorge—the "Aoi Stena"—at one of the few crossing points of the river near Antigonea (figure 6.1).[84] Here he would again show his astuteness when it came to planning, rapid execution of strategy, and ability to adapt to new challenges.[85]

The Battle of the Aous Gorge

Philip's position on the narrows of the gorge allowed him to block any Roman advance from Antipatrea to Pelium and cut the Roman lines of supply, while

83. He anticipated that Tappulus would take one of the three principal routes from Illyria into his kingdom along the valley of the Viossa (Aous) River from Apollonia south-east to Metsovo and beyond into Thessaly, with its tributary the Drin River providing a different route into Epirus: Walbank 1940, p. 148.

84. Livy 32.5.9–13. Location of Antigonea and Philip's position: Walbank 1940, pp. 149–150 n. 1; Hammond 1966b, pp. 47–51, and see pp. 39–42 on the geography of the Aoi Stena. On chronology, see Walbank 1940, pp. 319–320.

85. Hammond 1966b, p. 45, and see pp. 45–53 on the campaign of 198, with Walbank 1940, pp. 151–167.

FIGURE 6.2. Titus Quinctius Flamininus. © The Trustees of the British Museum.

ensuring that his own supplies through Parauaea, a region of Epirus, were secure.[86] Tappulus crossed over to the mainland and led an army to within five miles (eight kilometers) of Philip's camp, but there was little he could do other than hold fast because of the king's strong position. Then came an unexpected arrival: the new consul for 198, Titus Quinctius Flamininus, who had drawn Macedonia as his province and who would bring the Second Macedonian War to a triumphant end (figure 6.2).

Flamininus, not yet thirty, was energetic and ambitious. But despite his political backers in Rome, his inexperience in the east made him "an unknown quantity" as a diplomat and general.[87] He had arrived at Corcyra from Italy with 8,000 infantry and 500 cavalry; leaving some behind to catch up to him later, he had hastened to Tappulus' camp, who had little choice but to leave for Rome.[88] Livy recounts a battle in which Tappulus was said to have defeated Philip and caused him to flee, but this could not have taken place as Flamininus engaged Philip at Aoi Stena, and even Livy queries his source.[89]

86. Hammond 1966b, pp. 45–46.

87. Plutarch, *Flamininus* 2.1 (cf. 7.2 on his friends). Quote: Matyszak 2009, p. 77. On Flamininus, see Badian 1971; Eckstein 1976; Eckstein 2008, pp. 279–282; Pfeilschifter 2005; cf. Briscoe 1973, pp. 22–35. On Flamininus' early actions, see too Errington 1971a, pp. 144–151; Eckstein 1976, pp. 126–142; Matyszak 2009, pp. 76–82.

88. Livy 32.9.6–8; Plutarch, *Flamininus* 3.1–4. See too Eckstein 1976, pp. 127–128, on Tappulus' surprise and his reaction.

89. Livy 32.6.5–8.

Flamininus faced Philip's men and artillery on the opposite bank of the river. The river was now fast flowing and deep, so the only way across it would have been to build a bridge, leaving the workers vulnerable to missiles launched from the Macedonian troops. After considering various strategies, Flamininus decided to force his way across, but to no avail.[90] Forty days went by as he weighed his options of either invading Macedonia by a different route (perhaps as Galba had envisaged) or trying to cross the river again and storm Philip's position. Eventually, the Epirote League brokered a meeting between Philip and Flamininus to discuss peace—with each man standing on opposite banks of the river and shouting across it.[91] Philip offered to liberate any city he had himself captured but not those held by his ancestors and to accept arbitration in any compensation issues—these were similar terms to what Lepidus had offered him at Abydus in 200, which is perhaps why he offered them now.

But this was not the year 200. Backed by a Roman army on Greek soil, and with the Greeks sympathetic to Rome, Flamininus rejected arbitration and insisted on the surrender of all places outside Macedonia including Thessaly. His response was a red rag to bull—as if "in 1938 Adolf Hitler had demanded the 'liberation' of Scotland."[92] Flamininus probably had some negotiating flexibility as he was the man on the ground, but the Senate must have given him instructions about how to deal with Philip.[93] It was clear, then, that Flamininus or the Senate or both wanted Philip defeated and humiliated. Unsurprisingly, given his strategic need of Thessaly, Philip ended the negotiations with a furious question: "What heavier condition could you impose on a defeated man, Flamininus?"[94] It was just as well there was a river between them as Philip may have impetuously fought the Roman commander then and there.

Flamininus again tried to cross the Aous but was beaten back while his flanks were bombarded by missiles from Philip's catapults and stone-throwers. Eventually Charops brought him a local shepherd who spoke of a path that could be accessed at a different part of the river and came out above the

90. Livy 32.9.10–10.1.

91. Livy 32.10.1–8, with Walbank 1940, p. 151–152; Hammond 1967, p. 618; Eckstein 1976, pp. 128–131.

92. Errington 1971a, p. 146.

93. Walbank 1940, p. 152, but note Eckstein 1976, pp. 129–131.

94. Livy 32.10.7 (quote); Diodorus 28.1.

Macedonian line.[95] Flamininus sent 4,000 infantry with the shepherd one night to escape detection; when they arrived at the other end, they were to send a smoke signal. To fool Philip into thinking he was going to try to cross the river again, Flamininus had the men in his camp undergo training and drills. Just before dawn on the third day Flamininus spotted the smoke signal and in a tactic worthy of Alexander the Great he blitzed the Macedonians front and rear: 2,000 of their number were killed and the rest scattered, but no Roman losses are given in our sources.[96] Philip's casualty rates could even have been higher, given the training of the Romans.[97]

This battle at the Aoi Stena took place on June 25.[98] It was a minor one in the big picture, but it was a necessary one for Roman morale. The Romans captured Philip's camp and chased him for a day before Flamininus changed tack. Instead of ordering his troops up the Aous valley into northern Thessaly, he turned south to try to win over the Epirote League, which merely declared its neutrality although some Epirote soldiers joined his *auxilia*.[99] While it was to Flamininus' advantage to have the Epirote League on his side, his principal reason for turning south may have been to find a different route into Macedonia and create a new supply route for his army.[100]

Philip had retreated via Triphylia into the central Pindus range, where he waited for some days. He kept a sharp eye on Flamininus' movements, so when the latter moved into Epirus the king went to Thessaly, eventually basing himself at the impregnable Tempe pass. In Thessaly he resorted to a scorched-earth policy, devastating towns and capturing people along his way, which seems counterproductive at a time when he needed Thessalian support.[101] His reasoning may have been to prevent his enemies from occupying the same towns and to hinder their progress from lack of food. But after meeting Flamininus he might also have realized that his smaller army could not hold

---

95. Livy 32.11.1–4.

96. Livy 32.11.5–12.10; Plutarch, *Flamininus* 4.1–5.1 (the shepherd at 4.2); Appian, *Macedonian Wars* 5–6, with Briscoe 1973, pp. 187–188 on Livy 32.11.10, and Hammond 1966b, pp. 51–53, on the battle.

97. Walbank 1940, pp. 152–153.

98. Date: Walbank 1940, pp. 152, 319, and 321–322.

99. Livy 32.14.5–6.

100. Eckstein 1976, pp. 131–134.

101. Livy 32.13.1–9; Plutarch, *Flamininus* 5.2, with Walbank 1940, p. 153, for details; cf. Briscoe 1973, pp. 189–194.

Thessaly, and so sacking the cities was psychological to show he could act as he saw fit.[102] If so, we get an insight into his thinking: keeping Flamininus always guessing what Philip would do next as he strove to gain the upper hand.

Checkmate?

The upper hand never came Philip's way again. The Aetolians overran western Thessaly and Amynander finally captured Gomphi, which gave Flamininus a new supply line from the Gulf of Ambracia overland to Thessaly via Athamania and Gomphi.[103] Philip was also faced by a fleet of 100 Roman, Pergamene, and Rhodian warships, commanded by Flamininus' brother Lucius, which captured several Aegean islands and struck at Macedonian bases on Euboea. When Eretria fell despite the defense of the Macedonians in it, the Romans enslaved its population. Shortly after Carystus surrendered, but its Macedonian garrison was allowed to leave for a ransom of 300 sesterces per man but without any weapons.[104]

Flamininus, as we said, did not pursue Philip after the battle at the Aoi Stena and stayed in Epirus throughout July. In August, after summoning Amynander to him, he took his army into Thessaly.[105] In a relentless assault by day and night that overcame the exhausted 2,000 Macedonian defenders he captured the fortress at Phaloria by Mount Cercetium, commanding the western approaches to the Upper Peneus River Valley, and looted and razed it; several other cities quickly submitted to him. Flamininus' strategy was to intimidate the cities of western Thessaly while promising they would be spared if they surrendered to him.[106]

Not everyone was swayed by that message, however. After receiving provisions from the Ambracian Gulf at Gomphi, Flamininus invested Atrax, on the right bank of the Peneus in Perrhaebia, ten miles (16 kilometers) west of Larissa, which along with the fortress at Phaloria were vital for Philip's security. Atrax put up fierce resistance, with Flamininus experiencing firsthand the awesome ferocity of the Macedonian phalanx, which fought him there as the ground was level, and the inability of his legionaries to get anywhere

---

102. Walbank 1940, p. 154.

103. Livy 31.13.10–14.3.

104. Livy 32.16.4–17.3; Zonaras 9.16.2; cf. Pausanias 7.8.1 for Eretria.

105. Livy 32.14.8–15.1–9.

106. Eckstein 1976, pp. 134–136.

near the enemy because of the deadly sarissas.[107] His massive siege towers were also ineffective, and Atrax's inland location was far from nearby ports to land supplies. The siege dragged on into September 198, at which time Flamininus abandoned it, deciding instead to conquer Phocis, where several towns quickly fell to him though Elatea resisted.

To put further pressure on Philip, Flamininus and Attalus attended a meeting of the Achaean League assembly at Sicyon to try to persuade the Achaeans to take their side in the war.[108] The meeting was also attended by envoys from Rhodes, Athens, and Philip. Cycliadas had been exiled by then and replaced by Aristaenus as general for 199–198. Like many Achaeans, he was acutely aware that with Philip all but shut off behind Tempe he could not help them in their conflict with Nabis of Sparta. Another factor was that tucked away in Achaean territory was one of Philip's "fetters," Acrocorinth (the citadel of Corinth). The league did not take kindly to the Macedonian garrison there, and to help his appeal to the league Flamininus had ordered the fleet to besiege Corinth.

Aristaenus was all for backing Rome, making a vigorous speech to this effect, but the other member states were divided. For three days the issue was hotly debated, with the envoys speaking in a fixed order: first the Roman, then those from Attalus and Rhodes, then Cleomedon (Philip's delegate), and finally the Athenian. Since the Athenians had suffered the most thanks to Philip, their positioning was clearly intended to counteract Cleomedon's speech. But the biggest factor in the deliberations, surely trumping all considerations, was a Roman army on their doorstep.[109] That was enough for the Achaeans to throw their weight behind Rome, although three member states—Dyme, Megalopolis, and Argos—angrily refused and left the meeting.[110]

The siege of Corinth proved a difficult one. The defenders resisted robustly, helped by the arrival of Philocles and 1,500 reinforcements, which forced Flamininus to call it off.[111] The Macedonian garrison at Acrocorinth

---

107. Livy 32.15.8–9, 17.4–18.3.

108. Livy 32.19–23.3; Plutarch, *Flamininus* 5.3; Appian, *Macedonian Wars* 7; Zonaras 9.16.3; cf. Pausanias 7.8.2, with Walbank 1940, pp. 157–158; Briscoe 1973, pp. 200–212; Eckstein 1976, pp. 138–141; Gruen 1984, 442–447; Burton 2011, pp. 102–105.

109. Cf. Waterfield 2014, pp. 86–87.

110. The date is controversial, and an alliance might not have been made until the 180s: Gruen 1984, pp. 33–38 and 444–447.

111. Livy 32.23.4–13, and see Walbank 1940, p. 158; Errington 1971a, pp. 148–149.

therefore remained in place, much to the upset of the Achaeans. They had committed troops to the siege and perhaps naively thought that Rome would give Corinth to them as a thank-you gift. To make matters worse, Philocles took advantage of a group in Argos sympathetic to Philip and occupied its citadel, installing a garrison there. He allowed the roughly 500 Achaean troops to leave, although some, including their leader Aenesidemus of Dyme, fought to the end.[112]

These Macedonian successes were not enough. Attalus was now back on the scene, joining the fleet at the Piraeus while the Roman one sailed from Corinth to Corcyra. Flamininus, who had finally captured the troublesome Elatea to give him most of Phocis and eastern Locris, allowed the Macedonian garrison to leave unharmed and granted the people their freedom.[113] His action was perhaps to garner support by showing he was different from Philip, whose ruthlessness at Cius, Myrlea, and Thasos was still remembered. Then unexpectedly Flamininus received a herald from the king proposing a peace meeting, to which he "reluctantly" agreed.[114] The request turned out to be an excellent example of Philip's cunning, the sort of thing Philip II excelled in, and we have said several times how our Philip emulated that king.

As Matyszak rightly points out, Philip was no fool.[115] He knew he faced an uphill battle against the troop numbers that Rome could field, even though Macedonia was still secure and he had allies and strongholds in Thessaly, Corinth, and now Argos. He also knew that Roman consular commanders were replaced when their annual office ended, although their command could be prolonged when they were made proconsuls. But there was always uncertainty as to whether a commander would stay on or be recalled to Rome, and Flamininus was ambitious; he had shown that by arriving in Greece early to take up his command and sending Tappulus home.[116] The end of Flamininus' command was coming into sight and Macedonia was still undefeated in the war, so Philip gambled that if Flamininus were thinking he could not cover

---

112. Livy 32.25.

113. Livy 32.24; cf. Pausanias 10.34.4.

114. Livy 32.32.5–7.

115. Matyszak 2009, pp. 84–85. See too Walbank 1940, p. 159; Errington 1971a, pp. 149–150; Hammond and Walbank 1988, p. 428 with n. 1.

116. See too Eckstein 1976, pp. 129–131, who puts the terms at the Aous down to Flamininus' quest for his own *gloria*.

himself in glory by ending the war, he might settle for being the arbiter of peace, which his successor would have to follow.

The two men met toward the end of November at Nicaea in the Malian Gulf, not far from Thermopylae, in what turned out to be a three-day affair.[117] Flamininus and representatives from Pergamum, Rhodes, Aetolia, Achaea, and perhaps Athens (though there is no evidence of Athenian delegates speaking) as well as Amynander himself were already there when Philip arrived by ship. The king refused to disembark, despite Flamininus' urging, saying he was "afraid of no one but the gods, but he was suspicious of most of those present and especially of the Aetolians." When Flamininus said everyone present was exposed to the same danger, Philip haughtily retorted that he was wrong, as the Aetolians could soon replace their leaders, "but if Philip perished there was no one at present to occupy the throne of Macedonia."[118] These sorts of comments and retorts bring Philip alive for us; he had an air of self-entitlement, but who could blame him for that?

Flamininus must had a feeling of déjà vu: he had had to shout across to Philip at the Aous River, and now he was doing the same thing to the king on his ship! His terms were largely a repeat of what he said at the Aous: Philip was to withdraw all his troops and garrisons from the whole of Greece (Thessaly, significantly this time, was not mentioned). In addition, all deserters and prisoners had to be released, the area in Illyria Philip had occupied after the Peace of Phoenice was to be reinstated to Rome, and all places taken from Ptolemy V in Thrace were to be returned to him. The allies present at the meeting also named their own terms. Pergamum wanted Philip to hand back its ships and prisoners taken at Chios and the repair of monuments, including the temple of Aphrodite, he had destroyed in 201. Rhodes insisted on the removal of Philip's garrisons in Asia Minor. The Achaeans demanded they be given Argos and Corinth, and the Aetolians insisted that Philip vacate Greece and restore cities that had formerly been members of their league.

Philip was not going to bow meekly to these demands and defended himself vigorously. He agreed that the Achaeans should have Argos but refused to hand over Corinth, wanting to discuss the issue privately with Flamininus. He refused the Aetolian demands and sarcastically told the Pergamene envoys he

---

117. Polybius 18.1–10.4; Livy 32.32.8–37; Plutarch, *Flamininus* 5; Appian, *Macedonian Wars* 8; Justin 30.3.8; Zonaras 9.16.4 (all deriving from Polybius): see Walbank 1967, pp. 548–560; Briscoe 1973, pp. 227–243.

118. Polybius 18.1.7–8; cf. Livy 32.32.16.

would restore their temples and precincts by sending them gardeners! He also insisted on a written copy of Flamininus' demands.

Nothing much was decided by the end of the first day. On the second day Philip came ashore to meet Flamininus privately. He agreed to most of the demands but was determined to hold on to the "fetters" of Greece—Acrocorinth, Demetrias, and Chalcis—and to maintain a presence there. Therefore, he said, the Aetolians could have Pharsalus and Larissa, but not Phthiotic Thebes; Rhodes could receive back Carian territory, but not Iasus and Bargylia; the Achaeans could have Argos and the town of Corinth, but not Acrocorinth; he would return to Attalus his captured ships and crews from Chios; and finally, he would give Rome the places in Illyria that he had seized. The allies protested that Philip had said nothing about leaving Greece, but as the hour was late Philip proposed an adjournment, to which Flamininus agreed.

On the following day the parties met a little farther east near Thronium. Philip requested—perhaps at the instigation of Flamininus—a truce to send an embassy to Rome to discuss any matter that had not been satisfactorily settled.[119] Flamininus agreed to a truce of two months, though he did insist that Philip evacuate all of Phocis and Locris and urged the allies to send their own embassies to Rome, instructing Amynander to go there personally.[120]

Philip may have believed he had checked Flamininus when it came to his tenure as commander and organizing an end to the war. But Flamininus ended up checkmating the king, as was clear when the parties came before the Senate—indeed, Flamininus may even have arranged the truce to ensure that his command continued.[121] The hearing before the Senate was a sham.[122] Amynander spoke of the strategic location of the fetters that Philip refused to relinquish, and the others chimed in about Philip's reluctance to withdraw from Greece. The senators refused to allow Philip's envoys to deliver their prepared defense but simply asked them whether Philip was prepared to abandon these cities. Since the envoys had no authority to renegotiate any

---

119. Cf. Walbank 1940, p. 162.

120. Polybius 18.10.1–2, 7; Livy 32.36.8–10.

121. On Flamininus' subterfuge and truce, see Walbank 1940, p. 162; Hammond and Walbank 1988, p. 430.

122. Polybius 18.11; Livy 32.37.

terms without the king's approval, all they could answer was that "they had no instructions on the subject."[123]

They were ordered to leave, and Flamininus' command was extended. Now, as Livy soberly remarks, "Philip could see that the issue had to be decided in battle."[124]

123. Polybius 18.11.13.

124. Livy 32.38.1. Flamininus' command: Polybius 18.12.1–2; Livy 32.28.3–9.

7

Fall of the Phalanx

FLAMININUS AND HIS brother Lucius were given reinforcements to the tune of 6,000 infantry, 300 cavalry, and 3,000 allies from the Greek cities of South Italy as well as supplies to continue their war against Philip.[1] The king had had two months to regroup and rest his men, but Flamininus and the Senate had bettered him, and he had given up Phocis and Locris to boot. Rome's further embroilment in Greek affairs was now assured, for the Senate's decision to go to war "was a tacit, and to many unwelcome, admission that the future of the Greek states and of Macedonia lay in the hands of the Roman Senate and People."[2]

Prelude to Battle

When Philip found out there was no hope of peace, his immediate move was to increase his manpower. He had lost many men over his years of warfare, both at land and sea, and he also needed more troops for his many garrisons. At Corinth, for example, he had 1,500 Macedonians and a further 4,500 men; Chalcis had perhaps 5,000 men, Demetrias and Phthiotic Thebes possibly the same, and he also had garrisons in Caria, Thrace, and Illyria. In all, he had probably 20,000 to 30,000 men in garrisons in the year 200 alone.[3] He therefore resorted to an extraordinary recruitment measure. According to Livy (drawing on Polybius), he brought his manpower back up to strength by

---

1. Livy 32.28.10.

2. Hammond and Walbank 1988, p. 428.

3. Hammond and Walbank 1988, p. 431 n. 1, citing sources.

The Last Kings of Macedonia and the Triumph of Rome. Ian Worthington, Oxford University Press.
© Oxford University Press 2023. DOI: 10.1093/oso/9780197520055.003.0008

enrolling "recruits from the age of sixteen, and men whose service was over but who still possessed a modicum of vigor were also recalled to service."[4]

He was thus calling up veterans past fifty to fifty-five years of age and boys as young as fifteen or sixteen—there is disagreement as to whether the new recruits were sixteen or in their sixteenth year.[5] Often after a defeat, older citizens and veterans could be called on, so Philip's call to service now was not atypical.[6] But it must have been burdensome to those cities required to mobilize extra troops, hence he may have remitted taxes or offered other incentives, as a letter to the people of Amphipolis indicates.[7]

Philip's need for manpower may explain an act of hostility by Nabis of Sparta. Rebels at Argos were revolting, but as Philip could not spare troops to help them, he made a pact with Nabis to keep him on his side, which included marrying his daughter to Nabis' son. He agreed to hand Argos over to Nabis on the condition that if Philip lost the war with Rome the Spartan king kept the city, but if he won Nabis was to return it to him.[8] Shortly after, Nabis met with Attalus, Flamininus, and Nicostratus, the Achaean general for 198–197, at Mycenae. There, Nabis treacherously threw his weight behind the Roman cause, even offering to provide 600 Cretan archers for the allied army, and made a four-month truce with Nicostratus.[9]

Philip intended to take up a defensive position from Atrax to Phthiotic Thebes along a line of hills through which there were only two roads—one along the coast to Phthiotic Thebes and the other via Palaepharsalus (Krini) to Crannon.[10] He also intended to use his garrisons and bases (which he stocked with provisions over the previous winter of 198–197) at Demetrias, Phthiotic Thebes, Larissa Cremaste (in Phthiotis, not to be confused with the more important Larissa in Pelasgiotis), and Echinus to block the Roman army. To do so meant forcing it inland into southern Thessaly away from the sea, where he had a garrison at Pharsalus—hence these cities were crucial to

---

4. Livy 33.3.1–5. On this conscription *diagramma*, cf. Hatzopoulos 2001, pp. 25, 34, and 110; Sekunda 2013, pp. 104–105.

5. Ages: Hatzopoulos 2001, pp. 99–107.

6. Hammond 1989, p. 62, with references.

7. Hatzopoulos 1996, vol. 2, no. 14, pp. 38–39.

8. Livy 32.38.1–39.1, with Walbank 1940, pp. 163–164.

9. Livy 32.39.1–39.11. Walbank 1940, p. 166 n. 2, questions the four-month period.

10. On his route and strategy, see Hammond 1988, pp. 60–61.

his defense plan.[11] His control of ports such as Demetrias would deny landing access and impede supplies reaching the Romans. Finally, he needed to establish a good position on level ground so he could deploy his phalanx if need be. In all, his strategy was anchored in the hope that the Senate would grow tired of the war and make peace with him or, if battle ensued, his phalanx would defeat the Roman legion.

Flamininus probably anticipated Philip's strategy of wearing down the enemy and wanted a pitched battle on terrain disadvantageous to the Macedonian phalanx.[12] But first he decided to deal with the Boeotian League, Philip's last ally in central Greece. In mid-March 197 he summoned Attalus to him and took one legion south to Thebes, where he attended a meeting of the league's assembly.[13] At this meeting Attalus may have suffered a stroke and collapsed; he was taken back to Pergamum, where he died.[14] His loss removed one of Philip's principal foes, though it turned out that his successor, his son Eumenes, was as antagonistic to Macedonia as his father had been. Flamininus' presence at the assembly was enough of a distraction to allow 2,000 of his men to enter and take over Thebes. Rome had now subdued almost all of southern and central Greece up to Thessaly; only Acarnania was pro-Macedonian, and Flamininus had already sent his brother Lucius there to win it over.

Philip proceeded to Dium while Flamininus returned to Elatea to collect his other legions before heading north along the coast through Thermopylae to Heraclea for a meeting of the Aetolian League. It voted to give him 6,000 infantry and 400 cavalry, which joined him two to three days later at Xyniae in Phthiotis. Flamininus now intended to hit Philip where it hurt the most: his supplies. In a series of forced marches, picking up along the way Nabis' 600 Cretans and 1,200 Athamanians under Amynander, Flamininus besieged Phthiotic Thebes to block Philip's supply route through Demetrias.[15]

---

11. Importance of cities: Hammond 1988, p. 61.

12. Errington 1971a, pp. 144–151; Hammond and Walbank 1988, p. 432.

13. Livy 33.2. Date: Hammond 1988, p. 61 n. 3.

14. Livy 33.21.1.

15. Numbers and route: Walbank 1940, p. 67. Walbank 1940, p. 167 n. 4, proposed that the Cretan soldiers were what Nabis still owed Philip (cf. Livy 31.18.9), but see Briscoe 1973, p. 252, that the men from Apollonia are from Illyria and not the Apollonia in Crete. Also on numbers cf. Briscoe 1973, pp. 253–254.

In May or early June Philip headed south through Tempe and made the larger Larissa his base (map 6).[16] But when he heard that Flamininus had arrived at Phthiotic Thebes he left straightaway, setting up camp about four miles (6.5 kilometers) north of Pherae, and telling his men to expect battle the next day as their destination was only nine miles (15 kilometers) away.[17] Flamininus had abandoned his siege of Phthiotic Thebes and set up a fortified camp about six miles (10 kilometers) south of Pherae, which cut off Philip from his supply bases at Demetrias and Phthiotic Thebes.[18] He had also cleverly chosen an area of farmland with drystone walls and other obstacles on it that made it unsuitable for Philip's phalanx, though this type of terrain was also ill-suited for his own heavy infantry.[19]

It was only the following morning when scouts from each side made contact with each other that both commanders discovered how close their camps had been pitched. They warily stayed clear of each other, but a day later, probably at dawn when Philip broke camp, a fierce altercation occurred between some of his troops and the lighter-armored Aetolians, forcing his men back.[20] He was unwilling to commit his heavy infantry because of the ground but he was in need of supplies, especially fodder for his horses, so he did not have the same option as at the Aous River of playing the waiting game.[21] With that in mind, he turned west toward Scotussa in Pelasgiotis where there were plenty of crops as well as level ground for his phalanx, and where he had a garrison at Pharsalus and could use the road from Larissa to bring in food.[22]

On the same day, Flamininus also moved west once he heard that Philip had left, intending to destroy the crops at Scotussa before Philip arrived and force a battle. The king had a head start on him and covered the roughly 12 miles (20 kilometers) to Scotussa that day, whereas by day's end Flamininus

---

16. There is controversy because of conflicting accounts in the ancient sources on the geography and events in the next stages of the campaign and the actual battle site on one of the passes between Eretria and Scotussa. I follow the account of Hammond 1988, pp. 68–72, which is based on his observations from personally walking this region, with his fig. 2 on the site of battle; see too Walbank 1940, pp. 168–170; cf. Walbank 1967, pp. 576–581.

17. Polybius 18.19.3; Livy 3.3.11–14.3.

18. Hammond 1988, p. 63.

19. Livy 33.6.7–8.

20. Polybius 18.19.9–12.

21. On feeding horses and the problems faced, cf. Karunanithy 2013, pp. 64–66.

22. Polybius 18.20.1–2; Livy 33.6.8–9, and see Hammond 1988, p. 63; Hammond and Walbank 1988, p. 435.

had covered only about half that distance to put him south of Eretria (Tsangli); the two camps were about 7.5 miles (12 kilometers) apart, separated by the high Mount Karadag range.[23]

The next day Philip left Scotussa late and marched to Melambium, or rather Khalkiadhes, east of Scotussa.[24] That same day Flamininus' army covered about 12.5 miles (20 kilometers) into Pharsalian territory, setting up camp for the night around the "Thetideum" or shrine of Thetis, which, since she was the goddess of water, clearly had a good supply of water.[25] He would have encamped on the nearby River Enipeus so that he could prevent Philip from reaching Pharsalus and bring him to battle on favorable ground.[26] On both these days the two armies marched westward on roughly parallel lines, but they were unaware of the other's presence because of the mountain range between them; it was the crossing of a ridge there that brought about the battle on the third day, as Hammond's reconnaissance shows.[27]

On the night of this second day there was a torrential downpour and thunderstorm, causing the clouds to settle so low on the hills that, when dawn broke, visibility was virtually nonexistent.[28] Despite the conditions, Philip set off with his army before dawn, eager to get to the Pharsalus, but he was prevented by the thick fog and had to set up camp.[29] He sent an advance party to occupy the high ridge that separated him from his intended destination while a larger party foraged for supplies. Flamininus in the meantime sent 1,000 infantry and ten cavalry squadrons to locate his enemy. He warned them to be on the lookout for an ambush, but both sides were startled when they suddenly came upon each other on the same ridge; after sending back messengers to their respective camps, they attacked each other.[30]

This clash was the preamble to the battle that would determine Macedonia's future, for reinforcements from both sides were quickly deployed, and thanks

23. Polybius 18.20.3–5, and see Hammond 1988, pp. 63–64.

24. Livy 18.20.6; Livy 33.6.11. Location: Hammond 1988, p. 65; cf. Hammond and Walbank 1988, pp. 437–438.

25. Polybius 18.20.6; Livy 33.6.11.

26. Hammond 1988, p. 65.

27. Hammond 1988, pp. 68–72.

28. Polybius 18.20.7; Livy 33.6.12; Plutarch, *Flamininus* 8.1.

29. Polybius 18.20.8–9; Livy 33.7.1–3.

30. Polybius 18.21.1–8; Livy 33.7.4–8.

to the Aetolian troops the Romans were able to drive the Macedonians back.[31] The decisive battle took its name from the ridge tops running toward the plain that were called Dogs-heads—Cynoscephalae.[32]

The Battle of Cynoscephalae

Polybius is our major source for the details of the campaign outlined above as well as this pivotal battle; his account is the foundation of Livy's narrative and Plutarch's summary.[33] Polybius' account has errors when it comes to topography and even maneuvers, not just because of his bias toward Rome but perhaps also because he relied on Aetolian eyewitnesses who surely embellished their role in the battle at the expense of Philip's army; hence Livy's presentation of the battle is likewise suspect.[34]

Philip's army consisted of 23,500 infantry, comprising 18,000 Macedonian phalangites (including 2,000 peltasts), 5,500 light-armed troops (2,000 Thracians, 2,000 Illyrians, and 1,500 mercenaries of various nationalities), and 2,000 Macedonian and Thessalian cavalry. Flamininus fielded an army of slightly higher numbers—28,600 infantry (18,000 Romans and 8,000 Greek allies, most from the Aetolian League, as well as 2,000 Athamanians and 600 Cretans), 2,500 cavalry, and twenty war elephants, though if his legions had their full complement of 22,000 men he would have had 30,000 infantry.[35] The war elephants also gave him an advantage as Macedonian infantry did not have much experience with them and their size and smell frightened the cavalry horses. Also to his advantage was his men's battle experience, for many of his troops were hardened veterans from the previous season's campaign as well as the Second Punic War, whereas many of Philip's

---

31. May: Hammond 1988, p. 66. June: Walbank 1940, pp. 322–323 (though conceding on p. 322 that at the latest it was "in late May or early June").

32. On the identification of the ridges based on his personal reconnaissance, see Hammond 1988, pp. 67–72 and 80–81; cf. Hammond and Walbank 1988, pp. 437–440.

33. Polybius 18.21–26; Livy 33.7.6–10.5; Plutarch, *Flamininus* 8; Pausanias 7.8.7; Justin 30.4; Zonaras 9.16, with Walbank 1940, pp. 170–172; Walbank 1967, pp. 581–585; Briscoe 1973, pp. 256–266; Hammond 1988, pp. 72–76; Hammond and Walbank 1988, pp. 432–443; Matyszak 2009, pp. 91–94; Waterfield 2014, pp. 89–93.

34. Hammond and Walbank 1988, pp. 432–433 with n. 1 (p. 433), citing bibliography.

35. Livy 33.4.4–6, though his number of 600 for the Aetolian infantry is incorrect, while Plutarch, *Flamininus* 7.2, speaks of 6,000 and the Roman army as over 26,000. On numbers on both sides, see Walbank 1940, pp. 167–168; Hammond 1988, pp. 65–66; cf. Briscoe 1973, pp. 253–254; Hammond and Walbank 1988, pp. 436–437.

FIGURE 7.1. Cynoscephalae: view from ridge where Philip was stationed over the battle site. Photo credit: Robin Waterfield.

men were new recruits, as his earlier emergency recruitment edict reveals, whom the king still had to train daily.

When the opposing sides unexpectedly collided on the ridge the Macedonians drove back the Roman troops. As the mist rose Flamininus saw what was happening below him unlike Philip, whose camp was on the ridge (figures 7.1 and 7.2). He sent his troops reinforcements of 2,000 light-armed Roman and Aetolian infantry and 500 cavalry against the Macedonians, who were pushed back onto the higher ground above the ridge. Philip then deployed the Thessalian cavalry, one hipparchy of Macedonian cavalry, and all mercenaries except the Thracians. They drove their foes back downhill, although fierce Aetolian resistance saved them from being pushed all the way down to the level ground, presumably between the ridge and the Roman camp.

Philip was at a disadvantage from not seeing the action, which goes some way to explaining why he committed to pitched battle when a messenger brought him the welcome but inaccurate news that "the enemy are flying: do not lose the opportunity: the barbarians cannot stand before us: the day is yours now: this is your time."[36] He led half his phalanx to the other side of the ridge and ordered his general Nicanor to bring the other half. Flamininus

---

36. Polybius 18.22.8.

FIGURE 7.2. Cynoscephalae: long view of ridge and battle site. Photo credit: Robin Waterfield.

in turn instructed the legion to his right to stand firm with the elephants in front of it while the legion to his left drove the Macedonian light-armed infantry and cavalry back toward the ridge (see figure 7.3).

Philip had just arrived with the first half of the phalanx and deployed his men into line to his left facing south. He stationed himself on the right wing as was customary for a Macedonian king. The retreating light-armed men and cavalry took up a position to guard that wing. He then doubled the depth of his formation to sixteen men by moving his phalangites on the left, ordered the light-armed troops to cover that flank, and charged downhill into Flamininus and his legion. The sarissas wreaked havoc on Flamininus' line, and the sheer downhill force of his phalanx drove the Roman line back, leaving Flamininus no option but to move his other legion away from the battle and up to the right-hand ridge toward the watershed ridge. There, the rest of the Macedonian phalangites, the 2,000 Thracian light-armed troops, and the remainder of the cavalry were arriving in disorder from the higher ground, partly because of the terrain and partly because there was no commander to arrange their line. Here was Flamininus' chance: taking advantage of his enemy's disarray he ordered his elephants and the legions to attack and overcome them.

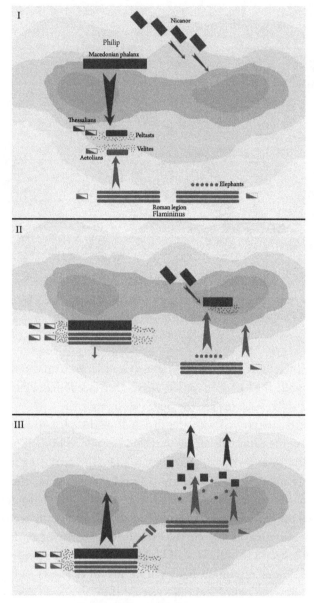

FIGURE 7.3. Battle of Cynoscephalae.

Two separate battles had now developed, for elsewhere Philip, still commanding his right wing, pushed the Roman left back as he came down the hill. In doing so the top of the hill was now undefended. That was when an unnamed Roman tribune of the second legion brilliantly spotted how to pair the two engagements together to Rome's advantage. He immediately wheeled twenty of his maniples ("handfuls" of about 120 men in 12 files and 10 ranks), who were faster moving and could form their own battle line, up the hill to charge the rear of the Macedonian phalanx that had just overcome Flamininus' line.[37]

The fatal flaw of the phalanx now came into play. The Macedonians, suddenly in between two offensive lines front and rear, could not maneuver easily because of their packed formation and their forward-pointing sarissas were too long to be turned quickly and easily for hand-to-hand fighting. With their sarissas now useless, the soldiers had only a small shield and a short sword or dagger, which were no match for the legionaries' large shields, javelins, and long swords. As the Macedonians were mercilessly cut down from behind, they raised their sarissas vertically in the air to show they were surrendering, but the Romans either did not realize what this action meant or did not care and continued to kill their enemy. To escape the carnage the Macedonians fled.

When Philip saw his left flank collapse he and the survivors (perhaps 5,000 to 7,000) fled to Tempe, where he established a defensive position and considered his future. The numbers of his dead and captured vary in different sources: either 8,000 killed and 5,000 captured (probably the most accurate figures), or 32,000 dead and 4,300 captured, or even 40,000 dead and 5,700 taken prisoner, whereas the Romans were said to have lost only 700 men.[38] It was the duty of the king to bury the fallen, yet the bodies of Philip's troops killed in action were said to have lain on the battlefield for six years before another Philip, a man from Megalopolis, gathered their bones and interred them beneath a burial mound.[39]

In many respects, neither side ought to have won the battle. That had nothing to do with the initial dense mist, or the terrain that kept the two armies out of sight of one another, or the surprise of the Roman and Macedonian scouting parties coming upon each other unexpectedly. Philip was facing low morale among his men after the defeat at the Aous River, and he had too many inexperienced young recruits as well as veterans past the customary age of service in his army. He was also facing high numbers of battle-hardened Roman legionaries and he had made some serious errors, not least by allowing Flamininus to cut him off from Demetrias and Phthiotic Thebes,

---

37. Polybius 18.26.1–3; Livy 33.9.8–9.

38. Polybius 18.27.6; Livy 33.10.6–10; Plutarch, *Flamininus* 8.5.

39. Livy 36.8.3–5; cf. 35.47.5–8; Appian, *Syrian Wars* 16.

and unusually for him not arranging enough provisions and so having to delay at Scotussa.

Flamininus was quicker than Philip, as when he took up his strategic position south of Pherae; he also had an organized supply system and showed good judgment in accepting defeat on the left but then attacking on his right.[40] Even so, the Roman victory was due more to the quick thinking of our unknown tribune than Flamininus; if that person had been elsewhere or simply not seized the opportunity he saw, things may have turned out differently.

Philip's casualty figures were great, and his army had been savaged. Another casualty of the battle was the phalanx after nearly two centuries of domination. It is a fall worth considering in more detail before we find out what the Senate was going to do to Philip and Greece.

The Demise of the Phalanx

The ferocity and maneuverability of the legion at Cynoscephalae revealed the fatal flaw of the phalanx, which Polybius wrote about in a long excursus on its advantages and disadvantages:[41]

> As long as the phalanx keeps its own formation and strength no one can resist it in a headlong clash or withstand its charge [he then describes the ranks of phalangites and sarissas]. . . . Why is it then that the Romans win, and why are those who use the phalanx defeated? The reason is that in war the times and places for action are unlimited, while there is only one time and one kind of place which enables the phalanx to perform at its best. . . . It is generally agreed that the phalanx needs ground that is level and open, and which in addition is free from obstacles—I mean such things as ditches, ravines, depressions, ridges, and river beds. All these are enough to hinder and break up that formation. Everyone would agree that it is more or less impossible, or at least extremely rare, to find a piece of country of twenty stades (about 2 miles or 3.5 kilometers) and sometimes even more in which none of these obstacles is to be found. But supposing one could find such places, if the enemy

---

40. Cf. Hammond 1988, p. 76; Hammond and Walbank 1988, pp. 434–435.

41. Polybius 18.28–32 (= Austin 2006, no. 83, pp. 170–172 abridged; trans. Austin); cf. Plutarch, *Flamininus* 8.4, with Walbank 1967, pp. 585–588. On the Roman legion, see Polybius 18.30.5–11.

refuse to come down to these but go round sacking the cities and the territory of one's allies, what is the use of such a formation? If it stays on the ground that suits it, it is unable to bring assistance to its friends and cannot even defend itself.... But if it leaves its proper ground and tries to take some action, it becomes an easy prey for the enemy.

For Polybius, the phalanx was only able to fight properly on flat ground with no obstacles and as a single massed unit. He was right. Cynoscephalae—and Pydna in 168 in Perseus' reign as we shall see—showed that on level ground the massed phalanx was more than a match for a looser legionary formation, and the long sarissas prevented the legionaries from getting close to the phalangites. But when the phalanx found itself on the uneven ground, it was a different story. Once unity was lost and the line was in disarray, the forward-facing hedge of sarissas was all but useless. On the other hand, the legions could not only maintain their order but also maneuver against the phalanx from behind and side on, cutting down the phalangites in close fighting who could not effortlessly turn their forward- and upward-pointing sarissas against attacks from these sides.

The sheer mass of the phalanx, which could be as many as thirty-two men deep, was also an issue. The legionaries took up only three rows, with each row divided into ten tactical units or maniples.[42] The frontline troops were new soldiers who were the youngest and fittest (called *hastati*); in the middle row were the veterans (*principes*), and in the rear line were the oldest and most experienced veterans (*triarii*). The *triarii* might never be needed if the front two lines overcame the opposing side—or as at Cynoscephalae, they were there to save the day when the Roman line was broken. Since a regular legion had 1,200 *hastati*, 1,200 *principes*, and 600 *triarii*—together with specialist auxiliaries, usually of Italian allies, and 300 cavalry—its number and arrangement ended up making it superior to the more inflexible mass of a Macedonian phalanx.

Then there was the weaponry. Nothing could block a sarissa ripping into a human body, but once unable to be thrust forward the sarissa became an ultra-long encumbrance. When that happened, as at Cynoscephalae, the other equipment of a phalangite paled against a legionary's two throwing spears (*pila*) and stabbing sword with its very sharp pointed end, which had to be twisted sharply out of an adversary's body, leaving a terrible and massive fatal hole.

---

42. Roman disposition: Polybius 18.30.5–11, with Walbank 1967, pp. 588–590. On the Roman military system, see too Polybius 6.19–42.

This last point leads into the manner of fighting, also of relevance. When Rome met Greece in war, it was "a military culture clash that was to leave both Greeks and Macedonians horrified by their grimly merciless opponents."[43] Greek wars were certainly brutal, and at times a captured city had its male population killed, its women and children enslaved, and was even razed to the ground. Yet the Greeks had rules to their warfare when it came to surrendering, ransoming prisoners, or how to collect the dead, and both sides generally avoided massacres on the battlefield.[44] The Romans were not interested in such conventions. They fought to win, and they did so more savagely than the Greeks—after all, for a victorious general to be granted a triumph in Rome his men had to have killed at least 5,000 of the enemy.

"Rome had revolutionized warfare, and the Macedonians had not kept apace," writes Carol King.[45] Why did Macedonian kings not deal with the weakness of the phalanx and try to match Rome's revolutions to warfare?[46] If Polybius could see it, then they surely could—as Matyszak sagely points out, an army needing a level plain was a bit of an anomaly anyway as Greece was such a mountainous country.[47] The heavy infantry of Macedonia and its enemies had been fighting battles on home ground and overseas since the days of Philip II in the second half of the fourth century, so well before Cynoscephalae in 197. Yet nothing was done.

The answer perhaps is complacency. When Philip deployed his phalanx on generally unsuitable terrain, he was certain that it would carry the day because it almost always had for nearly two hundred years. He learned the hard way this was not so, contributing to the demise of Macedonia's long-held military supremacy.

The Fate of Macedonia

Philip's defeat at Cynoscephalae had a ripple effect elsewhere. The Achaeans defeated Philip's general Androsthenes at Corinth even though Philip had

---

43. Matyszak 2009, p. 65.

44. See Rawlings 2007.

45. King 2018, p. 254.

46. There are many books on the Roman army; see, for example, Erdkamp (ed.) 2007, and in our period Connolly 1989. For general comments on the Macedonian and Roman armies, especially infantry, cf. Matyszak 2009, pp. 63–69; Waterfield 2014, pp. 128–134.

47. Matyszak 2009, pp. 67–69.

reinforced its garrison, the Rhodians eroded his gains in Asia Minor, and the Romans took over the whole of Acarnania.[48] To be on the safe side, he sent one of his hypaspists to Larissa to burn all his official documents.[49] Since he now had only one option left to him, to seek agreeable terms, he sent an envoy to Flamininus at Larissa. Here, the Aetolians unwittingly aided him, for after the battle they sacked Philip's camp while Roman troops were pursuing the fleeing Macedonians, annoying Flamininus greatly.[50] The Aetolians wanted Philip either expelled or executed, but Flamininus, to rile them, agreed to discuss terms and exhorted Philip to be in "good spirits," deliberately without consulting the Aetolians.[51]

Philip may have hoped to exploit the tension between Rome and the Aetolians.[52] Furthermore, he was likely aware that Flamininus was keeping a watchful eye on the activities of Antiochus of Syria, who by 198 controlled Phoenicia, had begun operations in Asia Minor and Thrace, and had arrived at the Hellespont with an army ostensibly to wrest Greek cities there from Ptolemy.[53] The Second Macedonian War might have ended Philip's seizure of Ptolemaic possessions, but that did not stop Antiochus, who was casting his eye across the Aegean. If Philip joined Antiochus, even after Cynoscephalae, the pair could still harass Rome's position in Greece.[54] This was another reason why Rome was so adamant that Philip give up the "fetters." Nor could Flamininus leave a seething Aetolian League in Greece if he had to deal with Antiochus.

Philip and Flamininus agreed on a fifteen-day truce, subject to the allies meeting at the entrance to the pass at Tempe. Flamininus made contact with them the day before Philip arrived and listened to their various views and demands. But his balanced stance incensed the Aetolians, with their representative Phaeneas accusing him of being bribed and demanding that Philip be deposed.[55] Flamininus cut off his protests by calling them nonsensical, making it clear that it would be he and the Senate deciding Philip's fate.

48. Livy 33.14–18; cf. Walbank 1940, p. 175.

49. Polybius 18.33.2; Livy 33.11.1, with Walbank 1967, pp. 591–592.

50. Polybius 18.27.4–5 and 18.34.1–2.

51. Polybius 18.34.3–8; Livy 33.11.3–10; Plutarch, *Flamininus* 9.1–4.

52. Cf. Walbank 1940, pp. 172–174.

53. Matyszak 2009, pp. 99–100.

54. Cf. Polybius 18.3–4; Livy 33.20.3. Antiochus' actions: Livy 33.19.8–20.12.

55. Polybius 18.36–37; Livy 33.12.1–13.

When Philip arrived the following day, he offered to concede all that had been demanded at the conference at Nicaea the previous year after the battle of Aoi Stena and to refer other matters to the Senate, which shows he wanted nothing to do with any Aetolian negotiators.[56] Yet at the same time he cleverly agreed to restore all towns to the Aetolians, gambling that Flamininus would over-rule him and so drive a further wedge between him and them. His gamble paid off as Flamininus conceded only Phthiotic Thebes to the Aetolians. Phaeneas protested that they should be receiving more, given the terms of their treaty of 211 with Rome, but Flamininus abruptly told him that that treaty was null and void once Aetolia had made peace with Philip in 206 (p. 92).[57]

Given the Greeks' dislike of the Aetolians, Flamininus' hardline attitude perhaps earned him some popularity. But the Romans were not welcomed everywhere. Flamininus and his allies had been promoting the rise of pro-Roman statesmen throughout Greece, but when the pro-Macedonian Boeotarch (chief official) of the Boeotian League, Brachylles, was gaining influence in Thebes he was assassinated with Flamininus' tacit approval.[58] In retaliation Brachylles' supporters killed 500 Roman soldiers, prompting the Roman general to invade Boeotia. Further bloodshed was avoided thanks to Athenian and Achaean diplomacy; Flamininus agreed to an indemnity of thirty talents and the surrender of the murderers.

Philip requested a further truce to allow him time to brief envoys and send them to the Senate. Flamininus agreed to one that lasted for four months— from the end of July to the end of October. However, the king had to pay an indemnity of 200 talents and surrender hostages, including his son Demetrius (who was later paraded in front of Flamininus' chariot at his triumph in Rome in 194 and in all spent six years in that city). If the Senate rejected his terms and peace was not made, the money and hostages were to be returned.[59]

During the truce Philip suffered two serious setbacks. The first came from the Dardanians, who devastated Upper Macedonia and central parts

---

56. Polybius 18.38.1–9; Livy 33.13, with Walbank 1940, p. 176; Errington 1971a, pp. 152–153; Briscoe 1973, pp. 273–274; cf. Errington 1989b, p. 269.

57. Polybius 18.38.1–2; Livy 33.13.11–12.

58. Polybius 18.43; Livy 33.27.5–29.12, with Walbank 1967, pp. 608–609; Walbank 1940, p. 178; Ager 1996, pp. 210–211; Hammond and Walbank 1988, p. 445.

59. Polybius 18.39.5–6; Livy 33.13.13–15; Plutarch, *Flamininus* 9.4; Dio 18.60; Appian, *Macedonian Wars* 9.2.

of the kingdom when they heard of his defeat at Cynoscephalae.[60] Philip's main army was still at Tempe, so he had to raise troops by conscription. With 6,000 infantry and 500 cavalry he was able to drive the invaders out of his kingdom, inflicting heavy losses on them around Stobi in Paeonia, close to modern Gradsko.[61] Then in the winter of 198–197 Orestis revolted, perhaps having already negotiated with Roman leaders in Illyria.[62] When Philip protested Orestis' decision to Flamininus the latter made no public comment but forwarded the dispute to the Senate.

Philip's envoys appeared before the Senate along with representatives from some of the Greek states. The Senate may have been under pressure to make peace because Antiochus, who was now Rome's most powerful eastern neighbor, and in tandem with the Rhodians had seized cities along the Asian coastline, which he gave to Rhodes.[63] To nip any threat from him in the bud, Flamininus the following year (196) told some of his envoys that Antiochus had to withdraw his troops from any city previously held by Ptolemy and Philip and not cross into Europe.[64]

The Senate made peace with Philip and imposed terms on him. Although the specifics have not survived, the conditions seem to have been similar to those discussed at Nicaea.[65] A difference though was that Rome made clear it was going to settle the affairs of Macedonia and Greece. The Senate's decision was probably in November 197, which then needed endorsement by the Comitia.[66] Ten commissioners were sent to Flamininus with a document outlining the terms; they arrived at Elatea early in 196, probably at winter's end.[67] This document contained only broad outlines, leaving Flamininus room to finesse the actual terms, and so should not be confused with the actual treaty.[68]

---

60. Livy 33.19.1–5.

61. Livy 33.19.1–5.

62. Walbank 1967, p. 616, has the defection in winter 198–197.

63. Errington 1971a, pp. 156–175; Errington 1989b, pp. 270–271; Eckstein 2008, pp. 342–381. On Rome's relations with Antiochus and the Seleucid kingdom, see Gruen 1984, pp. 611–671.

64. Polybius 18.47.1–3; cf. 18.49–52; Diodorus 28.12, with Walbank 1967, pp. 614–615.

65. Cf. Livy 33.30.1, with Walbank 1940, p. 177.

66. Hammond 1992, p. 350 n. 47, on chronology.

67. Dating: Walbank 1940, p. 324; see too Hammond and Walbank 1988, pp. 603–604.

68. Walbank 1940, p. 179. Document: Polybius 18.44; Livy 33.30 (less reliable); Appian, *Macedonian Wars* 9.3; Plutarch, *Flamininus* 10.1; Justin 30.4.17; Zonaras 9.16, with Walbank 1940, pp. 179–185; Walbank 1967, pp. 609–612; Gruen 1984, pp. 399–402; Hammond and

The document began with a general statement that all Greeks in Asia and Europe who were not under Philip's sway were to be free. It then went on to his punishment, which was surprisingly lenient: he was allowed to keep the throne, but had to stay in Macedonia proper (north of Mount Olympus); the cities and fortresses he held were to be handed over to Rome (meaning he had to give up Thessaly and the "fetters" of Greece); Macedonian garrisons in towns were to be removed (such as at Bargylia, Abydus, Thasos, and Perinthus) and fortifications razed; Flamininus was to negotiate with Prusias for the freedom of Cius; Philip was to relinquish his fleet apart from five light warships and one large warship; he was to pay Rome another war indemnity of one thousand talents, 500 at once and the rest in installments over a decade; and all prisoners and deserters were to be handed over to Flamininus. Nothing is said of the status of the cities that Philip took from Ptolemy or of the reparations demanded by Pergamum, though these details may have been lost in gaps in Polybius' text, hence our later authors had no record of them.[69]

Macedonia could have suffered far worse punishment, and significantly for Philip he remained king. True, his kingdom was almost reduced to what it had been in the days before Philip II, stretching only as far as the Strymon, and it was now a buffer zone of sorts between the tribes of the north and the Greek states. Nor did the king have a fleet anymore—not that that was a major loss, for since 200 his fleet had been largely confined to Demetrias, thanks to Rome and its allies dominating the seas.[70] But he was left with a sizeable army, no Roman troops occupied Macedonia, and it is worth repeating that the throne was not taken away from him.

Philip would be mixed up in disputes in Greece again, as well as working with Rome in its war efforts against Antiochus and Aetolia, as we shall trace in the next chapter, but for now he turned to deal with Macedonia's manpower, borders, and economic plight, rescuing his kingdom from years of devastation.

The Freedom of the Greeks

It is no surprise that the Aetolians were far from happy at these arrangements, which were not to their benefit. They expressed their disappointment and

---

Walbank 1988, pp. 603–604; Matyszak 2009, pp. 97–98. Philip, it seems, had already agreed to accept the general principles (Livy 33.24.6).

69. Walbank 1940, p. 180.

70. Cf. Walbank 1940, p. 183.

among other things demanded to know whether Rome intended to garrison the fetters of Greece.[71] Flamininus refused to comment but moved on to Corinth, where he and the Roman commissioners held a meeting to discuss the Aetolian claims and how to settle affairs in Greece. He persuaded his colleagues that a Roman withdrawal was necessary and as a sign of good faith to hand over Corinth to the Achaeans.[72] That he could do so supports the view that the Senate had sent him only the broad brushstrokes of a settlement, leaving him to draw up the final details.

The summer's Isthmian Games were about to take place at Corinth, and representatives from the Greek states as well as many spectators were there, so here was an excellent venue for Flamininus to deliver the news about what Rome was going to do with Greece. The Greeks must have been nervous, not only because of Rome's military strength but also they were still unclear about what Romans thought of them—they had "a mixed brew of anxiety and admiration, hopes and disappointments, anger, frustration, and plain bafflement."[73] In the end, Flamininus issued a surprisingly short proclamation:[74]

> The Senate of Rome and Titus Quinctius the proconsul, after defeating King Philip and the Macedonians, leave the following peoples free, without garrison, without tribute, and in full enjoyment of their ancestral laws: the Corinthians, Phocians, Locrians, Euboeans, Achaeans of Phthiotis, Magnesians, Thessalians, and Perrhaebians.

The audience was euphoric at what he said, clapping and crying out so loudly that the noise disrupted the airwaves and ravens flying overhead fell into the stadium.[75] States voted all sorts of honors on Flamininus, and even set up an equestrian statue of him at Delphi.[76]

---

71. Polybius 18.45.1–6; Livy 33.31.1–3; Plutarch, *Flamininus* 10.1–2.

72. Polybius 18.45.7–12; Livy 33.31.7–11.

73. Gruen 1984, p. 356, and see pp. 316–356 on what the Greeks made of the Romans.

74. Polybius 18.46 with the proclamation at 46.5 (= Austin 2006, no. 84, pp. 172–174; trans. Austin); Livy 33.32.4–5; Diodorus 28.13; Plutarch, *Flamininus* 10.3–4; Appian, *Macedonian Wars* 9.4, with Ager 1996, pp. 211–218. On the proclamation and Roman intentions, see Walbank 1940, pp. 180–181; Errington 1971a, pp. 153–155; Briscoe 1973, pp. 304–317; Gruen 1984, pp. 103 and 448–449; Errington 1989b, pp. 272–274; Eckstein 2008, pp. 283–302; Dmitriev 2011, pp. 153–165; Waterfield 2014, pp. 98–103; Worthington 2021a, pp. 155–157.

75. Polybius 18.46.6–15; Livy 33.32.6–10; Plutarch, *Flamininus* 10.5–6.

76. Honors: Sherk 1984, no. 6, pp. 7–8.

The people interpreted Flamininus' edict to mean that Greece was to be free, which by extension meant that the fetters were to be free and ungarrisoned. But the edict's content was mere propaganda as Greeks and Romans viewed "freedom" (*eleutheria*) differently.[77] In 167, as we shall see, Rome abolished the Antigonid dynasty and proclaimed Macedonia "free," which in practice meant free from a monarchy but not from Rome (chapter 11).

Flamininus had come to know the Greeks and their feelings for each other. That is why he intended his settlement to reduce the chances of their allying with Antiochus or of upsetting the balance of power he had tried to establish in northern and central Greece by making Macedonia a "political counter-weight" to the Aetolians.[78] Of course people saw the extent to which Rome was dominating affairs: as the slighted Aetolians said, "What was happening was a change of masters and not the delivery of Greece."[79]

Flamininus spent the next two years arranging necessary affairs in Macedonia and Greece.[80] He took considerable care over the arrangements he made in Greece, as a letter to the people of Chyretiae about the return of property indicates.[81] Thus, Orestis was made independent, as were Perrhaebia and Magnesia.[82] Lychnis and Parthus in southern Illyria were given to Pleuratus so that Philip's frontier was switched to the east side of Lake Lychnitis (Ohrid).[83] Amynander kept the forts he had won from Philip, and despite Aetolian protests the Acarnanian League received the Ionian island of Leucas. Corinth, Triphylia, and Heraea were given to the Achaean League while separate leagues were set up in Thessaly and Euboea. After a brief offensive by several Greek states, and with 1,500 troops contributed by Philip, against Nabis of Sparta over the retention of Argos, Flamininus announced he

77. See Gruen 1984, pp. 132–157 (especially pp. 145–148) and 448–456; Eckstein 2010, p. 237; Dmitriev 2011, pp. 166–199 and 228–282; Waterfield 2014, pp. 100–103; Burton 2017, pp. 34–35. See too Hatzopoulos 1966, vol. 1, pp. 224–226.

78. Errington 1971a, p. 152.

79. Polybius 18.45.6.

80. Polybius 18.47.6–48.3; Livy 33.34.5–35.14; Plutarch, *Flamininus* 12.2–3: see details in Walbank 1967, pp. 616–619; Walbank 1940, pp. 181–183. Rome was concerned about gaining the goodwill of Epirus and concluded a treaty at some point with the Epirote League: Hammond 1967, p. 623.

81. *SIG*³ 593 = Sherk 1969, no. 33, pp. 211–213, with Armstrong and Walsh 1986.

82. Polybius 18.47.6; Livy 33.34.6. Perrhaebia: *SIG*³ 593 = Sherk 1969, no. 33, pp. 211–213, with Walbank 1967, p. 616.

83. Dell 1977, p. 310.

would spare Nabis and hand over Argos and Acrocorinth to the Achaeans.[84] Despite all that, civil disorder eventually broke out in Thessaly, Aetolia, and Boeotia arising from debt problems and especially a serious grain shortage.[85]

Polybius goes on to describe a meeting at Tempe between Philip and one of the Roman commissioners, Gnaeus Cornelius Lentulus, who advised the king "to send an embassy to Rome to ask for an alliance, that they might not think he was watching for his opportunity and looking forward to the arrival of Antiochus."[86] Philip promised he would do so, and Lentulus took his leave. Nothing more is said about an alliance in our sources. If the exchange is true, the Senate had to decide what type of treaty—a formal alliance (*foedus* or *summachia*) or the more informal *amicitia*, which would allow Macedonia to be free and independent of Rome.[87]

Rome chose *amicitia*. Gruen's careful analysis shows a formal alliance would have been exceptional in Rome's dealings with outside states in this period.[88] Besides, when Philip's son Perseus became king and renewed his treaty with Rome in 171 the sources call it a *philia* in Greek, which is *amicitia* in Latin.[89] In any case, Rome's handling of Philip until his death shows he was disadvantaged in a way that would not be expected of a formal ally, especially after he gave support to Rome against the Aetolians, as we discuss in the following chapter.

Philip and Macedonia after Cynoscephalae

Philip had been localized to Macedonia; he did not stay there, as we will see in the following chapter. But one thing he made a priority in the eighteen years

---

84. On this and the following on Nabis and Greece, see conveniently Walbank 1940, pp. 187–197, citing sources.

85. Sherk 1984, p. 4, and see especially Walsh 2000.

86. Polybius 18.48.3–5; Livy 33.35.1–8.

87. Walbank 1967, p. 620, speaks of it "probably implying a regular *foedus*," and that Polybius' wording "suggests something firmer in the light of the danger from Antiochus." See further Gruen 1973, pp. 123–136; Gruen 1984, pp. 22 and 399–401; cf. Errington 1990, p. 205; *contra* Hammond and Walbank 1988, pp. 447 and 603–604; Eckstein 2008, pp. 208–341.

88. Gruen 1973, pp. 125–128 (noting on p. 126 that the first reference to a *foedus* with Aetolia was in 183/82). The *summachia* with the Aetolian League of 211 was because of the pressing circumstances in the First Macedonian War, as Gruen notes.

89. Polybius 25.3.1; Livy 40.58.8; cf. Diodorus 29.30; Pausanias 7.10.6; Zonaras 9.22, with Meloni 1953, pp. 68–73; Gruen 1973, pp. 134–135.

from Cynoscephalae to his death in 179 was addressing the problems affecting Macedonia.[90] The kingdom had suffered badly over the years; its economy had been battered, its army massively defeated, and thousands of its people had been captured by the Romans and sold as slaves.

Philip dealt with Macedonia's military problems first. He had lost 10,000 Macedonian soldiers at Cynoscephalae, another 1,000 with the defection of Orestis, and in all his army numbers may have been cut in half. He brought back the remaining garrisons from abroad (perhaps as many as 20,000, though some would be families of troops), acquired 5,000 of Antiochus' men, and "compelled all his subjects to bear children and raise them."[91] The last is interesting. Even if male children were born in 196, a year after Cynoscephalae, they would need to be at least sixteen and more likely eighteen years old before they could fight in the army, hence taking us to the years 180 to 178 at the earliest.

Philip's policy shows that he was looking ahead when it came to Macedonia's military, and he was successful. Livy claims that on the eve of the Third Macedonian War in 149 Perseus had 30,000 infantry and 5,000 cavalry, enough grain to last a decade, cash to hire mercenaries, and piles of arms and armor—in actuality, he could field 43,000 men, of whom 29,000 were Macedonians.[92] Those numbers were roughly the same as Alexander the Great's army, which included non-Macedonians, when he invaded Asia in 334, and at that time Macedonia was *the* power in the Mediterranean world.[93] Even allowing for exaggeration, Philip's accomplishment is obvious.[94]

Philip reorganized the structure of his kingdom by founding towns and transferring people from elsewhere in the kingdom (called *Makedones* in the sources) as well as Thracians, Gauls, and even Illyrians.[95] His objective here was twofold. First, he intended to buttress his western and northern frontiers, which had been pierced by Romans and Dardanians, by creating cities—presumably at the expense of the local Paeonians—with military populations that would protect routes from the north to central Macedonia and from

90. Cf. Polybius 25.3.9.

91. Livy 39.24.3–4.

92. Livy 42.51.3–11.

93. Alexander's army: Worthington 2014, pp. 139–140.

94. Walbank 1940, p. 256.

95. Polybius 23.10.4–5, and see Hammond and Walbank 1988, pp. 459–460; Hammond 1992, p. 359.

the Axius valley toward Pelagonia in Upper Macedonia. He may also have installed *Makedones* in another north-eastern area of Paeonia near Sveti Nikola and Kratovo (ancient Tranupara) as a bulwark against the Thracians. In this he was very much taking a leaf out of Philip II's book in establishing new towns along his north-west frontier and transplanting people from elsewhere to them.[96]

Second, transferring these peoples would help to bring about an economic revival.[97] Philip like many of his predecessors introduced harbor dues and other taxes and especially exploited the mines to a great extent. This included opening new ones "in many places," according to Livy, and using Thracians as miners who had much experience as Thrace had gold, silver, copper, iron, lead, and nickel mines.[98] Philip II had transformed Macedonia's coinage into the strongest in Europe, but that did not carry through to all kings after him.[99] The reason was probably due to Macedonia's mines not producing enough silver.

Philip likely faced a similar situation when he became king, but he eventually coined in gold and silver and minted new silver coin types, presumably benefitting from the new mines he opened if his local ones were not yielding enough metal.[100] His gold coins were known as the "Philippeioi," which went back to Philip II, and his silver tetradrachms from late in his reign were of two types. One featured the head of the hero Perseus wearing a winged helmet in the center of a Macedonian shield, and on the reverse Heracles' club inside an oak wreath, and the other had the head of the king sporting a beard, and on the reverse Athena with a thunderbolt (see figure 2.1).

The king's construction of new roads helped farmers and traders travel to the various towns, and Macedonia was able to export a surplus of cereals and timber (for shipbuilding), several precious metals, and even weapons for various markets. When in 167 the Roman general Paullus, who defeated Perseus in that year, seized the royal treasury he was said to have found the huge sum of 6,000 gold and silver talents in it.[101]

---

96. Hammond and Griffith 1979, pp. 653–657; Worthington 2008, pp. 109–110; cf. Dell 1970.

97. Walbank 1940, pp. 223–224, 229–230, and 265–266.

98. Livy 39.24.2–4, with Hammond and Walbank 1988, p. 460.

99. Kremydi 2011.

100. Hammond and Walbank 1988, pp. 461–468, citing bibliography on numismatic issues.

101. Polybius 18.35.4; Livy 45.40.1–3.

Macedonia's economy, which rested on multiple resources and areas as we traced in chapter 1, was therefore improved locally and nationally. Revenue rose significantly after years of little income, and by the time of Philip's death its population had grown significantly. Needless to say, our sources begrudge him any credit, with Livy stating that everything he amassed in peacetime "he could use in time of war whenever given the chance."[102] We will soon see how that view is incorrect, and how Philip's military buildup was not for further warfare with Rome, as our ancient writers and even some modern scholars think, but related to his borders. He was, to put it simply, looking after Macedonia's interests.

If the Romans thought that trying to restrict Philip to Macedonia meant that he was no longer a threat to them or their provisos for Greece, they were mistaken. He and his successor Perseus brought about a recovery of their kingdom and challenged Rome again. Curiously, though, they did not make any changes to the phalanx line and its protection, which would be to Perseus' detriment at Pydna in 168: the lesson of Cynoscephalae was not learned.

---

102. Livy 39.24.1–2.

8

Macedonia Renascent

THE SECOND MACEDONIAN War altered the balance of power in the eastern Mediterranean, for now only the kingdoms of Seleucid Syria, Attalid Pergamum, and Ptolemaic Egypt remained. Closer to home, the Greeks may have hoped to settle down to some peace and prosperity, but acrimonious bickering between various states soon broke out. By 192 the Aetolians and Antiochus III of Syria had had enough of their situations—the former still aggrieved at how Rome had treated them after Cynoscephalae and the latter resentful of Rome encroaching on his territory and telling him what to do. As a result, relations between Rome and Greece slumped and enabled Philip to make a comeback into Greek affairs. To see how he did, we need take only a broad-brushstroke approach to the complex events of the next few years before turning more closely to his final years as king.

Philip's Resurgency

Flamininus and the Roman army left Greece for Italy in 194; he took with him vast quantities of loot for his three-day triumph through the streets of Rome. But Antiochus had not been intimidated by Flamininus' warning in 196 to pull his troops from cities that Ptolemy and Philip previously held. He continued his campaign in Thrace, marching as far west as Aenus and Maronea (which took him closer to Macedonia), and to make matters worse, the previous year (195) he offered refuge to Hannibal at Ephesus. Nonetheless, in the winter of 194/93 he sent envoys to the Senate stressing his goodwill to Rome and seeking an alliance.[1] They were told in no uncertain terms that he had to

---

1. Rome's interactions with Antiochus that led to war: Walbank 1940, pp. 186–196; Gruen 1984, pp. 620–632; Eckstein 2006, pp. 292–306; Eckstein 2008, pp. 306–325; Dmitriev 2011,

The Last Kings of Macedonia and the Triumph of Rome. Ian Worthington, Oxford University Press.
© Oxford University Press 2023. DOI: 10.1093/oso/9780197520055.003.0009

withdraw from Thrace and that a Roman embassy would visit him to discuss his position.

This Roman embassy traveled via Pergamum, where Eumenes urged war on Antiochus, but met only with Antiochus' deputy at Ephesus in 193. Nothing was decided. If the Senate were smarting at the embassy's treatment then to rub salt into wounds, Philip took advantage of Rome's preoccupation with Antiochus and a growing rift in Greece thanks to the Aetolian League to return to the orbit of Greek affairs. In 193, the Aetolians, still aggrieved over their treatment after Cynoscephalae and whose initial hopes that Antiochus would support them had been dashed, decided to build a coalition against Rome. They sent envoys to Nabis, Antiochus, and—in an excellent illustration of the enemy of my enemy is my friend—Philip.[2]

It is no surprise that Philip was not receptive to the Aetolians, given his history with them, and Antiochus remained uncommitted. But Nabis did help their cause. In the spring of 192 he seized several Peloponnesian cities from the Achaeans, who had been tasked by Flamininus to protect Spartan cities, and besieged Gythium in Laconia, which had an Achaean garrison in it.[3] Philopoemen, the Achaean leader, was not standing for that. Despite a letter from Rome asking the Achaeans to wait for Roman reinforcements, he persuaded a league assembly to allow him to lead an army against the Spartan king, but he suffered a serious defeat and Gythium fell to Nabis. When a Roman fleet under the praetor Atilius Serranus landed in Greece, Roman and Achaean troops quickly recovered Gythium. Philopoemen, who was then besieging Nabis in Sparta, was not impressed when Rome ordered him to end his siege.

At a meeting of the Aetolian League Assembly in the same spring, which Flamininus also attended, the Aetolians belligerently reacted to Rome's criticism of them by summoning Antiochus to liberate Greece and arbitrate between Rome and Aetolia. Damocritus went even further by declaring that the Aetolians would next deal with Flamininus "from a camp pitched on the banks of the Tiber," which Livy calls "madness," and we cannot disagree with him.[4] They then began assaults on Demetrias, Sparta, and Chalcis,

---

pp. 209–223. On Antiochus, see too Errington 1971a, pp. 156–175; Errington 1989b, pp. 275–289; Grainger 2002; Matyszak 2009, pp. 99–113.

2. Livy 35.12–13.3, with Briscoe 1981, pp. 162–163.

3. Livy 35.25–30; Plutarch, *Philopoemen* 14–15.3; Justin 31.3.3–4, with Briscoe 1981, pp. 181–190.

4. Livy 35.33.7–11.

capturing Demetrias, which they offered to Antiochus. They failed to seize Chalcis, which Flamininus and Eumenes garrisoned, and Sparta, where Nabis was assassinated and Philopoemen installed a pro-Achaean government and made Sparta part of the Achaean League.

The Aetolians had not been helped by Sparta and Macedonia, but they did have Antiochus on their side, even telling him the fake news that the whole of Greece was ready to revolt from Rome and join him. In fact, states such as Boeotia, Thessaly, Achaea, and Athens remained resolutely neutral. In the fall of 192, Antiochus took 100 warships to Greece along with an army of 10,000 infantry, 500 cavalry, and six elephants; he landed at the Gulf of Pagasae, from where he was escorted to Demetrias.[5] The Aetolian general Phaeneas was concerned about the relatively small size of Antiochus' army compared to what the Romans could field, but he was disregarded; after making an exhortatory speech at Lamia, Antiochus was elected commander of the league's army.

In all Antiochus spent three months in Greece, although he did not play an influential role in the Aetolian war. He set to work at once to besiege Chalcis, which he overcame, and then turned to Boeotia. Although he massacred 500 Roman soldiers at Delium near Tanagra, the Boeotians showed little interest in him. He later personally visited Thebes and won over the Boeotian League as well as Amynander of Athamania, but failed with the Achaeans, who declared war on them. The Senate had already feared the worst and in the same fall had sent 3,000 Roman troops under the praetor Marcus Baebius Tamphilus to Apollonia. After the slaughter of the Romans at Dium it declared war, sending the new consul (for 191), Manius Acilius Glabrio, and two legions to Greece.

All eyes had been on Philip for some time, who was faced with a dilemma. If he joined Antiochus, whom he personally disliked, and the latter furnished reinforcements, then the formidable combination of Philip, Antiochus, the Aetolians, the Boeotians, and Amynander would probably draw in Epirus and Acarnania, which had defensive treaties with Rome.[6] In fact, the Epirotes did offer their cities and harbors to Antiochus but did not wish to be part

---

5. Campaign: Livy 35.43.3–50, 36.5–21.1; Diodorus 29.2–3; Plutarch, *Flamininus* 15, with Walbank 1940, pp. 197–204 and 328–332; Errington 1971a, pp. 168–171; Gruen 1984, pp. 632–643; Hammond and Walbank 1988, pp. 449–455; Green 1990, pp. 420–423; Grainger 2002; Eckstein 2008, pp. 325–336; Matyszak 2009, pp. 106–113; Waterfield 2014, pp. 117–122.

6. Both were made in 196: Hammond and Walbank 1988, p. 604.

of a war.[7] Philip therefore had a good chance of reasserting his influence in Greece and achieving a goal he had worked toward since the start of his reign: taking the Roman protectorate in Illyria. On the other hand, he had no ships to speak of and he knew that his land forces were no match for what Rome could deploy.[8] There was also the uncertainty of what Antiochus would do in Greece and Illyria or for that matter against Philip. Therefore, Philip played safe by sending envoys to Rome offering some of his troops, grain, and money for the war effort. These the Senate refused although it did ask him to assist Glabrio as needed.[9]

Philip's diplomacy with Rome was the right course of action in the end, for Antiochus in tandem with Amynander and the Aetolians attacked Thessaly. Seleucid incursions into Thrace were one thing, but Philip could not allow strategic Thessaly to fall to Antiochus. He sent word of this threat to Baebius at Apollonia and proposed a joint action against the Syrian king.[10] Philip and Baebius decided to establish a garrison in Larissa, which Antiochus was then besieging, as an advance base against the Aetolians.[11]

The people of Larissa were putting up a resistance, but it was saved by a ruse by the Roman commander Appius Claudius.[12] He lit numerous watch-fires on the surrounding hills, making it seem like the entire Roman army was encamped there. Antiochus prudently withdrew to Chalcis, using the oncoming winter as his excuse, allowing Claudius, who had only 2,000 men with him, to enter Larissa and install a garrison. The following spring (of 191) Antiochus raided Acarnania, enabling Philip and Baebius to invade Thessaly: in a blitzkrieg campaign lasting only three weeks they retook several cities, including the major fortress of Gomphi, before receiving reinforcements of 20,000 infantry, 2,000 cavalry, and fifteen elephants under Glabrio, as well as some Illyrian troops.[13] Glabrio eventually drove Antiochus back to

---

7. Polybius 20.3; Livy 36.5, with Hammond 1967, p. 623.

8. Cf. Walbank 1982, p. 233: "Naval power played no part in Philip's subsequent policies." Philip's last years: Gruen 1974 and the succinct discussion of Burton 2017, pp. 39–55.

9. Livy 36.4.1–4.

10. Livy 36.8.6, 36.10.10, and 36.13.1. Gruen 1973, pp. 129–132, that Philip's support of Rome did not point to an alliance after Cynoscephalae but was Philip looking out for his kingdom's interests.

11. Walbank 1940, pp. 200–201.

12. Livy 36.10.10–15.

13. Livy 36.13.1–14.9.

Thermopylae, leaving Philip to reflect on a successful Thessalian offensive that had netted him several key towns from the Aetolians.[14]

Perhaps it was Philip's successes that prompted him to allow many of Amynander's men from Larissa to depart unharmed, but that did not stop him from going on to conquer Athamania, with Amynander fleeing on his approach.[15] Antiochus—who was now largely fighting on his own, as the Aetolians committed only a few thousand troops out of fear that Philip would overrun their territory—could not withstand Glabrio's assault on his position at Thermopylae.[16] Philip was ill at the time and did not take part in the battle with Glabrio and his troops. One thousand of Antiochus' men deserted to Philip rather than remain in the Syrian army. Antiochus, who had had his teeth smashed by a rock during the fighting, realized his situation was hopeless and fled, first to Chalcis, and thence to Ephesus.

Philip had chosen the winning side, and after his successes in Thessaly and Athamania he expected to have a say in Greek affairs. Rome, however, had other ideas.

The Enemy of My Enemy

Glabrio left Thermopylae and launched a campaign to take Phocis, Boeotia, and Euboea, before in June besieging the Aetolian-controlled town of Heraclea while Philip invested Lamia as part of a push to end the Aetolian war.[17] There was an element of competition in these two sieges as both cities were only about seven miles (11 kilometers) apart. Philip was either slow or more likely faced greater resistance, for Glabrio took Heraclea but then told the king to end his siege of Lamia; this he resented, but there was nothing he could do.[18]

The Aetolians now sent an embassy seeking terms to the Roman commander at Hypata, Lucius Valerius Flaccus.[19] His demand of unconditional

---

14. The chronology is controversial, for Antiochus' defeat at Thermopylae could be in either April, May, or June: Walbank 1940, pp. 329–331.

15. Livy 36.14.7–9 and 39.23.10–11.

16. Livy 36.16–21.1; Appian, *Syrian Wars* 17–20; Plutarch, *Flamininus* 15.3; Zonaras 9.19.8–10; cf. Diodorus 29.3; see too Briscoe 1981, pp. 241–250.

17. Livy 36.22.4–25.8; Appian, *Syrian Wars* 21.94; Zonaras 9.19. Following campaigns: Walbank 1940, pp. 204–208; Matyszak 2009, pp. 115–119. Date of June: Walbank 1940, p. 331.

18. Livy 36.25.7–8 and 39.23.8–9.

19. Polybius 20.9–10; Livy 36.27–28, with Walbank 1979, pp. 77–83.

surrender was rejected, and the war continued. The Aetolians had earlier sent an unsuccessful embassy to Antiochus; its delegate Nicander (the same man who had tried to coax Philip over to the Aetolians in 193) was captured by some of Philip's scouts as he made his way home. The king invited him to dinner in his camp and released him unharmed, advising him that the Aetolians should reflect on how they had suffered so far because of their alliances and think about an alliance with Macedonia before it was too late.[20] His surprising response shows us two significant things: he viewed the Aetolians as less of a threat and more of an ally, and he was reaching the end of his tether with Rome, especially after Glabrio's high-handed treatment of him at Lamia.[21]

The Aetolian troops assembled at Naupactus on the north coast of the Gulf of Corinth. Claudius fought them there while Glabrio invested the city from August to September (of 191), during which time fighting in the Peloponnese ended. The Achaeans, to Flamininus' annoyance, had involved themselves in the Peloponnese, and when they attacked Messene he decided enough was enough. He ordered them to lift their siege, arranged for Messenia to join the Achaean League, and to obstruct the league's movements took over the island of Zacynthus, which Philip had previously given to Amynander, and turned it into a naval base.[22]

Philip had tactfully gained the permission of Glabrio to advance along the Malian road to Demetrias, taking various towns along the way including Magnesia.[23] At this point he was probably expected to link up with Glabrio and march to Thermum, but instead he made his way north to Perrhaebia and recovered any towns still defying him.[24] His maneuvers prompted Flamininus to intervene in Glabrio's ongoing siege of Naupactus, which he realized Philip was using as a distraction to rebuild his footing in Greece. Slowly but steadily, regardless of the terms imposed on him after Cynoscephalae, the king had added much of Thessaly to his territory. That winter, Flamininus granted the Aetolians a truce to send envoys to Rome to discuss peace, neatly preventing any pact with Philip.

Other embassies from the mainland were also at Rome, including one from Philip.[25] He emphasized his friendship to Rome and savvily dedicated a

---

20. Polybius 20.11.5–7; Livy 36.29.4–11.

21. Walbank 1940, p. 206.

22. On the preceding: Livy 36.30–31.

23. Livy 36.33.1–7.

24. Walbank 1940, p. 207 n. 3, on confusion in the routes.

25. Polybius 21.3; Livy 36.35.11–14, with Walbank 1979, p. 91.

gold crown weighing one hundred pounds to Jupiter Optimus Maximus, for which the senators released his sixteen-year-old son Demetrius and promised to remit the last installments of the indemnity imposed after Cynoscephalae— as long as Philip remained loyal to Rome.[26] An Achaean embassy, by contrast, was treated with brusqueness and its demands rejected. The senators were likewise unwelcoming of the Aetolians, demanding that they surrender their foreign policy to Rome and pay an indemnity of one thousand talents. This was not what the Aetolians wanted to hear, and despite their worries they resolved to continue the war.[27]

Antiochus was a bigger issue for Rome. In the spring of 190 a Roman army of 8,000 troops commanded by Scipio Africanus (victor over Hannibal in the Second Punic War) and his brother Lucius Cornelius Scipio was sent against Antiochus, and first landed in Illyria.[28] The Scipios traveled through Thessaly to Amphissa to try to end the continuing Aetolian war, granting the Aetolians a six-month truce (May to October) to send another round of envoys to the Senate, and then returned to Thessaly. They sent Tiberius Sempronius Gracchus to organize their army's route through Macedonia.[29] Gracchus traveled from Amphissa to Pella at great speed and came upon a Philip "well into the wine" at dinner, which he took as a good sign. Still, Philip was quick and sober enough to agree to help the Scipios.

Philip had not been asked to provide any troops for the campaign against the Aetolians, but he was careful. He knew the value of being a friend (*amicus*) of Rome, and the demise of Antiochus was to his advantage.[30] But he also could not risk endangering the remission of the enormous war indemnity, and may well have realized much rested on what he provided for the Roman army in his territory.[31] Accordingly, he gave the Scipios supplies, repaired bridges and roads to aid their march, welcomed them to his court,

---

26. Polybius 21.3; Diodorus 28.15.1.

27. Polybius 21.2; Livy 37.1.1–6; Diodorus 29.4; Zonaras 9.19.14. The demand of money is interesting, perhaps arising from Antiochus' gift to the Aetolians, about which Philip may have quietly informed the Senate: Matsyzak 2009, p. 117.

28. Walbank 1940, pp. 209–212; Errington 1971, pp. 175–178; Hammond and Walbank 1988, pp. 449–450. Date of March 18: Walbank 1940, p. 332.

29. Livy 37.7.8–16; Appian, *Macedonian Wars* 9.5; Appian, *Syrian Wars* 23.100, with Walbank 1940, pp. 210–211; Briscoe 1981, pp. 301–303.

30. Gruen 1973, pp. 132–133; cf. Gruen 1974, p. 225.

31. Walbank 1940, p. 210.

and provided an escort as far as the Hellespont.[32] He also struck up a genuine friendship with Scipio Africanus.

The Aetolian envoys eventually stood before the Senate. Their arrogant tone did not endear them to the senators, who refused to consider anything but an unconditional surrender and ordered them to leave Italy within fifteen days.[33] But now Amynander, an exile in Aetolia, caused problems in Greece.[34] He was still seething that Philip had held Athamania since 191, and in December 190 he invaded his kingdom with 1,000 Aetolian troops, urging his people to revolt and expel the Macedonian garrisons. Philip, taken by surprise, reacted instantly. He reached Gomphi with 6,000 men, left 4,000 of them there, and pushed on to Athenaeum to evaluate the extent of the revolt and take towns in the area before returning to Gomphi. In a counterattack, however, he was trapped in a pass, but managed to scramble back to Gomphi with some difficulty. Amynander now sent envoys to the Senate and to the Scipios in Asia Minor seeking peace, excusing his dependence on the Aetolians, and blaming Philip for forcing him to act as he had.

Amynander's success spurred the Aetolians to take many of Philip's possessions in southwest Thessaly. But their hopes of continued success were dashed when news reached Greece that the Scipios had defeated Antiochus that winter (190–189) at Magnesia on the Maeander River in Lydia.[35] The resulting Treaty of Apamea in 188 ended hostilities between Antiochus and Rome; the king suffered an enormous indemnity of 15,000 talents, handed over most of his fleet and all his elephants, and in a significant reduction of the size of the Seleucid Empire surrendered all his lands in Thrace and Asia west of the Taurus range.[36]

A further blow to the Aetolians was the arrival in Greece that summer (of 189) of another army under the consul Marcus Fulvius Nobilior, who quickly besieged the large fortress of Ambracia (Arta) in Epirus, held by the

---

32. Livy 37.7.13–16.

33. Livy 37.49; cf. Diodorus 29.9.

34. Polybius 21.25.1–2; Livy 38.1–3.2, with Walbank 1940, pp. 213–214.

35. Polybius 21.25.3–8; Livy 37.37–44.2; Appian, *Syrian Wars* 30–37; Justin 31.8.6–7; Zonaras 9.20.5–8. Succinctly summarized by Walbank 1940, pp. 211–212; cf. Briscoe 1981, pp. 343–358.

36. Polybius 21.16–17, 21.42, 21.45; Livy 37.45.4–21; Diodorus 29.10; Appian, *Syrian Wars* 38; Justin 31.8; Zonaras 9.20.9. On the negotiations and treaty see too Errington 1971a, pp. 178–183; Briscoe 1981, pp. 358–362; Gruen 1984, pp. 640–671; Ager 1996, pp. 266–267; Eckstein 2008, pp. 333–335; Waterfield 2014, pp. 134–136.

Aetolians for many years. The defenders resisted stoutly, helped by two waves of Aetolian soldiers.[37] They also used a type of poison gas in tunnels through which the Romans were trying to breach the city, filling jars with feathers, burning charcoal at the rims, and using bellows to blow the choking smoke at the enemy.[38] But the end was drawing in sight for the Aetolians, thanks to Philip. Still playing the dutiful ally of Rome, he and his son Perseus, now in his early twenties, led an army into Dolopia and Amphilochia in northern Aetolia, forcing the Aetolians to divert a relief force to Ambracia, while the Achaeans and Illyrians raided the Aetolian coast.

Unable to wage a war on three fronts, the Aetolians approached Nobilior for peace. The Athenians, Rhodians, and Amynander appealed on their behalf for lenient terms, to which Nobilior agreed.[39] Among other things, Aetolia was to give up all its conquests apart from Amphilochia in northwest Aetolia, despite Philip's protestations; surrender forty hostages to Rome; pay an indemnity of 500 talents (200 upfront and the balance over six years); surrender all prisoners and deserters; and have the same friends and enemies as Rome, fighting them when Rome deemed necessary. Significantly, there is no mention of Rome doing the same thing for them.

Down But Not Out

Philip was presumably anticipating a reward for supporting Rome over the last few years. Instead, he got nothing, other than the bitter experience of how Rome acted as it saw fit.[40] The Romans had needed Philip on side after Cynoscephalae; with both Antiochus and the Aetolian League no longer a threat after 189, the Senate saw no reason to continue its courtship of Macedonia. Philip may have had an inkling of this when no Roman troops in Greece helped him in his campaign against Amynander, and when he appealed to his friends in Rome to support claims to territory formerly held

---

37. Polybius 21.26.1–6, 21.27–28, 29.6–15; Livy 38.3.9–38.4.13, with Briscoe 2008, pp. 36–52. Campaign: Walbank 1940, pp. 214–216; Hammond 1967, pp. 139–149; see too Walbank 1979, pp. 123–128.

38. Polybius 21.28—the procedure is described at 21.28.12–18; cf. Livy 38.7.11–13, with Walbank 1979, p. 127.

39. Polybius 21.25.10–11 (envoys seeking support), 21.29–32 (negotiations and peace); Livy 38.10–11, with Walbank 1979, pp. 128–136; Gruen 1984, pp. 25–33; Hammond and Walbank 1988, pp. 604–605.

40. Walbank 1940, pp. 216–217; Hammond and Walbank 1988, p. 454; Hammond 1992, p. 358.

by the Aetolians he was ignored.[41] His treatment, the lack of support against Amynander, and even being told to abandon the siege of Lamia made him furious—according to Livy, here were the seeds of the war between his son Perseus and Rome, whose "origins go back to Philip and had he lived longer he would have fought the war himself."[42]

Philip was also not consulted about the peace terms imposed on the Aetolians, which were all to his disadvantage. In his agreement with Baebius he had been told he could hold onto any town he captured, hence he expected to retain those in Perrhaebia, Thessaly (including the strategic Demetrias), and Athamania. But the Senate reneged on the deal—though in fairness, if it gave him these places it would contravene the terms of the settlement of 196. In fact, Rome had reconstituted the Thessalian League, which would soon replace the Aetolian League as Philip's southern foe. Even worse was that closer to home the frontier road between Thrace and Macedonia was redrawn inland to exclude the two Thracian coastal cities of Maronea and Aenus, which Philip had seized along with others.[43] Maronea and Aenus were only fifty miles (80 kilometers) from his border, so the redrawn boundary might tempt hostile Thracians down onto his coast.

Soon after Roman troops left Greece, though Rome cautiously kept Cephallenia, which had been excluded from the peace and was taken shortly after by Nobilior, and Zacynthus as naval bases.[44] The Senate's arrangements in the Balkans and in Asia Minor (in which Eumenes and Rhodes received much of Antiochus' kingdom) showed it had no interest in international law nor felt any sense of duty to its allies. For Philip, Rome's terms imposed on him after he was defeated in battle in 197 were one thing; its reneging on promises after all his help was another. After the First Illyrian War Rome had snubbed Antigonus III by not sending a good faith embassy to him. Now Rome was again conducting itself high-handedly—which would not have been lost on the next king, Perseus.

If the Romans could treat Philip badly, then, given his nature and spirit, so could he them. In the fall of 188 the consul Gnaeus Manlius Vulso, one of the negotiators at Apamea, was traveling back through Thrace on his way

---

41. Polybius 21.31.3–4.

42. Livy 39.23.5; cf. 39.29.3. Philip's fury: Livy 39.23.6–13.

43. Livy 39.24.6–9. Gruen 1974, p. 226 with n. 18, suggests this was an ad hoc arrangement as Maronea and Aenus were not in the terms of the Peace of Apamea.

44. On Nobilior taking Cephallenia at this time, see Briscoe 2008, pp. 104–109.

home when four Thracian tribes ambushed him. He lost many men and much booty but then fell victim to the same tribes a second time, though he managed to stave off his attackers before reaching Macedonia and from there Apollonia.[45] The rumor was soon circulating, despite no proof, that Philip had instigated the Thracian attacks.[46] Now, Vulso had not contacted Philip beforehand for assistance—as had the Scipios via Gracchus—which did leave him vulnerable. However, Philip must have had news of what had happened; presumably he could have sent men to escort the consul safely through his kingdom, but his disregard may have been because of his treatment at Rome's hands.

By 187 (or 186 at the latest) Philip began pushing boundaries—literally— when he unilaterally retweaked his eastern boundary to put Maronea and Aenus again in his kingdom.[47] His move need not imply any expansionist policy, but simply—as so often—shielding his borders against hostile forces.[48] But Eumenes interpreted his act as a direct threat and the Thessalians had long been apprehensive that Philip was going to deal with them next, so they turned to the Amphictyonic League (the various Greek states that looked after the Delphic oracle). Glabrio had freed this body from Aetolian dominance in 191, and tasked Thessaly and Athens with reorganizing it, which they did between 186 and 184 with senatorial approval.[49]

Philip was never a member of the Amphictyony.[50] Membership had been bestowed in 346 on Philip II and his successors though not on Macedonia itself. It may have been suspended when Alexander IV was murdered in 310 and reinstituted under Demetrius I, but when the Amphictyony was reorganized in 186 Philip was excluded from it.[51] This is not surprising, given the Thessalians' hatred of the king, for they never had an issue complaining

---

45. Livy 38.40–41, with Walbank 1940, pp. 217–218.

46. Livy 38.40.8.

47. Livy 39.27.10.

48. Walbank 1940, pp. 223–224.

49. Walbank 1940, pp. 225–226; Habicht 1987. Sherk 1969, no. 1, pp. 21–25; cf. nos. 37–39, pp. 221–232, on Roman diplomatic dealings with Delphi and moves against the Aetolians.

50. Walbank 1977, pp. 89–90. Giovannini 1970 argues that Philip did not lose his place on the council.

51. For Poliorcetes being admitted onto the council, see Pugliese 2014, p. 150 with n. 18.

to the Senate about him.[52] Their attitude was clearly different toward Perseus, however, who was admitted to it (p. 186).

The Thessalians now persuaded envoys from the Amphictyonic Council to make the journey to Rome in the winter of 186–185, where they discovered others already there from Perrhaebia, Thessaly, Amynander, and Eumenes—and Philip himself.[53] The Senate did not seem especially bothered by those from Perrhaebia, Thessaly, Amynander, or the Amphictyony. But there was disquiet when the Pergamene delegates spoke of Philip's activities in Thrace, bolstering their case by producing refugees from Maronea (they said), who also spoke of Philip holding Aenus as well.[54] Philip must have expected retribution, yet the Senate did not punish him.[55] Instead it sent a commission comprising Quintus Caecilius Metellus, Marcus Baebius Tamphilus, and Tiberius Sempronius Gracchus to Greece, who called a meeting at Tempe to hear everyone's complaints against the king.[56]

Philip did not have an easy time, for "the Romans took their seats as judges, the Thessalians, Perrhaebians and Athamanians quite clearly as the prosecution, and Philip as the defendant."[57] The complaints rained down on him, all to do with the cities he had taken as part of his agreement with Rome.[58] Among other things, the Thessalians and Perrhaebians believed he should hold only those cities that had been originally Aetolian and not in the first instance Thessalian or Perrhaebian and then brought into the Aetolian League—such as Gomphi, Tricca, Phaloria, and Eurymenae.[59] They alleged that he intended to sack these cities, that he could not be trusted when it came to Thessaly, and that all Thessaly was so terrified of him that Rome had to do something to remain true to its proclamation of freedom. Many of their

---

52. *SIG*³ 613, lines 33–35 = Sherk 1984, no. 1 (Delphi). Philip and the league: cf. Walbank 1940, p. 248.

53. Livy 39.24.6–12; Zonaras 9.21.5, with Walbank 1940, pp. 226–227.

54. Walbank 1979, p. 184, states they were "probably a faction which supported Eumenes."

55. Gruen 1974, pp. 226–227, argues that Philip expected no retaliation over these moves, as the critiques all came from Greek embassies; *contra* Walbank 1940, p. 227, that Rome wanted to take a more "drastic remedy."

56. Polybius 22.6.5–6; Livy 39.24.13–14.

57. Livy 39.25.1, with Walbank 1940, pp. 227–228.

58. Livy 39.25.2–17.

59. Eurymenae was taken by Philip in 191 apparently from Amynander, who was working with the Aetolians at that time: Livy 36.13.5–6, with Walbank 1940, p. 228 n. 1.

allegations were without merit and likewise the Athamanians could only repeat rhetorical warnings of future dangers from Philip.[60]

These verbal attacks did not sit well with someone like Philip as we might
expect. When it was his turn to speak, "to give the appearance of being ac-
cuser rather than defendant," he launched into a series of counter-charges, accusing his adversaries, especially the Thessalians, of seizing and keeping towns
and territories to which they were not entitled, rebutting claims against him
that he had detrimentally affected the Thessalian economy, and underscoring
that his agreement with Rome allowed him to hold onto any city he took
from the enemy.[61] He was in the right, for Tamphilus was the same man who
had negotiated with Philip in 191, so the latter was not likely to lie about the
terms of the agreement in his presence.[62]

There was uproar when Philip finished speaking, but he had not done himself any favors with the Romans when he courageously announced the sun
had not yet set on him, which the Thessalians and the Senate took as a threat
directed against them.[63] Not that his words mattered. The commissioners
were not interested in legality, not least because Philip viewed the conference
as time-wasting and had made his feelings known. They ordered him to do
away with his garrisons in all cities under dispute and to limit his kingdom
to its "ancient" frontiers, taking him back to a similar situation as in 196, although he continued to hold Demetrias and some Achaean towns.[64]

An exception was made about the status of Maronea and Aenus, which
was to be decided at a second meeting in Thessalonica so that envoys from
Eumenes and exiled Maroneans (perhaps those who had been in Rome the
previous winter) could speak.[65] When everyone duly gathered at Thessalonica,
Eumenes made it plain that Maronea and Aenus should either be independent or given to him, and the Maroneans spoke of Philip and his garrison
dominating their city and exiling any opponents. Though angry, Philip forced
himself to be more restrained than at Tempe. He listed his grievances, beginning with the Romans leaving Orestis independent, how he had been robbed
of his territories in Thessaly, Perrhaebia, and Athamania despite what Glabrio

---

60. Cf. Walbank 1940, pp. 228–230.

61. Livy 39.26.1–10 (quote at 26.1); cf. Diodorus 29.16.

62. Gruen 1974, pp. 227–228.

63. Livy 39.26.9.

64. Livy 39.26.14, with Errington 1971a, pp. 196–197; cf. Walbank 1940, pp. 230–232.

65. Livy 39.27.2–28.14.

had promised him, why Eumenes did not deserve Maronea and Aenus since Philip had supported Rome more, including providing safe passage for the Scipios' army, and stressed that as a friend of Rome he should have justice.

The commissioners seemed swayed by Philip's arguments—after all, he had right on his side. But they were mindful of not upsetting Eumenes, so they referred the matter back to the Senate.[66] In early 184, that body sent Appius Claudius at the head of yet another commission. Its mission was to ensure that Philip had returned disputed cities to Thessaly, Perrhaebia, and Athamania as well as withdrawn his garrisons from Maronea and Aenus, which were declared independent, and that the entire Thracian coastline was free from Macedonian influence.[67] In fact, the Senate had been placed in a difficult position, hence it returned to the core of its settlement of 196.[68]

To complicate matters further a gruesome incident at Maronea took place, which had repercussions for Philip.[69] A group of Thracian marauders stormed the city and massacred many of the inhabitants, prompting the king to keep his garrison there as protection. Our sources accuse him of ordering his governor of Thrace, Onomastus, and a certain Cassander (perhaps the *epistates* or overseer of Maronea) to instigate the Thracian attack out of anger over the Senate's decision. There is no evidence that he was to blame, and indeed he may have complied with the Senate's directive, leaving Maronea undefended and a sitting duck for any Thracians to exploit.[70] He protested his innocence to the commissioners when they arrived, blaming the massacre on local factions, and offering to hand over Onomastus and Cassander for interrogation. When the commissioners demanded that they be sent to Rome, Philip went to some lengths to convince Claudius that Onomastus needed to stay. Cassander was not so lucky: while en route to Rome he suddenly died in Epirus, for which Philip unsurprisingly was blamed. Perhaps, then, he did have something to hide.

The Senate's decision about Philip's possessions, justified or not, caused a rift with him.[71] Although he is not blameless, he must have recognized how the Senate was siding with Eumenes and the Greeks, especially the Thessalians,

66. Livy 39.29.1–2, with Walbank 1940, pp. 233–234.

67. Polybius 22.11.2, 4; Livy 39.33—after checking on Philip the commissioners were to go to the Peloponnese to meet with the Achaeans.

68. Walbank 1940, pp. 224–235.

69. Polybius 22.13–14.6; Livy 39.34.

70. Hammond and Walbank 1988, p. 457; cf. Errington 1971a, p. 198; Gruen 1974, pp. 230–231. Walbank 1940, p. 235, believes Philip instigated the attack.

71. Just: Walbank 1940, pp. 234–236. Unreasonable: Errington 1971a, p. 197.

over him, even though he had an *amicitia* with Rome! He was now faced with a problem. The assault on Maronea (assuming he was not behind it) showed the risk to his eastern border with Thrace. Since it was obvious that Rome would care little if he fell victim to any Thracian incursion and that Eumenes would capitalize on his misfortune, he decided to take over Thrace to shore up his eastern border. The Senate was not going to be impressed.

Expansion in Thrace

Philip's Thracian campaign was a tribute to his military planning and diplomacy (map 4).[72] He first opened diplomatic contacts with the people of Byzantium, who had been paying a tribute to Amadocus, king of the Odrysian Thracians inland of Aenus. The Byzantines eagerly accepted Philip's offer to attack him in return for friendship, and that summer Philip defeated and took Amadocus prisoner.[73] Probably now Philip married one of his daughters to Teres, Amadocus' successor, presumably hopeful of also using his troops.[74] Political marriages organized by kings were nothing unusual; here we see a similarity with Alexander the Great marrying his half-sister Cynane to the king of the Agrianians in the upper Strymon region of Paeonia, whose troops became an integral part of his army.[75]

Philip next opened negotiations with two other Thracian adversaries, the Bastarnae, a tribe living well north of Byzantium between the Carpathian Mountains and the Dnieper River, and the Scordisci in the region of Belgrade.[76] On top of building up a coalition against Thracian aggression, he wanted the Bastarnae to migrate west and help him once and for all put down the Dardanians on the Thracian-Illyrian border by settling in their territory.

The king was astute enough to know that the more he did, the more vocal the complaints against him. And indeed, during the winter of 184–183 various embassies from Pergamum, Thessaly, Perrhaebia, Epirus, Athamania, and Illyria denounced Philip before the Senate.[77] Eumenes' delegates included his brother

---

72. On the campaign, see Walbank 1940, pp. 236–238; Hammond and Walbank 1988, pp. 468–471.

73. Polybius 22.14.12, 23.8.4–7; Livy 39.53.4, 12–14.

74. Diodorus 32.15.5.

75. Arrian 1.5.4, as noted by Hammond and Walbank 1988, p. 469.

76. Justin 32.3.5.

77. Polybius 23.1–4.16; Livy 39.46.6–9; Appian, *Macedonian Wars* 9.6; Justin 32.2.3, with Walbank 1979, pp. 214–220; cf. Dell 1977, pp. 310–311.

Athenaeus, who complained of Philip's sending troops to Prusias of Bithynia in advance of his campaign against Eumenes and that the Macedonian garrisons at Aenus and Maronea were still in place.[78] To try to appease the Senate Philip sent his son Demetrius on a good faith mission to Rome.[79]

For three days the Senate listened to charges brought by the opposing side. Then it called Demetrius. Perhaps because of his age and inexperience he was allowed to read from prepared notes Philip had sent with him.[80] Demetrius stressed that his father was being unjustly hurt, that his accusers deserved blame, and that he had not contravened any agreement. In many respects, this was true. He was, for example, entitled to lead his men into Thrace and as far afield as Byzantium, for under the terms of the settlement he had not been debarred from the northern Balkans and most of Thrace.

The Senate sided with Demetrius, not because of the king's word but apparently because it was delivered by Demetrius.[81] It still needed to appease Eumenes though, so it sent another commission led by Quintus Marcius Philippus to make sure Philip was vacating towns he held in Thrace including the long-suffering Maronea and Aenus.[82] Philip must have known he was lucky not to be subject to greater repercussions, yet by all accounts he was affronted that Flamininus and the Senate favored Demetrius so much, and may even have viewed him as the next Macedonian king, to which we return below.[83]

The Roman commission arrived in spring 183, with Philippus reporting back that Philip had followed the Senate's directive "in a sullen and grumbling spirit and with many sighs" and only until he could go to war again.[84] The king's attitude was justified, but he was hardly planning a war with no fleet and diminished troop numbers.

That summer Philip embarked on a campaign against the Odrysians (again), the Dentheletae near the Strymon, and the Bessi on the Hebrus

78. Polybius 23.1.4, 23.3.1–2; Livy 39.46.9.

79. Polybius 22.14.7–11, 23.1.5, 2.1–10; Livy 39.35.1–3, 39.47, with Gruen 1974, pp. 231–232 with n. 36, on Polybius' presentation of Philip's motive.

80. Gruen 1974, p. 233, suggests this was part of a prearrangement.

81. Polybius 23.2.10, 23.3.4–5; Livy 39.47.11.

82. Polybius 23.4.16; Livy 39.48.5, 39.53.10–11; Justin 32.2.3–5.

83. Cf. Livy 39.53.

84. Polybius 23.8.1–2 (quote at 8.1), 23.9.4–7; Livy 40.3.1–2.

River, in which he captured the town of Philippopolis (Plovdiv) and installed a garrison, though it was expelled by the Odrysians.[85] From there he marched to Paeonia, where in a plain called Deuriopus, whose location is not known but perhaps north of the Monastir gap, he founded a new town, Perseis.[86] It was named after his eldest son Perseus, presumably to show he was his successor.[87]

The main tribes of central Thrace, and especially their troops, were now under Philip's control.[88] In the fall of 183 occurred what Polybius considered a dark episode, brought on by Fortune, when Philip transported an unknown number of his people from coastal cities to the borders of Paeonia, and in their place settled Thracians and mercenaries to shore up his defenses against the Dardanians and secure support in key areas.[89] Polybius saw this action as a terrible misfortune for Philip and Macedonia, with those forced to move despairing at their fate, especially as Philip was said to have ordered critics of his transpopulation policy and their sons and daughters imprisoned.[90] Yet Philip's movement of people was no different from what Philip II had done in the 350s to safeguard the border with Illyria.[91]

However, the presentation of these affected people as always distressed and rulers caring little for their feelings has been challenged.[92] Our ancient writers may have imposed images of suffering on the settlers, and in doing so unfairly lambasted kings like Philip II and Philip V.[93] For one thing, no

85. Polybius 23.8.4–7; Livy 39.53.12–14.

86. Livy 39.53.15–16.

87. Meloni 1953, pp. 16–23 and 34–38.

88. Cf. Walbank 1940, p. 246, that Philip even wanted to forge a Balkan empire.

89. Polybius 23.10.1–6; Livy 40.3.3–4; cf. 39.24.4, with Walbank 1940, pp. 243–244 with n. 3; Dreyer 2013, p. 202.

90. Polybius 23.10.7–16; Plutarch, *Moralia* 53e; cf. Livy 40.4.1–5.1 if the episode refers to this time. Polybius 23.10.15 names Samus, Pyrrhicus, and Ademetus, which are found on inscriptions: see Habicht 1970, p. 270; Galles 1977. See further below.

91. Justin 8.5.7–6.2; cf. Demosthenes 19.89.

92. Hammond 1992, p. 360; cf. Dreyer 2013.

93. Cf. Justin 8.5.7–6.2 on Philip II's transpopulation policy to his north-western frontier in the 350s and the people looking "wistfully now at the tombs of their forefathers, now at their ancient family deities, now at the houses in which they had been born and had themselves produced children, sorrowing at one moment for their own fate for having lived to see that day, and at the next for that of their children, for not having been born after it," with Worthington 2008, pp. 109–110.

displaced people as far as we know seized the opportunity of Philip's death in 179 to return home, and as late as 167 we find foreigners still living on their own lands in Macedonia.[94] Likewise, we hear of no mass exodus of people who were supposedly forced to move by Philip II when that king died in 336.

Despite Philip's movements, in the winter of 183–182 the Senate sent him a message of goodwill while ominously warning him to avoid anything "which might give the *appearance* of opposition to Rome."[95] Yet Rome never gave Aenus and Maronea to Eumenes, and perhaps also its seemingly benevolent attitude was in part due to the Greeks being less vocal in their criticisms. As Gruen notes, despite Philip's exploits in Greece and Thrace, Rome's policy toward Macedonia after 196 was "remarkable not for its aggressiveness but for its passivity."[96]

In the spring of 182 Philip reached an agreement with the Bastarnae, which included marrying one of their princesses to Perseus, who was none too happy with this plan.[97] The marriage may have been to keep this pact permanent, and it was a sign of how important Philip regarded his policy in Thrace, though he was hardly planning a Balkan empire as has been suggested.[98] He had been carefully expanding in the east—the only direction he could go after what had been determined in 196 and Rome's hold over Illyria—and his alliances with tribes like the Bastarnae were meant to safeguard Macedonia against Dardanian and other threats. Nor did they contravene his treaty with Rome as its terms allowed him to campaign outside Macedonia without senatorial permission.[99]

Philip's plans in Thrace and against the Dardanians seemed to be working out to his satisfaction. However, he was now facing problems with his two sons Demetrius and Perseus, which form the backdrop to Philip's last years and death.[100]

---

94. Livy 45.30.5, with Walbank 1940, pp. 243–244.

95. Gruen 1974, p. 238, drawing on Polybius 23.9.7; cf. Walbank 1940, pp. 226–232.

96. Gruen 1974, p. 245. Dell 1983 concurs with Gruen's argument that Rome was not to blame but sees Philip's Thracian campaigns as causing conflict and bringing about Demetrius' end.

97. Livy 40.5.10–11, with Walbank 1940, pp. 237–238; Meloni 1953, pp. 34–41. Perseus was later accused of murdering her: Livy 42.5.4.

98. Walbank 1940, p. 246.

99. The clause apparently requiring approval at Livy 33.30.6 is a spurious addition: Burton 2017, p. 82 n. 22; cf. Briscoe 1973, pp. 7 and 306.

100. Livy 40.6.4 on the age difference.

The Quarrel of Philip's Sons

The sources' veracity is suspect about the last years of Philip's life and his relations with his sons. Tensions had been growing between Demetrius and Perseus (who was five years older than his brother and Philip's heir) over their differing attitudes to Rome, the succession, and even Demetrius' popularity.[101] Perseus and Philip ostensibly resented Demetrius' favor with the Senate in 183 when he went on the goodwill mission from his father as discussed above. Flamininus seems to have personally liked Demetrius, which Philip and Perseus apparently interpreted as Rome preferring him as the next king and not Perseus, whose very legitimacy was questioned.[102] As a result, the two brothers became rivals and drew Philip into their altercation, eventually leading the king to put Demetrius to death at Perseus' instigation.

Edson has pointed out there is no evidence of serious animosity between the two brothers.[103] The details speak otherwise. In the spring (probably March) of 182 the annual festival of the hero Xanthus took place. It included the ceremonial purification of the army, in which the king led his entire army between the two halves of a sacrificial dog.[104] Afterward, a mock battle was held, with each brother leading one half of the army. But the fighting got out of hand and a bruised Perseus refused to attend his brother's banquet that evening. It was just as well, for one of his friends was assaulted at it, and his attackers rushed out to track down Perseus—who barred his quarters for protection, forcing them to leave.

The next day Perseus accused his brother before Philip of trying to kill him. All three were said to have given long speeches: both brothers denounced each other, Perseus protested his innocence, and Philip bemoaned the strife in his family.[105] Their speeches are highly stylized, and their reliability is debatable.[106] But Philip had concerns about Demetrius' self-regard after his

---

101. Livy 40.5–16.3, 20.3–21.11, 23.24.8, 54.1–2; cf. 39.53.1–10. See on the sources: Walbank 1938, noting from his discussion that "Polybius' account of these last years of Philip [makes it] one of the least satisfying in his whole work" (on p. 67); Walbank 1979, pp. 233–235; Briscoe 2008, pp. 417–453; Dreyer 2013. On the whole affair of the sons, see Edson 1935; Walbank 1940, pp. 240–241 and 246–248 (cf. pp. 334–335 on chronology); Meloni 1953, pp. 29–60; Gruen 1974; Adams 1982; Dell 1983; cf. Burton 2017, pp. 47–54.

102. Polybius 23.3.4–6, 23.7.4–7; Livy 39.53.1–7, 39.53.9, 40.5.2–5, 40.9.2, 40.10.8–11.4, 40.16.3; cf. 41.23.11.

103. Edson 1935, p. 194.

104. Livy 40.6–7. Chronology: Walbank 1940, pp. 334–335.

105. Livy 40.8–16; cf. Polybius 23.11.

106. Walbank 1979, pp. 234–235; cf. Edson 1935, p. 196; Walbank 1979, pp. 229–235; Gruen 1974, pp. 240–241.

visit to Rome and possible aspirations to succeed him. He therefore decided to send the same two Friends, Philocles and Apelles, who had accompanied Demetrius to Rome in 183 back there to find out more about his son's dealings with Flamininus over the succession.[107] To be on the safe side, Demetrius downplayed any association he had with Rome, not even writing letters to friends there. Evidently, he did not want Perseus and his father to have any reason to suspect him. Then again, his behavior might indicate he knew that Flamininus and the Senate favored his accession.[108]

By the spring of 181 Philip had returned to Paeonia and the territory of the Maedi. Livy states the campaign was to keep the army active and show he was not thinking of going to war with Rome, but there are no grounds for accepting the latter view.[109] With a picked body of troops, Philip climbed to the summit of what Livy calls Mount Haemus, today Mount Musala, the highest peak of the Rila mountain range at over 9,840 feet (3,000 meters). There he sacrificed to Zeus and the Sun, a sacrifice that had political and religious symbolism as the mountain was sacred to the Thracians.[110]

The climb was no easy feat, given the steep slopes and forests higher up, freezing temperatures at night, and constant mist. From the top of the mountain, he could see every surrounding mountain range, as is the case today, but not the Adriatic, the Black Sea, the Danube, and the Alps, as our sources tell the story. On his return, and short of provisions, he put down pockets of resistance among the Dentheletae, foraged for food, and in the Strymon valley besieged the Maedian city of Petra, which capitulated and surrendered hostages, before returning home to Pella.[111]

Both of his sons accompanied him on this campaign, but at Stobi Demetrius returned to Pella.[112] Perhaps relations between them were strained and Demetrius wanted to take further care not to feed his father's suspicions.

---

107. Livy 40.20.3–4; cf. 40.11.1–4.

108. Polybius 23.3.4–9; Livy 40.20.5–6, with Walbank 1940, p. 247.

109. Livy 40.21.1–3, 40.22.1–7.

110. Name of the mountain: Walbank 1940, pp. 249–250. Sacredness: Hammond and Walbank 1988, p. 469.

111. Livy 40.22.8–15. On Philip's route and the topography, see Walbank 1940, pp. 249–250; Hammond and Walbank 1988, p. 469 n. 2.

112. Livy 40.21.4–8, with Walbank 1940, p. 250 n. 4. The claim that Demetrius was sent back from Stobi because Philip was finessing plans to invade Italy and did not want him to warn Rome about them is wrong: Livy 40.21.7.

Then again, Philip might not have wanted to risk the lives of both his sons, for Livy tells us that since the king was taking Perseus with him, he sent Demetrius back "to safeguard his hopes for the future and protect the realm."[113]

Significantly, though, Philip sent Didas, his governor of Paeonia, back with Demetrius to try to find out more about his son's views on Rome and the Macedonian throne.[114] Didas sent a message to Perseus that Demetrius was planning to flee to Rome, which Perseus immediately reported to Philip, who at the time was besieging Petra. The king did not act, preferring to wait for the return of Apelles and Philocles from Rome with their news, but he ordered that Demetrius be put under surveillance.

When Apelles and Philocles finally returned they brought with them a letter they said was from Flamininus, which stressed that Demetrius did not intend to harm any family members and urged Philip to be lenient toward him as his youth and desire for the throne had led him astray.[115] This was damning evidence, and to corroborate it Philip had one of his son's close friends, Herodorus, tortured, who gave no particulars about Demetrius' treachery. The letter, however, was a forgery, which even Livy states, with Apelles and Philocles having "earlier worked out in Macedonia the report they would make from Rome."[116] Possibly there may have been some type of correspondence that was wrongly interpreted by Livy's source (not Polybius).[117] Still, Perseus continued to use the letter as evidence to denounce his brother to Philip, though the king still refused to do anything.[118] Ultimately, however, Demetrius was doomed from the moment the two brothers quarreled.[119]

In the spring of 180 Philip left Thessalonica for Demetrias in Thessaly.[120] He sent Perseus to Amphipolis to receive Thracian hostages and Demetrius and Didas to Astraeum in Paeonia, ostensibly instructing Didas to kill

---

113. Livy 40.21.6, with Gruen 1974, pp. 241–242; cf. Meloni 1953, p. 48.

114. Livy 40.21.9–11, 40.23.1–4.

115. Livy 40.23.6–8.

116. Livy 40.23.6.

117. Walbank 1940, p. 251; Meloni 1953, p. 52; Gruen 1974, pp. 243–244; cf. pp. 223–224. Perhaps his source was Achaean: Edson 1935, pp. 196–198; Walbank 1938, p. 65 n. 51; Walbank 1940, p. 251.

118. Livy 40.24.1–2.

119. Walbank 1940, pp. 251–252; Meloni 1953, pp. 29–34 and 41–55; Errington 1971a, pp. 199–200; Adams 1982, pp. 242–244.

120. Livy 40.24.3.

Demetrius.[121] Didas called Demetrius to a sacrifice at Heraclea and had him poisoned at the dinner. Realizing what had happened, Demetrius managed to stagger to his room in great pain but was still alive sometime later as two men were said to have suffocated him with his bedding.[122] Possibly poison and smothering are meant to exaggerate the cruelty of Philip's agents.[123]

The whole episode is problematic and raises several questions: How did the Senate view Demetrius, and did he aspire to the kingship? Might Perseus have planned to remove Demetrius out of jealously or, if he were illegitimate, fear that Demetrius would challenge him for the throne? Did Perseus manipulate his father to execute Demetrius? Or was their dispute about something else?

Whether Rome occupied itself in Macedonia's dynastic affairs and Demetrius had his eyes on the throne are contentious issues. In late 183 (or perhaps early 182) Philip executed several leading Macedonians, possibly having to do with dissatisfaction over his relocation of peoples or some sort of conspiracy involving Demetrius; he even arrested their children and put them to death.[124] Clearly something caused him to act as he did, but whether it was about the succession is unknown. Demetrius may well have been more sympathetic to Rome than Perseus, perhaps because of the six years he had spent there as a hostage from 197 to 191, but that does not mean he was the preferred successor.[125] And even if Flamininus did like Demetrius as a person, it is too much of a leap to say he intended to form some sort of "Roman party" in Macedonia or that the Senate intended Demetrius to be a client king.[126]

---

121. Livy 40.24.3–4.

122. Livy 40.24.5–8; cf. Diodorus 29.25.

123. Walbank 1940, p. 252.

124. Polybius 23.10.8–11, 23.10.15; cf. Livy 40.3.7–5.1; Plutarch, *Moralia* 53e, naming Samus, Pyrrichus, and Ademetus. Polybius 23.10.9 claims they were executed, but he may have assumed this because under Macedonian law relatives of those executed for treason could also be put to death (Curtius 8.6.28). A conspiracy over his transpopulation move is believed by Walbank 1940, pp. 244–245.

125. Gruen 1974. Golan 1989, pp. 117–118, believes Perseus underwent some type of reeducation to make him favor Rome.

126. Edson 1935, pp. 191–193 and 201 (quote on p. 193); Walbank 1940, pp. 239 and 241; Meloni 1953, pp. 29–34 and 41–60; Errington 1971a, pp. 198–199; Adams 1982, pp. 243–245; Waterfield 2014, pp. 161–164, accept that the Senate had this plan; *contra* Gruen 1974, pp. 234–235. There is also the question of whether Flamininus had the Senate's support, on which see Edson 1935, pp. 193–194 and 200–201; cf. Dell 1983, pp. 74–75.

Likewise, the idea that Perseus had his brother killed because of his illegitimacy is also doubtful as his father's actions showed him to be heir to the throne, for which he needed to be legitimate.[127] Finally, there is no evidence about what caused the brothers' falling out. It may even have been something personal—for example, Perseus did not seem keen to marry the princess of the Bastarnae, as we mentioned above. What if he had caused the rift by proposing Demetrius, who was not heir to the throne, as her husband? Demetrius, who had a high opinion of himself, might have taken umbrage over Perseus' move, leading to enmity between the two. Finally, we cannot ignore that Demetrius died from natural causes and the sources seized on his death to disparage Philip and Perseus, given both were Rome's enemies.[128]

A postscript to the affair is that during his stay at Demetrias in the winter of 180–179, a grieving Philip was told that Apelles and Philocles had forged the letter from Flamininus. Subsequently, their secretary, Xychus, who had accompanied them to Rome, testified to their guilt rather than suffer torture. Philip ordered the seizure of the two men—Philocles was caught but Apelles fled for safety to Italy though he was later hunted down and killed.[129] Philip, it was said, was even more distressed over putting his son to death and because Perseus, who kept his distance from him, was still alive.[130]

Philip's Death

Always a risk for Philip was a Dardanian invasion of Macedonia. In 179 he moved from Demetrias to Thessalonica and thence to Amphipolis, from where he planned an ambitious offensive in tandem with the Bastarnae against the Dardanians, after which Livy fantastically stated that Philip would send the Bastarnae to plunder in Italy.[131] Philip wanted to overrun the territory of the Dardanians and for the families of the Bastarnae to occupy the Polog, the region of Dardania closest to Macedonia, and so be his friendly

---

127. Livy 40.5.2–5; cf. 39.53.5–6; Plutarch, *Paullus* 8.11–12, from Polybius (that part of his work is missing).

128. Given the details about the court in the later writers, Polybius' sources must have had knowledge of it, so may have been Macedonian "court sources," who were anti-Perseus: Walbank 1940, p. 252; Gruen 1974, pp. 224–225, citing bibliography, to which add Dreyer 2013.

129. Livy 40.54.9–55.8, 42.5.4.

130. Livy 40.55.8.

131. Livy 40.57; Justin 23.3. That Philip planned to invade Italy is "absurd": Hammond 1992, p. 361 n. 16. See Burton 2017, pp. 99–100, also in doubt and quoting equally skeptical scholars.

neighbors. He had arranged with the Thracian kings for the Bastarnae's safe passage through central Thrace but sent as overseer Antigonus, a nephew of Antigonus III Doson—the same man who had brought him the news at Demetrias about Apelles and Philocles and the forged letter of Flamininus. Perseus went with the vanguard into Thrace, with Philip leading the main army from Amphipolis.

The problem for Philip with this campaign was that the Dardanians were friends of Rome, so he risked Roman troops returning to Greek soil. But his foreign policy was directed to his borders even if it did cause tension with Rome. It is likely that this Dardanian operation is what our hostile sources confuse (deliberately or not) with preparations for another war against Rome, which his son Perseus inherited when he succeeded his father the same year (chapter 9).[132] But at this point in his reign such thoughts cannot have been in Philip's mind: our sources are again projecting a wrong image of him.

The Bastarnae set out in the summer of 179 and sent their messengers to meet Philip at Amphipolis. But not far from there they received the surprising news that Philip had died, which, says Livy, was fortuitous—presumably for Rome and the Dardanians.[133] The advancing Bastarnae were now in limbo and unsure what to do.[134] The deal that Philip had with the Thracians collapsed, and Antigonus could not prevent fights from breaking out between both peoples. On top of that, one night a huge thunderstorm so terrified the Bastarnae that many of them returned home. Still, at least 30,000 under a man named Clondicus forged ahead and eventually settled on Dardanian land.[135]

Philip died at the age of fifty-eight. The cause of his death, if we believe our sources, was due to a rapid mental illness beginning at Amphipolis from feelings of guilt over ordering Demetrius' death and as a result suffering insomnia and anxiety.[136] If we follow one ancient source, he died in November–December 179, hence he reigned a little over forty-two years.[137] November though was too late in the year for the planned Dardanian campaign, and

---

132. Polybius 22.18.8–11; Livy 41.23.9, 41.23.11; cf. Walbank 1940, p. 254; Walbank 1977, p. 81; Adams 1982, pp. 239–240; Errington 1990, p. 210.

133. Livy 40.57.2, with Briscoe 2008, p. 561.

134. Livy 40.57.3.

135. Livy 40.58.1–8.

136. Livy 40.56.8–9; Diodorus 29.25; Plutarch, *Paullus* 8.9.1; Justin 32.3.4–5.

137. Porphry, *BNJ* 260 F 31.9.

given Philip's other commitments in the last few months before his death, he likely died in the summer or early fall of 179.[138]

"Excellent and Loyal Conduct"

Pausanias quotes an oracle that was said to have foretold the rise of Macedonia under Philip II and its fall under our Philip:[139]

> O Macedones, boasting of your Argead kings,
> To you the reign of a Philip will be both good and evil.
> The first will make you kings over cities and peoples;
> The other will lose all your honor,
> Defeated by men from west and east.

It is hard to dispute that Philip II was "good" for Macedonia, given his legacy, but was our Philip "evil"? Should he even be compared to the earlier Philip, when several kings in between—including Alexander the Great—had not served their kingdoms well (cf. chapter 2)?[140] Leaving aside Pausanias' further dig that Philip was attracted to his namesake predecessor because of his use of deception and treachery, their worlds were greatly different. That is why Diodorus, writing in the first century and looking back to the context of the Romans' defeat of Antiochus and Philip V, can say that they were "the greatest monarchs of that age."[141] For his time, Philip V is deserving of a better press, given his achievements no matter his flaws.[142]

The principal criticisms of Philip are of course his loss to Rome in the Second Macedonian War, and then the settlements in Macedonia and Greece. We might even blame him for his alliance with Hannibal in 215, the possible catalyst for Rome's involvement in Greece. But Rome had been busy in Greece since the days of the First Illyrian War, sometime before Hannibal came on the scene, and Philip's defiance of Rome was to be expected of any

---

138. Walbank 1940, p. 295.

139. Pausanias 7.8.8–9 (adapted from Loeb).

140. Worthington 2014 for the reigns of Philip II and Alexander the Great, with critical appraisal of the latter not as a general or leader of men but as king of Macedonia.

141. Diodorus 31.8.

142. Pausanias 7.7.5–6. See the concluding remarks on Philip of Walbank 1940, pp. 258–275; Hammond and Walbank 1988, pp. 472–487; D'Agostini 2019, pp. 157–166.

king seeking to safeguard his realm and remain independent. The priority he gave to border security was seen in the way he reacted without hesitation to Illyrian, especially Dardanian, invasions, and his plan of taking back Illyria from Rome, but the Romans were not going to let that happen.

The simple fact was that once the Senate decided on something, nothing would stop it from doing it. Had Philip II or Alexander the Great or Antigonus II faced the Romans we might write a different account of their reigns. That Philip V was able to hold Rome at bay for so long was a tribute to his qualities as king and general, not to mention the fighting prowess of the Macedonian army. Falling to Rome was inevitable for anyone, for the Romans were unstoppable, and coexistence and cooperation as equals with them impossible. Philip's stance, perverted by our literary writers, was something to be lauded, given who he was up against. So too is his stoical way of looking at things: in the post-Cynoscephalae period, it must have been difficult for him to support Rome as he did and then be treated so contemptuously. Again, his personal character comes to the fore, which was always a driving force in the way he conducted himself as a man and as a king.

Philip was at war for thirty-four years of his forty-two-year reign. As a general, he rightly knew how vital it was to maintain his supply lines while disrupting those of his enemy. He was also a formidable and daring strategist, decisive in action, quick to seize opportunities in the field, and always in the thick of battle. Even after his defeat at Cynoscephalae he embarked on further campaigning as if he—like Alexander the Great—could not cope with anything but a life of military activity. Perhaps this was also to keep the loyalty of his army, especially after Cynoscephalae when he remained king only by virtue of the Senate. Philip's hold on the kingship after 197 was very different from what it had been before then.

He was also unlucky, as when he bolted thinking a large Roman navy was heading toward him in his attack on Apollonia or the inclement weather on the day of Cynoscephalae. He also failed himself and his army on that day by not managing his phalanx more effectively. But even after his loss, what troops he had remained loyal to him as his campaigns in Thrace show. Nor was there any challenge to his extraordinary measure to increase troop numbers by forcing his people to bear children for the future of the army.

As a king, he was diplomatic, as in his dealings with the Achaeans and Rome until the latter's strong-arm tactics ended dialogue. But he was also ruthless, not only toward captured places like Cius, Myrlea, and Thasos, but also toward those who opposed him, including their families.[143] Nor can

---

143. Livy 40.4.1–5.1.

we forget the steps he took to free himself of his guardians inherited from Antigonus III once he decided he no longer needed them. But at the end of the day, any king had to take steps to maintain his kingship, the loyalty of his subjects, and to rule in his own right.

Equally significant, Philip knew his limitations. Polybius speaks of him having the grand ambition of universal rule, for which defeating Rome was a necessary step. But Philip's resources, in particular his navy, were never up to taking on Rome's legions and its huge and numerous war vessels, even when Rome was in dire straits during the Second Punic War. Indeed, it could be argued that the aftermath of the battle of Cannae (216) and his alliance with Hannibal (215) presented Philip with a golden opportunity to take on Rome. That he did not shows he never had that intention. Hellenistic kings generally were aggressive and ambitious, but that is not the same as craving universal dominion.[144]

For Philip, Hannibal's value was in taking Rome's attention away from his principal objective: getting possession of Illyria. He ended up misjudging what he would get out of that alliance and underestimated the resilience of Rome, but at the time he could hardly have known this. When he added to his fleet it was nothing to do with any imperialistic aims but to counter the Ptolemies and Seleucids and then Rome at sea, but even then, his navy in Illyria and in the Aegean failed dismally and was either destroyed or curtailed.[145] This record did not bode well for any Italian venture, and in any case, as has been rightly said, "Once the Romans had intervened decisively east of the Adriatic in the Second Macedonian War, one can no longer speak of a meaningful Macedonian naval policy."[146]

We might criticize Philip for not attending to socio-economic grievances plaguing Macedonia until after his defeat at Cynoscephalae. Yet he remained an efficient administrator throughout his reign, as his various edicts and letters to officials in towns throughout his kingdom illustrate. He showed an acute understanding of problems that needed to be addressed and moved to do so quickly and resolutely when dissatisfaction occurred, as his *diagramma* (edict) about infantry organization and management of war booty of 218 proves. After 196, he revived the economy by stimulating

---

144. Cf. Walbank 1983. Hellenistic kings generally were bellicose and aggressive: Eckstein 2006, pp. 79–117, on kings, though Eckstein 2010, p. 230, exaggeratedly claims that "there is little reason to doubt that Philip himself had vast ambitions, including even universal rule."

145. Walbank 1982, pp. 225–233 and 234–235.

146. Walbank 1982, p. 234.

agricultural and timber production, reviving and opening new mines, and introducing new coinage, so much so that Perseus inherited a robust and prosperous kingdom. It is a pity Philip did not devote the same consideration to reforming the phalanx after its signal defeat at Cynoscephalae. If he had, then the Third Macedonian War between Perseus and Rome may not have had a different outcome, but Rome would have been more bloodied in it (chapter 10).

Philip should be rated for his successes in reconstructing Macedonia.[147] He certainly does not deserve the way that Polybius and other writers present him because of their personal biases toward Rome, nor be cast as a tragic figure acting emotionally rather than rationally.[148] Likewise, judging Philip's policies and actions with hindsight leads to a warped picture: they need to be assessed as and when they occurred. Then the picture changes.

Some scholars echo Polybius that at the end of his reign Philip was an old man, unable to sleep, broken-hearted over the death of Demetrius, and racked with guilt because of all his cruelty.[149] Old he may have been, perhaps even beside himself at what had happened to Demetrius, though that is supposition. But he was not a disillusioned and worn-out man. When he died he had turned his kingdom around from its weak position in 197, widening Macedonia's sphere of influence in Thrace, increasing his manpower reserves, planning for the future, and was on the eve of launching a major attack on the Dardanians. These are the signs of a ruler adapting to a new normal while bolstering his kingdom and continuing to be a warrior king. It is worth remembering that out of his reign of forty-two years, only about eight were when he was at peace.

Philip was a hard-drinking and hard-living individual, who at times was reckless and prone to emotion, yet he was no different from other Macedonian kings, and he had a penchant for turning adversity to advantage. That quality cannot be learned but is inherent. He should not be seen as a disappointing king whose grandiose and unrealistic aspirations steered Macedonia to defeat at the hands of Rome and in the process ended the history of one of the most formidable armies of antiquity. His reign is not a mere postscript to his predecessors and an episode in the sad decline of Macedonia. He deserves to

---

147. Walbank 1940, pp. 255–257.

148. See Walbank 1938 (with observations on Polybius' view of tragedy); cf. Walbank 1970, but see Dreyer 2013.

149. Walbank 1940, p. 258; Burton 2017, p. 54, drawing on Polybius 23.10.1–3, 23.12–14.

be brought out of the shadow of previous great kings and rated as a ruler who strove to preserve his kingdom's independence and ensure its safety, no matter the odds. After all, we should not forget that it was Rome that declared war in 200, and Philip was expected to defend his kingdom's liberty.

As a counter to Pausanias' oracle quoted at the start of this section, the last word on Philip should be from those who knew him best: the Macedonians themselves. They held him in high esteem and paid him special honors, perhaps even deifying him on death.[150] But the inscription on a dedication at Delos says it all: "The community of Macedones (honors) king Philip, son of king Demetrius, for his excellent and loyal conduct."[151]

---

150. See Hammond and Walbank 1988, p. 487 n. 12, with reference.

151. *SIG*³ 575, trans. Hammond and Walbank 1988, pp. 486–487. Economic recovery and coinage: Hammond and Walbank 1988, pp. 458–468; foreign policy: Hammond and Walbank 1988, pp. 468–472; general assessment of Philip's reign: Walbank 1938; Walbank 1940, pp. 258–275; Gruen 1974; Hammond and Walbank 1988, pp. 472–487; Dreyer 2013.

9

Perseus: Last of the Antigonids

PERSEUS' SHORT REIGN (179–168) saw plenty of action, including moves to improve Macedonia's influence in Greece and warfare with Rome, beginning in 171 (the Third Macedonian War). Although he was not as adept a statesman or military commander as his father, he refused to bow to anyone, including the Romans. He also had a long memory, for he was hostile to Rome before he became king, and not especially enamored of the Athenians. As with his father, our ancient writers are malicious, besmirching Perseus' character and damning him for waging war on Rome, hence challenging the city's rise to world power.[1] We must therefore be cautious in accepting what they say about Perseus.

Early Years

Details of Perseus' birth and early life are largely unknown (figure 9.1). He was born in the latter part of the 210s, perhaps even 212, for he was in his early twenties in 189 when he commanded a contingent of troops in his father's campaign against the Aetolians.[2] His mother Polycratea was a member of a distinguished family from Argos in the Peloponnese.[3] Yet some sources suggest he was the bastard and unloved son of his father and

---

1. Pugliese 2014. On sources, see Hammond and Walbank 1988, pp. 488–490 and 532–533; Dileo 2003; Scuderi 2004; Pugliese 2014, and cf. the appendix.

2. Meloni 1953, pp. 1–4 (arguing for 212).

3. Meloni 1953, pp. 4–15.

The Last Kings of Macedonia and the Triumph of Rome. Ian Worthington, Oxford University Press.
© Oxford University Press 2023. DOI: 10.1093/oso/9780197520055.003.0010

FIGURE 9.1. Perseus. © The Trustees of the British Museum.

an Argive woman.[4] Since Philip intended Perseus to succeed him, he was clearly legitimate.

Like other boys, Perseus would have been raised in the Macedonian tradition, hence learning to fight, ride a horse, and hunt from an early age, and he would have been a Royal Page from fourteen to eighteen years old. Presumably he was well educated and a philhellene like his predecessors. Polybius states that he was different from his father as he did not chase after women or drink excessively, ate moderate amounts of food, kept himself fit by all manner of physical exercise, and generally had showed a royal dignity and "gravity and composure not unsuited to his years." In the next breath Polybius adds that all these attributes applied only at the start of his reign.[5]

4. Livy 40.5.5, 40.5.7–9; Plutarch, *Paullus* 8.11–12.

5. Polybius 25.3.5–8.

Perseus had been groomed by his father as his successor. For example, in 199 (when only a young boy!) he was given command of a force in the north against the Dardanians, then served with his father's troops against Galba, and in 189 we find him fighting in Aetolia.[6] In 183 Philip had founded and named a city, Perseis, after him, presumably to show he was heir. There is a bizarre story that Philip was so grief-stricken and incensed when he discovered that Perseus had tricked him into ordering the death of his younger son Demetrius that the king refused to have anything to do with Perseus; instead, he decided that a certain Antigonus the son of Echecrates, one of Antigonus III Doson's nephews, would succeed him.[7] He even took him on a tour of his kingdom to introduce him to the people, and had it not been for Philip's doctor secretly sending news of Philip's death to Perseus, Antigonus might have assumed the throne.[8] Antigonus might have endeared himself to Philip, but the story is surely false and may have been a product of pro-Roman circles to discredit Perseus. One of Perseus' first actions on becoming king was to execute Antigonus, though this was probably not to remove a potential opponent but because he had failed to protect the Bastarnae from the Thracians (p. 174).[9]

Accession and First Years

Perseus received word that Philip's condition was deteriorating rapidly in a secret communication sent by the royal doctor Calligenes.[10] He was in Thrace at the time and rushed back to Amphipolis to find his father was already deceased. Philip had died on the eve of his campaign against the Dardanians, with his allies the Bastarnae marching to support him. If news of his death became known, the Dardanians might well turn on the Bastarnae, and worse, taking advantage of Perseus' absence, strike at Macedonia. In fact, when news of Philip's death broke, the Sapaeans of Thrace ravaged eastern Macedonia, as

6. Livy 38.5.10, 38.7.1; see too Walbank 1940, pp. 242–246; Meloni 1953, pp. 16–29. On his first command at only about twelve years old, Antigonus I Gonatas did something similar for his son, the future Demetrius II, at the end of the Chremonidean War in 261, as Robin Waterfield pointed out to me.

7. Livy 40.56.1–11.

8. Livy 40.56.1–11. On Antigonus as successor, see Edson 1935, pp. 199–200; Walbank 1940, p. 253; cf. Matyszak 2009, p. 125, accepting the story.

9. Livy 40.58.9; see Walbank 1940, p. 255; Hammond and Walbank 1988, p. 491 (treason).

10. Livy 40.56.7; see too Meloni 1953, pp. 55–60.

we shall see. It was better, then, for Perseus not to disclose what had happened to Philip but to assume command of the army and return to Pella to take the throne before anyone realized what had happened.

Perseus was the last Antigonid king.[11] It is often thought that he immediately sent a diplomatic mission to the Senate to renew his father's alliance (*amicitia*), but there may not have been time as Appian tells us that he was hit with problems affecting Macedonia's border security and mining interests, directly impacting its economy.[12] He would more plausibly have dealt with these first, before any interaction with Rome.

Seizing advantage of Philip's death, Abrupolis, the king of the Thracian tribe of the Sapaeans, to Macedonia's east close to Abdera, attacked eastern Macedonia as far as Amphipolis and raided the precious Mount Pangaeum mining region. Reacting with the same speed and decisiveness as his father, Perseus led an army against the invaders and expelled Abrupolis from his throne, a risky venture as that Thracian king was a friend and ally (*socius et amicus*) of Rome.[13] However, the Romans did not berate Perseus nor help the unfortunate Abrupolis, though they did exploit the matter later.[14] Perseus' campaign is also cited in inscriptional evidence, for in a dedication set up at Amphipolis we hear of "the campaigns into Thrace," the plural indicating there was more than one.[15] Another inscription (from Delphi) lists Rome's grievances against Perseus in 172 and refers to separate undertakings against Thrace and Abrupolis.[16]

Perseus could now comfortably open channels with Rome. Fearing the Senate might have a critical view of him, given his father's history with Rome and the death of his popular brother Demetrius, he sent an envoy to stress his friendship and ask for the renewal of the *amicitia* between Rome and his

---

11. Reign: Meloni 1953; Errington 1971a, pp. 202–226; Gyioka 1975 (not seen); Hammond and Walbank 1988, pp. 488–558; Hammond 1992, pp. 362–381; Matyszak 2009, pp. 126–156; Waterfield 2014, pp. 165–167 and 173–193; Burton 2017, pp. 56–175; cf. Derow 1989, pp. 301–319; Errington 1990, pp. 212–217; Eckstein 2010, pp. 240–246; King 2018, pp. 256–260. See too Golan 1979/80; Bousquet 1981; Pugliese 2014.

12. Appian, *Macedonian Wars* 11.6; cf. Walbank 1979, p. 275.

13. Polybius 22.18.2–3; Livy 42.13.5; Diodorus 29.33; Pausanias 7.10.6. See too Meloni 1953, pp. 61–67.

14. Polybius 22.18.2; Diodorus 29.33; Pausanias 7.10.7.

15. *SEG* 31.614, with Koukouli-Chrysanthaki 1981, p. 233.

16. *SIG*³ 643, with Hammond and Walbank 1988, p. 492.

father.[17] It was normal in Hellenistic monarchies for a new king to renew any of his predecessor's treaties, hence his move need not be interpreted as pandering to Rome.[18] Despite this goodwill mission our sources accuse him of treachery in renewing the *amicitia* as he had already decided to make war on Rome.[19] Nonetheless, the Senate reaffirmed the *amicitia*, though perhaps not until the following year (178), and it remained active until 171 when war broke out.[20] The delay of several months perhaps indicates the Senate's disdainful stance toward Macedonia—no different from its treatment of his father, which Perseus would not have forgotten.

Now secure on the throne, Perseus turned to other matters affecting his people. He issued a general recall of exiles to Macedonia, even those banished for treasonable offenses, and restored their property, cancelled all state debts, and released prisoners.[21] There is some disagreement on the scope of the debt cancellation, with scholars arguing that he meant only state-owed debts and not individual ones as well; the matter cannot be resolved with certainty.[22] What we can say is that his decree was welcomed for obvious reasons. He may have intended it to distance himself from his father, though again a new king was expected to show benevolence to his subjects.[23]

Also in 178, after the renewal of the *amicitia*, Perseus married Laodice, the daughter of Seleucus IV of Syria, the successor to Antiochus III.[24] It seems that his previous wife, a princess of the Bastarnae, had died before then—by his own hand, it was said.[25] The Syrians could not march an army through Asia

---

17. Polybius 25.3.1; Livy 40.58.8; cf. Diodorus 29.30; Zonaras 9.22, with Meloni 1953, pp. 68–73; Adams 1982, p. 245; Gruen 1984, p. 403. Gruen 1973, pp. 134–135, notes that renewal of the *amicitia* shows that Philip did not have a formal alliance (*summachia*) with Rome in 196. Livy 41.24.6: he was saluted as king by the Romans. Livy 41.45.93: the Senate recognized him as king.

18. Errington 1971a, p. 106.

19. Cf. Walbank 1979, p. 275; Pugliese 2014, p. 152.

20. Polybius 25.3.1; Livy 42.25.4, 42.25.10; Diodorus 29.30 ("deceiving the deceiver on his own ground"); Appian, *Macedonian Wars* 11.5; Zonaras 9.22.2, with Meloni 1953, pp. 68 and 70–72; Gruen 1984, p. 403; Hammond and Walbank 1988, p. 493; Burton 2017, p. 57 with n. 1. Briscoe 2012, p. 235, that the treaty was not renewed.

21. Polybius 25.3.1–3, with Walbank 1979, pp. 275–276; see too Meloni 1953, pp. 74–77.

22. For example, Mendels 1978, pp. 56–59 (state only); Meloni, pp. 76–77 (everyone).

23. Gruen 1984, p. 404. Customary: Golan 1979/80, pp. 120–121.

24. Livy 42.12.3. Referred to as Queen Laodice in a Delian inscription: *SIG*³ 639.

25. Livy 42.5.4.

Minor or sail to Greece under the terms of the Treaty of Apamea (188), hence the Rhodians, with whom Perseus quickly cultivated a friendship (perhaps learning from his father's clashes with their powerful fleet), brought Laodice to him; he gave each rower in the vessel carrying his bride a gold headband as reward.[26] This political marriage made Perseus an ally of Syria. If, however, he was anticipating Syrian backing in any of his ventures, he never received it, for once Seleucus died his successor was more interested in Egypt.[27] Probably Perseus also married off his sister Apame to Prusias II, king of Bithynia, the son of Philip's ally Prusias I, who had died in 182. These marriages further widened Perseus' network of alliances, though it hardly follows they were made with the intention of attacking Rome.[28]

Perseus and the Greeks

Perseus publicized his recent pardons to exiles and those in debt in the sanctuaries of Apollo at Delos and Delphi and in the shrine of Itonian Athena in probably Coronea in Boeotia.[29] Delphi was an especially prominent site in Greek religion, visited by countless Greeks and foreigners every year, and several Macedonian kings had made donations to the god or set up their own monuments there for religious and propaganda reasons.[30] Perseus therefore was not establishing any precedents but following a tradition. At the same time, the prestige of Delphi allowed him to promote himself and his dynasty.

To begin with, he set up a gilded statue of himself by the temple of Apollo along with copies of Demetrius II Poliorcetes' letters and treaties inscribed on a series of prominent sculptures.[31] Since Prusias II of Bithynia and Eumenes II of Pergamum had statues at Delphi, it made sense for the geographically closer

---

26. Polybius 25.4.8–10.

27. See Helliesen 1981 for the argument that the Antigonid and Seleucid dynasties were bound together before this marriage.

28. Livy 42.12.3; Appian, *Macedonian Wars* 11.1, 7; cf. Burton 2017, pp. 103–110, on Rome not concerned about the dynastic alliances.

29. Polybius 25.3.2, with Mendels 1978, pp. 55–59. The shrine at Coronea: Hammond and Walbank 1988, p. 493, but Walbank 1979, p. 276, suggests the one near Halus in Thessaly. Polybius 25.3.1 says his benevolences were intended to gain popularity in Greece; his policy was *Ellenokopein* or "to play the Greek" (*Ellenokopein*): Derow 1989, p. 301; see too Walbank 1979, pp. 81 and 275; Burton 2017, p. 59 with n. 12.

30. See Miller 2000.

31. Gilded statue: Plutarch, *Paullus* 28.4. On the measures, see Jacquemin, Laroche, and Lefèvre 1995; Lefèvre 1998; cf. Kousser 2010, p. 528.

Macedonian king to have one as well for all to see.[32] Why he had sculptures displaying his great-grandfather's letters and treaties rather than, say, a statue of Antigonus I Monophthalmus, to whom the Antigonid line traced its ancestry, strikes us as odd. Perhaps his measure gives us an insight into which of his ancestors he admired or even emulated.

Another reason might have to do with Athens, which was still an influential city and the one to which Macedonian kings paid special attention. The Athenians had bestowed various extravagant honors on Monophthalmus and Poliorcetes for liberating them from Demetrius of Phalerum's rule in 307. These had included a gold statue of the pair in the city and one at the entrance to the sanctuary in Delphi.[33] In 303–302 they erected another "liberation monument" to Poliorcetes when he took up residence in the city, this time an expensive equestrian statue.[34] But then in 200 they had smashed the statues in the city when they cursed Philip V and kings before him (pp. 113–114).[35] Their act may have rankled Philip more than we think, and by extension Perseus. The latter therefore seized the opportunity to showcase Poliorcetes, who had been an actual king of Macedonia—unlike Monophthalmus—at this prime location.

Delphi had another appeal as well: the Amphictyonic League. Philip had not been a member of this august body, but inscriptional evidence shows that by 178 two Macedonian envoys "from King Perseus" sat on its council.[36] This was a tribute to Perseus and his kingdom's prestige.[37] Perseus' diplomatic use of the Amphictyony was why in 172 Rome wanted him banned from sacred ceremonies at Delphi, hence taking his membership of the council, as we shall see.[38]

---

32. See too Miller 2000, pp. 279–280.

33. Pausanias 10.10.2.

34. Brogan 2003, pp. 198–205, citing bibliography.

35. Fragments of an equestrian statue, perhaps that of Poliorcetes, were discovered in a well during excavations in the Agora in 1971: Shear 1973, pp. 165–168 and plate 36; Brogan 2003, pp. 198–203.

36. SIG^3 636, lines 5–6, with Meloni 1953, pp. 94–104; Walbank 1977, pp. 89–90; Hammond and Walbank 1988, pp. 493–494 with n. 1; Pugliese 2014, pp. 149–150. Giovannini 1970 argues that Philip did not lose his place on the council, hence Perseus' accession brought no change to Macedonia's position in central Greece, but against this see Walbank 1977, pp. 89–90.

37. Gruen 1984, pp. 403–408; Hammond and Walbank 1988, pp. 494–495; Derow 1989, p. 302; Pugliese 2014, p. 150.

38. Adams 1982, p. 247 with n. 73, claims that Perseus did not view the league in this way, but Rome's reaction shows this cannot be.

Further afield in Greece, Perseus was likely capitalizing on the rampant suffering affecting both rich and poor and even *stasis* in several states from social conflicts and economic problems linked to grain shortages and monetary debt.[39] For example, in 173 he apparently ended the party strife that had broken out the previous year in Aetolia, and then cancelled all debts plaguing the Achaeans and in Perrhaebia and Thessaly to avoid further civil unrest.[40] Boeotia was also in severe disarray thanks to rival factions wanting either to abolish or maintain the Boeotian League.[41] Perseus approved of the latter and concluded a treaty with the league in either 174 or 173.[42]

As with his father, there is nothing to suggest his actions stemmed from ideological motives nor is there actual evidence that he interfered so directly in Achaea, Perrhaebia, and Thessaly—these allegations were likely the product of Roman propaganda to justify going to war against him, as we discuss below.[43] Perseus, like Philip, was an opportunist who "was quite ready to fish in troubled waters, and to do so without pursuing any consistent social programme."[44]

Perseus actively engaged in Greece only once, when in 174 he marched against his subjects in Dolopia north of Aetolia, who had tortured and murdered his governor there, to reestablish Macedonian authority.[45] After that campaign he returned to Pella via Delphi, where he stayed for three days, perhaps checking on the progress of the monuments mentioned above, and Thessaly. Eumenes would later claim that Perseus' presence in Greece helped "the worst cause" and was designed to "crush" the aristocratic, pro-Roman factions as the king was out to win over everyone.[46] That is not so. Perseus took the route he did as a "publicity move" to allow the Greeks to meet the

---

39. Livy 42.5.7–10. See Sherk 1984, p. 4, and see especially Walsh 2000.

40. Livy 42.5.7–12 (from Polybius: Briscoe 2012, p. 168); Diodorus 29.33; cf. Meloni 1953, pp. 104–112; Deininger 1971, pp. 135–191; Mendels 1978, pp. 59–62; Briscoe 2012, pp. 168–171; Pugliese 2014, p. 148; Burton 2017, pp. 117–119.

41. Polybius 20.6.1–6; see too Gruen 1976, pp. 43–46; Deininger 1971, pp. 135–191; Hennig 1977, pp. 119–148; Burton 2017, pp. 117–119.

42. Meloni 1953, pp. 148–149 (dating the aid to 173); Deininger 1971, p. 153 n. 1; Golan 1979/80, pp. 128–133; Burton 2017, p. 61.

43. Mendels 1978; cf. Gruen 1976; Pugliese 2014, pp. 147–151.

44. Walbank 1977, p. 87, and see pp. 87–88.

45. Livy 41.22.4, 42.13.8; Appian, *Macedonian Wars* 11.6, with Meloni 1953, pp. 131–135.

46. Livy 42.13.8–9, but see Livy 41.22.7–8.

new king.[47] Then again, in visiting Delphi and marching through Thessaly, he had taken an army well beyond his borders and so could be accused of a show of strength.[48]

Aside from publicity, border security was always paramount to kings; Perseus was no different. He was acutely aware that a Roman army could easily march through Thessaly, which had been granted independence in the settlement after Cynoscephalae, and in tandem with the Aetolians, who were subject to Rome, launch an attack on Macedonia's southern border.[49] He needed to keep a sharp eye on his relations with northern Thessaly and increase his influence in Greece to protect Macedonia and, taking a leaf out of his father's book, impede enemy supply lines.[50] To this end he sent several embassies to the Greek states and found favor with many of them, much to the upset of Eumenes, who was likewise courting the Greeks.[51]

Eagerness to increase his standing in Greece is why in 174 Perseus attempted to bury the hatchet with the Achaean League, which had enacted a law in 198 after it had gone over to Rome's side forbidding any Macedonian from setting foot in Achaea.[52] He dispatched an embassy offering his friendship as well as his willingness to return any escaped slaves who had taken refuge in Macedonia, which was meant to sway their previous owners.[53] But despite these overtures, to which some were favorably disposed, he was rebuffed by the pro-Roman Aetolian leader Callicrates. In a passionate speech Callicrates spoke of the king's hostile actions since he took the throne and that supporting him would lead to war with Rome, claiming that Perseus had inherited a war from his father.[54] An opposing speech by a certain Archo

---

47. Livy 41.22.5–6. Gruen 1984, p. 406; see too Meloni 1953, pp. 131–135. *SIG*³ 643 dates his visit to Delphi in the Olympic year 174/73.

48. Cf. Polybius 22.18.4, and see Adams 1982, p. 247; Waterfield 2014, p. 167. Show of force: Derow 1989, p. 304.

49. Graninger 2010.

50. Meloni 1953, pp. 196–397.

51. Livy 42.5.1.

52. Livy 41.23.1–2, 41.23.6, with Briscoe 2012, p. 119.

53. Livy 41.23.3 (cf. 41.23.4), with Errington 1971a, p. 205; Burton 2017, pp. 60–61.

54. Livy 41.23.4–24.20, with Meloni 1953, pp. 135–141; Adams 1982, p. 248. Achaea's role in the preliminaries and war discussed at Gruen 1976, pp. 32–35.

spoke in favor of reconciliation with Macedonia, but worry about retribution from Rome carried the day.[55]

The Senate did not react adversely to Perseus at this time, though some senators must have been perturbed when he turned to Thrace and the Bastarnae, which were outside his borders.[56] In probably the early winter of 175–174, the Dardanians and the Bastarnae living in their territory went to war. The latter defeated a contingent of Dardanians but a camp where the families of the Bastarnae were staying was captured and pressure perhaps applied to the men to return home.[57] The Bastarnae suffered another setback in early 174 when many members of a large raiding party in Dardania drowned when the ice of the Danube broke under them. Orosius, who gives us this account, claims that Perseus had instigated the raid as a precursor of all things to an invasion of northern Italy.[58] However, with no navy and Rome at full strength the king was hardly able to contemplate, let alone execute such a plan.

More certain is Perseus' policy in central Thrace in the later 170s, which continued that of his father.[59] Appian claims that Thrace was his "base of operations," implying he held all of it, but that is exaggeration.[60] He made a secret alliance with Cotys, the king of the Odrysians, which gave him access to the main trade route, via the Hebrus valley, to the central plain and Black Sea coast.[61] Diplomatically, he steered clear of the coastal Greek cities of Maronea and Aenus, whose status had been the source of much dispute between Philip and Rome. Perseus was taking care not to antagonize Rome, but his relations with the city were about to deteriorate.

---

55. Livy 41.24.

56. Though Giovannini 1969 argues that the visit to Delphi and appeal to the Greeks were a turning point in his relations with Rome; *contra* Walbank 1977, pp. 86–92.

57. Livy 41.19.7–11, with Meloni 1953, pp. 83–84, and Hammond and Walbank 1988, p. 496, that families were in the camp and used as leverage (Briscoe 2012, p. 102, seems doubtful).

58. Orosius 4.20.34–35 (*auctore Perseo*), with Meloni 1953, pp. 78–86; *contra* Gruen 1984, pp. 405–406; Hammond and Walbank 1988, p. 496. No navy noted too by Gruen 1984, p. 417 n. 106.

59. Meloni 1953, pp. 86–92; Hammond and Walbank 1988, pp. 496–497 and 611–613.

60. Appian, *Macedonian Wars* 11.1; cf. Hammond and Walbank 1988, p. 497, for possessions and routes.

61. Livy 42.29.12.

Tensions with Rome

For the first years of his reign Perseus and Rome were on good terms; as we noted, the Senate renewed its *amicitia* with Macedonia. But when a Dardanian embassy went to Rome to complain that Perseus had linked up with the Bastarnae against the Dardanians, the Senate dispatched an investigative commission led by the ex-consul Aulus Postumius Albinus.[62] No evidence of Perseus joining or even conspiring with the Bastarnae was discovered.

Endeavoring to reassure Rome of his friendship, Perseus sent his own envoys to Rome to stress that he had no desire to endanger what had been determined in 196. The Senate took no direct action against him, nor could it as it had no legal grounds to restrict him, but it ordered him to "make it appear" that he was respecting the treaty with Rome.[63] As has been pointed out, this reaction was a "crude attempt to cow a young ruler and can only have rankled."[64] Rankle it probably did, but for now Perseus followed a careful diplomatic line.

In 173 the Senate dispatched a commission led by the ex-consul Marcus Claudius Marcellus to Greece to try to restore Roman confidence. After managing to bring some peace (albeit short-lived) in Aetolia, Marcellus addressed the Achaeans, complimenting Callicrates for maintaining the exclusion ban on Macedonians.[65] Appius Claudius Pulcher was sent to Perrhaebia and Thessaly, where Flamininus' earlier measure of setting up a group of wealthy nobles to manage affairs had backfired because of mounting debt and exploitation.[66] Pulcher introduced fairer regulations about debt repayment and interest—a sign that Perseus had not solved these issues—but this was a case of too little too late as dissatisfaction with Rome continued.[67]

Another state was contending for the friendship of the Greeks, one that had plagued Philip in his reign: Pergamum. Its king Eumenes II was alarmed at Perseus' dynastic alliances, for Prusias of Bithynia was a bitter rival and the Seleucids wanted to recover their losses in Asia Minor. He was also anxious

62. Polybius 25.6.2–6.

63. Livy 41.19.5–6.

64. Waterfield 2014, p. 167.

65. Aetolia: Livy 42.5.10–6.1. Achaeans: Livy 42.6.1–2.

66. Derow 1989, p. 305.

67. Livy 42.5.9–10, with Meloni 1953, pp. 141–150.

about Perseus' rising popularity in Greece at the cost of his own.[68] In 173 Eumenes reverted to the tried-and-trusted warning to the Senate that Perseus was preparing for war; in response, it sent a commission of five men, led by the consul Gaius Valerius Laevinus, to Macedonia. Finding nothing, and in a snub to Eumenes, the commissioners as per senatorial orders renewed Rome's friendship (*amicitia*) with Antiochus IV and Ptolemy VI.[69]

That did not silence Eumenes. In 172 (perhaps April) he personally went to Rome to condemn Perseus and was well received.[70] Among other things, he claimed that Perseus had been planning a war against Rome for some time as he had inherited it from his father, that he had been conspiring with the Bastarnae, stocking up on supplies, boosting troop numbers, extending his influence in Greece and Asia Minor, and arranging dynastic marriages to challenge Pergamum and Rome.[71] As Appian says, "Of the things that could excite [the Senate's] jealousy, envy, and fear even more strongly than direct accusations, Eumenes omitted nothing."[72] He even warned the Senate that Perseus would invade Italy so it needed to act first.[73] His speech profoundly affected the senators, who voted to keep its contents private.[74]

Perseus sent his own delegate to Rome, a man named Harpalus. The Senate refused to let him answer Eumenes face to face and only allowed him to speak when the Pergamene king had left. A few days later Harpalus finally got to make his plea to the senators that Perseus had neither said nor done anything against Rome, but Harpalus was greeted with skepticism.[75] Nonetheless,

---

68. Gruen 1984, p. 406 with n. 53; Adams 1982, p. 246; see too Kertész 1993, pp. 672–674; Burton 2017, pp. 67 and 102–110. Popularity: Livy 42.5.2–3; cf. Burton 2017, p. 87.

69. Livy 42.6.1–3.

70. Livy 42.11–13.12; Appian, *Macedonian Wars* 11.1, with Meloni 1953, pp. 150–166; Gruen 1984, pp. 409–410; Briscoe 2012, pp. 186–202. See further on Eumenes, Adams 1982, pp. 250–253; Gruen 1984, pp. 550–563; Eckstein 2010, pp. 241–242; Waterfield 2014, pp. 173–174; Burton 2017, p. 67. The passage in Livy is perhaps derived from Polybius, who in turn heard about it from senators, and so is not based on any official recording: Hammond and Walbank 1988, p. 498 with n. 3; see too Gruen 1984, pp. 550–563.

71. Livy 42.11.5–14.1; Appian, *Macedonian Wars* 11.3.

72. Appian, *Macedonian Wars* 11.2.

73. Livy 42.13.11.

74. Livy 42.14.1.

75. Livy 42.14.2–4; Appian, *Macedonian Wars* 11.3; though Diodorus 29.34.1 claims that Harpalus "made no reply." On the discrepancy, cf. Briscoe 2012, pp. 198–199.

some states were not pleased with Eumenes' accusations, especially Pereus' ally Rhodes, which sent its own embassy to Rome to support the Macedonian king.[76]

As he made his way back to Pergamum, Eumenes decided to consult the Oracle of Apollo at Delphi. While walking through a narrow defile there he was struck on the head and shoulders by falling rocks and knocked unconscious.[77] He recovered quickly enough but took advantage of the situation to accuse Perseus of trying to kill him. Livy adds all manner of detail, such as Perseus hiring a Cretan mercenary captain and three Macedonians to assassinate Eumenes so he could go to war against Rome. The plot now thickens with the return of Laevinus and the other commissioners, bringing with them two men. One, Praxo of Delphi, told the story that Eumenes' would-be assassins had stayed at what must have been his guesthouse and let slip that Perseus had hatched the plot against Eumenes. The other was a man from Brundisium, who claimed that Perseus had tried to get him to poison Romans traveling on official business when they stayed with him.[78]

It does not follow that there was an actual attempt on Eumenes' life as opposed to his being a victim of bandits or even a simple rock fall. Livy's account cannot be corroborated, and the allegation may be one made up later.[79] Even more sensational are the stories (which must be from an annalistic account) implicating Perseus in plots against Roman officials. No matter how fantastic the claims, Perseus' fate was sealed, with Polybius explicitly stating that the attack on Eumenes marked the outbreak of the war.[80] The Senate declared him a *hostis* (enemy) and sent an embassy to inform him it had ended the *amicitia*. It also ordered two legions of allied infantry and cavalry and a fleet of fifty ships to sail from Brundisium to Apollonia and await the arrival of the main army under the new consuls the following year.

76. Livy 42.14.5–10; Appian, *Macedonian Wars* 11.3. On Rhodes in this period, see Gruen 1975.

77. Livy 42.15–16; cf. 42.40.8; see too Meloni 1953, pp. 162–164; Briscoe 2012, pp. 202–210; Burton 2017, p. 68.

78. Livy 42.17; Appian, *Macedonian Wars* 11.7, with Gruen 1984, pp. 409–410; Briscoe 2012, pp. 210–211; Burton 2017, pp. 87–88.

79. Cf. Gruen 1984, p. 409; Hammond and Walbank 1988, p. 499 with n. 1, Briscoe 2012, pp. 202–203; Burton 2017, p. 87. Assassination attempt: for example, Meloni 1953, p. 164; Adams 1982, pp. 252–253.

80. Polybius 22.18.8; cf. 22.18.5; Livy 42.18.1–2; cf. 42.25.1, with Burton 2017, pp. 197–201, on the embassy.

Eumenes likewise began to prepare for war.[81] So did others, including Ariarathes IV of Cappadocia, who placed his sons under Rome's care.[82] In addition, two Roman commissioners were sent to Asia and islands including Crete and Rhodes urging their loyalty to Rome and warning Perseus to keep his distance from Roman allies.[83] The Rhodians, it seems, were not intimidated, though later they decided to play safe and declared their friendship to Rome. The Senate also sent envoys to Perseus' ally Genthius, the Ardiaean king north of Lissus; he was preparing to invest Issa, which had an *amicitia* with Rome, and was warned to steer clear of Rome's allies in Illyria.[84]

There was still the issue of Greek discontent that might be to Perseus' favor. To win over the Greeks, the Senate resorted to a devious propaganda move when in the summer of 172 it sent a letter to Greece listing charges against Perseus so far-fetched that "the very quantity of alleged misdeeds undermines their credibility."[85] As Burton importantly notes, most of them were not applicable to Perseus at this particular time, but were "raked up by his enemies later on, when a case against him was being constructed and a pattern of hostility going back to the beginning of his reign was being sought."[86] The charges are an excellent instance of "fake news" in the ancient world, used to embellish Perseus' actions and blacken his motives to justify going to war against him, as we shall now see.

Roman Duplicity

Two fragments of an inscription found at Delphi detail Perseus' so-called offenses as outlined in an official senatorial letter to drum up support against him. This was presumably addressed to the Delphic Amphictyony, given its broad implications for all Greeks. The summary of the charges below is taken from Hammond and Walbank (square brackets indicate restorations):[87]

---

81. Livy 42.17.3–5.

82. Livy 42.19.3–6.

83. Livy 42.19.7–8; see too Meloni 1953, pp. 166–185.

84. Livy 42.26.2–6; see too Dell 1977; Gruen 1984, pp. 419–423; Burton 2017, p. 69 (Burton 2011, pp. 136–141, on the treaty between Rome and Issa).

85. Gruen 1984, p. 409. See Burton 2017, p. 81 nn. 7–14, for similar sentiments by other scholars (for example, "absurd," "comic," "flimsy," "ludicrous").

86. Burton 2017, p. 81.

87. *SIG*³ 643 = Austin 2006, no. 93, pp. 185–186 = Sherk 1969, no. 40, pp. 233–239 = Sherk 1984, no. 19, pp. 18–20. The points in my text are from Hammond and Walbank 1988, p. 501.

1. Perseus is to be banned from sacred ceremonies at Delphi.
2. He has brought barbarians from beyond the [Danube] to enslave [Greeks].
3. He has broken the [sworn agreement].
4. The Thracians attached to us . . . and Abrupolis has been expelled from his kingdom by Perseus.
5. Envoys travelling to Rome on the matter of alliance [have been abused by Perseus].
6. He committed an act of desperation in [trying to poison senators].
7. [The Dolopians] were deprived of freedom.
8. In Aetolia he planned civil war and massacre.
9. He was continually . . . corrupting the leading men and he was causing revolutions.
10. This has led to disasters in Pe[rrhaebia etc.] and in the barbarians becoming more a cause of fear.
11. Perseus is eager for war and intendeds to enslave [Greece].
12. [?His involving of Genthius].
13. Perseus impiously attacked Eumenes the king [at Delphi].

The last part of the inscription is lost. Pugliese suggested that it accused Perseus of murdering Artetaurus of Illyria, a Roman ally, of supporting Byzantium against Rome, and of making an alliance with Boeotia.[88]

It has been suggested that the list of grievances was the work of the members of the Amphictyonic League attempting to endear themselves to the Romans, given the likely return of a Roman army.[89] Yet the similarities between the list and Eumenes' earlier speech to the Senate, which the senators kept confidential until later, are so striking that the list surely derives from his speech. Eumenes' charges may have stretched credibility, but as has been

---

Burton 2017, pp. 79–91, has the most detailed analysis of each one, but see too Meloni 1953, pp. 241–243; Hammond and Walbank 1988, pp. 500–502; Derow 1989, pp. 301–315. Bousquet 1981 adds to the epigraphic evidence with a fragment from a Roman official's letter ordering the list be set up at Delphi for all the Greeks to see (*SIG*³ 613B). Hammond and Walbank 1988, p. 500 n. 3, citing bibliography, argue that it was inscribed in 172 rather than 171 (so Bousquet) because Rome took the diplomatic initiative and Perseus drew up his letter as a reply to it. On chronology, see too Meloni 1953, pp. 176–184; cf. Pugliese 2014, p. 156. See Hammond and Walbank 1988, p. 501, for where these points appear in our literary sources, and how they are treated; cf. Gruen 1976, p. 36 with n. 66.

88. Pugliese 2014, p. 156 n. 42.

89. Sherk 1969, p. 239, citing other bibliography.

said, "If they were not all believed at Rome, they were at least adopted as official Roman propaganda."[90] Sending the letter to the Amphictyony addressed
many Greek states in one fell swoop, but Delphi was where Perseus wanted
to erect his memorials to Macedonian might, hence Rome was also seen to be
clipping his wings.

Some of the Roman grievances in their "charge sheet" against Perseus
were valid, the majority not so.[91] Perseus did, for example, campaign against
Abrupolis and Dolopia as well as offer military help to Byzantium and
Aetolia. But he did not overwhelm Perrhaebia or capture Thessalian cities or
have Theban envoys en route to Rome to protest his alliance killed. Nor did
he plan to enslave Greece or cause a civil war there, and there is nothing to
suggest he was behind a plot to kill Eumenes or poison senators. In fact, it is
hard to make a compelling argument that Perseus was out to wreck the settlement of 196, given the extent of Greek self-interest in war.[92]

There were civil strife and class conflicts in areas of Greece, as we noted
above.[93] However, their causes were not bound up in any ideological struggle
between aristocrats and the masses but arose from massive debts affecting poor
and rich alike.[94] Likewise, the claim that Rome backed the rich over the poor
in Greece, and that Perseus may have seen the disenchanted masses turning to
him against Rome, does not ring true.[95] For example, in 175/74, rival factions in
Aetolia called on Perseus to send an army to restore order, but then they asked
for arbitrators from Rome, who had only limited success and internal strife
broke out again.[96] Rome was simply spinning known social conflicts to em-
broil Perseus and castigating him egregiously to turn the Greeks against him.

Tensions were escalating dramatically between Perseus and the Senate,
as when he ordered Roman envoys, sent to him over the status of his treaty

90. Derow 1989, p. 307.

91. Burton 2017, pp. 80–91 ("charge sheet" term on p. 87).

92. Giovanni 1969; cf. Meloni 1953, pp. 104–109 and 237–238, but against this theory see
Walbank 1977, pp. 86–92. Greek self-interest: Gruen 1976; Mendels 1978; Gruen 1984, pp.
505–514; cf. Adams 1982, pp. 238–239.

93. See Mendels 1977 and Gruen 1981, focusing on the time of Philip V, but their comments are
relevant before and after the king's reign also.

94. Mendels 1978, pp. 61–72.

95. For example, Deininger 1971, pp. 159–164; cf. Meloni 1953, pp. 141–142 and 254–256, that
Rome supported the upper and lower classes as and when it suited its interests.

96. Meloni 1953, pp. 145–146; Gruen 1976, pp. 35–39; Mendels 1978, pp. 60–61.

with Rome, to leave his kingdom within three days.[97] In the meantime, other Roman envoys went to seek military and diplomatic support from Greece, Illyria, Pergamum, Cappadocia, Numidia, and Egypt. Philip's own allies were dwindling. A Roman mission to Prusias of Bithynia was not successful as he thought it wrong to ally with Rome against his wife's brother. Cotys of Thrace was already in a secret agreement with Perseus, while Genthius' neutrality, despite Rome's earlier warning to him, made the senators suspicious of his stance.[98]

In the same year, 172, a five-man mission to Illyria and Greece led by Quintus Marcius Philippus and 1,000 troops arrived at Corcyra. There, they received a letter from Perseus wanting to know why Roman troops were sailing to Greece and occupying Oricum, Apollonia, Dyrrhacium, and Epidamnus.[99] Philippus' reply was a verbal one: it was because Rome was looking after these cities; in other words, Perseus had no business asking and faced Rome's military might. From Corcya, the envoys spent the following months visiting Epirus, Acarnania, Aetolia, Boeotia, Thessaly, the Peloponnese, and even Genthius to ensure their support against Perseus.[100] In major coups the Thessalian League was won over, as was the Boeotian (apart from the three towns of Haliartus, Thisbe, and Coronea) and the Epirote, which committed 400 soldiers to defend Orestis against Perseus.[101] But what really caused the Greeks to throw in their lot with Rome was the arrival of Roman troops on Greek soil and fear of Roman reprisals.[102] Now, in October or perhaps the start of November 172, while the Roman envoys were still on their mission to the Greek states, Perseus requested a meeting with Philippus, emphasizing the personal relationship Philippus had had with his father.[103]

Perseus met Philippus close to the Vale of Tempe.[104] Livy's report of the meeting is questionable as he has Philippus repeat many of the accusations

---

97. Livy 42.25.1–13; cf. 43.9.4.

98. Livy 42.29.

99. Livy 42.37.1–6.

100. Polybius 27.1; Livy 42.37.7–38.7, with Briscoe 2012, pp. 270–305; cf. Meloni 1953, pp. 245–249; Harris 1979, pp. 227–233; Gruen 1984, pp. 411–412; Hammond and Walbank 1988, pp. 507–510; Pugliese 2014, p. 155; Burton 2017, pp. 69–70.

101. See Hammond 1967, pp. 625–633, on the Epirote League in Perseus' reign.

102. Polybius 24.9.6 uses the phrase "out of fear."

103. Livy 42.8–10. Chronology: Walbank 1941, pp. 82–85; Meloni 1953, pp. 185–191.

104. Livy 42.39–43.3, with Meloni 1953, pp. 185–190; Derow 1989, p. 509.

against Perseus that Eumenes made to the Senate in 172 and which were included in the list proclaimed at Delphi. Still, Perseus spoke his mind and the two of them did agree to a truce of two months so that Perseus, on Philippus' advice, could send envoys to Rome. Philippus was acting underhandedly though. He was out to buy time until the main Roman army arrived and caught Perseus by surprise, not to mention that he and his colleagues were still intent on attracting other Greeks to their side and were about to leave for Boeotia.[105] But his conduct came back to haunt him. When he returned to Rome the older senators did not appreciate his "new cunning" (*nova sapientia*) to gain an advantage as they felt it was dishonorable and betrayed their ancestors' beliefs.[106] The younger, more ambitious senators disagreed.

Perseus, unaware of Philippus' duplicity, sent letters to the Greeks, Byzantines, and Rhodians protesting Rome's propaganda effort against him and claiming that in defending his kingdom he was in the right when it came to international law and legal justice.[107] He was probably correct about his rights, but the Senate was not interested in legal niceties, something even the Greeks recognized. Hence it is no surprise that only Rhodes and Coronea, Thisbe, and Haliartus in Boeotia responded to Perseus' appeal for allies—though he evidently looked down on the Boeotians: when they asked for Macedonian garrisons to defend themselves against avenging Thebans he refused and told them to defend themselves as best they could.[108]

The Senate refused to hear Perseus' embassy for some months—not until March 171. It rejected all attempts at appeasement and ordered the envoys to leave Rome at once and Italy within thirty days.[109] The reason for its action was that early in the same year (171) the Comitia Centuriata had voted for the consuls' motion to go to war against Perseus for violating the treaty he had

---

105. Errington 1971a, p. 210; Waterfield 2014, p. 178; Burton 2017, pp. 71–72. Hammond and Walbank 1988, p. 510 with n. 2, note that "standstill" is better than "truce" or "armistice" in Polybius 27.5.7–8; see too Warrior 1981, pp. 5–6 and 45; Burton 2017, p. 75 with n. 87. Polybius 27.6.1–3 speaks of the king's envoys being summoned to Rome.

106. Livy 42.47.1–9, with Briscoe 1964; Gruen 1984, p. 415; Petzold 1999; Briscoe 2012, pp. 313–318; cf. Meloni 1953, pp. 202–203; Errington 1971a, pp. 210–212; Waterfield 2014, p. 179.

107. Polybius 27.4; cf. 27.7; Livy 42.46.1–5, with Walbank 1979, pp. 296–297; Golan 1979/80 (at pp. 133–136); Pugliese 2014, pp. 157–158; Burton 2017, pp. 74–75. Perseus had his letter to the Rhodians delivered by two ambassadors (*presbeutai*), a sign of the importance he attached to diplomatic relations with that island; cf. Pugliese 2014, p. 157.

108. Polybius 27.5; Livy 42.46.6–10, with Walbank 1979, pp. 296–299.

109. Polybius 27.6.1–4; Livy 42.48.1–4; cf. Diodorus 30.1, with Walbank 1979, pp. 299–301; Briscoe 2012, pp. 308–313; Pugliese 2014, pp. 159–160.

with Rome, invading the territory of Rome's allies, and preparing to wage war on Rome. The Senate ordered a large-scale deployment of troops and ships for the new consul tasked with fighting Perseus, Publius Licinius Crassus (ancestor of the triumvir with Julius Caesar and Pompey the Great).[110] We discuss the various motives for war below so as not to interrupt this narrative of events.

Livy gives two different versions of the Senate's reaction to the Macedonian envoys, which is a salutary warning about the nature of our sources.[111] He recounts the Senate's behavior toward the embassy, yet has already told us that Perseus' envoys were denied entry to Rome as war had been declared. They delivered their speech in the temple of Bellona, urged the Senate to recall its troops, and emphasized that Perseus was willing to come to terms, but nonetheless were ordered to leave Italy under military escort within eleven days.[112] This latter account is from an unworthy annalistic source and is discarded by modern scholars whereas the former, derived from Polybius, is preferred.[113]

The Senate ordered a Roman fleet to the base at Cephallenia in the Ionian Sea, and Crassus took the main army to join the vanguard force near Apollonia.[114] Despite no actual fighting yet, in Rome state diviners were already forecasting "victory, triumph, and enlargement of the realm."[115]

The Blame Game

"Assessing the myriad causes of the Third Macedonian War proffered by historians is a particularly perilous exercise—as indeed it was in antiquity."[116] Never a truer word was spoken, for modern scholars have put forward a

---

110. Reasons for war in detail: Livy 42.30.10–31.1. Troop numbers: Livy 42.31. See too Hammond and Walbank 1988, p. 509 n. 2. On chronology, see Gruen 1984, pp. 413–414 n. 85; Briscoe 2012, pp. 8–12.

111. Pugliese 2014, pp. 159–160; cf. Meloni 1953, pp. 191–210; Hammond and Walbank 1988, p. 505. On confusion in Livy 42, see Warrior 1981; Briscoe 2012, pp. 23–25.

112. Livy 42.36.1–8.

113. Livy 42.48.1–4; cf. Diodorus 30.1 (also thirty days). Likewise, Appian, *Macedonian Wars* 11.5–9, records two sets of envoys, one being ordered to leave Rome the same day and Italy within eleven days (11.9), clearly drawing on the doublet in Livy: Pugliese 2014, pp. 159–160.

114. Livy 42.48.5–49.

115. Livy 42.30.8.

116. Burton 2017, p. 78.

dizzying array of theories.[117] For example, did Perseus inherit the war from his father; did his dynastic marriages pose a threat to Rome; did war occur because of his actions, especially in Greece, which flouted the settlement of 196; did an aggressive Senate from the outset intend to conquer Macedonia, hence war was inevitable; was it a case that no matter what he did or did not do he could never redeem himself in Rome's eyes; did he exploit a possible Celtic raid on Italy to try to conquer Rome; to what extent did Perseus' enemies, especially Eumenes, influence the Senate; or was it a combination of these factors or something else?

We can reject the idea that Perseus inherited the war from his father.[118] Polybius and Livy speak of its origins in Rome's dismal treatment of Philip in the 180s, and while that may have rankled Perseus, that motive was surely not enough.[119] Moreover, our ancient writers mistook (accidentally or not) Philip's preparations against the Dardanians toward the end of his reign as a move against Rome. Given the need for border security and the risk the Dardanians posed throughout his father's reign, it made sense for Perseus to prepare troops and provisions at the start of his reign in case of invasion. This is a far cry from mobilizing an army to attack Rome.

Nor does it follow that his dynastic marriages were meant to build up a coalition of kings against Rome, forcing the Senate to act before it was too late.[120] One argument is that that body, fearful that Perseus and Antiochus IV would turn against Rome, took advantage of Syria's preoccupation with its conflict against Egypt (the Sixth Syrian War) to declare war on Macedonia. But the Senate heard of the Sixth Syrian War most probably in 170, by which

---

117. Bickerman 1953, pp. 492–506; Meloni 1953, pp. 61–209; Giovannini 1969; Gruen 1976; Walbank 1977; Werner 1977; Mendels 1978; Adams 1982; Gruen 1984, pp. 408–419; Hammond and Walbank 1988, pp. 497–504; cf. Briscoe 2012, pp. 5–18, especially pp. 13–15. See now Burton 2017, pp. 78–123, for detailed analysis of the various modern theories.

118. Polybius 22.18.8–11; Livy 41.23.9, 41.23.11; cf. Gruen 1974, pp. 221–225; Walbank 1977, p. 81; Gruen 1984, p. 408; Pugliese 2014, pp. 153–154, noting that Polybius elsewhere attributes others to starting wars—for example, Hannibal commanded the enemy in the Second Punic War but its origins lay with Hamilcar (3.9.6). Golan 1989 argues that Polybius carefully styled his account, given his personal experiences of being taken to Rome as a prisoner after the battle of Pydna in 167, to show that Rome not Perseus was the aggressor.

119. Livy 39.23.6–13, 39.29.3; cf. 40.16.3.

120. Meloni 1953, pp. 122–125, and see pp. 115–127 on Perseus' foreign networking; Burton 2017, pp. 101–110, on a coalition of kings and Roman views of Antochus; against this: Giovannini 1969, p. 855; Gruen 1975, pp. 66–67; Gruen 1984, p. 404.

time the Third Macedonian War was in full swing.[121] The senators anyway did not view the dynastic marriages with concern as they knew they were a common feature of Hellenistic kingdoms.

Another argument is that in 171 the Senate was suddenly alarmed by a possible barbarian invasion of Italy, including Cisalpine Gaul, so the consul Gaius Cassius Longinus mobilized his army to defend Italy's northeastern frontier.[122] True, that border was always a weak spot—there may have been a worry earlier of Philip V allying with Celtic tribes (p. 110).[123] Hence the Senate feared Perseus joining with the Celts and demanded his submission. But Perseus—like his father—was in no position to begin hostilities against Italy without a navy, and he was more worried about dealing with Rome on his own soil.

On the face of it, Perseus was doing everything he could to alleviate any senatorial anxieties about him, including his three delegations to Rome, his deferential request to recognize his kingship, his personal meeting with Philippus, and his adherence to the truce despite the Senate's abysmal attitude to his own envoys.[124] His careful policy in these years contradicts one scholarly opinion that his "comparative youth and diplomatic inexperience made him far less careful than Philip had been to avoid offending the Senate and far less ready to make concessions to Rome."[125] If anything, the reverse was true.

Yet the Senate clearly mistrusted him. The question is from when.[126] Burton argues strongly for as early as 175 or 174, given Perseus' exploits in Greece that led to embassies to the Senate about him. That may be true, for the Senate had a slow build-up to declaring war which hastened once it was deluged with envoys from protesting Greeks and especially Eumenes.[127] Worried lest Perseus' marital contracts with the Seleucids and Prusias of

121. Bickerman 1953, pp. 479–506; *contra* Walbank 1977, pp. 82–86. On Rome's attitude to Antiovhus (as not a factor) see especially Burton 2017, pp. 103–110.

122. Twyman 1993.

123. Twyman 1986.

124. Cf. Adams 1982, pp. 242–245 and 254–255; for a harsher summary of Perseus' moves, see Errington 1971a, p. 212. Note Meloni 1953, pp. 185 and 202, that Perseus should not have honored the truce or tried for a peaceful settlement.

125. Errington 1971a, p. 204.

126. Burton 2017, pp. 96–100 (reviewing others' arguments for various dates, e.g., the execution of Demetrius: Edson 1935, p. 20; Waterfield 2014, p. 166); cf. Meloni 1953, pp. 148–149, 444–451.

127. Cf. Warrior 1981, pp. 1–14; Gruen 1984, pp. 416–417.

Bithynia would challenge him and having had his sights set on Macedonia since Philip's era, Eumenes turned to Rome to bring down Perseus.[128]

Eumenes is arguably the key to the Senate's decision, given how his scare-tactic rhetoric played on Roman anxieties and even paranoia about Perseus. Once the senators had been beguiled by Eumenes' jingoistic rhetoric in his speech of 172, war was inevitable: Livy's remark that their minds could not be swayed when it came to conflict with Macedonia is apposite.[129] Perhaps even individual senators play a role here if some saw war as a chance for fame and reward and even thought of the eastern Mediterranean as Rome's possession.[130] On top of that was the lure of income from Rome's conquests: it was already substantial, but there was always room for more.[131]

Perseus had put himself in an unwinnable situation with the Senate because of his reassertion of Macedonia's position in Greece that was at odds with what Rome wanted in 196.[132] Even though his campaigns against the Dardanians and in Thrace and Greece did not break the terms of the settlement of 196, despite the spin that the Senate later put on them, he could never redeem himself. It thus appears that the Senate was the aggressor for never giving him the benefit of the doubt.[133]

Was Perseus taken aback by Rome's decision? I think not. In 189, Rome had concluded its war with the Aetolian League, in which Philip V and a young Perseus had fought on Rome's side. Philip, however, was never consulted about the terms, which disadvantaged him greatly, despite his services to Rome. He had turned for help to personal friends in Rome, including Philippus, but to no avail. Perseus thus experienced firsthand that the Senate cared little about doing the right thing by its friends and allies when it came to advancing Rome's interests, and the same thing was happening now.

---

128. Walbank 1977, pp. 93–94; Kertész 1993, pp. 672–674; see too Warrior 1981, pp. 1–14; *contra* Gruen 1984, pp. 409–410, that he had this impact, especially as the meeting with the Senate was behind closed doors.

129. Livy 42.48.3. Attitude of senators: Burton 2017, pp. 110–113.

130. Walbank 1977, p. 93; Harris 1979, p. 252; Adams 1982, pp. 249–250; cf. Briscoe 2012, pp. 13–15, but see now Burton 2017, pp. 114–115 on "glory-seeking" senators (and cf. pp. 110–115). Note Gruen 1982, that the settlement after the battle of Pydna in 167, at which Rome defeated Perseus, showed that Rome did not intend to control Macedonia (see my chapter 0000). On Roman attitudes to empire and its benefits, see Gruen 1984, pp. 273–315.

131. Gruen 1984, pp. 288–315.

132. Derow 1989, pp. 302–303.

133. Harris 1979, p. 227, and cf. pp. 227–233; but see now Burton 2017, pp. 110–117.

When he assumed the throne in 179, Perseus was aware of two things. First, the Romans were naive if they thought that their arrangements in 196 would bring peace to Greek cities whose history was anchored in warfare with one another. Second, when things fell apart, Rome would return to Greece, at which time Macedonia would be in its cross-hairs, no matter what Perseus did or did not do—especially if Rome had wanted his brother Demetrius to succeed Philip.

Accordingly, Perseus remained loyal to the *amicitia* with Rome, but he carefully maintained an army, fully equipped and with plenty of supplies, ostensibly for border protection, and took steps via the Amphictyony to widen his standing in Greece. Most likely Roman involvement in the east in tandem with Eumenes' warnings influenced the Senate's thinking, for Eumenes and the Senate could not tolerate another influential ruler in the Mediterranean.[134] Thus, when he became king, Perseus did not intend war with Rome, but he suspected one would be coming, and he prepared for it for the sake of his kingdom.

If so, then it explains the changes he made to his coinage after 174.[135] He reduced the weight of his silver tetradrachms, didrachms, and drachms to the more popular Rhodian standard since Rhodian and Pergamene coinage was the strongest in the eastern Mediterranean, similar to Argead fifth-century practice.[136] This devaluation was not just to make exchange easier, but would save him a substantial amount of money when paying his own troops and mercenaries the same rates of pay. The logical reason for his change was for the eventuality of war. It was just as well that he did.

---

134. Appian, *Macedonian Wars* 11.3, with Pugliese 2014, p. 154.

135. See Hammond and Walbank 1988, pp. 503–504; Hatzopoulos 1996, vol. 1, pp. 253–254, citing bibliography.

136. Kremydi 2011, p. 175.

10

The Third Macedonian War

THE THIRD MACEDONIAN War, lasting from 171 to 168, was considered by Polybius the stepping-stone to Rome's dominion of the Greek world.[1] The Senate's aggressive policy has drawn parallels to the modern era and threat elimination, specifically US military activity, following a period of relative passivity in the late twentieth century, in Iraq and Afghanistan after the September 11, 2001, attacks on the World Trade Center and Pentagon.[2] When the Third Macedonian War was over, and despite severe repercussions for Macedonia and the end of the Antigonid dynasty, the Senate still hoped for a new settlement that would enable the people to govern themselves as far as possible. In similar fashion, there was every intention that Iraq would see local rule bringing with it peace and prosperity. Regardless of the validity of analogies like these, they serve as another reminder of what we can learn from the ancient world and especially what to avoid.

Macedonia on the Eve of the War

In late April 171 Perseus' envoy returned to him with the grim news that Rome was at war with him.[3] The king called a meeting of his Friends at

---

1. But Golan 1989, e.g., pp. 115–116, argues that Polybius' experience as one of the 1,000 Achaeans sent after Pydna as prisoners to Rome—where he spent sixteen years, during which time his father (also a prisoner) died—led him to express his views more cautiously on Rome's aggression.

2. Burton 2017, p. 16; cf. Briscoe 2012, p. vii.

3. On the war, see Meloni 1953, pp. 211–431; Errington 1971a, pp. 213–226; Errington 1974b; Gruen 1976, especially pp. 32–46; Walbank 1977; Harris 1979, pp. 227–233; Adams 1982; Gruen 1984, pp. 408–419, 423–429, and 505–514; Hammond and Walbank 1988, pp. 505–557; Derow 1989, pp. 310–316; Matyszak 2009, pp. 131–156; Eckstein 2010, pp. 243–245; Waterfield

The Last Kings of Macedonia and the Triumph of Rome. Ian Worthington, Oxford University Press.
© Oxford University Press 2023. DOI: 10.1093/oso/9780197520055.003.0011

Pella.[4] They agreed to support him if he decided to fight fire with fire.[5] Like his father, Perseus was not going to bow to any threats to his kingdom; his sacrifice of one hundred cattle to the Macedonian goddess of war, Athena Alcidemus ("Defender of the People") showed his decision. All the same, he needed his army on his side. He traveled to Citum to hold a military review and described Rome's injustices to himself and his father.[6] The choice, he said to his assembled troops, was either to fight for liberty or to accept subjugation—what should he do? The men clamored for the former, no surprise there, hence the matter was settled. Afterward, envoys came from the various cities in Macedonia offering him as much grain and money as they could put together, all of which he refused—he had been building up reserves for the past few years.[7]

Justice may well have been on Perseus' side for not breaking his treaty with Rome nor the recent truce with Philippus, but justice mattered little to the bellicose Senate. The Roman fleet of fifty quinquiremes carrying 10,000 troops had now sailed across the Adriatic, with the bulk of the vessels going on to Chalcis to be joined by ships from Eumenes carrying 6,000 infantry and 1,000 cavalry. Fifty-four *lembi* from Genthius were sent to the Roman fleet based at Epidamnus, but since Genthius' loyalty was suspect they may have been commandeered.[8] Rome's supply lines across the Adriatic to the north-western coast of Greece and around the southern Peloponnese, as well as from the eastern Aegean to Chalcis, were assured.

By now the consular army under Crassus of 30,000 troops and 2,000 cavalry had made its way at speed through Epirus and Athamania to the strategic town of Gomphi in south-western Thessaly. His men and horses were exhausted when they reached Gomphi, but his march had been a notable achievement, though to a large extent it had been helped by a lack of opposition along the route as Perseus was still adhering to the truce rather than

---

2014, pp. 181–193; Burton 2017, pp. 124–172; cf. Warrior 1981 (events from 173 to the end of the campaigning season of 171); Briscoe 2012, pp. 21–29.

4. Timing: Hammond and Walbank 1988, p. 514 n. 3.

5. Livy 42.50–51.2, with Briscoe 2012, pp. 326–330.

6. Livy 42.51.2–53.1 with details of numbers and different units, including Thracian, Paeonian, and Agrianian troops, who perhaps had been moved by Philip V in the fall of 183 (see my p. 0000): see, further, Briscoe 2012, pp. 330–341.

7. Livy 42.53.4.

8. Cf. Meloni 1953, pp. 212–213 with n. 1; Walbank 1979, p. 337; Briscoe 2012, p. 321; Burton 2017, p. 125 with n. 8, and p. 142 on Genthius.

trying to confine the Romans in the northwest.[9] Perseus was now faced by a hostile army on his doorstep, for Crassus' position meant that Macedonia could face invasion from Thessaly as well as Illyria.

Perseus had about 43,000 men in his army, including 26,000 Macedonian infantry (21,000 phalangites and two elite groups, one of 2,000 and the other of 3,000) and 3,000 first-rate Macedonian cavalry.[10] These high numbers show Philip's success in replenishing the manpower losses since Cynoscephalae twenty-six years prior. The rest of Perseus' army was made up of 1,000 Odrysian cavalry and 13,000 infantry: 3,000 Paeonians, Agrianians, and Thracians (the last living in Macedonia), 3,000 Thracians living outside the kingdom, 3,000 Cretans, 2,000 Gauls, 1,000 Odrysians, 500 Aetolians and Boeotians, and 500 other Greeks.

All the infantrymen were seasoned soldiers and led by experienced commanders. In this respect the Macedonian army had the edge over the Roman, which had a large number of new recruits in it and was nothing like the army that had fought and defeated Hannibal.[11] But Perseus' army had a major weakness: it was "a once-for-all army, irreplaceable if it suffered a severe defeat."[12] He therefore had to make sure that if he went into battle against the Romans he would win, which explains his caution at times. Rome on the other hand had abundant troops and a powerful navy that could mount its own operations. Perseus' lack of a fleet was another weakness as he was unable to put constant pressure on all of Rome's supply lines. Still, from the outset he showed a strategic prowess and ability to think and act quickly that he inherited from his father and was reminiscent of Alexander the Great.

The First Year of the War

In the fall of 171, at the head of his army, he set off to seize the two main passes of Volustana and Tempe that afforded entry from Thessaly into Macedonia

---

9. Hammond and Walbank 1988, p. 513.

10. Livy 42.51.3–11 = Austin 2006, no. 94, pp. 186–187. On units and numbers and the textual issues in Livy, see Hammond and Walbank 1988, p. 515 n. 1; Briscoe 2012, pp. 331–335 and 357–358; cf. Meloni 1953, p. 217. Matyszak 2009, pp. 131–132, contrasts their fighting prowess with those at Cynoscephalae. On the allied forces during the war, see especially Sekunda 2013, pp. 114–124. The number of Macedonian cavalry for this campaign is the highest for all the Antigonid period for which we have evidence: Sekunda 2013, p. 74.

11. Hammond and Walbank 1988, p. 515; cf. Matyszak 2009, p. 133.

12. Hammond and Walbank 1988, p. 515.

(map 6). His invasion of Thessaly was as efficient as it was effective.[13] Perseus marched through Eordaea and Elimiotis, stopping off at Boceria on the east side of Lake Begorritis for the night as there was plentiful water to be had.[14] The next day he covered forty miles (64 kilometers) to the Haliacmon River, carefully taking routes to keep him hidden from Roman outposts at the Volustana pass. A swift advance into Perrhaebia followed, in which he defeated the Perrhaebians and took Volustana.

Tempe was next. Advancing down the Europus valley in Bottiaea he besieged Chyretiae, which was at the very least sympathetic to Rome because Flamininus had returned property to it in 194.[15] The city capitulated on the second day. Two days later Perseus was besieging the Perrhaebian town of Mylae, at the narrow entry to the valley; when it surrendered, he sacked it and sold its surviving population into slavery. It made sense to build up his liquid capital when the opportunity presented itself. A rapid march east to Phalanna followed, where he learned that an enemy army, including the general of the Thessalian League no less, was encamped at Gyrton to block his advance.

Perseus was not ready to fight until he controlled the Tempe pass, so he besieged Phalanna relentlessly. When it fell to him, he took a route to the south of pass, surprising the two towns of Elatea and Gonnoi and camping at Sycyrium in the foothills of Mount Ossa. Here was a route by Larissa, and the Vale of Tempe to Mount Olympus, with abundant water and ample crops and fodder for his horses in the surrounding fields.[16] The Volustana and Tempe passes reinforced the safety of his border with Thessaly and just as importantly gave him a supply line either by wagon through Tempe or by water up the Peneus River, which flowed from the Pindus range to the Aegean, northeast of the Vale of Tempe.

Perseus' fast marches and quick thinking when it came to changing the routes he chose was not lost on Crassus, who knew he had to end the king's momentum. He moved his men to the Peneus and built a fortified camp on its south bank about five miles (eight kilometers) from Larissa.

---

13. Meloni 1953, pp. 223–251; Hammond and Walbank 1988, pp. 516–519; Matyszak 2009, pp. 135–140; Briscoe 2012, pp. 341–348.

14. Livy 42.53.5–54.11.

15. See Armstrong and Walsh 1986, rightly arguing how Flamininus' letter to the people there (*SIG*³ 593) shows the care he took over his settlement of Thessaly.

16. Livy 42.54.10–11, 42.56.8–9.

Attalus of Pergamum, who had crossed over to Chalcis, joined him there with reinforcements of 4,000 Pergamene infantry and 1,000 cavalry, 500 Aetolian League cavalry (its entire complement), 300 Thessalian cavalry, 100 infantry from Apollonia, and 1,500 light-armed infantry from the Achaean League.[17] Crassus' numbers were now roughly equal to those of his enemy.

For the rest of 171 Perseus enjoyed the upper hand, disrupting the Romans' supply routes from the Gulf of Pagasae to central Greece and denying them the chance to forage for provisions in the territory of Pherae by laying waste to it.[18] In this he was following his father's policy of wearing down his foes. But then came victory over the Romans in a surprising battle.

One morning the Macedonian king quietly led his troops to the Roman camp near a hill called Callinicus about three miles (five kilometers) from Larissa. Crassus was holding a planning meeting with his senior staff when he received the shocking news that Perseus' army was bearing down on him wanting to do battle.[19] The Roman commander sent out a cavalry detachment, but it was soon overcome with the loss of 30 cavalrymen. The next day Perseus formed his battle line, putting most of the Macedonian cavalry on the flanks and himself at the center—perhaps he had learned the lesson from Cynoscephalae not to position himself on a wing as Philip had done. He also interspersed his lighter-armed infantry and the remaining cavalry along his line—if the Romans broke through it, his infantry could still fight them on the rough ground around the hill. Because of the unsuitable terrain and his need to protect his troop numbers, he held his phalanx back; when late in the ensuing battle the phalangites rushed out to fight of their own accord he ordered them back to the camp.

Crassus also decided to keep his legions in his camp, instead sending out 12,000 Roman and allied cavalry and light-armed infantry. Perseus, with about the same number of men, charged first, with such ferocity that his cavalry almost routed the Romans in the first few minutes, but 400 gallant Thessalians grittily stood their ground and allowed their defeated cavalry comrades to escape back to camp. The Romans lost 200 cavalry and 2,000 infantry and had 600 of their number taken prisoner to the Macedonians' loss of 60 men.

17. Livy 42.55.8–10. Crassus' earlier route and camp: Livy 42.55.1–7.

18. Livy 42.56.8–9.

19. Livy 42.56.4–60.2, with Meloni 1953, pp. 230–236; Matyszak 2009, pp. 136–137; Burton 2017, pp. 128–132; Briscoe 2012, pp. 353–364.

The Romans were demoralized, and Crassus blamed the Aetolians for the loss and sent five of their leaders to Rome—though these five were not especially pro-Roman anyway.[20] But then Perseus lost his advantage that night because he did not post enough lookouts, allowing Crassus, on Eumenes' quick thinking, to cross to the river's north bank and build a fortified camp.[21] The Peneus River was now between the Roman and Macedonian armies, and Crassus soon received reinforcements from Numidia of 22 war elephants (which the Macedonian horses were not trained to face) and 2,000 infantry and cavalry.

Perseus rightly blamed himself for Crassus' escape and had to switch his campsite closer to Larissa. Perhaps to save some face and raise his men's morale he meted out the spoils from the battle and exhorted his troops to keep fighting.[22] His Friends, however, thought this would not be enough. They persuaded him not to push his luck and send an envoy to Crassus seeking peace with Rome and even offering to pay a war reparation if both sides could go back to the status quo of 179.[23] Crassus demanded unconditional surrender and for Perseus to accept whatever the Senate decided about Macedonia.[24] An unimpressed Perseus unsurprisingly withdrew to Sycyrium. Since he had compromised the Romans' supply line from western Thessaly and Epirus, he escalated his attacks on their troops searching for food.

A delegation from the Epirote League now sought an alliance with Perseus. It was blocked by a younger politician named Charops, the grandson of the Charops who had alerted Flamininus about the path around the Aous Gorge (p. 120).[25] The Epirote overture and the hostile attitude of the Greeks, together with the unacceptable Roman reverses, galvanized the Senate to take more drastic action against Perseus. It first rejected an offer from Ptolemaic Egypt to mediate between the two sides—the first of four attempts by third

---

20. Livy 42.60.9; cf. Polybius 27.15.14, with Errington 1971a, p. 214; Deininger 1971, pp. 168–170; Waterfield 2014, p. 184.

21. Livy 42.60.3–4.

22. Livy 42.61.

23. Livy 42.62.3–10.

24. Polybius 27.8; Livy 42.62.11–13; Appian, *Macedonian Wars* 9.12; Justin 33.1.4. See too Meloni 1953, pp. 236–251; Derow 1989, pp. 310–311; Burton 2017, p. 133. Matyszak 2009, p. 138, who also says Perseus expected Crassus to refuse.

25. Polybius 27.15; Diodorus 30.5, with Errington 1971a, p. 215; Hammond 1967, pp. 627–628; and Hammond and Walbank 1988, p. 520 n. 1.

parties to mediate in the war.[26] Then it issued a decree in October 170 against the three Boeotian towns that had supported Perseus after Philippus' visit in 172: Coronea, Thisbe, and Haliartus (p. 196).[27]

In 171 the praetor Gaius Lucretius Gallus besieged Harliartus.[28] When it fell, many of its people were slaughtered; those who surrendered were sold into slavery, its treasury was seized, and the city was razed to the ground. Thisbe yielded without a struggle; nevertheless, Gallus expelled its pro-Macedonian government and installed one sympathetic to Rome, which dominated public affairs for the next ten years, and those of its population not sold as slaves needed a permit to travel to Phocis or Aetolia.[29] Coronea fell to assault in the fall of 171. Livy's account of its demise is missing, but a fragmented senatorial decree speaks of members of a pro-Roman party fortifying the Acropolis and regaining their possessions—presumably they had been driven out when the city had earlier defied Rome.[30]

Even Chalcis was not safe despite it being the Roman naval base, for when the fleet returned there in 170 its crews looted temples, seized private homes, and kidnapped citizens to sell.[31] The Romans' brutality when it came to conquered cities turned many Greeks away from Rome to Macedonia, so to prevent further discontent the Senate sanctioned its commanders and ordered its troops to respect the Greeks' liberty.[32] Ominously, at the same time it was made clear that any recalcitrant city would be better off as a friend of Rome.[33]

Perseus in the meantime had unsuccessfully attacked the Roman camp north of the Peneus River—he made too much noise on his approach, so the enemy was ready for him, and he was beaten back to Sycyrium.[34] The Romans moved camp to Crannon south of the river, where plenty of crops were to be

---

26. Eckstein 1988, p. 427; on all attempts, see Eckstein 1988, pp. 426–444; cf. on mediation Gruen 1984, pp. 111–119 (p. 118 for the third war). An earlier Rhodian embassy to Rome ordering the Romans to end the war is incorrect: Eckstein 1988, p. 426.

27. *SEG* 19.374 = Sherk 1969, no 2, pp. 26–31, with Meloni 1953, pp. 240–246.

28. Livy 42.56.4–5, 42.63.3–11.

29. *SIG*[3] 646 = Austin 2006, no. 95, pp. 187–189; Sherk 1969, no. 2, pp. 26–31; Sherk 1984, no. 21, pp. 68–70.

30. Sherk 1984, no. 3, pp. 32–33; see too Errington 1974b; Burton 2017, p. 208.

31. Livy 43.7.5–11.

32. Meloni 1953, pp. 261–267; Burton 2017, pp. 139–140.

33. Meloni 1953, pp. 261–265; Errington 1971a, pp. 215–217; Eckstein 2010, p. 244 (the Romans treated their Greek friends "with a new arrogance").

34. Livy 42.64.1–6.

had. Although Perseus tried to coax them to battle, they refused his bait and he returned to Sycyrium.[35] He decided to apply more pressure on the Roman forces by setting up his camp at Mopselus, close to their own, forcing them to move to Phalanna. When word reached him that they were foraging for food, he took 1,000 cavalry and 2,000 Thracian and Cretan infantry and attacked them. He captured 600 of their number and 1,000 wagons loaded with grain and their horses, forcing the rest of the enemy to take refuge on a nearby hill.[36]

Unfortunately, any advantage Perseus suddenly had was lost when Crassus came to the rescue of his beleaguered men. Ordering the legions to follow at their own pace he sped ahead with cavalry and Roman and allied light infantry, including the Numidian troops and elephants, to find Perseus waiting for him, his phalanx already deployed. Thus began what has been called the battle of Crannon, at which Perseus used a new weapon called a *kestros* or sling-dart.[37] The odds favored Perseus, but in the fighting he lost 24 cavalrymen and 300 infantry, and his line began a retreat. Somehow his phalanx became entangled with the recently seized Roman prisoners and wagons of grain that were in its path. When Crassus saw the chaos, he gave the order to charge. The Macedonian army was unable to resist this concerted attack: 8,000 Macedonians were killed and 2,800 taken prisoner to the Romans' 4,300 men. The Roman victory, in the big picture, was not a deciding one, but it was crucial for morale.[38] It also showed again the weakness of the phalanx when disrupted.

Perseus returned to Macedonia, sending his army into winter quarters before leaving for Thessalonica with Cotys. Despite his loss at Crannon, there had been some positive gains over the year, especially with his capture of the passes into Macedonia and parts of Perrhaebia and Thessaly. But there had been serious setbacks that were part of a worrying trend: his inability to capitalize after victory at Callicinus by allowing the Romans to escape, his botched attempt to capture the Roman camp, and the mayhem when phalanx and line of booty collided at Crannon due to lack of leadership.[39] All of this would not have been lost on Crassus.

---

35. Livy 42.64.7–10.

36. Livy 42.65.1–6.

37. Livy 42.65.7–66.10; on the name, cf. Burton 2017, p. 137. On the *kestros*, see Burton 2017, p. 136 n. 47.

38. See Burton 2017, p. 137, noting how Roman propaganda turned it into a momentous battle.

39. Cf. Burton 2017, pp. 138–139, noting also that Crassus' unfamiliarity with the terrain and the lack of deployment of the Roman fleet benefited Perseus—he was lucky then.

The Second Year of the War

During the winter of 171–170 Perseus and Crassus steered clear of each other. Perseus removed his garrison from Larissa, which Roman troops quickly overran before recovering Perrhaebia, and marched into Boeotia for the winter.[40] In 170 Crassus was succeeded by the consul Aulus Hostilius Mancinus and Gallus by the praetor Lucius Hortensius. That spring, two members of the Epirote League, Theodotus and Philostratus, conspired to kidnap Mancinus in Epirus on his way from Corcyra to Thessaly and hand him over to Perseus as a sign of Epirus' loyalty. But Perseus was delayed at the Aous River as he marched to them and Mancinus was warned; he bypassed Epirus for Anticyra and sailed safely from there to Thessaly.[41] The plot led to a split in league members, with the Molossian state and a couple of others allying to Perseus and the rest led by the Thesprotians supporting Rome.[42]

Perseus had gained some strategically valuable allies in Epirus, which in turn robbed Mancinus of his best supply route from Epirus to Thessaly via the Zygos pass. The king followed up his diplomatic win by launching a sudden assault from Demetrias on the Roman naval base at Oreus in northern Euboea. He captured four quinquiremes and twenty merchant vessels, along with their cargoes of grain intended for the Roman army in Thessaly.[43] Hortensius now had to obtain supplies from along the Thracian coastline, but his men's activities caused only anger.

At Abdera (a friend of Rome), for example, the people wanted to send envoys to Mancinus and even the Senate protesting the demand for 100,000 *denarii* and 50,000 *medimnoi* of grain. Undeterred, Hortensius attacked the city, beheaded the leading citizens, and sold everyone else as slaves.[44] The Senate issued damning criticisms of Mancinus and Hortensius, fining the latter one million asses.[45] But the damage had been done: the nearby Greek cities of Maronea and Aenus, which had been a source of dispute between Philip and Rome, shut off their harbors to Hortensius' fleet for their own safety.

---

40. Livy 42.57.6–11.

41. Polybius 27.16.1–6; Diodorus 30.5a; cf. Walbank 1979, pp. 316–317.

42. Hammond 1967, pp. 628–629; cf. Burton 2017, p. 141 n. 68.

43. Plutarch, *Paullus* 9.3.

44. Livy 43.4.8–13.

45. Livy 43.8.1–3, 43.9–10.

Throughout 170 Perseus was active and successful on various fronts even though all the details are not known due to gaps in Livy's text.[46] Mancinus invaded Macedonia twice but both times was beaten back by the king, who even defeated the Roman commander in battle as he tried to invade from Elimiotis.[47] Regardless of the Roman army so close by, Perseus went on to capture several cities in Perrhaebia, thereby undoing recent Roman successes there.[48] He even marched north against the Dardanians, killing 10,000 of their number and taking a great deal of booty.[49]

Perhaps at this time the Macedonians massacred 500 opposition troops "whether of their own accord or under orders of the king," who had surrendered under a promise of safe conduct.[50] This was not the first time a Macedonian king had resorted to such treachery. In 326 Alexander the Great had promised safety to the Assaceni population of Massaga in the Lower Swat Valley of India if their mercenaries joined his army. As soon as they did, he killed all of them, for which even our ancient writers condemned him.[51] It was not just the Romans who had a savage side.

During all this time the Romans continued to try to win over the Greeks with high-profile envoys visiting the Boeotians and the Achaean and Aetolian Leagues, but to no avail.[52] In all, 170 was another good year for Perseus, and a morale boost for all his people. That feeling was soon going to change.

Slowing Momentum

Both sides would normally cease operations during winter because of the harsh conditions. But Perseus was eager to campaign further in Illyria, keep the Dardanians at bay, and perhaps even win over Genthius, whom the Senate mistrusted.[53] Since the Romans were not going to try to cross the

---

46. Cf. Burton 2017, p. 139, with bibliography about the second year in n. 59.

47. Plutarch, *Paullus* 9.4.

48. Livy 45.3.7.

49. Plutarch, *Paullus* 9.5, though Meloni 1953, p. 273, queries Plutarch's number. On the campaign: Meloni 1953, pp. 273–278.

50. Diodorus 30.4.

51. Arrian 4.27.3–4; Diodorus 17.84; Plutarch, *Alexander* 59.3–4, with Worthington 2014, pp. 238–239.

52. Burton 2017, p. 143.

53. Campaign: Livy 43.18.3–23.8.

snow-laden passes, some as high as 4,700 feet (1,450 meters), from Thessaly into Macedonia, that winter (170–169) he took an army of 10,000 infantry, 2,000 light-armed troops, and 500 cavalry to besiege Uscana in southern Illyria, home to the Penestae people and strategically located on a main route between Perseus and Genthius (map 3).[54] He could not allow Uscana to fall into Roman hands as that would give Rome a base closer to Dardania, not to mention open up Macedonia to invasion by Romans and Illyrians from the west and Dardanians from the north.

He stopped off at Styberra in Deuriopus (the same area where Perseis, named after him, was located), and on the third day he arrived at Uscana and besieged the city.[55] Taken by surprise, the people had no choice but to surrender. Perseus allowed the Roman troops in the city to depart unharmed though he confiscated their arms and armor, but the Illyrian soldiers and the rest of the people, whom he considered traitors, were sold as slaves at Styberra.[56] Why he spared these Romans is not known, especially as he went on to capture twelve other fortresses and take their 1,500 Roman garrison troops prisoner.

Perseus' swift campaign was a tribute to his tactical skills. A case in point was the heavily fortified town of Oaeneum in the Artatus (Velcka) valley, where he built a ramp higher than its walls allowing his men to overcome the defenders. All the adult males were put to death, the remaining people were taken prisoner, and his men shared the booty.[57] He had also added to his defenses, for he left behind garrisons in Uscana and probably also in the other fortresses he took, which successfully resisted Roman counter-attacks in the spring of 169.

To strengthen his ties further throughout the north he sent envoys to Genthius seeking an alliance.[58] They arrived at Scodra, where Genthius

---

54. Polybius 28.8; Livy 43.18.3–11; Plutarch, *Paullus* 9.5. Location of Uscana: Hammond and Walbank 1988, p. 522 n. 2, citing bibliography; see too Dell 1977, pp. 311–312.

55. Location of Macedonian Styberra: Hammond and Walbank 1988, p. 524 n. 1.

56. Livy 43.19.2. See also Dell 1977, pp. 312–313; Burton 2017, p. 144; Milivojevic 2019; numbers: cf. Briscoe 2012, p. 453.

57. Livy 43.19.2–4, 43.7–12. This siege was reminiscent of Alexander the Great's at Gaza in 332, when he built an artificial hill to match Gaza's height and set his siege engines atop it: Worthington 2014, pp. 178–179.

58. Polybius 28.8.4–9.1; Livy 43.19.13–14; Diodorus 30.9.2; Plutarch, *Paullus* 9.6, with Walbank 1979, pp. 336–341.

summoned them to Lissus.[59] He admired the way Macedonia even in Philip's time conducted itself against the Illyrians and perhaps believed it had an edge over Rome.[60] But he refused to help not because he lacked the spirit to fight Rome, he said, but because he did not have money. Perseus was told this and sent the envoys back to renew the plea for an alliance, but because he made no mention of giving Genthius money the latter remained unmoved.[61]

Perseus therefore helped his Epirote allies the Molossians by garrisoning Phanote in the Thyamis valley on the border between Molossia and Threspotia.[62] A Roman attack, in tandem with the Chaonians and Thesprotians, on Phanote was defeated by a Macedonian and Molossian army, forcing the enemy troops back to Illyria for safety.[63] The Macedonian commander, Cleuas, then moved into Chaonia; helped by 500 Molossians, he ambushed the garrison at Antigonea, the main city of the Chaonians, killing a large number of them and taking prisoners.

The next target was the city of Stratus as its Aetolian garrison commander Archidamus had agreed to betray it to Perseus.[64] Control of Stratus would give him a strategic base in enemy territory, but his plan was to return the city to the Acarnanians to lure them into an alliance with him against Rome.[65] In March 169 Perseus set off with 10,000 infantry and 300 cavalry across the snow-laden passes of the Pindus range, his men and pack animals suffering terribly in the freezing conditions. That they survived is a tribute to Perseus' leadership skills. His achievement evokes Alexander the Great again, when he crossed the frozen Hindu Kush (which the Greeks called the Caucasus) via the high Khawak pass in winter 329, his men having to eat the pack animals raw when their food ran out as it was too damp to light fires to cook them.[66]

On the fourth day Perseus reached the plain of Ioannina, where the Molossians gave him food and some troops, On the fifth day came a long

---

59. Polybius 28.8.4–5; Livy 43.20.1–3.

60. Dell 1970, p. 125.

61. Polybius 28.9.3–8; Livy 43.20.3.

62. Identification of Phanote: Hammond 1967, p. 676, but see Meloni 1953, pp. 256–257 n. 4; note though Hammond and Walbank 1988, p. 525 n. 1.

63. Livy 43.21.4–5.

64. Livy 43.21.5–22.7.

65. Meloni 1953, pp. 279–284; see too Hammond 1967, pp. 281 and 630–631.

66. Worthington 2014, p. 221.

march through the Kiafa pass to the River Arachthus in eastern Epirus, north of Ambracia, home to a Roman garrison.[67] His progress was slowed, however, because the bad weather and height of the Arachthus meant he had to wait until his engineers built a timber bridge across it. Eventually a series of forced marches brought him to Stratus, but his plan to capture the city was thwarted by the Roman commander Gaius Popillus, who beat him there with 1,000 troops. That prompted an Aetolian support force of 600 troops, on which Perseus was counting, to change plan and go over to the Roman side. If Perseus was not aware of the Aetolians' rising disillusionment with him, their conduct now made it obvious. He was left with no choice but to return to Macedonia, along the way taking Aperantia, a mountainous area in northeast Aetolia, where he left an 800-strong garrison.[68]

What had Perseus' costly campaign achieved?[69] The answer is not much. He had failed to take Stratus, and he had not yet defeated the Roman army decisively nor won over key Greek states. Worse, he had to leave some of his "irreplaceable" army in Penestia to keep the people there in check as well as in distant Aperantia and even Cassandrea on the Pallene peninsula because of Roman naval activities.[70] To make matters worse, in 169 the Senate sent 6,000 Romans and 6,000 Latin allies for the legions and 250 Roman cavalry and 300 Latin cavalry to Macedonia, as well as reinforcements for the navy. Still, Perseus had reinforced his north-western frontier and made inroads into Illyria, sold prisoners and booty for income, continued to pose a risk to Rome on several fronts, and showed his leadership abilities and clever planning.

A curious episode takes place during the winter of 169–168 when Eumenes and Antiochus were said to have made overtures to Perseus with the logical argument that if Rome conquered Macedonia, then Pergamum and Syria would be next, given the Romans' natural hostility to monarchy as a form of government.[71] By now the consul Lucius Aemilius Paullus had been appointed to lead a large army against Perseus, as we shall see in the next chapter, so it made sense for Perseus to ally with these kings. But nothing happened, not least

---

67. Perseus' route: Hammond and Walbank 1988, p. 525.

68. Livy 43.22.8–11.

69. See the criticisms in Hammond and Walbank 1988, p. 526.

70. Livy 43.23.7.

71. Polybius 29.8; Livy 44.24.1–7; Appian, *Macedonian Wars* 18.1.

because Eumenes wanted a huge monetary sum either to remain neutral or negotiate peace, which Perseus refused to pay.[72]

Eumenes' extraordinary change of heart stretches credibility. He had been pushing Rome to war against Perseus since 173, so why he wanted to do anything that benefitted Perseus and ran counter to the Senate makes little sense. Closer to the truth is that the story was fabricated by Polybius and followed by later writers as an example of Perseus' alleged miserliness, which cost him strategic alliances. Polybius projects Perseus elsewhere in his narrative as penny-pinching and hence a poor leader—for example, his refusal to pay Genthius money, as noted above, which cost him Genthius' support. Later, when faced by a large Roman army under Paullus, as we discuss in the next chapter, Perseus was said to have promised Genthius 300 talents and made a down payment of ten.[73] But then he grew suspicious of Genthius and refused to hand over the rest, losing a valuable ally.

Perseus' alleged stinginess is evident in his dealings with Clondicus, the leader of the Bastarnae, who agreed to bring 10,000 cavalry and the same number of men to Perseus in return for ten gold pieces for each cavalryman, five for each infantryman, and one thousand for Clondicus himself. He and Perseus with roughly half of his army were to meet in early 168 at the Paeonian city of Bylazora, from where Perseus presumably intended to attack the Dardanians and possibly the Romans in northern Illyria.[74] When Clondicus arrived he demanded full payment, which the king's Friends and commanders were in favor of, but Perseus refused. He told Clondicus he needed only 5,000 cavalry, and in disgust Clondicus returned home, ravaging parts of Thrace along the way.

The image of Perseus in these dealings must be viewed skeptically as once again Polybius could be guilty of character denigration at the cost of veracity. On the other hand, Perseus may have worried about over-extending

72. Polybius 29.8–9; Livy 44.24.7–25.12: either 500 talents or 1,000 talents for remaining neutral or not joining Rome or 1,500 talents for negotiating peace; Appian, *Macedonian Wars* 18.1: 1,000 talents. See too Meloni 1953, pp. 335–341; Walbank 1979, p. 366; Schleussner 1973, pp. 119–123; Gruen 1984 pp. 558–563; Eckstein 1988, pp. 428–429; Briscoe 2012, pp. 546–549; Burton 2011, pp. 181–182 and 293–294.

73. Livy 44.23.2–8, 44.27.8–12; Appian, *Macedonian Wars* 18.1; cf. Polybius 28.8.4–9.8, Diodorus 30.9.2; Plutarch, *Paullus* 9.6. See Hammond and Walbank 1988, pp. 530–531, on Genthius' coinage at this time.

74. Livy 44.26.2–27.3; Diodorus 30.19; Appian, *Macedonian Wars* 18.1–3; Plutarch, *Paullus* 12.4–8 and 13.1–2, with Meloni 1953, pp. 329–335; Walbank 1979, pp. 369–370; Hammond and Walbank 1988, pp. 534–535; Briscoe 2012, pp. 550–555; Burton 2017, p. 160 with n. 130.

his finances, given the vagaries of a rolling economy and his expenses over the previous years. Along with that, Genthius' loyalty was suspect; facing increasing Roman aggression, he might declare against Perseus to save himself and his kingdom. Likewise, there was no guarantee that Clondicus would not switch allegiance to Rome if offered enough money, leaving Perseus trapped between two enemy lines were Clondicus to attack him from the north.[75] But all these factors do not make Perseus a miser with short-sighted leadership.

The Return of Philippus

The year 169 saw both the third year of the war and the return of the sixty-year-old Quintus Marcius Philippus to Greece—the same man who had misled Perseus at Tempe in 172 (p. 197). Now consul, he led 12,000 troops and 550 cavalry to Actium. He tapped his cousin Gaius Marcius Figulus to command the fleet at Chalcis and after meeting with his predecessor Hortensius at the Roman base at Palaepharsalus in Thessaly kept him on staff.[76] To maintain Roman support, especially considering the reputed plot to kill Mancinus, he sent envoys with messages of goodwill to the Achaeans, Aetolians, and Acarnanians, but received little back.[77]

Philippus thought he could deal with Perseus as easily as he had hoodwinked him in Tempe or dealt with his father over the status of Maronea and Aenus in 183 (p. 166). He decided not to waste any more time but to invade Macedonia by land while Figulus raided the coast of Pieria. But Perseus anticipated his plan and blocked Philippus by establishing a base at Dium near the Petra pass. He then secured the three other passes into his kingdom by sending 12,000 men under Hippias to Lapathus near the Tempe pass, 10,000 light-armed troops under Asclepiodotus to the Volustana pass, and another force (under an unknown commander) to hold Otobulus, while ordering his cavalry to patrol the coastal plain and prevent any raids there.[78]

The Romans decided to break through Lapathus into Macedonia and join their navy off Pieria. With 30,000 men Philippus hiked 7 miles

75. See Hammond and Walbank 1988, p. 535.

76. Livy 44.1.4, with Briscoe 2012, p. 467 (on Livy wrongly calling him a proconsul). See Burton 2017, p. 148 with n. 95, on numbers.

77. Derow 1989, pp. 312–314. Philippus and the following activities: Meloni 1953, pp. 285–301, for example.

78. Livy 44.2.1–2.12, with Briscoe 2012, p. 471.

(11 kilometers) a day for three days over the rugged terrain of the Lapathus saddle before reaching the top. The exhausted men were allowed a day's rest there. Hippias' camp was roughly one mile (1.5 kilometers) away, visible across the ridge. Hippias at once took some infantry but did not engage the enemy although he did hurl some missiles at them. The next day saw more serious fighting among the light infantry as the narrowness of the ridges prevented a full-scale deployment of troops, with each side suffering considerable casualties.[79]

Philippus had made no headway after two days and was in urgent need of supplies. He had two choices: retreat ignominiously or find another way to reach Figulus at the coast to stock up on provisions. He chose the latter, making his way down a precipitous route through the Karavidha gorge to the Pierian plain. This was a bold move, but the descent was a nightmare, with pack animals lost, panicked elephants trumpeting so loudly they scared off horses, and the men constantly slipping and falling over because of the steep slopes. In all, their route was perhaps 12 miles (19 kilometers), but it took them four days to cover it before they reached the plain. There they built a fortified camp between Heracleum (Platamona) and Leibethra at the foot of Mount Olympus and received some supplies from Figulus.[80]

Perseus was caught off-guard by Philippus crossing this formidable mountain and camping within his kingdom. Livy (from another lost passage in Polybius) claims that he was taking a bath at Dium when a bodyguard rushed to tell him the enemy was on his doorstep, causing him to jump out of his bath lamenting he had been defeated without even a fight.[81] Whether he was really bathing and reacted the way he did may be character assassination by our sources. Then again, if they wanted to show a panicked king they could just as easily have had him dining, sleeping, or otherwise engaged, hence he may well have been in the bathtub.

In a panic Perseus reeled off a barrage of orders.[82] He told everyone at Dium and in the area around the southern end of the plain to relocate to Pydna on the Pierian coast, thereby abandoning the Petra pass. Next, he

---

79. Livy 44.3.1–4.6.

80. Livy 44.4.7–5.13; on the camp, cf. Briscoe 2012, pp. 481–482.

81. Livy 44.6.1; Diodorus 30.10.2.

82. Livy 44.6.2–4; Diodorus 30.11, on which cf. Burton 2017, p. 151 n. 105. See Hammond and Walbank 1988, p. 529 n. 1, with reference to a fragmentary inscription on a statue base, which restored could be to Philip and Perseus.

ordered that the treasures in the palace at Pella were to be dumped into the sea, the dockyard at Thessalonica burned, his garrison troops to be withdrawn from the Volustana and Tempe passes as well as Lapathus, and the gold statues of the kings removed from Dium. Burning the dockyard and ditching the treasures are dubious, though the Roman fleet could hardly take over a destroyed dockyard as a base.[83] In any case, they were not burned, and the treasures, if ditched, were recovered. The instructions to abandon the passes must have been given, because he charged Hippias and Asclepiodotus with dereliction of duty and executed them to cover his strategic blunder (and cowardice, so Livy).[84]

Philippus thus had an easy entry to Dium, going into areas northwest of Pydna, receiving the surrender of various towns there and granting them their freedom, before moving north to the River Ascordus and returning to Dium. Meanwhile the Roman fleet landed on the coast but brought too little food for his men, as Perseus anticipated. Philippus therefore withdrew to Phila where he could acquire grain brought by sea and overland from Thessaly, enabling Perseus to reoccupy Dium and establish a defensive position on the steep north bank of the River Elpeus about 5 miles (8 kilometers) away.[85]

As winter was drawing close both armies stood fast, separated only by the wide Elpeus River, which ran beneath the towering slopes of Mount Olympus. Perseus had chosen an exceptional position as the season made the river deep and treacherous to cross. The Roman ships had landed ravaging parties on the coasts of the Thermaic Gulf, even threatening Thessalonica, but were often driven back by Macedonian soldiers. An attempt by a Roman commander, Gaius Marcius, along with Eumenes and Prusias of Bithynia (who had clearly abandoned his policy of neutrality), on Potidaea failed, with the defenders killing 600 Romans in a bitter clash. The Romans suffered another defeat when they tried to take Meliboea and Demetrias thanks to reinforcements from Perseus, at which point Eumenes returned home. Eventually, the Roman

83. Meloni 1953, p. 302; Burton 2017, p. 152; doubted by Hammond and Walbank 1988, p. 528 n. 2.

84. Livy 44.10.1–4; cf. 44.7.8–9; Diodorus 30.11, with Briscoe 2012, p. 498; Burton 2017, pp. 152–153.

85. Livy 44.7.1–7, 44.8.1–7, with Walbank 1957, p. 627, and Briscoe 2012, p. 491, on the name. Note the criticism of Philippus for putting himself in a dangerous and vulnerable position: Matyszak 2009, pp. 144–146. On the topography and terrain, see Hammond 1984, p. 32; Hammond and Walbank 1988, pp. 542–544.

fleet sailed to winter at Sciathos in the northwestern Aegean and Oreus on Euboea, while Philippus, bruised and beleaguered, moved to Heracleum.[86]

The year 169 had been another good one for Perseus. Although southern Macedonia was exposed to a Roman army, he and his allies had inflicted some significant defeats on enemy troops, suffering few casualties themselves, and Philippius had not been able to act effectively with the Roman navy. Perseus' momentum worried the Senate, as did Rome's declining fortunes in Greece and even at sea.[87] On top of that, Antiochus was taking advantage of Rome's preoccupation with Perseus to invade Egypt, which had appealed for help to Rome.

At some point the Rhodians and Prusias separately sent envoys to the Senate offering to mediate between Perseus and Rome.[88] The senators were not interested: they had decided it was time for decisive action and would not even hear them until after Perseus was defeated.

---

86. Livy 44.9.1–11. Campaigns: Burton 2017, pp. 155–157.

87. Hammond and Walbank 1988, pp. 536–537.

88. Polybius 28.17.9–15; Livy 44.14.5–12. On the embassies, see Hammond and Walbank 1988, p. 533; Eckstein 1988, pp. 434–437; Burton 2017, pp. 156–157. Prusias prostrated himself before the Senate in the winter of 167/66, not in fear of any retaliation for favoring Perseus but seeking additional territory; the Senate renewed its *amicitia* with him and gave him money and possibly warships: Eckstein 1988, pp. 437–442.

11

Dismembering Macedonia

IN 168 THE new consul, Lucius Aemilius Paullus, whose father had defeated
Demetrius of Pharos in the Second Illyrian War and who had died fighting
at Cannae against Hannibal, received Macedonia as his province (figure 11.1).
He persuaded the Senate to send a commission to Macedonia and Illyria to
gauge Greek support for Rome and assess its military strength over there.[1]
Its report led to the crafting of three offensives to topple Perseus and restore
Roman influence in Illyria. The first was against the worrying Genthius in
Illyria, who was showing signs of favoring Perseus over Rome, despite his
earlier rebuff over money he had demanded from the king (p. 214). The
second offensive was in the Aegean, and the third was in Pieria, where the
Romans were in an inferior position and separated from Perseus by the Elpeus
River. The praetor Gaius Octavius was to command the fleet, and another
praetor, Lucius Anicius Gallus, took over from Cento (who stayed in Illyria).
All of them arrived on the mainland by spring 168.

The Offensives

Gallus was in charge of the first offensive against Genthius. He conducted his
campaign with surgical precision. It lasted only thirty days, though Livy's account is so fragmented that we know only a few details.[2] Genthius mustered
15,000 men and ships at Lissus, the southernmost city of his kingdom. From
there he marched five miles (eight kilometers) to besiege Bassania, a Roman

---

1. Livy 44.18.1–5, 44.19.1–3, and 44.20.2–7. On Paullus, see Reiter 1988.

2. Livy 44.30.1–32.5; Appian, *Illyrian Wars* 9 (twenty days), with Hammond and Walbank
1988, pp. 537–538; Briscoe 2012, pp. 561–568; see too Meloni 1953, pp. 326–329 and 358 n. 4;
Matyszak 2009, p. 150; Waterfield 2014, pp. 188–189.

The Last Kings of Macedonia and the Triumph of Rome. Ian Worthington, Oxford University Press.
© Oxford University Press 2023. DOI: 10.1093/oso/9780197520055.003.0012

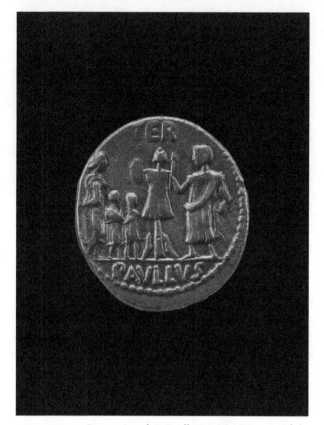

FIGURE 11.1. Lucius Aemilius Paullus. © The Trustees of the British Museum.

ally (*socius*) from the days of the Illyrian Wars. His half-brother Caravantius attacked the territory of the Cavii, while eighty *lembi* ravaged the lands around Epidamnus and Apollonia. Gallus, commanding two legions (10,400 infantry), 600 cavalry, and several thousand Italian allied troops, went north from Apollonia to join Cento at the River Genusus (Shkumbin).

Gallus captured many of Genthius' *lembi*, defeated him in a battle, and invaded his kingdom. Genthius retreated to his capital Scodra and negotiated a three-day truce when Gallus arrived to invest the city. If Genthius hoped Caravantius would come to his rescue, he was mistaken, leaving no choice but to surrender on the last day of the truce. He and other members of his family were sent to Rome, though the Romans took no other prisoners. The Ardiaean monarchy was ended, and Rome now dominated the entire coastline, compromising Perseus' western frontier.

We also know little about the second offensive in the Aegean.[3] Perseus had tasked his commanders Antenor and Callippus to patrol the Aegean, and they had conducted a series of raids and overcome a Pergamene fleet.[4] Now the Roman fleet under Octavius, with ships from Eumenes, ended these Macedonian raids and confined their vessels to their bases at Cassandrea, Pella, and Demetrias. They also seized any merchant vessels and their cargoes they found sailing to Macedonia. Thus, Roman ships carrying supplies to the army in Thessaly and Pieria were now free to sail without fear of attack. If we believe Livy, Perseus thought the Roman navy was just as dangerous as the army.[5] He therefore stationed a garrison of 2,000 at Thessalonica to protect its dockyards, 1,000 cavalry at Aenea to prevent raids on the countryside, and 5,000 troops to the Petra pass. In all, he may have deployed as many as 10,000 troops on these missions, taking them away from his main army.[6]

Paullus himself oversaw the third offensive, to bring down Perseus. Even though the Macedonian army had been shattered at Cynoscephalae in 179, in the decade since then its numbers had been built up, and its phalanx was just as deadly. Paullus knew he could not risk fighting on level ground where the phalanx would be in its element, so he needed to draw Perseus into a pitched battle on uneven ground. Perseus was equally aware that he needed to steer clear of that at all costs, so terrain became the driving need of a battle site.

During the winter Perseus fortified his camp atop the steep left bank of the Elpeus River with palisades and stone walls and set up torsion catapults and stone-throwing machines on top of wooden towers.[7] Wanting to wear out Paullus, he took special care with his supply line. He brought in what he needed by wagon from Pydna via Dium, with women from nearby towns carrying the food on their backs, and his horses could feed on the nearby pastures. He had good reason to be optimistic as his position, while defensive, was still stronger than that of his father at the Aous River Gorge.[8] Moreover,

---

3. Livy 44.32.5–8.

4. Livy 44.28; cf. 29.

5. Livy 44.32.6.

6. Hammond and Walbank 1988, p. 539.

7. Livy 44.32.10–11; Plutarch, *Paullus* 13.5. See the description of the topography and terrain in Hammond 1984, p. 32; Hammond and Walbank 1988, pp. 542–544; on the fighting, see Burton 2017, pp. 162–165.

8. Hammond 1984, p. 32.

his men were probably in good spirits—after all, apart from reversals at sea they had generally had the upper hand in clashes with Roman troops.

Paullus had with him 39,000 infantry, of whom perhaps 26,000 were legionaries, 4,000 cavalry (1,200 from Italy), and some war elephants from Masinissa of Numidia.[9] Perseus commanded nearly 40,000 infantry, consisting of 21,000 phalangites; 15,000 light-armed infantry of Thracians, Paeonians, Gauls living in Macedonia, Agrianians, and Cretan specialist archers; and a special unit of "elephant fighters" (*elephantomachai*), with angled sharp spikes on their helmets and shields designed to tackle the war elephants.[10] He also had 2,000 Macedonian heavy cavalry and 1,000 Odrysian light cavalry. But at this time key alliances with Antiochus and Eumenes had not been made, assuming they made overtures to him, and likewise with Genthius and Clondicus of the Bastarnae, all because of his reputed miserliness, as we discussed in the previous chapter.[11] If true, which is hard to accept in all cases, we should agree with Livy that Perseus needed to sacrifice money in the best interests of his kingdom.[12]

Perseus had sent 5,000 troops to guard the Petra pass, but he made a mistake by not deploying infantry further north to protect his line of supply if a Roman fleet landed on the coast there. This was an oversight that Paullus exploited when he arrived at the Peneus River in early June (probably the 7th).[13] There he fortified his own camp and learned of Genthius' defeat in the first offensive.[14] The Peneus was relatively dry because it was late in the spring; hence, as Matyszak notes, its bed served as a "formidable trench" between the two sides.[15] Both commanders took their time to decide what to do next.[16]

---

9. Numbers: Hammond and Walbank 1988, pp. 539–540 n. 2; cf. Burton 2017, p. 159.

10. Numbers: Plutarch, *Paullus* 13.4, with Hammond and Walbank 1988, pp. 540–542. On the elephant unit (Livy 44.41.4), cf. the note of Briscoe 2012, p. 597.

11. On Perseus leaving the Elpeus to meet separately with Genthius and Clondicus: Polybius 29.4.4–5; Livy 44.23.7, 44.26.5. On Perseus' dealings with Genthius, see Polybius 28.8.4–9.8; Livy 43.19.13–14, 43.20.3, 44.23.2–8, 44.27.8–12; Diodorus 30.9.2; Plutarch, *Paullus* 9.6. For his dealings with Clondicus, see Livy 44.26.2–27.3.

12. Livy 44.26.1–2.

13. On the timetable of the following events, see Hammond 1984, p. 41; Hammond and Walbank 1988, pp. 545–547.

14. Plutarch, *Paullus* 13.5; cf. Livy 44.33–34.

15. Matyszak 2009, p. 148. Robin Waterfield points out to me that despite what Livy says, the river never ran completely dry.

16. Meloni 1953, pp. 376–377; Walbank 1979, p. 381.

Paullus knew that he could not rush Perseus' line, for his men would be sitting ducks as they tried to cross the river, but he also could not hold fast and allow Perseus to dictate the course of events. Since he had a good knowledge of the area's geography, he ordered a substantial number of Roman vessels to bring him provisions and take up a position to the rear of the Macedonian line. Perhaps at this point Perseus realized his error in not sending additional troops up there as he now had to deal with an enemy on land and at sea.

Paullus next devised a plan to surprise his adversary by sending Publius Scipio Nasica and Quintus Fabius Maximus with perhaps 5,000 men toward Pythium in Perrhaebia to attack the Macedonian army there between 3 and 6 a.m. on the third day after they left (which would be June 14).[17] They were to march first to Heracleum as if they were rendezvousing with the fleet under Octavius to sail against Thessalonica, hence away from Perseus' position. That was a hoax. Instead, the men were to take rations that Octavius was bringing and secretly march back to Pythium.[18] Paullus hoped that Perseus would fall for his trick, which meant his foes would be trapped between two very size-able hostile lines.

To lend credence to this plan and give Nasica and Maximus time to get into position, Paullus lulled Perseus into thinking he was ready to try to break his enemy.[19] At dawn on the 12th, Roman light-armed troops fought the Macedonians' light-armed troops in the riverbed until noon when Paullus recalled them after suffering casualties. The same thing happened the next day, the 13th, with the Romans suffering losses thanks to Perseus' artillery. The king thought—reasonably enough—that these attacks were to pin him down to allow the troops under Nasica and Maximus to march safely to join the fleet. The latter were doing no such thing, for on that same day (13th) they had stealthily returned under cover of darkness to the woods around the Lapathus ridge and taken up their position. There they waited for the prearranged time the following morning.

In the early hours of the next day (the 14th), as ordered, this contingent burst through the sleeping Macedonians at the head of the Petra pass, and overcame two other Macedonian contingents to clear the pass and encamp

17. Livy 44.35.8–24. Plutarch, *Paullus* 15.6–7 (from Scipio Nasica), gives 8,320, but this is from an apparent letter Nasica sent to "one of the kings," which exaggerates his own importance and the numbers involved: see, further, Walbank 1979, pp. 379–383; Hammond 1984, p. 43; Hammond and Walbank 1988, p. 545 n. 3 and p. 546.

18. See Burton 2017, pp. 163–164. Route: Walbank 1979, pp. 381–383.

19. Livy 44.35.16–24.

at the foothills east of Katerini in Pieria.[20] When Perseus heard this news, he realized he was surrounded north of the river so broke camp, pushing his men on a forced march of 15 miles (24 kilometers) to a new position just south of the fortified city Pydna on the Pierian coastline.[21] He moved from his camp the next day intending to deal with the men under Nasica and Maximus west of Katerini. The Romans came down into the plain and marched along the main coastal road toward Pydna, expecting Perseus to be inside its walls and ready to defend it, but unexpectedly came upon him in the plain in front of the city with his line already deployed.[22]

Perseus' scouts had already reported dust clouds in the distance. He rightly took these to be from his enemy and deployed his line as he intended "to confront the Romans as soon as they came up."[23] He was already on the level plain, which suited his phalanx perfectly, and the surrounding ridges benefitted his light-armed troops.[24] The flatness of the plain remains today, which is mostly farmland (figure 11.2).

To make matters worse for the Romans, the king's line faced south, allowing him to block an enemy advance northward. Perseus must have thought that the odds were finally in his favor.

The Battle of Pydna

Our principal sources for the details of the preliminaries to the battle and the actual fighting are unfortunately fragmentary—Polybius, a memoir by Scipio Nasica, who fought on the Roman right flank, and the Hellenistic historian Posidonius (who wrote about Perseus in several books). As a result, we must rely on the accounts of Livy and Plutarch, who drew on the other three, though we cannot say how closely they followed them or imposed their own interpretation on events.[25] This is particularly the case with Nasica's largely

---

20. Plutarch, *Paullus* 15–16.3; cf. Polybius 29.15.2–3, with Walbank 1979, pp. 383–386. Livy's account of the following action is lost.

21. Plutarch, *Paullus* 16.4–9; Zonaras 9.23. On the site of Pydna, see Hammond 1984, pp. 31–32.

22. Livy 44.37.1, 44.38.11; Plutarch, *Paullus* 17.2 (cf. 16.7–9), with Hammond 1984, pp. 33–34, for example. Location of Perseus' camp: Meloni 1953, p. 394; Walbank 1979, p. 385; McDonald 1981, p. 252; Hammond 1984, p. 37; Hammond and Walbank 1988, p. 552.

23. Plutarch, *Paullus* 16.7.

24. Topography of the plain: Hammond and Walbank 1988, p. 547.

25. See Walbank 1979, pp. 378–379, on sources; cf. Hammond and Walbank 1988, pp. 548–549, detailing various passages in Livy and Plutarch where they drew on Nasica (e.g., Livy

FIGURE 11.2. Pydna: site of the battle. Photo credit: Robin Waterfield.

personal account of his role in the battle and so written from the Roman viewpoint. The following discussion is derived from Hammond's classic analysis of the battle.[26]

Paullus quickly saw that Perseus' commanding position on the plain made his troops vulnerable, even more so as they were exhausted and hot from their march there.[27] He gave orders for his men to pull back from Perseus' line to give them some distance, then quickly deployed his legionaries into three formations, one behind the other.[28] The first formation, which faced Perseus' advancing line, was made up of wedge-shaped units with the points of the wedges facing their foes to disrupt the uniform line of a charging phalanx. The gaps between wedges were filled with light-armed skirmishers who kept making sorties ahead of their own comrades to delay and even deter the opposite side from launching a full-on attack.

44.36.8–14 and Plutarch, *Paullus* 17.1–4, where Nasica wishes to engage Perseus and Paullus not doing so), and that Polybius likely incorporated some of Nasica's stories into his own account while adding his own comments. On Nasica's memoir to do with Pydna, see further Burton 2017, pp. 214–218.

26. Hammond 1984. See too Burton 2017, pp. 166–169 and 214–218.

27. Livy 44.36.1–7.

28. Livy 44.38.1–4.

How Paullus arranged his other two formations we do not know, but all his men retreated unharmed to the surrounding foothills, where he set up a fortified camp. Apparently from where he sat in his tent he could look down on the plain and see the enemy army.[29] Perseus had let slip a golden opportunity to crush the Roman army. If he had pounced on Paullus' startled troops when he first saw them and covered the roughly half-mile (1 kilometer) between the two sides at speed, the chances are that his phalanx would have proved unstoppable. By the time he gave the order to advance, it was too late, for Paullus' troops were onto the ridge.

The only Roman troops in the plain now were the skirmishers and some cavalry, but Perseus' phalanx was still advancing along the level ground. Paullus hit on a daring tactic, ordering the cavalry to gallop from the left wing past the front of the phalanx with the cavalrymen hanging their shields in such a way that they broke off the points of the sarissas.[30] The phalangites presumably could not have aimed their weapons at the cavalrymen's shields and may have tried to use them to trip or impale the horses, but they would not have been able to maneuver their cumbersomely long sarissas quickly enough because of the speed of the galloping horses.[31]

A break in the fighting allowed Perseus to build a fortified camp in the plain between the Roman one and the coast, thereby cutting off Paullus' seaborne supplies and reinforcements and forcing him to forage for provisions. At the same time, Perseus made sure his own supply line from Pydna was not affected, perhaps even hoping that Paullus and his men would weary of their situation and leave. Perseus' plan was a clever one, and a lesser commander might well have withdrawn, but Paullus was all out to kill or capture the king.

A delay of some days followed. On the night of June 21 there was a lunar eclipse.[32] Our sources give differing accounts of the men's superstitious reaction to this phenomenon, such as banging bronze vessels and waving blazing torches at the sky to charm the moon back, and the different spins put on

---

29. Plutarch, *Paullus* 17.13, with Hammond 1984, pp. 34–35, on the terrain.

30. Frontinus, *Strategematica* 2.3.20.

31. Hammond and Walbank 1988, pp. 550–551 with n. 1, correcting Meloni 1953, p. 393, that this contact was in the final battle, hence Frontinus is wrong. Development of the battle: Hammond 1984, pp. 38–42.

32. Polybius 29.16; Livy 44.37.5–9; Plutarch, *Paullus* 17.7–10; see too Zonaras 9.23 and Justin 33.1.7 (presumably from Polybius), with Walbank 1979, pp. 386–388; see too Hammond 1984, pp. 43–44; Hammond and Walbank 1988, p. 545 n. 2; Briscoe 2012, pp. 584–586; Burton 2017, pp. 166–167 and 216–217.

it. For example, the Macedonians thought the worst and the Romans conversely the best as both saw it as the end of Macedonia. Paullus, who was "not altogether without knowledge and experience of the irregularities of eclipses," sacrificed twenty oxen the next morning to Heracles but failed to obtain favorable omens until "with the twenty-first victim the propitious signs appeared and indicated victory if they stood on the defensive."[33]

The battle began the next day (the 22nd) in accidental fashion thanks to a horse breaking away from the Roman line and running free.[34] As it galloped away across a river, some Thracians on Perseus' side seized it, but a Roman force sent to retrieve the horse killed one of them, causing 800 of their comrades to attack them. During this time the Macedonian and Roman heavy infantry remained in their respective camps, but as more troops became involved in this skirmish Perseus and Paullus deployed their heavy infantry and formed their lines.

Livy, following Polybius (and echoed later by Zonaras), put the outbreak of battle down to Chance: "Fortune, which is stronger than human planning, brought on the battle."[35] Plutarch insists it was preplanned, with Paullus cunningly releasing a horse toward the enemy line to draw out its light infantry when the sun would not be shining in his soldiers' eyes.[36] All these explanations may simply be stories as Paullus could hardly have anticipated that a loose horse would not only provoke a conflict but escalate it into actual battle.[37] But perhaps a horse had broken loose and ended up unwittingly playing a role in the battle's mythology—after all, on his victory monument at Delphi Paullus added a frieze depicting the battle, which featured a riderless horse (see figure 11.5).

Each side fielded, as noted before, roughly 40,000 men.[38] The Macedonian line, on level ground, stretched over two miles (3.5 kilometers), with the

---

33. Plutarch, *Paullus* 17.8.11.

34. Livy 44.40.4–10; Plutarch, *Paullus* 18.1–2; Zonaras 9.22.5.

35. Livy 44.40.3.

36. Plutarch, *Paullus* 18.1–4 (from Nasica); Zonaras 9.23. The position of the sun (supposedly in the evening) is doubted by Hammond 1984, p. 37.

37. On the horse story, see Meloni 1953, pp. 383–384; Hammond 1984, pp. 44–45. Matyszak 2009, p. 152, doubts it.

38. Hammond 1984, pp. 45–46. Numbers: Plutarch, *Paullus* 13.4. The actual Roman numbers are not known, but Hammond 1984, p. 46; cf. Burton 2017, p. 167 n. 155, suggests less than 40,000 but not by much.

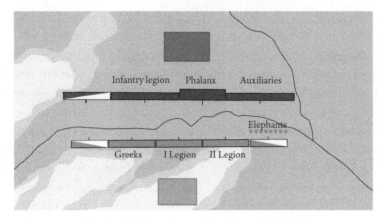

FIGURE 11.3. Battle of Pydna. Licensed under a CC BY-SA 4.0 License (https://creativecommons.org/licenses/by-sa/4.0/).

phalanx taking up half of that at a depth of sixteen men.[39] Perseus' 21,000 phalangites were probably arrayed in fourteen brigades, perhaps of 1,500 each as in Alexander the Great's army. On each wing were cavalry squadrons, which, if the deployment was the same as at Callinicus, would be the so-called Sacred Squadrons. On either side of them were Royal Squadrons, and the *agema* led by the king was on the right. Additionally, there were 1,000 Odrysian light cavalry, who usually fought in an open formation as light-armed infantry were often interspersed in their ranks (figure 11.3).[40]

Evidently not influenced by his father's mistake at Cynoscephalae, Perseus put himself with some squadrons of Sacred Cavalry on the right wing. This was a customary position, but as events proved, he was too far away to rally his line when the Romans began to gain the upper hand. Paullus lined himself and one legion up against Perseus' "bronze shield" phalanx (*chalkaspides*) and his other legion under an ex-consul named Albinus against the "white shield" phalanx (*leukaspides*)—their names presumably were from the color of their shields.[41]

39. Calculations: Hammond 1984, p. 39. Deployment of lines: Hammond 1984, pp. 45–46.

40. Battle: Livy 44.41–42.8; Plutarch, *Paullus* 18–22.2, with Walbank 1940, pp. 378–391; Meloni 1953, pp. 359–409; McDonald 1981, pp. 252–254; Hammond 1984; Hammond and Walbank 1988, pp. 547–557; Matyszak 2009, pp. 152–155; Briscoe 2012, pp. 568–600; Waterfield 2014, pp. 188–190; Burton 2017, pp. 167–169.

41. Sekunda 2013, pp. 95–96, but see now his comments about the latter regiment on pp. 108–113.

The Macedonians attacked first, making the surrounding hills "resound with their loud battle cries," and Paullus, who had never faced the Macedonians in battle, made the comment some years later that "he had never seen a sight more fearful" as when he confronted the massed Macedonian phalanx bearing down on him.[42] The Macedonian peltasts and the phalangites linked up with the light-armed troops on their flanks to form a continuous line and charged the legionaries, their sarissas piercing the Romans' shields, cuirasses, and bodies. The Pelignians, Italian allies on the right of the Roman line, tried to push the sarissas aside with their swords and shields, even trying to seize them with their hands, but they could do little against the long pikes.

The Pelignians did, however, buy Paullus valuable time, and they opened gaps in the phalanx's long line, which left some infantry still on the flat ground and others on the ends of the steep ridge ends, where the terrain was to their disadvantage.[43] Paullus seized his chance to exploit their sudden vulnerability. He ordered his legionaries to advance not in one continuous line but separately in maniples of about 120 men, and then charge through the gaps in the phalanx line and encircle it. The phalangites were still gripping their forward-pointing sarissas and did not have the room to turn to ward off this new enemy attack on their sides and rear. In brutal hand-to-hand fighting, the legionaries' long slashing swords and tall oblong shields, which reached to their feet, were far superior to the phalangites' small daggers and light shields. Perseus' phalangites were cut to pieces.

Paullus' war elephants and light cavalry had already charged into Perseus' cavalry and light-armed troops and inflicted terrible damage. The elephants' size and smell always spooked horses (on both sides); Perseus had tried to prepare his own animals by exposing them to dummy elephants and even simulating their trumpeting, but the real thing was too different.[44] Moreover, the *elephantomachai* (anti-elephant unit) were never deployed against the giant beasts, and so were completely ineffectual.[45] The Macedonians' horses were spooked by the elephants and fled as the infantry was routed and cut down. The entire battle was over in less than an hour.[46]

---

42. Plutarch, *Paullus* 19.2; see too Polybius 29.17.1.

43. Walbank 1940, pp. 292–293; Meloni 1953, pp. 387–389.

44. Polyaenus 4.21.

45. Walbank 1979, p. 389; cf. Burton 2017, p. 168 n. 157.

46. Plutarch, *Paullus* 22.1; cf. Hammond 1984, pp. 46–47.

Aftermath

At least 20,000 of Perseus' army were killed on the battlefield and were denied burial. Some of the surviving phalangites rushed to the coast and swam out to sea, but Roman sailors in small boats sent out from the warships killed them without mercy, even those who raised their arms in surrender. Some turned back to shore but were trampled to death by the elephants, which Paullus had ordered to the water's edge to catch any enemy combatants trying to return.[47] As Livy soberly notes, the Roman army had never killed so many Macedonians in any other single battle.[48] Over the following days 5,000 stragglers were rounded up, and 6,000 who had taken refuge in Pydna were captured; all 11,000 were sold as slaves. Roman losses were put at around 100, a figure thought accurate, given that the Romans kept formation, and had better arms and armor.[49]

Perseus survived the battle, though he was said to have been wounded by a javelin. Less flattering accounts have him fleeing early on from fright or having to retire hurt because he had been kicked by a horse the day before—presumably his act of cowardice originates in Polybius and should be ignored.[50] But the battle was such a quick one that any withdrawal by Perseus could have been seen as a flight.[51]

Should Perseus be condemned for the Macedonian defeat?[52] He certainly did make critical errors and lost several advantages, such as his position on the Elpeus River or in front of Pydna or between the Roman camp and the coast, and he blundered by not charging Paullus when he caught him unawares approaching Pydna. His position on the right wing instead of the center on the day of battle was also costly as he could not protect the phalanx and keep it on level ground: "one feels that a more capable king would have led his phalanx."[53] Perseus ought to have known better. We might even blame him

---

47. Livy 44.42.4–6.

48. Livy 44.42.7.

49. Numbers: Livy 44.42.7, which are accepted by Hammond 1992, p. 378 n. 61.

50. Polybius 29.17.3–4, 29.18, 29.19; Livy 44.42.2; Plutarch, *Paullus* 19.4 (cowardice), 7–10 (his injuries from the more credible Posidonius). See Walbank 1979, pp. 389–390, for debunking the claim that Perseus acted cowardly; cf. Hammond and Walbank 1988, pp. 556–557.

51. Burton 2017, p. 169 n. 159.

52. Meloni 1953, pp. 313–314.

53. Hammond 1984, p. 47 n. 56.

for making no changes to the phalanx's formation and maneuverability with the result that, as at Cynoscephalae, the penetration of the phalanx by the maniples was decisive and turned defeat into victory. After Cynoscephalae the phalanx had limped on, but its death knell sounded at Pydna, "spelling doom before the many-headed Hydra of Latin manpower."[54]

Yet Paullus can also be criticized. He had not sent scouts ahead of his army on June 16 to determine where Perseus' army was, he was slower setting up his line than Perseus on the day of the battle, and luck played a role in weakening the Macedonian phalanx to the extent that he could exploit it and gain victory. Our sources unsurprisingly find only praise for him and excuse his defects, such as not wishing to attack on the 16th or delaying on the 22nd because of his piety in making sacrifices.[55]

Perseus fled to Pella, perhaps at night, with only 4,000 cavalry and probably a few thousand light-armed troops, although the details of his flight were elaborated by our sources.[56] The Macedonian cavalrymen—who had been cursed by the infantrymen with them for their cowardice in not engaging the enemy—dispersed to their own homes. At Pella Perseus quickly gathered money and some treasure, and then with the Royal Pages (who unusually did not accompany him but were waiting for him at the palace), a few of his friends, and 500 Cretans as escort he set out the next night to Amphipolis.[57] He had called for help from the Bisaltae people of the lower Strymon area west of Amphipolis, but to no avail. Leaving Amphipolis, which immediately surrendered to Paullus, he crossed to the sacred island of Samothrace in the north Aegean, where he was soon blockaded by Octavius and the Roman navy.[58]

From there, he sent envoys and letters to Paullus suing for peace and seeking mercy. The latter, so the story goes, was distressed over Philip's fate—until he read a letter that defiantly (or naively?) began, "King Perseus to the Consul Paullus, greetings." At that point Paullus refused to have anything

---

54. See the comments of Karunanithy 2013, pp. 232–234 (quote on p. 233).

55. For example, Livy 44.36, 44.38–39; Plutarch, *Paullus* 17.11.

56. On his flight and eventual surrender: Livy 44.43, 44.45, 44.46.10, 45.4.2–6.12; cf. Polybius 29.20; Diodorus 30.21.1–2 (with the story, perhaps doubtful, of the king betraying his followers because of his greed); Plutarch, *Paullus* 23, 26.1–6; Justin 33.2.5, and see Walbank 1979, pp. 392–393; Hammond and Walbank 1988, p. 549.

57. The Pages at the palace and not at Pydna: Livy 44.43.5.

58. Livy 45.5.1–2.

else to do with the king until he surrendered.[59] Perseus tried to make a deal with a Cretan captain on Samothrace to take him and his treasure to Crete, but the man treacherously sailed off once he had the money and left the king behind.[60]

Less than a week had passed since the battle of Pydna and the end for Perseus was in sight. Octavius offered the few Friends with Perseus and the Pages their freedom if they surrendered to him. With no other option they did so, taking with them Perseus' younger children. They were followed by Perseus and his eldest son Philip, who were sent back to Amphipolis.[61] It was there and in nearby cities that the Roman army was billeted for the winter of 168–167. There is no mention of Perseus' wife Laodice, whom the Senate may have returned her to her uncle Antiochus so as not to risk alienating him.[62]

Settling Greece and Illyria

Paullus' ruthless treatment of the defeated army showed he intended "to impose on Macedonia a total and undeniable defeat," as did his orders for his cavalry to ravage and plunder the countryside.[63] His troops did so from Pydna to Pella. Pydna was looted and sacked by the army, even though it surrendered to Rome, and likewise Meliboea on the coast of Magnesia in Thessaly by the navy. Pella suffered a similar fate, with Paullus stealing all manner of precious objects including silver and gold statues and paintings from the palace's royal quarters, which he took to Rome for his triumph in 167. Perseus had, however, already emptied the royal treasury that was located on Phacus (an island in Lake Loudias separated from the city walls by part of the river) of all but about 300 talents.[64]

Perseus was brought before Paullus, who was surrounded by Roman troops and numerous local spectators.[65] Paullus asked him why he went to war against Rome and received no answer, at which point he demanded the king's

59. Livy 45.4.27.

60. Livy 6.2–6.

61. Livy 45.6.7–12.

62. Briscoe 2012, p. 625.

63. Hammond and Walbank 1988, p. 559.

64. Livy 44.46.1–10.

65. Livy 45.8.

unconditional surrender and that his kingdom be at the mercy of the Roman People. Thus ended the Third Macedonian War, prompting Livy to reflect on the fall of Macedonia from its days of greatness under previous kings.[66] Late in 168 the Senate extended the commands of Paullus and Gallus for another year so they could supervise the settlements in Illyria and Macedonia. These must be dated to 167, for the senators decided the fate not only of Macedonia and its Greek allies but also of all states in the war, including Rome's allies.

The Senate decided to weaken any league, kingdom, or city that it felt might constitute a threat unless it deferred to Rome's satisfaction.[67] Allies and helpers again discovered to their cost that the Senate looked only after itself. Masinissa and his sons, for example, had provided at Rome's request war elephants, cavalry, infantry, and crops, and Eumenes ships, cavalry, infantry, and supplies, but the Senate would not allow Masinissa to visit Rome and it endeavored to weaken Pergamum by favoring Eumenes' brother Attalus rather than him.[68]

The Rhodians scrambled to prevent any punitive measures against them by executing those who had supported Perseus and profusely emphasized their allegiance and friendship to Rome. In response, the Senate confiscated some of Rhodes' possessions, including the important trading island of Delos, which in 167 it gave to Athens. That city had been prospering, but acquisition of the island benefitted it even more.[69] By contrast, the Rhodian economy went into a slump, so much so that the people found it hard to maintain a navy.[70]

Cities in Greece decided to be on the safe side and expel or kill Macedonian sympathizers and even those who had shown only a lukewarm feeling for Rome.[71] Most notable was the massacre of 550 leading Aetolians at the end of a meeting of their league, the banishment of others, and the confiscation of their property, which Roman troops condoned. Deportation also happened. For example, at the instigation of the pro-Roman Callicrates, 1,000 suspect

---

66. Livy 45.9.2–7; cf. 45.6.3, on Perseus having the radiance of Philip II and Alexander the Great; see too Briscoe 2012, pp. 629–631.

67. Gruen 1984, pp. 191–198; Hammond and Walbank 1988, pp. 560–563; Waterfield 2014, pp. 194–197.

68. Burton 2017, pp. 181–182 and 183–184.

69. Worthington 2021a, pp. 169–171, citing bibliography.

70. Gruen 1975, pp. 59–63; Gruen 1984, pp. 39–42; see too Burton 2012, pp. 178–181.

71. Errington 1971a, pp. 233–236; Gruen 1984, pp. 514–523.

members of the Achaean League, who included Polybius, were shipped to Italy. They were kept without trial for seventeen years and when only 300 "at most" survived they were sent home, Polybius among them.[72]

Early in 167, most probably, the Senate ordered the leaders of all communities in Illyria to Scodra where Gallus would announce what it had decided to do.[73] Illyria was to be divided into three separate districts, cut off from one another by restrictions on intermarriage, property ownership, and trade, and each one was bound to Rome in various ways. How these districts functioned administratively is not known, but perhaps in the same way as Macedonia, as we shall see. Half of the taxes previously paid to Genthius were now to be paid to Rome, though loyal tribes and cities were exempted from it, and all Roman garrisons were withdrawn to Italy. The Illyrians were cynically told they were free—free to do Rome's bidding, that is.

In the summer of 167 Paullus went on a tour of Greece, during which he visited Athens with his son Scipio Aemilianus (who later destroyed Carthage at the end of the Third Punic War in 146). Paullus endeared himself to the Athenians as he was a genuine philhellene or lover of Greek culture and even asked for an Athenian tutor for his children and a painter to depict his triumphal procession in Rome.[74]

Paullus also went to Delphi, where he came upon Perseus' still unfinished propaganda monuments that he had ordered at the start of his reign to commemorate his earlier benefactions (pp. 185–186). He decided to use the column-bases set aside for Perseus' statue for a spectacular equestrian statue of himself atop a column, 30 feet (9 meters) high, in front of the temple of Apollo (figure 11.4). As Plutarch says, "The conquered should make room for their conquerors."[75] He erased Perseus' Greek dedication and added his own in Latin inscription: *L. Aimilius L. f. imperator de rege Perse Macedonibusque cepet* ("Lucius Aemilius, son of Lucius, Imperator, took this from King Perseus and the Macedonians").[76]

---

72. Pausanias 7.10.7–12 (numbers at 7.10.11–12).

73. Livy 45.26.11–15; Diodorus 31.8.2–5, with Gruen 1984, p. 424; Hammond and Walbank 1988, p. 562 with n. 3; Derow 1989, p. 317; Briscoe 2012, pp. 690–691; Burton 2017, p. 175.

74. Tour of Greece: Livy 45.27.5–28.5; cf. Polybius 30.10.3–6, with Walbank 1979, pp. 432–433; Briscoe 2012, pp. 692–699. Paullus in Athens: Worthington 2021a, pp. 168–169.

75. Plutarch, *Paullus* 28.4.

76. Kähler 1965; Jacquemin and Laroche 1982; Hammond and Walbank 1988, pp. 613–617; Jacquemin, Laroche, and Lefèvre 1995; Miller 2000, pp. 280–281; Koussser 2010, pp. 528–531; Taylor 2016.

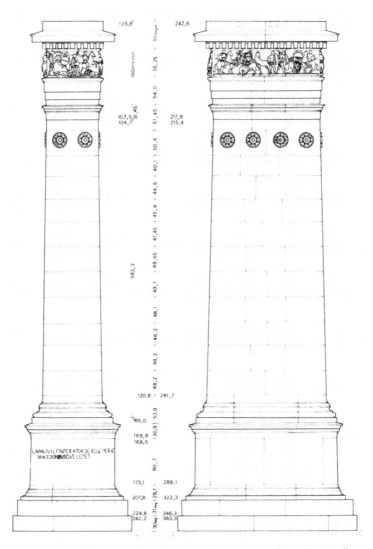

FIGURE 11.4. Reconstruction drawing of monument of Aemilius Paullus at Delphi, c. 167 B.C. Reproduced from A. Jacquemin and D. Laroche, "Notes sur trois piliers delphiques," *BCH* 106 (1982): 191–218.

In keeping with his victory at Pydna, he had a continuous frieze sculpted along all four sides of the pillar depicting his victory and Macedonia's defeat at the battle of Pydna, which included a riderless horse (figure 11.5).

Perseus had intended his memorials to portray Macedonia's greatness under the Antigonids; Paullus' takeover and his statue showed Macedonia's collapse before the power of Rome. The historical narrative surrounding his

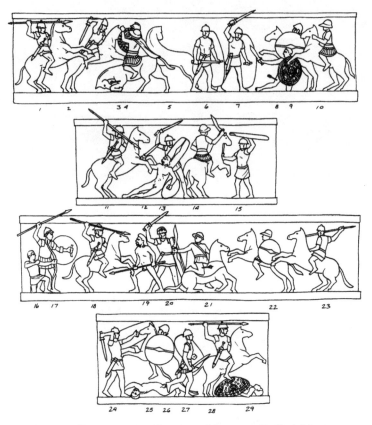

FIGURE 11.5. Reconstruction drawing of frieze on Paullus' Monument at Delphi. Illustrated by Albert Nguyen. Reproduced from M.J. Taylor, "The Battle Scene on Aemilius Paullus' Pydna Monument: A Reevaluation," *Hesperia* 85 (2016): 559–576.

monument could not be more marked: anyone visiting Delphi would have immediately grasped what used to be and who was now in charge.

The End of the Macedonian State

In the fall of 167, Paullus announced the details of the settlement of Macedonia at a conference at Amphipolis attended by ten leading men from each city. He spoke in Latin and Octavius repeated the terms in Greek. The chronology is disputed, but the reappointments in late 168 of Paullus and Gallus must show that Macedonia like Illyria received its terms in 167, for after his announcement in Illyria Gallus rejoined the army, which was still in its winter quarters.

Also, in summer 167 Paullus toured Greece; the settlement of Macedonia was later than his tour, hence it may be placed in the fall, well over a year after the battle of Pydna.[77]

The Senate's ruling on Macedonia was akin to that on Illyria.[78] It did not turn Macedonia into a province, perhaps because of Rome's unfortunate experiences in having to wage war in the Spanish provinces virtually every year since it created them in 197.[79] If Rome could rule some other way, with the onus on the conquered peoples to govern and a reduced Roman presence, it was going to do so. Unsurprisingly, the Antigonid dynasty was ended, but Roman garrisons were withdrawn, the people could keep their own lands and cities, follow their own laws, elect their own magistrates, and pay Rome half the tribute the king had demanded; like Illyria, Macedonia was declared free.[80]

At first sight the Macedonians were treated leniently as they could have suffered far worse punishment. But in reality, monarchic rule was swapped for imperial rule as the Romans cynically gave the eternal slogan of "freedom and autonomy" a new twist: freedom only from monarchy.[81] Further, Macedonia was partitioned into four self-governing regions or republics (*merides*), each one independent of the other, with its own capital, assembly, and officials, but all subject to Roman laws (figure 11.6).[82] These regions were not haphazard

---

77. Chronology: Hammond and Walbank 1988, p. 563 n. 2. Meloni 1953, p. 408 n. 3, p. 417 n. 3, and p. 468, puts Paullus' tour in fall 168 and the settlement in spring 167.

78. Roman settlement: Livy 45.18, 45.29–30, 45.32.1–7 (= Austin 2006, no. 96, pp. 189–192); Diodorus 31.8.6–9; Plutarch, *Paullus* 28.6; Justin 33.2.7, all deriving from Polybius, whose account has not survived; cf. Briscoe 2012, pp. 658–662 and 701–711. See further, Aymard 1950; Meloni 1953, pp. 409–431; Errington 1971a, pp. 221–224; Harris 1979, pp. 143–146; Gruen 1982; Gruen 1984, pp. 423–429; Hammond and Walbank 1988, pp. 563–569; Derow 1989, pp. 317–318; Errington 1990, pp. 216–217; Hatzopoulos 1996, vol. 1, pp. 221–230; Matyszak 2009, pp. 157–158; Eckstein 2010, pp. 245–246; Pugliese 2014, pp. 162–168; Waterfield 2014, pp. 190–193; Vanderspoel 2015.

79. Cf. Errington 1971a, p. 222.

80. On the tribute and its collection, see Gruen 1982, pp. 264–266. Plutarch, *Paullus* 28.6, puts the amount at 100 talents, which seems very low: Hammond and Walbank 1988, p. 564 n. 2. Gruen 1984, p. 428 n. 169, doubts an annual tribute.

81. Idea of freedom: Meloni 1953, pp. 418–419; Walbank 1967, pp. 610–620; Gruen 1984, pp. 132–157 and 448–456; Hatzopoulos 1996, vol. 1, pp. 224–225; Dmitriev 2011, pp. 227–282; Pugliese 2014, pp. 164–165.

82. Livy 45.18.7, 45.29.5–9, 45.30.3–8; Diodorus 31.8.8–9, with Hatzopoulos 1996, vol. 1, pp. 231–260 and vol. 2, pp. 473–486; see too Meloni 1953, pp. 420–430; Gruen 1982, pp. 261–262; Burton 2017, pp. 173–175 and 188–191. The structure had existed earlier, before the time of Philip II, but Vanderspoel 2015, pp. 199–200, suggests the model was Italy.

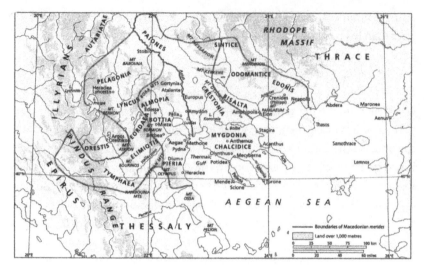

FIGURE 11.6. Macedonia showing the *merides*. Reproduced from P.J. Burton, *Rome and the Third Macedonian War*, Cambridge University Press, 2017. Reproduced with permission of The Licensor through PLSclear.

but carefully drawn up, using the Nestus, Strymon, and Axius Rivers as natural barriers to make travel from one to another difficult, especially as the Romans controlled the passes.

The westernmost *meris* comprised Upper Macedonia, including Elimiotis, Eordaea, Lyncus, Pelagonia, Tymphaea, and Atintania around Lake Lychnidus, with the capital in Pelagonia, and Orestis remaining independent. The old Lower Macedonia between the Peneus and the Axius and including Paeonia west of the Axius constituted another *meris*, with Pella the capital. The third *meris* was between the Axius and the Strymon, including Paeonia east of the Axius and the Chalcidice, but excluding Bisaltia, and had Thessalonica as capital. Finally, the easternmost *meris* stretched from the Strymon to the Nestus River, including Bisaltia, and had Amphipolis as capital (figure 11.6).

The Roman division muzzled geographic, political, economic, military, and even social contacts, and was carefully crafted to destroy the unity on which the kings had relied.[83] Any central assembly was banned, as were intermarriage, mining silver and gold (though copper and iron were allowed), and cutting timber for shipbuilding, while the regions could not engage in trade

---

83. Errington 1971a, p. 223; Gruen 1982, pp. 258–259.

with each other to reduce economic activity and prevent any resurgence.[84] Only the *merides* bordering on "barbarian" tribes were allowed to have guards on their frontiers.[85] These military restrictions meant that Macedonia could not defend itself against external threats, perhaps deliberate on Rome's part to keep the former kingdom cowed.[86]

A few days later Paullus dictated a code of laws for the four republics, in itself not a break with the past as there had been local administration under the monarchy.[87] The difference now is that the laws came from Rome. He required an immediate election in each *meris* of annual councilors (*synedroi*) and a chief magistrate (*archegos*) to oversee the taxes due to Rome. Presumably these officials held office in the center of each region, that is Amphipolis, Thessalonica, Pella, and Pelagonia.[88] In effect a new ruling class and administrative structure had been created in the four republics, each dependent on the Senate's will.

He then read out a list of chief royal advisers, nobles, generals, admirals, and garrison commanders, who, together with their sons over the age of fifteen, were to be deported to Italy, perhaps also along with the Royal Pages: anyone resisting would be put to death.[89] These people probably never returned home, leaving Macedonia bereft of capable citizens who could assume positions of responsibility in the so-called free elections.

The settlement of Macedonia was also intended to rupture the tripartite balance of power in the eastern Mediterranean of Antigonid Macedonia, Seleucid Syria, and Ptolemaic Egypt. And it did. But if the Romans were convinced that dismembering Macedonia would be accepted by the people and that no ambitious leader would ever bring about a revolt against them, they were in for a shock.

---

84. The issue of mines is controversial. Hammond and Walbank 1988, p. 564 and Errington 1990, pp. 199–200, consider the Senate shut the mines immediately. Papazoglou 1979, p. 305, claims that the Romans merely confiscated the mines to make them their own. Gruen 1982, pp. 262–264, and Gruen 1984, pp. 426–427, sees a gradual process, but with provisions to close the gold and silver mines to prevent exploitation on the part of Roman tax farmers (*publicani*) and to prevent the Macedonians having the resources to mount an insurrection; see too Briscoe 2012, pp. 659–661.

85. Diodorus 31.8.9.

86. Vanderspoel 2015, p. 200.

87. Livy 45.31.1; cf. 32.1–7. See Hatzopoulos 1996, vol. 1, pp. 47–216, 259–269, and 372–429, for example.

88. Hammond and Walbank 1988, p. 566.

89. Livy 45.32.3–7, with Briscoe 2012, p. 716, making an analogy here with the de-Ba'athification of Iraq after the fall of Saddam Hussein (2003).

Andriscus aka Philip VI and the Fourth Macedonian War

POLYBIUS AND LIVY unsurprisingly presented Rome's settlement in 167 in a rosy light.[1] Among other things, the Macedonians no longer needed to endure slavery by living under a king; Paullus' law code was significantly better than having the Macedonian nobility telling them what to do; the ban on mining was a relief for oppressed miners; and the people were now happy living in their own regions. In 167, Roman troops left Greece, and by 158 the Senate allowed an easing of restrictions in Macedonia by removing some of the commercial embargoes, permitting intermarriage, and even allowing the gold and silver mines to reopen, all supporting the view that Rome did not want to absorb Macedonia or Greece after Pydna.[2] The reality, however, was quite different.

The Sacking of Epirus

Paullus eventually left Amphipolis for Epirus, where the Molossians had openly defied Rome by backing Perseus in the war. The Roman army camped outside their capital Passaron, from where Paullus sent orders to the ten leading men in each Molossian city to bring all gold and silver to the main treasury, and then meet with him at Passaron.[3] Since Rome's Illyrian and Macedonian settlements had not involved bloodshed, the Molossians were not especially

---

1. Polybius 26.17.13; Livy 45.30.1–2; cf. Diodorus 31.8.2 and 4, with Eckstein 2010, pp. 245–246.

2. Errington 1971a, pp. 229–231; Gruen 1984, pp. 425–429; Matyszak 2009, pp. 159–164; Eckstein 2010, p. 246.

3. Livy 45.34.1–3.

The Last Kings of Macedonia and the Triumph of Rome. Ian Worthington, Oxford University Press.
© Oxford University Press 2023. DOI: 10.1093/oso/9780197520055.003.0013

worried, and they may have already put to death pro-Macedonian leaders or sent them to Italy for trial to endear themselves to Rome.

Their response would not be enough. The Senate may have secretly communicated to Paullus that he was to take revenge on the Molossian cities for their treachery and that his men could keep any booty they seized. Without giving anything away, Paullus sent detachments of troops to collect all the gold and silver and proclaimed the people were free; then one morning the soldiers went on a prearranged rampage.[4] They sacked about seventy cities and townships, destroying fortification walls where they existed, and seized enormous amounts of booty, including art works, as well as 150,000 inhabitants who were sold as slaves predominantly in Italy.

Central Epirus was largely depopulated, though if the Romans had wanted to kill or capture the entire population Paullus would have sent his troops in at night or at dawn. By the middle of the morning when he launched his assault many of the people were at work in the fields and could flee for safety.[5] For all that, the settlement of 167 was a façade considering the ruthlessness and self-serving nature of the Romans.

Perseus in Retrospect

What happened to Perseus after he was sent to Amphipolis? He, along with his sons Philip and Alexander, his daughter, and some of his leading Friends, were taken to Rome and led in chains before Paullus' chariot as part of his lavish triumph later that year (167).[6] Over three days large numbers of wagons displayed statues, sculptures, expensive plates and goblets, a variety of armaments, gold and silver bullion, before finally, on the third day, the chariot of Perseus with his armor and diadem, his enslaved children, and then Perseus himself dressed as a countryman in a cage were all paraded to cheering crowds. At that time Rome awarded Paullus the name *Macedonicus*.

---

4. Polybius 30.15; Livy 45.34.4–6; Appian, *Illyrian Wars* 9.28; Plutarch, *Paullus* 29, with Walbank 1979, pp. 438–439; Hammond 1967, pp. 634–635; Errington 1971a, pp. 225–226; Gruen 1984, pp. 516–517; Hammond and Walbank 1988, pp. 567–568; Waterfield 2014, pp. 201–204. Estimate of the enormous booty from Macedonia and Epirus: Meloni 1953, pp. 433–435. That the Senate had so instructed Paullus is stated by Plutarch and Appian: Briscoe 2012, pp. 720–721.

5. Hammond 1967, p. 642.

6. Livy 45.40.1–6; Diodorus 31.8.9–13; Plutarch, *Paullus* 32–34, with Meloni 1953, pp. 437–440. Triumph: Waterfield 2014, pp. 204–206. Paullus apparently had to argue for a triumph as one was not immediately granted: Livy 45.35.3–42.1, with Briscoe 2012, pp. 724–754.

Afterward, Perseus was incarcerated in Alba Fucens, a central Italian town at the foot of Mount Vellino about 60 miles (96 kilometers) east of Rome. He was at first locked into a small dungeon, starved to such a degree that the other prisoners pitied him and gave him some of their food, and then thrown a sword and a noose to kill himself. Eventually, the Senate let him move to a house though he was not allowed to venture out. There, he either starved himself to death in 166 or his guards, who had been forbidden to beat him, refused to let him sleep so that he eventually died of exhaustion.[7] His son Philip died in prison two years later; his other son, Alexander, survived, and eventually became a Roman magistrate's secretary.[8]

How does Perseus rate as a Macedonian king? After his defeat at Pydna in 167, the Antigonid dynasty came to an end, as did the single Macedonian state and national army. We might well conclude that Perseus failed as a king and certainly we cannot excuse him for not preparing his army better for that inevitable showdown with the Romans at Pydna. To Polybius the king's fall was easily explicable: it was due to Fortune once, like his father, he had defied Rome. Fortune had helped Alexander the Great topple the Persian Empire; it was not the same ally of Perseus against the Roman Empire.[9]

Yet we should not call Perseus a failure or describe his reign a postscript to that of his father in the big picture of Roman involvement in Macedonia. Perseus became king in a world very different from when his father had assumed the throne. After Cynoscephalae in 197 the capacity for Macedonian expansion even in Illyria was gone, yet he still had to fight on several fronts, including against Rome in the Third Macedonian War, and he faced constant undermining from the likes of Eumenes of Pergamum. Like his father he had a distrust of Rome because he had experienced firsthand its underhanded nature and duplicity with its allies, including Macedonia, and its readiness to rebuff them without a second thought.

Perseus was guided by these personal experiences. From the outset he worked to allay the Senate's suspicions of him, not because he was eager to be Rome's friend but because he recognized that anything that had been drawn up in 196 was going to be ephemeral because of the nature of the Greeks and the Aetolians' resentment of Rome's scorning of them. He knew that

---

7. Livy 45.42.4–5; Diodorus 31.9; Plutarch, *Paullus* 37.1–3; Zonaras 9.24.5; cf. Polybius 36.10.3, with Walbank 1979, p. 669. For a reason that he was not to be harmed because of his time on sacred Samothrace, see Burton 2017, p. 173 n. 1.

8. Plutarch, *Paullus* 37.4; cf. Porphyry, *BNJ* F 3, 18.

9. Polybius 29.21; cf. Livy 45.9.2.

escalating tensions in Greece would prompt the Senate either to reinstate the status quo or create something new. That would mean the return of Roman troops to Greek soil, and when that happened, Perseus wanted to be ready in case Rome had plans for him.

To this end, he continued to bring economic and other benefits to his kingdom as his father had done, built up his resources, and tried to coax Greek cities and foreign rulers to his side. His diplomacy led to the Senate's giving him this time, for it made no move against him until 172, and only then perhaps because of Eumenes' confrontational rhetoric. The list of charges it publicized at Delphi in the same year, most of which were unjust, marked the formal change in its relations with the Macedonian king and showed to all and sundry that once it set its mind on something it resorted to any means to achieve it regardless of relationships. It is no surprise that Perseus prepared for war: he was left with no other choice, for surrendering without a fight was unthinkable for a Macedonian warrior king.

In the war, Perseus proved himself at times to be an excellent strategist and leader of men. But he must be held to account for losing opportunities that while they would not have brought about Rome's defeat in the long run, they would have bloodied and pressured his enemy more. But like the Greeks at Chaeronea in 338 or his father at Cynoscephalae in 197, Perseus was fighting for a noble ideal: freedom. Like his father, he never paused from trying to protect his kingdom from foreign incursion and to maintain its liberty, even knowing how stretched his own resources and manpower were compared to the Romans. It was the right thing for both kings to do.

Theirs was a David-and-Goliath struggle, and although both times Goliath won, as kings Perseus and his father acquitted themselves with honor. They do not deserve the character denigration of Polybius and Livy.

Andriscus aka Philip VI

Gruen has argued that such things as the Roman withdrawal of troops, only temporary mine closures, and administrative changes were meant to create a new political class so that the Romans did not need to concern themselves with Macedonian affairs, and further, that even the tribute payments would not be onerous as no source says they were to be ongoing.[10] Vanderspoel has

---

10. Gruen 1982, pp. 257–267 (pp. 264–266 for the tribute); cf. Gruen 1984, pp. 425–428; Pugliese 2014, pp. 163–164 n. 71 (that the sources confused Perseus offering to pay a war

likewise drawn attention to what he sees as Rome's "apparent disinterest" in Macedonia after Pydna. He contrasts that city's imperialistic ventures in the western Mediterranean and Spain and argues that in 168 Rome did not see Macedonia as a danger, unlike the resurgence of its formidable rival in the west, Carthage.[11]

Both scholars may be right in their arguments as they pertain to Rome in 167. But the fact that another war broke out two decades later, the Fourth Macedonian War, which we discuss below, reveals the myopia of the Senate. What that body did not consider was the mood of the Macedonians and Greeks to outside rule and enforced change. The rosy picture painted by Polybius and Livy of the settlement of 167 belied reality. After centuries of monarchy and unification Macedonia could not suddenly become a country of four independent republics—even Polybius admits that the people were not used to this type of system and were in a state of civil war.[12]

Discontent was widespread. In probably 162, for example, a certain Damasippus murdered the members of the city council of Phacus (by Pella) and fled with his family to Egypt.[13] Economic problems persisted, for the closure of mines and reduction in mining revenues actually made it harder to pay half the tribute than the full amount under the kings when mining was in full swing, hence local economies suffered further.[14] Even worse was that border security, the one thing that kings had always striven to safeguard, was compromised. The abolition of the single Macedonian army led to attacks on the borders of the *merides*, which the token defense forces could not prevent. This was a return to the days before Philip II.

In 164 or 163 the Senate diverted a commission en route to Syria to Macedonia to investigate the problems. Perhaps to restore some order the Senate decided to reopen the gold and silver mines four years later.[15] In 151 some pro-Roman leaders, fearing the increasingly belligerent people, decided to bypass the Senate and sought help directly from the young Scipio

---

indemnity—e.g., Livy 42.62.10; Justin 33.1.4—with a perpetual one imposed by Rome). See too Vanderspoel 2015; cf. Harris 1979, pp. 143–146.

11. Vanderspoel 2015, especially pp. 201–206.

12. Polybius 31.2.12–14. On later Macedonia (down to AD 14), see Daubner 2018.

13. Polybius 31.17.2.

14. Hatzopoulos 1996, vol. 1, pp. 221–222, citing bibliography; for a critique of life after the settlement, see pp. 222–230, with Gruen 1984, pp. 429–431; Burton 2017, pp. 184–186.

15. See MacKay 1970.

FIGURE 12.1. Andriscus. © Classical Numismatic Group, Inc. Licensed under a CC BY-SA 2.5 License (https://creativecommons.org/licenses/by-sa/2.5/deed.en).

Aemilianus; he showed no interest and went to Spain, but the senators must have been anxious at how and why they were bypassed.[16]

The civil discord set the scene the following year (150) for a man named Andriscus to declare himself a son of Perseus and garner enough support to become king, eventually going to war with Rome (figure 12.1). We know next to nothing about Andriscus, who renamed himself Philip (VI) when he took the throne for dynastic reasons, hence Polybius refers to him as the "false Philip" and "a Philip fallen from the skies."[17] He had been brought up in Adramyttium in Aeolis, now Turkey, but his parentage cannot be known for sure. He cannot have claimed he was Perseus' actual son Philip, who had died in Italy in 163, for that identification could be challenged.[18] Instead, he made himself out to be an illegitimate son of Perseus and one of the king's courtesans, hence not a true Antigonid. This was not as far-fetched as it sounds. Macedonian kings had numerous affairs that must have produced illegitimate children, and in 308 Ptolemy I of Egypt, for example, claimed to be a bastard son of Philip II to lend weight to his attempted takeover of Macedonia and Greece.[19] Ptolemy would not have resorted to such a measure if he thought he would have been mocked. The same presumably holds true for Andriscus in 150.

---

16. Polybius 35.4.10–12.

17. Polybius 36.10.2, and see Helliesen 1986, pp. 309–310.

18. Polybius 36.10.3.

19. Worthington 2016a, pp. 151–154.

The Romans did not see Andriscus as a menace for some time, which is probably why our sources felt little need to discuss him until he suddenly became king.[20] The first we hear of him is in 152 when he was a mercenary in Antioch in the service of Demetrius I of Syria, which among other things would have brought him into contact with ex-soldiers from Perseus' army and other Macedonians living in the east.[21] Demetrius I, it was said, grew worried that Andriscus resembled Perseus' son Philip, even jokingly calling him "son of Perseus," so he had him arrested and sent to Rome.[22] The Senate ordered him to live in a town (the name is unknown) in Italy, but he escaped from there and went via Miletus to Thrace. There, Teres, who had married a daughter of Philip V, claimed to recognize him as part of the royal family. It was enough for a bid for the Macedonian throne. In the spring of 149, Andriscus won a battle on the eastern borders of Macedonia with Thracian support, surely helped by the weakening of borders and reduction in military numbers after 167.[23]

Andriscus' success ties in with Polybius' comment that the Macedonians were never comfortable with the way that their kingdom had been carved up and their new way of life.[24] However, we should not over-estimate the people's approval of him—as has been pointed out, without the backing of Thrace, he would not have won Macedonia.[25] Andriscus abolished the four independent republics, reestablished the one kingdom of Macedonia, and conducted a bloody purge of opponents as well as the Roman-backed officials. He then set his sights on Thessaly, which appealed for help not to Rome but to Achaea.[26]

By now, affairs in Greece were unstable.[27] In the mid-150s the Athenians continued their decade-long clash with the Boeotians over the town of Oropus on Attica's northern border with Boeotia. They sent, in 155, an embassy to

---

20. Polybius 36.10; Diodorus 31.40a, 32.9a, 32.15; Pausanias 7.13.1. Andriscus: Errington 1971a, pp. 231–233; Gruen 1984, pp. 431–436; Helliesen 1986; Matyszak 2009, pp. 163–168; Eckstein 2010, pp. 246–248; Waterfield 2014, pp. 219–220; Burton 2017, pp. 186–188; cf. Walbank 1979, pp. 668–669; Papazoglou 1979, pp. 304–306.

21. Helliesen 1986, pp. 310–314.

22. Diodorus 31.40a, 32.15.1.

23. Polybius 36.10.4, and see Errington 1971a, p. 232.

24. Gruen 1984, p. 432.

25. Kallet-Marx 1995, pp. 33–36.

26. Polybius 36.10.5. Purge: Polybius 26.17.13.

27. Cf. Errington 1971a, pp. 233–236.

Rome consisting of the heads of the three philosophical schools in Athens: Carneades of Cyrene (Academy), Critolaus of Phaselis in Lycia (Lyceum), and Diogenes from Seleucia on the Tigris (Stoicism). This "philosophers' embassy" found favor with the Senate.[28] More ominously, the Achaean League was again trying to reassert its influence in the Peloponnese, contravening the settlement of 196 that had guaranteed the independence of cities there. The Achaeans clashed with Sparta, sending exiles from the latter in 149 to the Senate for support.[29]

Rome was now embroiled in the outbreak of the Third Punic War against Carthage (149–146). But events in Greece and especially Andriscus' actions prompted the Senate to act. It sent only one legion, commanded by the praetor Publius Iuventius Thalna, who had no experience of serving in the east, to deal with Andriscus. Perhaps only one could be spared because of the conflict with Carthage. On the other hand, "the Romans evidently felt that if two legions under Paullus had been enough to sweep away the highly-trained army of Perseus, a single legion should disperse whatever rabble Andriscus had put together."[30] Thus was triggered the short Fourth Macedonian War of 149 to 148.[31] Andriscus' army, which presumably included former soldiers from Perseus' army, was hardly a rabble: it defeated Thalna's men in 148, killing Thalna in the fighting, after which Andriscus marched south to win over Thessaly.

The Fourth Macedonian War

Thalna's defeat had to be avenged and Greece pacified. Since the consuls for 148 were busy fighting elsewhere, the Romans sent one of the praetors for that year, Quintus Caecilius Metellus, this time with two legions, and possibly even with consular *imperium*.[32] Like Thalna, he had no experience of serving in the east; for Rome to send two inexperienced commanders against Andriscus

---

28. Worthington 2021a, pp. 171–172, citing references.

29. Errington 1971a, pp. 236–240; Harris 1979, pp. 240–244; Gruen 1984, pp. 481–502; Derow 1989, pp. 319–323; Matyszak 2009, pp. 169–173; Dmitriev 2011, pp. 313–350; Waterfield 2014, pp. 222–225.

30. Quote: Matyszak 2009, p. 166. Thalna's inexperience in the east shows that the Romans did not always send out informed commanders: Gruen 1984, pp. 212–213, and see pp. 203–249 on military and diplomatic appointments to the east.

31. Eckstein 2010, pp. 246–248; Waterfield 2014, pp. 218–220.

32. See in detail Morgan 1969, with pp. 423–425 on his actual powers.

shows the toll that the Third Punic War was taking on them. Metellus sent a sharp rebuke to the Achaeans, who were making his life difficult by deciding to crush Sparta. They ignored his request to delay, defeating a Spartan army in battle and establishing garrisons throughout Laconia, though they did not sack Sparta.

Metellus dealt with the self-styled Philip VI first. He broke through a Macedonian army in Thessaly, which was presumably meant to block his advance, effectively splitting the enemy army into two, one part in Thessaly and the other at Pydna. Andriscus' cavalry was able to slow Metellus' progress, but a further problem for him was the arrival of a Pergamene fleet to support Metellus. Andriscus was compelled to steer clear of the coast in case it landed troops to his rear. Eventually he and Metellus did battle at Pydna in 148.

In this second battle of Pydna, the details of which are largely unknown, Andriscus was defeated, perhaps because so many of his troops were still in Thessaly. His men had taken flight from the battlefield once Metellus crushed their line, and Andriscus himself went to Thrace. He was able to regroup and prepare to do battle again in the same year, but Metellus' army had followed him and were waiting: Andriscus' army was attacked and defeated even as it made its way onto the battlefield. Andriscus fled again, but a Thracian prince named Byzes, evidently seeing that it paid to be friendly to Rome, handed him over to Metellus, after which he disappears from history. Thus ended the Fourth Macedonian War. The fate of the Macedonian troops in Thessaly is unknown, but they may have simply surrendered to Metellus.[33]

Late in 148 Metellus could send word to the Senate that Macedonia and Thessaly were again in Roman hands. For his victory he—like Paullus after the first battle of Pydna in 167—was awarded the appellation "Macedonicus" and allowed to celebrate a triumph in Rome. Metellus now had to wait for the Senate's decision on Macedonia and Greece. Possibly its response did not reach him until at least January 147, as the winter would have slowed the progress of the senatorial commissioners to him.[34] If so, then Metelleus himself was not responsible for implementing the Senate's orders. Since he also had to deal with a short-lived and opaque pretender threat in Macedonia stretching

---

33. Mastyzak 2009, p. 168, that they "quietly" disbanded themselves.

34. Timetable: Morgan 1969, pp. 428–429.

into 147 as well as intervention in the Achaean League's war with Sparta, he may have had no time to carry out the Senate's dictates anyway.[35] Most likely, then, it was left to the commander of the Roman troops in Greece in 146, Lucius Mummius, to make formal arrangements.[36]

Provincia Macedonia

For our purposes, the identity of the Roman official and the year are not crucial, for it is safe to say that Andriscus' loss at Pydna in 148 brought Rome down far harder on Macedonia than after Perseus' defeat in 168. Although we have few details as our evidence, much from later, is not conclusive, in all likelihood Macedonia was turned into a province under actual governors.[37] The reverse has been argued on the basis that no source refers to any reorganization as a province, that the term "province" is too "legalistic" as the *merides* continued to exist and cities were self-governing for another two centuries, and that there is no list of governors per se other than men who were posted there to attend to border security.[38]

Yet would Rome simply try to reimpose a settlement along the lines of that in 167 and hope for no future insurrections? It did not leave the Greeks to their own devices after the end of the Achaean War in 146 (see below), so why would Macedonia be treated differently? The *merides* were a useful means to administer the former kingdom and could continue to be so as a province, and at some point, an annual governor was appointed to oversee Macedonia and a permanent regular tribute imposed.[39] All of this spelled a new era for Macedonia, with Roman control evidenced by the construction of one of the most famous roads. This was the Via Egnatia, beginning in Dyrrachium

---

35. Pretenders: Morgan 1969, pp. 430–431. Metellus watching Greek affairs: Morgan 1969, pp. 433–442.

36. Morgan 1969.

37. Velleius Paterculus 1.1; Zonaras 9.28, with Papazoglou 1979, pp. 303–308; Gruen 1984, pp. 433–436; Kallet-Marx 1995, pp. 11–41, especially 11–18 and 30–41; Matyszak 2009, pp. 177–178; Vanderspoel 2010, pp. 255–259; Waterfield 2014, pp. 220–222; Vanderspoel 2015, especially pp. 201–206. There was another pretender threat (details unknown but the person called himself Alexander V, son of Perseus) in 142: Zonaras 9.28.

38. Gruen 1984, pp. 433–436 and 524, and see especially pp. 434–435 n. 202. Others: Morgan 1969, pp. 441–442; Papazoglou 1979, pp. 305 and 309–311; Eckstein 2010, p. 248. Against Gruen see, for example, Baronowski 1988; cf. Kallet-Marx 1995, pp. 12–41.

39. Porphyry, *BNJ* 260 F 3.19, with the commentary of Toye *ad loc.*; Gruen 1984, p. 435 n. 206.

(Durrës) on the Adriatic and stretching via the new capital Thessalonica across Thrace to Byzantium, in all about 700 miles (1,100 kilometers) long.[40]

There was still instability in Greece caused by the Achaeans, who resented Rome's interference into their attempts to reassert influence and make Sparta a member of their league. Tensions led to warfare between the Achaean League and Rome in 146.[41] When the Third Punic War with Carthage ended in the same year, the Romans were quick to send troops to Greece under the consul for that year Lucius Mummius. He lost no time in defeating the Achaeans. On the Senate's orders, Mummius sent shock waves throughout the Greek world by razing Corinth, the epicenter of the anti-Roman coalition, to the ground, killing any males still alive, selling the women and children into slavery, and plundering artworks.[42] Corinth was only rebuilt in 44 on the orders of Julius Caesar.

It was time to decide what would happen to Greece. It was obvious— as Perseus had known—that what had been crafted in 196 would never be durable because of the nature of the Greeks and their views of Rome.[43] Something more long-term was needed, so the Senate made Greece an official province of Rome, which was called Achaea, supervised by the Roman governor of Macedonia. Thus began a new era in the country's history, with large numbers of Romans visiting Greece, especially Athens, attracted to its schools of philosophy and rhetoric, and Rome appropriating many aspects of Greek culture for its own political and cultural needs.[44]

---

40. Polybius 34.2–10. See, for example, Hammond 1972, pp. 19–58; Hammond and Hatzopoulos 1982; Hammond and Hatzopoulos 1983; Vanderspoel 2010, pp. 264–267.

41. Polybius 38.9–18. Morgan 1969, pp. 442–446; Errington 1971a, pp. 236–241; Gruen 1984, pp. 520–523; Derow 1989, pp. 319–323; Green 1990, pp. 448–452; Matsyzak 2009, pp. 169–173; Waterfield 2014, pp. 222–225.

42. Polybius 39.2–3; Pausanias 7.16.7–17.1 (= Austin 2006, no. 100, pp. 195–196 = Sherk 1984, no. 35, pp. 34–35 abridged); Diodorus 22.26.5; Dio 21.72, with Errington 1971a, pp. 239–240; Gruen 1984, pp. 520–528; Kallet-Marx 1995, pp. 84–88; Matyszak 2009, pp. 175–176.

43. Harris 1979, pp. 240–244; Gruen 1984, pp. 523–527; Derow 1989, pp. 319–323; Kallet-Marx 1995, pp. 42–96; cf. Matyszak 2009, pp. 169–173; Dmitriev 2011, pp. 313–350; Waterfield 2014, pp. 225–232. See too Baronowski 1988.

44. A by-product of the philosophers' embassy (see above) was to unveil their philosophical systems to the Romans for the first time. After Romans had experienced the "allure" of Hellenism they wanted a literary and artistic tradition akin to that of the mainland Greeks, which led to prominent Romans and their sons going to study and even live in Athens, as well as appropriating aspects of Hellenism for their own cultural needs: Perrin-Saminadayar 2011; Worthington 2021a, pp. 218–221, 252–257, 263–264, citing bibliography.

FIGURE 12.2. Roman Forum and Agora, Thessalonica. Photo credit: Marco Verch. Licensed under a CC BY-SA 4.0 License (https://creativecommons. org/licenses/by-sa/4.0/).

Macedonia's days as a superpower of the ancient world, going back to Philip II and even more spectacularly under Alexander the Great, were well and truly over. Its decline and fall were nothing to do with *Tyche* (Chance) as Polybius would have it. Rather, it was a combination of many things, from the relentless grip of Rome on Greek affairs to defeats in key battles to the defiance of the Macedonians, whose reaction against the isolationism of the *merides* and quickness to embrace Andriscus' union of a single kingdom was something that the Senate could not allow.[45] In many respects, the Macedonian kingdom had run its course once Rome came on the scene, so its end was inevitable.

From 148 we have *Provincia Macedonia*. Its capital was Thessalonica, which was both imperial residence and provincial center—the remains of its impressive forum and agora testify to its size and importance (figure 12.2). As the centuries passed, the province enjoyed stability and prosperity until the emperors Diocletian and Constantine split it up further in the fourth century AD.[46]

---

45. But see Burton 2017, pp. 188–192.

46. Papazoglou 1979; Vanderspoel 2010; Daubner 2018 (to AD 14).

The three kings of this book have fared less well in history not because they failed to establish a great empire or invaded Italy or anything like that but because, unlike kings before them, they faced the unstoppable force of Rome. It is a testament to Philip's and Perseus' strength, resilience, cunning, diplomacy, bravery, and drive to retain their kingdom's independence that despite the odds they held the Romans at bay for so long. Andriscus did not remain on the throne long enough and never led a united Macedonia, so he never stood a chance against Rome. Still, it is obvious from his anti-Roman stance and attitude toward the Greeks that he intended to elevate Macedonia's standing, for which he too deserves praise.

To view this period as a postscript to Macedonia's Classical greatness or these three kings merely as collateral damage in the story of Rome's ascendancy in the east is an injustice. Our sympathies lie with the kings, for what the biased Polybius has to say of Perseus applies to all three: Perseus was the sort of underdog mismatched against a greater opponent that spectators cheer for when they watch an uneven contest between two athletes—and at times even deride the superior one to give the other support.[47]

---

47. Polybius 27.9–10.

"Fake News": The Sources on Philip V and Perseus

Despite the importance of this period in Mediterranean and indeed world history, our sources are not plentiful, and what literary ones we have are often inconsistent with one another and, even worse, have significant gaps in their accounts.[1] We deal with these below as they are crucial for the presentation of Philip and Perseus, but first some comments on the archaeological, epigraphical, and numismatic evidence.

The archaeological evidence most obviously consists of the remains of towns, houses, palaces, tombs, and graves, for example, which throw light on the lifestyles, beliefs, and tastes of the rulers and the people. Mention has been made of these finds and their value for artistic and cultural life or religious attitudes at various parts of this book, but for recent and succinct summaries of the rich finds and what they tell us about life in the cities, see the relevant chapters in Lane Fox 2011a, which cite further bibliography.

Inscriptional material, though not extensive, is significant: the collection in Hatzopoulos 1996 is invaluable. Of special note is Philip's military *diagramma* (edict) of 218, which gives us insight into military organization within his army and general fairness when it came to dividing up spoils: see p. 23. We could even say it indicates the degree to which the king was a micro-manager. Finally, the iconography of the coinage is valuable not only for giving us an image of what the kings looked like but also for their propaganda usage. Some of Philip V's coins recall those of Alexander the Great and Pyrrhus of Epirus, allowing us to say that he wanted to identify with them and even acknowledge his ties to Epirus, from where his mother came.

---

1. Cf. Walbank 1940, pp. 278–288.

The works of several literary writers from different periods have come down to us, though they are far from complete. They include Diodorus Siculus (of Sicily), who worked in later first century BC Rome and wrote an expansive universal history from mythological times to Julius Caesar's campaigns in Gaul in 54.[2] Diodorus' history was in forty books, but only fifteen are extant, and those that deal with the Hellenistic era are fragmentary. Also in the first century, Gnaeus Pompeius Trogus wrote a history of the Macedonian empire from the time of Philip II, though it has not survived. Fortunately, it was epitomized at some time in the second to fourth century AD by a certain Marcus Junianus Justinus (Justin).[3] Unfortunately, Justin's narrative of our period is also fragmentary, and since we do not have Trogus' original work we do not know how faithfully Justin followed it—or for that matter how reliable Trogus was.

We are lucky to have Appian of Alexandria's history of Rome's rise to power, written in twenty-four books, several of which are extant along with considerable fragments.[4] Appian's chronicle of Rome's wars with Macedonia and Illyria is relevant to our period, but since he was living and working in the early second century AD, long after the events in question, he needs to be read with care. He also wrote from the Roman perspective, and at times contradicts other accounts.[5] Writing even later—in the early third century AD—was Cassius Dio.[6] His monumental history of Rome spanned over a millennium, from mythological times with the arrival of Aeneas in Italy from Troy to AD 229, and many of its eighty books survive. Like Appian, he wrote from the Roman point of view, and he used a variety of sources he does not name.

The first- to second-century AD biographer Plutarch wrote lives of various prominent Greeks and Romans; for us, the *Lives* of Aratus, Flamininus, Philopoemen, and Aemilius Paullus are germane.[7] Again, we have an author writing centuries after our period, and because of his genre he was more interested in sensationalism and the moral worth of his characters than historical

---

2. Diodorus: Sacks 1990; Sacks 1994.

3. See Yardley 2003.

4. On Appian, see Gowing 1992; cf. Gabba 1956.

5. Walbank 1940, pp. 285–287; Meloni 1955; Bivona 1957; Mastrocinque 1975/76; Klaudianou 1977; Pugliese 2014, pp. 159–160.

6. See Millar 1964; the essays in Lange and Madsen (eds.) 2016 and in Burden-Strevens and Lindholmer (eds.) 2018; cf. Gowing 1992.

7. On Plutarch, see Russell 1973; Duff 1999; Pelling 2002.

accuracy. His biographies are lively reading, but he often uses earlier sources uncritically, and we need to treat what he says with care. Finally, there is the Byzantine chronicler and theologian Joannes Zonaras of the twelfth century AD, whose *Extracts of History* ambitiously stretched from the creation of the world to the death of the Byzantine emperor Alexius I Comnenus in AD 1118. Zonaras often uses the works of Cassius Dio, which impacts his accuracy.[8]

It is Polybius and Livy we rely on the most for our history of the last Macedonian kings and their relations with Rome, yet their veracity is often doubtful, as I highlight many times in this book.[9] Polybius was born in Megalopolis in Arcadia in about 200; he was a prominent member of the Achaean League and its cavalry commander for 170/69.[10] Given his lifetime and activities in Greece and Rome, he was able to see documents such as copies of treaties and was personally present at some events and able to interview eyewitnesses of others. His *Histories* in forty books covered the period from 220 to 146, focusing on Rome's rise to world power and its clashes with Macedonia. He began it after 167 when he was taken to Rome as a hostage and lived there for seventeen years until 151. Unfortunately, only the first five books dealing with events to 216 (shortly after the end of the Social War) are intact. The remaining books, roughly three-quarters of the whole work, are fragmentary; as such, we are missing much of Perseus' reign, especially the battle of Pydna and resulting settlement of Macedonia, and we have only a few scattered mentions of Andriscus' kingship and its aftermath.[11]

Titus Livius (Livy) wrote a monumental history of Rome and its people in 142 books from the founding of the city to the first emperor, Augustus. Livy started it in the later first century BC and was probably still working on it when he died sometime in the period AD 12–17. He devoted much of his work to Roman politics and expansion in the west, which in turn overshadowed his treatment of events in Macedonia and Greece, but unfortunately his narrative is missing after 167, the year after the first battle of Pydna. Livy drew heavily

---

8. See Banchich and Lane 2009.

9. On Polybius, see Pedech 1964; Walbank 1970; Walbank 1972; Sacks 1981; Green 1990, pp. 269–285; Eckstein 1995; McGing 2010; Baronowski 2011; Dreyer 2011; Dreyer 2013; and the essays in Walbank 1985; Walbank 2002; Gibson and Harrison (eds.) 2013; and Grieb and Koehn (eds.) 2013; cf. Walbank 1957, pp. 1–37. For a commentary, see the still indispensable Walbank 1957; Walbank 1967; and Walbank 1979. On Livy, see Walsh 1961; Dorey 1971; Chaplin 2000; Mineo (ed.) 2014; see too Warrior 1988; Warrior 1996; cf. Briscoe 1973, pp. 1–48. For a commentary, see the excellent Briscoe 1973; Briscoe 1981; Briscoe 2008; and Briscoe 2012.

10. Polybius 28.6.9.

11. Pugliese 2014, pp. 151–152.

on Polybius, whose entire *Histories* would have been available to him, but that reliance tainted the way he wrote about the kings' reigns. Nor does it help that he used questionable accounts by anti-Macedonian Roman annalists who deliberately deprecated Perseus, and the firsthand memoir of Scipio Nasica for the first battle of Pydna, which embellishes all sorts of things to elevate Nasica's standing.

Despite the advantages of the sources Polybius used and his methodology, his personal bias against Philip and Perseus mars his work and influences authors after him, especially Livy. The reasons for Polybius' bias are several. He remained a loyal supporter of the Achaean League and admired all things Achaean, hence anyone who caused it and its leaders like Aratus upset was always at fault.[12] That of course led to his hatred of its enemy the Aetolian League, not to mention Philip's adviser Apelles. He was also profoundly affected by his stay in Rome. He became friendly with several leading Romans and that, plus his view of Macedonia, led him to write his work from Rome's viewpoint.[13] Also underlying his work is his belief that Rome's elevation in the world was due to *Tyche* (Chance or Fortune); in other words, it was predestined.[14] To him, Philip and Perseus were caught up in the spread of Roman imperialism and foolishly stood in its way, bringing about their own downfalls. They therefore did not stand a chance.

Perhaps if Polybius had kept to the dubious predestination explanation, we would still be able to evaluate Philip and Perseus as kings. But Polybius' dislike of them for defying Rome, along with their clashes with the Achaeans, led to him portraying them in a harsh and often rhetorically twisted light. They are seen as venal, ignoble, suspicious, cruel, self-serving, petty, miserly, and even paranoid, who started their reigns well, but then suffered a moral decline. Certainly, they were guilty of ruthless and impious acts and their characters may well be unsavory. However, in that day and age they were not alone in what they did or why, yet we seldom hear of equally grievous actions on the part of others.

To take one example here, though more are discussed in this book: We have Polybius twisting Philip's destruction of Thermum, the Aetolians'

---

12. Gruen 1972; Haegemans and Kosmetatou 2005; Walbank 2000.

13. Walbank 1970.

14. *Tyche*: Walbank 1940, pp. 128–129; Walbank 1957, pp. 16–26; Walbank 1972, pp. 58–65; Walbank 1994, pp. 356–337; Eckstein 1995, pp. 254–271; Eckstein 2005, pp. 228–242; Deininger 2013. Other writers also used Fortune in explain things, such as Paullus' speech on Fortune and human affairs at Plutarch, *Paullus* 27.

religious center, to condemn his immorality.[15] In a long passage he calls the attack on Thermum irrational and even illegal and he compares the king to Philip II and Alexander the Great, who he says had higher moral standards and did not stoop to the sorts of wanton acts Philip did.[16] Yet Polybius says nothing about the actions of the Aetolian League in sacking Dium and Dodona, and Alexander in Asia was guilty of many religious atrocities, including massacring an entire town of Brahman holy men.[17]

For Polybius Philip does not even act in a noble manner. A case in point is his stay in Argos, where he dressed like a commoner and had multiple affairs with married and unmarried women.[18] But so what? Macedonian kings dressed in similar fashion to ordinary people and plenty of kings had numerous affairs, even fathering children from them—Ptolemy I circulated the rumor that he was an illegitimate son of Philip II.[19] Indeed, Philip II's court, declares Demosthenes (admittedly a hostile source), was characterized by its drunkenness, debauchery, and lewd dancing.[20] Demetrius I Poliorcetes moved into the sacred space of the Parthenon, Athena's temple, in Athens and held orgies with courtesans and young men in it.[21] Some might disapprove of our Philip for his lifestyle, but he was a typical Macedonian who loved his wine, women, and song, and needs to be accepted for that.

Polybius' psychological approach to Philip skews his presentation of the king. He saw Philip as a decent young man when he first became king and in his relationship with his guardians, but then incompetent, which unfairly colors his assessment of him.[22] The king became corrupted by power, suffered a dramatic moral deterioration (*metabole*) in his character, foolishly waged war on Rome, and died a pitiable old man, racked by guilt and heartbreak over what he had done to his son Demetrius and his people.[23]

---

15. Polybius 5.8.3–9.7.

16. Polybius 5.10–12.8.

17. Dium: Polybius 4.62.1–3. Dodona: Polybius 4.67.1–4; Diodorus 26.4.7. Alexander: Worthington 2014, pp. 241, 256, and 305.

18. Polybius 10.26.1–6; Livy 27.31.3–6; cf. 27.31.9.

19. Pausanias 1.6.2.

20. Demosthenes 2.18–19.

21. Plutarch, *Demetrius* 23.2–24.1, 23.26.3; cf. Athenaeus 3.128a, 6.253a.

22. McGing 2013; see too Walbank 1994, pp. 38–40.

23. Corrupted: Polybius 4.77.1–4, 7.11.1–11; cf. Plutarch, *Aratus* 49. Death: Polybius 23.10.1–3, 23.12–14; cf. Polybius 10.26.7–10.

When did Philip's alleged moral deterioration occur? For Polybius it was the massacre at Messene in 215 (pp. 75–78).[24] Yet as we have seen, there is nothing to suggest that Philip encouraged the killing in the city, and Polybius' stance is likely the result of the king's argument with Aratus there as he became his own man and leaned less heavily on the Achaean general. What we have is not the historical Philip, or rather, only aspects of the historical king. Polybius' history takes on a literary rather than historical bent, reflected also in the rhetorical speeches he includes to reflect Philip badly.[25] He has been rightly accused of indulging in "tragic history," using the rhetoric of tragic and literary techniques to make moralizing assertions about Philip's later character and attributing the defeat of his kingdom to his tragic flaws.[26] The assessment of Philip's reign in chapter 8 rebuts this image.

Polybius' take on Perseus follows similar lines. Perseus was a good king when assuming the throne, largely because he renewed his father's treaty with Rome, endeavored not to provoke that city, and had a higher lifestyle and standards than Philip.[27] Yet Polybius qualifies his positive assessment by saying Perseus was like this only at the start of his reign—it is not a surprise that he disparages the king as his reign progresses and Macedonia goes to war against Rome.

Perhaps the most startling criticism of Perseus is his stinginess at the cost of his kingdom's security. If we accept Polybius' account, Perseus had the opportunity to make alliances with Eumenes of Pergamum, Genthius of Illyria, and Clondius of the Bastarnae and benefit from a boost to his manpower and resources, especially as a powerful Roman army under Lucius Aemilius Paullus was readying to bring him to battle. Yet Perseus was apparently too miserly to pay each of the three leaders what they demanded for their assistance, costing him these strategic alliances.[28] In speaking of the dealings with

---

24. Polybius 7.11–14, with Walbank 1967, pp. 59–60.

25. For example, the negotiations leading to the Peace of Naupactus in 217: see D'Agostini 2019, pp. 134–138. Livy is much the same: Briscoe 1973, pp. 17–22.

26. Polybius and the tragic, see especially Walbank 1938; Dreyer 2013; cf. Marincola 2013 on Polybius and tragic history.

27. Polybius 25.3.5–8.

28. Eumenes: Polybius 29.8–9; Livy 44.24.7–25.12; Appian, *Macedonian Wars* 18.1 (three different figures of 500, 1,000, or 1,500 talents depending on Eumenes' services). Genthius: Polybius 28.8.4–9.8; Livy 43.19.13–14, 43.20.3, 44.23.2–8, 44.27.8–12; Diodorus 30.9.2; Appian, *Macedonian Wars* 18.1; Plutarch, *Paullus* 9.6. Clondicus: Livy 44.26.2–27.3; Diodorus 30.19; Appian, *Macedonian Wars* 18.1–3; Plutarch, *Paullus* 12.4–8 and 13.1–2.

Eumenes, Polybius gives an excursus on Perseus' ignorance and failure to pay proper attention to his kingdom because he was cheap; hence he has major character flaws as a king and as a man.

Since Polybius experienced the king firsthand as he took part in some of Perseus' campaigns and acted on behalf of the Achaean League, his views should have value. Yet we can be skeptical. Perseus, like Philip, was always concerned about his finances, given the Macedonians had a rolling economy and may not have had enough money on hand. Eumenes' offer in any case is odd coming from an ally of Rome, and there was no guarantee that Genthius and Clondicus would remain loyal to him.

Polybius, followed by other sources, accused Perseus of cowardice in the battle of Pydna when he fled the battlefield.[29] The king certainly had made critical errors and let opportunities slip against the Roman army that led to the Macedonians' eventual defeat in the battle. But like his father and his predecessors going back to Philip II and Alexander the Great he was a warrior king and fought alongside his men. Moreover, after Cynoscephalae a defeated Philip had been allowed to keep the throne and his army, eventually expanding in Greece and Thrace. When he saw his army defeated, Perseus might well have hoped to regroup and so left the field.[30]

Polybius' partiality for the Achaeans and Rome influenced his views about Philip and Perseus. In similar fashion Livy, as a Roman, naturally saw Philip and Perseus as the enemies of his state.[31] He often compresses events or imposes his own take on them with his Roman audience in mind—his account of the battle of Cynoscephalae, for example, differs in several places from that of Polybius.[32] Likewise, while Polybius claims that Philip was planning a new war against Rome at the end of his reign, which Perseus inherited, Livy by contrast states that Perseus provoked the war and was responsible for everything that happened in it.[33]

Livy and other authors follow Polybius' moralizing approach, especially toward Perseus. They give a negative image of Perseus from the outset,

---

29. Polybius 29.17.3–4, 29.18, 29.19; Livy 44.42.2; Plutarch, *Paullus* 19.4.

30. Cf. Burton 2017, p. 169 n. 159, that the battle was so short (one hour) that Perseus' retreat was confused with flight.

31. Hammond and Walbank 1988, pp. 488–490 and 532–533; Dileo 2003; Scuderi 2004; Pugliese 2014; Burton 2017, pp. 214–218.

32. Livy 33.7.6–10.5; cf. Polybius 18.21–26; Plutarch, *Flamininus* 8; Pausanias 7.8.7; Justin 30.4; Zonaras 9.16.

33. Polybius 22.18.8–11; Livy 41.23.9, 41.23.11.

accusing him of being illegitimate, of cynically renewing the *amicitia* with Rome although he was planning war, and even being suspicious and resentful of his brother Demetrius to the extent that he manipulated his father into putting Demetrius to death.[34] Livy also has Perseus change—in his case, from a cautious leader to one who, among other things, is mindless and incompetent, prone to panic disastrously, and blames others for his errors instead of himself.[35]

Polybius' attributions of Philip's and Perseus' apparent immoral characteristics—greed, meanness, madness, and ignorance—became a topos in our literary sources, questioning their reliability and leaving us with subjective rather than objective accounts of the kings.[36] It is therefore not going too far to say that their presentation of Philip and Perseus is one of the fake-news stories of antiquity, justifying a reappraisal of these kings' reigns as this book sets out to do.

---

34. Illegitimate: Livy 40.5.2–5; cf. 39.53.5–6; Plutarch, *Paullus* 8.11–12. Cynical renewal: Polybius 25.3.1; Livy 42.25.4, 42.25.10; Diodorus 29.30; Appian, *Macedonian Wars* 11.5; Zonaras 9.22.2. Deception: Livy 39.53.1–7, 39.53.9, 40.5.2–5, 40.9.2, 40.10.8–11.4, 40.16.3; Polybius 23.3.4–6, 23.7.4–7 (also having Philip equally resentful of his son).

35. Mindless: Livy 44.2.12. Panic: Livy 44.6.2–4. Blaming others: Livy 44.10.1–4; cf. 44.7.8–9.

36. Pugliese 2014, pp. 152–153; cf. Hammond and Walbank 1988, pp. 526–527.

Bibliography

I have used the original publications and paginations for articles reprinted in collections of scholars' works (for example, Walbank 1985; Walbank 2002).

Adams, W.L., "Perseus and the Third Macedonian War," in W.L. Adams and E.N. Borza (eds.), *Philip II, Alexander the Great, and the Macedonian Heritage* (Washington: 1982), pp. 237–256

Adams, W.L., "The Successors of Alexander," in L.A. Tritle (ed.), *The Greek World in the Fourth Century* (London: 1997), pp. 228–248

Adams, W.L., "Alexander's Successors to 221 BC," in J. Roisman and Ian Worthington (eds.), *A Companion to Ancient Macedonia* (Malden: 2010), pp. 208–224

Ager, S.L., *Interstate Arbitrations in the Greek World, 337–90 B.C.* (Berkeley and Los Angeles: 1996)

Andronikos, M., "The Royal Tombs at Aigai (Vergina)," in M.B. Hatzopoulos and L.D. Loukopoulos (eds.), *Philip of Macedon* (London: 1980), pp. 188–231

Andronikos, M., "Art during the Archaic and Classical Periods," in M.B. Sakellariou (ed.), *Macedonia, 4000 Years of Greek History and Civilization* (Athens: 1983), pp. 92–110

Andronikos, M., *Vergina: The Royal Tombs and the Ancient City* (Athens: 2004)

Anson, E.M., "Macedonia's Alleged Constitutionalism," *CJ* 80 (1985a), pp. 303–316

Anson, E.M., "The Hypaspists: Macedonia's Professional Citizen-Soldiers," *Historia* 34 (1985b), pp. 246–248

Anson, E.M., "The Evolution of the Macedonian Army Assembly (330–315)," *Historia* 40 (1991), pp. 230–247

Anson, E.M., "Macedonian Judicial Assemblies," *CPh* 103 (2008), pp. 135–149

Anson, E.M., "The Introduction of the Sarisa in Macedonian Warfare," *Ancient Society* 40 (2010), pp. 51–68

Antonetti, C., *Les Étoliens: Image et Religion* (Paris: 1990)

Archibald, Z.H., *The Odrysian Kingdom of Thrace: Orpheus Unmasked* (Oxford: 1998)

Archibald, Z., "Macedonia and Thrace," in J. Roisman and Ian Worthington (eds.), *A Companion to Ancient Macedonia* (Malden: 2010), pp. 326–341

Armstrong, D. and J.J. Walsh, "The Letter of Flamininus to Chyretiae," *CPh* 81 (1986), pp. 32–46

Austin, M.M., *The Hellenistic World from Alexander to the Roman Conquest. A Selection of Ancient Sources in Translation*² (Cambridge: 2006)

Aymard, A., "L'Organisation de la Macédoine en 167 et le régime représentatif dans le monde grec," *CPh* 45 (1950), pp. 96–107

Aymard, A., "Philippe II de Macedoine otage à Thébes," *REA* 56 (1954), pp. 15–36

Badian, E., *Roman Imperialism in the Late Republic* (Ithaca: 1968)

Badian, E., "The Family and Early Career of T. Quinctius Flamininus," *JRS* 61 (1971), pp. 102–111

Banchich, T. and E. Lane, *The History of Zonaras from Alexander Severus to the Death of Theodosius the Great* (London: 2009)

Baronowski, D.W., "The Provincial Status of Mainland Greece after 146 B.C.: A Criticism of Erich Gruen's Views," *Klio* 70 (1988), pp. 448–460

Baronowski, D.W., *Polybius and Roman Imperialism* (London: 2011)

Bickerman, E., "Notes sur Polybe III. Initia belli Macedonici," *REG* 66 (1953), pp. 479–506

Billows, R., *Antigonus the One-Eyed and the Creation of the Hellenistic State* (Berkeley: 1990)

Bivona, L., "Appiano *Mac.* XII," *Kokalos* 3 (1957), pp. 129–135

Borza, E.N., "The Natural Resources of Early Macedonia," in W.L. Adams and E.N. Borza (eds.), *Philip II, Alexander the Great, and the Macedonian Heritage* (Lanham: 1982), pp. 1–20

Borza, E.N., *In the Shadow of Olympus. The Emergence of Macedon* (Princeton: 1990)

Bosworth, A.B., *The Legacy of Alexander: Politics, Warfare and Propaganda under the Successors* (Oxford: 2002)

Bosworth, A.B., "Alexander the Great and the Creation of the Hellenistic Age," in G.R. Bugh (ed.), *The Cambridge Companion to the Hellenistic World* (Cambridge: 2007), pp. 9–27

Bousquet, J., "Le roi Persée et les Romains," *BCH* 105 (1981), pp. 407–416

Braund, D., "The Emergence of the Hellenistic World, 323–281," in A. Erskine (ed.), *A Companion to the Hellenistic World* (Malden: 2003), pp. 19–34

Briscoe, J., "Q. Marcius Philippus and *Nova Sapientia*," *JRS* 54 (1964), pp. 66–77

Briscoe, J., *A Commentary on Livy. Books XXXI–XXXIII* (Oxford: 1973)

Briscoe, J., "The Antigonids and the Greek States, 276–196 B.C.," in P.D.A. Garnsey and C.R. Whittaker (eds.), *Imperialism in the Ancient World* (Cambridge: 1978), pp. 145–157

Briscoe, J., *A Commentary on Livy. Books XXXIV–XXXVII* (Oxford: 1981)

Briscoe, J., "The Second Punic War," in A.E. Astin, F.W. Walbank, M.W. Fredericksen, and R.M. Ogilvie (eds.), *Cambridge Ancient History*² 8 (Cambridge: 1989), pp. 44–80

Briscoe, J., *A Commentary on Livy. Books XXXVIII–XL* (Oxford: 2008)

Briscoe, J., *A Commentary on Livy. Books XLI–XLV* (Oxford: 2012)

Brizzi, G., "Lo scacchiere internazionale: Annibale e Filippo V," *Hesperia* 17 (2003), pp. 63–78

Brogan, T.M., "Liberation Honors: Athenian Monuments from Antigonid Victories in Their Immediate and Broader Contexts," in O. Palagia and S.V. Tracy (eds.), *The Macedonians in Athens, 322–229 BC* (Oxford: 2003), pp. 194–205

Bugh, G.R. (ed.), *The Cambridge Companion to the Hellenistic World* (Cambridge: 2007)

Burden-Strevens, C. and M.O. Lindholmer (eds.), *Cassius Dio's Forgotten History of Early Rome: The Roman History* (Leiden: 2018)

Burstein, S.M., *The Hellenistic Age from the Battle of Ipsos to the Death of Kleopatra VII* (Cambridge: 1985)

Burton, P.J., *Friendship and Empire: Roman Diplomacy and Imperialism in the Middle Republic (353–146 BC)* (Cambridge: 2011)

Burton, P.J., *Rome and the Third Macedonian War* (Cambridge: 2017)

Byrne, S.G., "The Athenian *Damnnatio Memoriae* of the Antigonids in 200 B.C.," in A. Tamis, C.J. Mackie, and S.G. Byrne (eds.), *Philathenaios. Studies in Honour of Michael J. Osborne* (Athens: 2010), pp. 157–177

Cabanes, P., "Histoire Comparée de la Macédoine, de l'Épire et de l'Illyrie Méridionale (IVe–Iie s. a.C.)," *Ancient Macedonia* 5 (Institute for Balkan Studies, Thessaloniki: 1993), pp. 293–311

Cambridge Ancient History[2], vols. 7–9 (Cambridge: 7.1: 1984; 7.2: 1989; 8: 1989; 9: 1994)

Camia, F., *Roma e le poleis. L'intervento di Roma nelle controversie territoriali tra le communità greche di Grecia e di Asia minore nell II secolo c. C.* (Athens: 2009)

Carney, E.D., "Hunting and the Macedonian Elite: Sharing the Rivalry of the Chase (Arrian 4.13.1)," in D. Ogden (ed.), *The Hellenistic World: New Perspectives* (London: 2002), pp. 59–80

Carney, E., "The Role of the *Basilikoi Paides* at the Argead Court," in T. Howe and J. Reames (eds.), *Macedonian Legacies: Studies in Macedonian History and Culture in Honor of Eugene N. Borza* (Claremont: 2008), pp. 145–164

Ceka, N., *The Illyrians to the Albanians* (Tirana: 2013)

Champion, C. "The Nature of Authoritative Evidence in Polybius, and the Speech of Agelaus at Naupactus," *TAPA* 127 (1997), pp. 111–128

Champion, J., *Pyrrhus of Epirus* (Barnsley: 2012)

Champion, J., *Antigonus the One-Eyed: Greatest of the Successors* (Barnsley: 2014)

Chaplin, J.D., *Livy's Exemplary History* (Oxford: 2000)

Christesen, P. and S.C. Murray, "Macedonian Religion," in J. Roisman and Ian Worthington (eds.), *A Companion to Ancient Macedonia* (Malden: 2010), pp. 428–445

Cloché, P., *Histoire de la Macedoine jusqu' à l'avènement d'Alexandre le Grande* (Paris: 1960)

Connolly, P., "The Roman Army in the Age of Polybius," in J. Hackett (ed.), *Warfare in the Ancient World* (New York: 1989), pp. 149–168

Coppola, A., *Demetrio di Faro: Un Protagonista dimenticato* (Rome: 1993)

D'Agostini, M. "Il discorso del re: Filippo V in Giustino," in C. Bearzot and F. Landucci (eds.), *Studi sull'Epitome di Giustino II. Da Alessandro Magno a Filippo V di Macedonia* (Milan: 2015), pp. 121–144

D'Agostini, M., *The Rise of Philip V: Kingship and Rule in the Hellenistic World* (Edizioni dell'Orso: 2019)

Daskalakis, A., *The Hellenism of the Ancient Macedonians* (Thessaloniki: 1965)

Daubner, F., *Makedonien nach den Königen (168 v. Chr.–14 n. Chr.)* (Stuttgart: 2018)

Deininger, J., *Der politische Widerstand gegen Rom in Greichenland, 217–86 v. Chr.* (Berlin: 1971)

Deininger, J., "Bemerkungen zur Historizität der Rede des Agelaos 217 v. Chr. (Polyb. 5.104)," *Chiron* 3 (1973), pp. 103–108

Deininger, J., "Die Tyche in der pragmatischen Geschichtsschreibung des Polybios," in V. Grieb and C Koehn (eds.), *Polybios und seine Historien* (Berlin: 2013), pp. 71–111

Dell, H.J., "The Western Frontier of the Macedonian Monarchy," *Ancient Macedonia* 1 (Institute for Balkan Studies, Thessaloniki: 1970), pp. 115–126

Dell, H.J., "Macedon and Rome: The Illyrian Question in the Early Second Century B.C.," *Ancient Macedonia* 2 (Institute for Balkan Studies, Thessaloniki: 1977), pp. 305–315

Dell, H.J., "The Quarrel between Demetrius and Perseus: A Note on Macedonian National Policy," *Ancient Macedonia* 3 (Institute for Balkan Studies, Thessaloniki: 1983), pp. 66–76

Derow, P.S., "Polybius, Rome, and the East," *JRS* 69 (1979), pp. 1–15

Derow, P.S., "Rome, the Fall of Macedon, and the Sack of Corinth," in A.E. Astin, F.W. Walbank, M.W. Fredericksen, and R.M. Ogilvie (eds.), *Cambridge Ancient History*[2] 8 (Cambridge: 1989), pp. 290–323

Derow, P.S., "Pharos and Rome," *ZPE* 88 (1991), pp. 261–270

Derow, P.S., "The Arrival of Rome: From the Illyrian Wars to the Fall of Macedon," in A. Erskine (ed.), *A Companion to the Hellenistic World* (Malden: 2003), pp. 51–70

Dileo, G., "Tra Polibio e Livio: Diodore e la presunta avarizia di Perseo," *Syngraphe* 5 (2003), pp. 89–105

Dmitriev, S., *The Greek Slogan of Freedom and Early Roman Politics in Greece* (Oxford: 2011)

Dorey, T.A., *Livy* (London: 1971)

Dow, S. and C.F. Edson, "Chryseis, A Study of the Evidence in Regard to the Mother of Philip V," *HSCPh* 48 (1937), pp. 127–180

Dreyer, B., *Polybios—Leben und Werk im Banne Roms* (Hildsheim: 2011)

Dreyer, B., "Frank Walbank's *Philippos Tragoidoumenos*: Polybius' Account of Philip's Last Years," in B. Gibson and T. Harrison (eds.), *Polybius and His World: Essays in Memory of F.W. Walbank* (Oxford: 2013), pp. 201–211

Drougou, S., "Vergina—The Ancient City of Aegae," in R. Lane Fox (ed.), *Brill's Companion to Ancient Macedon* (Leiden: 2011), pp. 243–256

Duff, T., *Plutarch's Lives: Exploring Vice and Virtue* (Oxford: 1999)

Dzino, D., *Illyricum in Roman Politics, 229 BC–AD 68* (Cambridge: 2010)

Eckstein, A.M., "T. Quinctus Flamininus and the Campaign against Philip in 198 B.C.," *Phoenix* 30 (1976), pp. 119–142

Eckstein, A.M., "Rome, the War with Perseus and the Third-Party Mediation," *Historia* 37 (1988), pp. 414–444

Eckstein, A.M., "Polybius, Demetrius of Pharus, and the Origins of the Second Illyrian War," *CP* 89 (1994), pp. 46–59

Eckstein, A.M., *Moral Vision in the Histories of Polybius* (Berkeley and Los Angeles: 1995)

Eckstein, A.M., "Greek Mediation in the First Macedonian War," *Historia* 51 (2002), pp. 268–297

Eckstein, A.M., "The Pact between the Kings, Polybius 15.20.6, and Polybius' View of the Outbreak of the Second Macedonian War," *CP* 100 (2005), pp. 228–242

Eckstein, A.M., *Mediterranean Anarchy, Interstate War, and the Rise of Rome* (Berkeley and Los Angeles: 2006)

Eckstein, A.M., *Rome Enters the Greek East. From Anarchy to Hierarchy in the Hellenistic Mediterranean, 230–170 BC* (Malden: 2008)

Eckstein, A.M., "Macedonia and Rome, 221–146 BC," in J. Roisman and Ian Worthington (eds.), *A Companion to Ancient Macedonia* (Malden: 2010), pp. 225–250

Edson, C.F., "Perseus and Demetrius," *HSCPh* 46 (1935), pp. 191–202

Edson, C.F., "Early Macedonia," *Ancient Macedonia* 1 (Institute for Balkan Studies, Thessaloniki: 1970), pp. 17–44

Ehrhardt, C., "Demetrios Ho Aitolikos and Antigonid Nicknames," *Hermes* 106 (1978), pp. 251–253

Engels, J., "Macedonians and Greeks," in J. Roisman and Ian Worthington (eds.), *A Companion to Ancient Macedonia* (Malden: 2010), pp. 81–98

English, S., *The Army of Alexander the Great* (Barnsley: 2009a)

English, S., *The Sieges of Alexander the Great* (Barnsley: 2009b)

Erdkamp, P. (ed.), *A Companion to the Roman Army* (Malden: 2007)

Errington, R.M., "Philip V, Aratus, and the 'Conspiracy of Apelles,'" *Historia* 16 (1967), pp. 19–36

Errington, R.M., "From Babylon to Triparadeisos," *JHS* 90 (1970), pp. 49–77

Errington, R.M., *The Dawn of Empire: Rome's Rise to World Power* (London: 1971a)

Errington, R.M., "The Alleged Syro-Macedonian Pact and the Origins of the Second Macedonian War," *Athenaeum* 49 (1971b), pp. 336–354

Errington, R.M., "Macedonian Royal Style and Its Historical Significance," *JHS* 90 (1974a), pp. 20–38

Errington, R.M., "*Senatus consultum de Coronaeis* and the Early Course of the Third Macedonian War," *RFIC* 102 (1974b), pp. 79–86

Errington, R.M., "The Nature of the Macedonian State under the Monarchy," *Chiron* 8 (1978), pp. 77–133

Errington, R.M., "Rome and Greece to 205 B.C.," in A.E. Astin, F.W. Walbank, M.W. Fredericksen, and R.M. Ogilvie (eds.), *Cambridge Ancient History*² 8 (Cambridge: 1989a), pp. 81–106

Errington, R.M., "Rome against Philip and Antiochus," in A.E. Astin, F.W. Walbank, M.W. Fredericksen, and R.M. Ogilvie (eds.), *Cambridge Ancient History*² 8 (Cambridge: 1989b), pp. 244–289

Errington, R.M., *A History of Macedonia*, transl. C. Errington (Berkeley and Los Angeles: 1990)

Erskine, A. (ed.), *A Companion to the Hellenistic World* (Malden: 2003)

Ferrary, J.L., *Philhellénisme et impérialisme. Aspects idéologiques de la conquête romaine du monde hellénistique* (Paris: 1988)

Fine, J.V.A., "The Mother of Philip V of Macedon," *CQ* 28 (1934), pp. 99–104

Fine, J.V.A., "The Background of the Social War of 220–217 B.C.," *AJP* 61 (1940), pp. 129–165

Fuller, J.F.C., *The Generalship of Alexander the Great* (London: 1960)

Gabba, E., *Appiano e la storia delle Guerre Civile* (Florence: 1956)

Gabbert, J., *Antigonus II Gonatas: A Political Biography* (London: 1997)

Gabriel, R.A., *Philip II of Macedon: Greater Than Alexander* (Washington: 2010)

Galles, K.I., "Chrusologonos Ex Edesses: Larisaikon Timetikon Psephima," *Ancient Macedonia* 2 (Institute for Balkan Studies, Thessaloniki: 1977), pp. 33–43

Garlan, Y., *Recherches de poliorcétique grecque* (Paris: 1974)

Garoufalias, P.E., *Pyrrhus, King of Epirus* (London: 1979)

Gibson, B. and T. Harrison (eds.), *Polybius and His World: Essays in Memory of F.W. Walbank* (Oxford: 2013)

Gilley, D. and Ian Worthington, "Alexander the Great, Macedonia and Asia," in J. Roisman and Ian Worthington (eds.), *A Companion to Ancient Macedonia* (Malden: 2010), pp. 186–207

Giovannini, A., "Les rigins de la troisième guerre de Macédoine," *BCH* 93 (1969), pp. 853–861

Giovannini, A., "Philipp V., Perseus und die delphische Amphiktyonie," *Ancient Macedonia* 1 (Institute for Balkan Studies, Thessaloniki: 1970), pp. 147–154

Golan, D., "Two Letters of Perseus to the Greeks," *SCI* 5 (1979/80), pp. 118–136

Golan, D., "Polybius and the Outbreak of the Third Macedonian War," *AC* 58 (1989), pp. 112–129

Gowing, A., *The Triumviral Narratives of Appian and Cassius Dio* (Ann Arbor: 1992)

Grainger, J.D., *Seleukos Nikator: Constructing a Hellenistic Kingdom* (London: 1999)

Grainger, J.D., *The League of the Aitolians* (Leiden: 1999)

Grainger, J.D., *The Roman War of Antiochus the Great* (Leiden: 2002)

Grainger, J.D., *The Rise of the Seleukid Empire (323–223 BC): Seleukos I to Seleukos III* (Barnsley: 2014)

Grainger, J.D., *Kings and Kingship in the Hellenistic World, 350–30 BC* (Barnsley: 2017)

Graninger, D., "Macedonia and Thessaly," in J. Roisman and Ian Worthington (eds.), *A Companion to Ancient Macedonia* (Malden: 2010), pp. 306–325

Green, P., *Alexander to Actium: The Historical Evolution of the Hellenistic Age* (Berkeley and Los Angeles: 1990)

Greenwalt, W.S., "Polygamy and Succession in Argead Macedonia," *Arethusa* 22 (1989), pp. 19–45

Greenwalt, W.S., "Why Pella?," *Historia* 48 (1999), pp. 158–183

Greenwalt, W.S., "Macedonia, Illyria, and Epirus," in J. Roisman and Ian Worthington (eds.), *A Companion to Ancient Macedonia* (Malden: 2010), pp. 279–305

Grieb, V. and C. Koehn (eds.), *Polybios und seine Historien* (Berlin: 2013)

Gruen, E.S., "Aratus and the Achaean Alliance with Macedonia," *Historia* 21 (1972), pp. 609–625

Gruen, E.S., "The Supposed Alliance between Rome and Philip V," *CSCA* 6 (1973), pp. 123–136

Gruen, E.S., "The Last Years of Philip V," *GRBS* 15 (1974), pp. 221–246

Gruen, E.S., "Rome and Rhodes in the Second Century B.C.: A Historiographical Enquiry," *CQ* 25 (1975), pp. 58–81.

Gruen, E.S., "Class Conflict and the Third Macedonian War," *AJAH* 1 (1976), pp. 29–60

Gruen, E.S., "Philip V and the Greek Demos," in H.J. Dell (ed.), *Ancient Macedonian Studies in Honour of C.F. Edson* (Thessaloniki: 1981), pp. 169–182

Gruen, E.S., "Macedonia and the Settlement of 167 B.C.," in W.L. Adams and E.N. Borza (eds.), *Philip II, Alexander the Great, and the Macedonian Heritage* (Washington: 1982), pp. 257–267

Gruen, E.S., *The Hellenistic World and the Coming of Rome* (Berkeley and Los Angeles: 1984)

Gyioka, P.G., *Perseus, ho teleutaios basileus ton Makedonon* (Thessaloniki: 1975)

Habicht, C., "Epigraphische Zeugnisse zur Geschichte Thessaliens unter der Makedonishen Herrschaft," *Ancient Macedonia* 1 (Institute for Balkan Studies, Thessaloniki: 1970), pp. 265–279

Habicht, C., *Studien zur Geschichte Athens in hellenistischer Zeit* (Göttingen: 1982)

Habicht, C., "The Role of Athens in the Reorganization of the Delphic Amphictyony after 189 B.C.," *Hesperia* 56 (1987), pp. 59–71

Habicht, C., *Athens from Alexander to Antony*, transl. D.L. Schneider (Cambridge: 1997)

Haegemans, K. and E. Kosmetatou, "Aratus and the Achaean Background of Polybius," in G. Schepens and J. Bollansée (eds.), *The Shadow of Polybius: Intertextuality as a Research Tool in Greek Historiography* (Leuven: 2005), pp. 123–129

Hamilton, C.D., "The Origins of the Second Macedonian War," *Ancient Macedonia* 5 (Institute for Balkan Studies, Thessaloniki: 1993), pp. 559–567

Hammond, N.G.L., "The Kingdoms in Illyria circa 400–167 BC," *BSA* 61 (1966a), pp. 239–253

Hammond, N.G.L., "The Opening Campaigns and the Battle of the Aoi Stena in the Second Macedonian War," *JRS* 56 (1966b), pp. 39–54

Hammond, N.G.L., *Epirus* (Oxford: 1967)

Hammond, N.G.L., "Illyris, Rome and Macedon in 229–205 B.C.," *JRS* 58 (1968), pp. 1–21

Hammond, N.G.L., *A History of Macedonia* 1 (Oxford: 1972)

Hammond, N.G.L., "Training in the Use of the Sarissa and Its Effect in Battle 359–333 BC," *Antichthon* 14 (1980), pp. 53–63

Hammond, N.G.L., "The Battle of Pydna," *JHS* 104 (1984), pp. 31–47

Hammond, N.G.L., "The Campaign and the Battle of Cynoscephalae in 197 BC," *JHS* 108 (1988), pp. 60–82

Hammond, N.G.L., "Casualties and Reinforcements of Citizen Soldiers in Greece and Macedonia," *JHS* 109 (1989), pp. 56–68

Hammond, N.G.L., "Royal Pages, Personal Pages, and Boys Trained in the Macedonian Manner during the Period of the Temenid Monarchy," *Historia* 39 (1990), pp. 261–290

Hammond, N.G.L., *The Macedonian State: Origins, Institutions, and History* (Oxford: 1992)

Hammond, N.G.L., "What May Philip Have Learnt as a Hostage in Thebes," *GRBS* 38 (1997), pp. 355–372.

Hammond, N.G.L. and G.T. Griffith, *A History of Macedonia* 2 (Oxford: 1979)

Hammond, N.G.L. and M.B. Hatzopoulos, "The Via Egnatia in Western Macedonia" (1), *AJAH* 7 (1982) [1985], pp. 128–149

Hammond, N.G.L. and M.B. Hatzopoulos, "The Via Egnatia in Western Macedonia" (2), *AJAH* 8 (1983) [1986], pp. 48–53

Hammond, N.G.L. and F.W. Walbank, *A History of Macedonia* 3 (Oxford: 1988)

Hansen, E.V., *The Attalids of Pergamon* (Ithaca: 1971)

Hanson, V.D. (ed.), *Hoplites: The Classical Greek Battle Experience* (London: 1991)

Hardiman, C.L., "Classical Art to 221 BC," in J. Roisman and Ian Worthington (eds.), *A Companion to Ancient Macedonia* (Malden: 2010), pp. 505–521

Harris, W.V., *War and Imperialism in Republican Rome, 327–70 B.C.* (Oxford: 1979)

Hatzopoulos, M.B., "Succession and Regency in Classical Macedonia," *Ancient Macedonia* 4 (Institute for Balkan Studies, Thessaloniki: 1986), pp. 279–292

Hatzopoulos, M.B., *Cultes et rites de passage en Macédoine* (Athens: 1994a)

Hatzopoulos, M.B. (ed.), *Macedonia from Philip II to the Roman Conquest* (Princeton: 1994b)

Hatzopoulos, M.B., *Macedonian Institutions under the Kings*, 2 vols. (Athens: 1996)

Hatzopoulos, M.B., *L'organisation de l'armée macédonienne sous les Antigonides. Problèmes anciens et documents nouveaux* (Athens: 2001)

Hatzopoulos, M.B., "Macedonia and Macedonians," in R. Lane Fox (ed.), *Brill's Companion to Ancient Macedon* (Leiden: 2011a), pp. 43–50

Hatzopoulos, M.B., "Macedonians and Other Greeks," in R. Lane Fox (ed.), *Brill's Companion to Ancient Macedon* (Leiden: 2011b), pp. 51–78

Hatzopoulos, M.B., "Vies parallèles: Philippe V d'après Polybe et d'après ses propres écrits," *Journal des Savants* (2014), pp. 99–120

Hatzopoulos, M.B., "Federal Makedonia," in H. Beck and P. Funke (eds.), *Federalism in Greek Antiquity* (Cambridge: 2015), pp. 319–340

Hatzopoulos, M.B., "Une deuxième copie du diagramma de Philippe V sur le service dans l'armée de campagne, la loi éphébarchique d'Amphipolis et les politarques macédoniens," *Mediterranean Archaeology* 19 (2016), pp. 203–216

Hatzopoulos, M.B., *Ancient Macedonia* (Berlin: 2020)

Heckel, W., "A King and His Army," in W. Heckel and L. Tritle (eds.), *Alexander the Great: A New History* (Malden: 2009), pp. 69–82

Heckel, W., T. Howe, and S. Müller, "The Giver of the Bride, the Bridegroom, and the Bride: A Study of the Murder of Philip II and Its Aftermath," in T. Howe, S. Müller, and R. Stoneman (eds.), *Ancient Historiography on War and Empire* (Oxford: 2017), pp. 92–124

Helliesen, J., "Demetrius I Soter: A Seleucid King with an Antigonid Name," in H.J. Dell (ed.), *Ancient Macedonian Studies in Honor of Charles F. Edson* (Thessaloniki: 1981), pp. 219–228

Helliesen, J., "Andriscus and the Revolt of the Macedonians, 149–148 B.C.," *Ancient Macedonia* 4 (Institute for Balkan Studies, Thessaloniki: 1986), pp. 307–314

Hennig, D., "Die Bericht des Polybios über Boiotien und die Lage von Orchomenos in der 2 Hälfte des 3. Jarhunderts v. Chr.," *Chiron* 7 (1977), pp. 119–148

Hiller von Gaertringen, F., *Die Inschriften von Priene* (Berlin: 1906)

Hoyos, D., "The Age of Overseas Expansion (264–146 BC)," in P. Erdkamp (ed.), *A Companion to the Roman Army* (Malden: 2007), pp. 63–79

Jacquemin, A. and D. Laroche, "Notes sur trois piliers delphiques," *BCH* 106 (1982), pp. 191–218

Jacquemin, A., D. Laroche, and F. Lefèvre, "Delphes, le roi Persée et les Romains," *BCH* 119 (1995), pp. 125–136

Juhel, P.O., "On Orderliness with Respect to the Prizes of War: The Amphipolis Regulation and the Management of Booty in the Army of the Last Antigonids," *BSA* 97 (2002), pp. 401–412

Kähler, H., *Der Fries vom Reiterdenkmal des Aemilius Paullus in Delphi* (Berlin: 1965)

Kahrstedt, U., "Städte in Makedonien," *Hermes* 81 (1953), pp. 85–111

Kalléris, J.N., "L'armee macedoine sous Alexandre I, Le Philhellene," in J. Servais, T. Hackens, and B. Servais-Soyez (eds.), *Stemmata: Melanges de philologie, d'histoire et d'archeologie grecques offerts Jules Labarbe* (Liege: 1987), pp. 317–331

Kalléris, J.N., *Les anciens Macédoniens. Etude linguistique et historique*, 2 vols. (Athens: 1988)

Kallet-Marx, R.M., *Hegemony to Empire: The Development of the Roman Imperium in the East from 148 to 62 B.C.* (Berkeley and Los Angeles: 1995)

Karunanithy, D., *The Macedonian War Machine. Neglected Aspects of the Armies of Philip, Alexander and the Successors 359–281 BC* (Barnsley: 2013)

Kertész, I., "The Attalids of Pergamon and Macedonia," *Ancient Macedonia* 5 (Institute for Balkan Studies, Thessaloniki: 1993), pp. 669–677

Keyser, P.T., "The Use of Artillery by Philip II and Alexander the Great," *Ancient World* 15 (1994), pp. 27–49

King, C.J., "Kingship and Other Political Institutions," in J. Roisman and Ian Worthington (eds.), *A Companion to Ancient Macedonia* (Malden: 2010), pp. 374–391

King, C.J., *Ancient Macedonia* (London: 2018)

Klaudianou, J., "Appiano (*Maced.* XI,9) e l'espulsione di Macedoni da Roma," *Annali della Facolta di Lettere e Filosofia* 18 (1997), pp. 17–23

Kleu, M., *Die Seepolitik Philipps V. von Makedonien* (Bochum: 2015)

Kleu, M., "Philip V, the Selci-Hoard and the Supposed Building of a Macedonian Fleet in Lissus," *AHB* 31 (2017), pp. 112–119

Kottaridi, A., "The Palace of Aegae," in R. Lane Fox (ed.), *Brill's Companion to Ancient Macedon* (Leiden: 2011), pp. 297–333

Koukouli-Chrysanthaki, C., "Politarchs in a New Inscription from Amphipolis," in H.J. Dell (ed.), *Ancient Macedonian Studies in Honor of Charles F. Edson* (Thessaloniki: 1981), pp. 229–241

Kousser, R., "Hellenistic and Roman Art, 221 BC–AD 337," in J. Roisman and Ian Worthington (eds.), *A Companion to Ancient Macedonia* (Malden: 2010), pp. 522–542

Kremydi, S., "Coinage and Finance," in R. Lane Fox (ed.), *Brill's Companion to Ancient Macedon* (Leiden: 2011), pp. 159–178

Kuzmin, Y.N, "King Demetrius II of Macedon: In the Shadow of Father and Son," *Ziva Antika* 69 (2019), pp. 59–84

Kuzmin, Y.N., "Phila and Phthia: The Names of Antigonid Queens in Two Recently Published Athenian Decrees," *ZPE* 221 (2022), pp. 113–120

Lane Fox, R. (ed.), *Brill's Companion to Ancient Macedon* (Leiden: 2011a)

Lane Fox, R., "Philip of Macedon: Accession, Ambitions, and Self-Presentation," in R. Lane Fox (ed.), *Brill's Companion to Ancient Macedon* (Leiden: 2011b), pp. 335–366

Lane Fox, R, "Dating the Royal Tombs at Vergina," in R. Lane Fox (ed.), *Brill's Companion to Ancient Macedon* (Leiden: 2011c), pp. 1–34

Lane Fox, R., "'Glorious Servitude…': The Reigns of Antigonos Gonatas and Demetrios II," in R. Lane Fox (ed.), *Brill's Companion to Ancient Macedon* (Leiden: 2011d), pp. 495–519

Lange, C.H. and J.M. Madsen (eds.), *Cassus Dio: Greek Intellectual and Roman Politician* (Leiden: 2016)

Lazenby, J.F., *Hannibal's War* (Warminster: 1989)

LeBohec, S., "Phthia, mère de Philippe V: Examen critique des sources," *REG* 94 (1981), pp. 34–46

LeBohec, S., "Démétrios de Pharos, Scerdilaidas et la Ligue hellénique," in P. Cabanes (ed.), L'Illyrie méridionale et l'Epire dans l'Antiquité (Clermont-Ferrand: 1987), pp. 203–208

LeBohec, S., *Antigone Dôsôn roi de Macédoine* (Nancy: 1993)

LeBohec, S., "Remarques sur l'Âge de la Majorité chez les Rois de Macédoine," *Ancient Macedonia* 5 (Institute for Balkan Studies, Thessaloniki: 1993), pp. 779–788

Lefèvre, E., "Traité de paix entre Démétrios Poliorcète et la confédératon étolienne (en 289?)," *BCH* 122 (1998), pp. 109–141.

Lévèque, P., *Pyrrhos* (Paris: 1957)

Lloyd, A.B., "Philip II and Alexander the Great: The Moulding of Macedon's Army," in A.B. Lloyd (ed.), *Battle in Antiquity* (London: 1996), pp. 169–198

Longaretti, L., "L'alleanza tra Annibale e Filippo V di Macedonia," *RIL* 123 (1989), pp. 183–192

Loreto, L., "Polyb. 10.17.1–5 e il regolamento militare macedone. Norme ellenistiche in materia di saccheggio e di bottino di guerra," *Index* 18 (1990), pp. 331–366

Ma, J., "Kings," in A. Erskine (ed.), *A Companion to the Hellenistic World* (Malden: 2003), pp. 177–195

Ma, J., "Court, King, and Power in Antigonid Macedonia," in R. Lane Fox (ed.), *Brill's Companion to Ancient Macedon* (Leiden: 2011), pp. 521–543

MacKay, P.A., "The Coinage of Macedonian Republics, 168–146 b. Chr.," *Ancient Macedonia* 1 (Institute for Balkan Studies, Thessaloniki: 1970), pp. 256–264

Manni, E., *Demetrio Poliorcete* (Rome: 1951)

Mari, M., "The Ruler Cult in Macedonia," *Studi Ellenistici* 20 (2008), pp. 219–268

Mari, M., "Traditional Cults and Beliefs," in R. Lane Fox (ed.), *Brill's Companion to Ancient Macedon* (Leiden: 2011), pp. 453–465

Marincola, J., "Polybius, Phylarchus, and 'Tragic History': A Reconsideration," in B. Gibson and T. Harrison (eds.), *Polybius and his World: Essays in Memory of F.W. Walbank* (Oxford: 2013), pp. 73–90

Marsden, E.W., "Macedonian Military Machinery and Its Designers under Philip and Alexander," *Ancient Macedonia* 2 (Institute for Balkan Studies, Thessaloniki: 1977), pp. 211–223

Mastrocinque, E., "Eumene a Roma (172 a. C.) e le fonti del libro Macedonico di Appiano," *AIV* 134 (1975/76), pp. 25–40

Matyszak, P., *Roman Conquests: Macedonia and Greece* (Barnsley: 2009)

McDonald, A.H., "Studies on Ancient Macedonia in Honor of Charles F. Edson. With Perseus at Pydna," in H.J. Dell (ed.), *Ancient Macedonian Studies in Honor of Charles F. Edson* (Thessaloniki: 1981), pp. 243–254

McDonald, A.H. and F.W. Walbank, "The Origins of the Second Macedonian War," *JRS* 27 (1937), pp. 180–207

McGing, B.C., *Polybius' Histories* (New York: 2010)

McGing, B.C., "Youthfulness in Polybius: The Case of Philip V of Macedon," in B. Gibson and T. Harrison (eds.), *Polybius and His World: Essays in Memory of F.W. Walbank* (Oxford: 2013), pp. 183–199

Meeus, A., "The Power Struggle of the Diadochoi in Babylonia, 323 BC," *Ancient Society* 38 (2008), pp. 39–82

Meloni, P., *Perseo e la Fine della Monarchia Macedonia* (Rome: 1953)

Meloni, P., *Il valore storico e le fonti del libro macedonico di Appiano* (Rome: 1955)

Mendels, D., "Polybius, Philip V, and the Socio-Economic Question in Greece," *Ancient Society* 8 (1977), pp. 155–174

Mendels, D., "Perseus and the Socioeconomic Question in Greece (179–172/1 B.C.). A Study in Roman Propaganda," *Ancient Society* 9 (1978), pp. 55–73

Mendels, D., "Messene 215 B.C. An Enigmatic Revolution," *Historia* 29 (1980), pp. 246–250

Merker, I.L., "The Ancient Kingdom of Paionia," *Balkan Studies* 6 (1965), pp. 35–54

Mikalson, J., *Ancient Greek Religion* (Oxford: 2005)

Milivojevic, F., "Uscana, Perseus and the Romans: Livy and the Chronology of War Operations in the Third Macedonian War," *Ziva Antika* 69 (2019), pp. 85–108

Millar, F., *A Study of Cassius Dio* (Oxford: 1964)

Miller, S.G., "Macedonians at Delphi," in A. Jacquemin (ed.), *Delphes: Cent ans après la Grande Fouille* (Athens: 2000), pp. 263–281

Millett, P., "The Political Economy of Macedonia," in J. Roisman and Ian Worthington (eds.), *A Companion to Ancient Macedonia* (Malden: 2010), pp. 472–504

Milns, R.D., "Philip II and the Hypaspists," *Historia* 16 (1967), pp. 509–512

Milns, R.D., "The Army of Alexander the Great," in E. Badian (ed.), *Alexandre le Grand. Image et réalité* (Geneva: 1976), pp. 87–136

Mineo, B. (ed.), *A Companion to Livy* (Malden: 2014)

Mitchell, S., "The Galatians: Representation and Reality," in A. Erskine (ed.), *A Companion to the Hellenistic World* (Malden: 2003), pp. 280–293

Moretti, L., *Iscrizioni storiche ellenistiche*, 2 vols. (Florence: 1967–75)

Morgan, M.G., "Metellus Macedonicus and the Province Macedonia," *Historia* 18 (1969), pp. 422–446

Morison, W.S., *Theompompus, BNJ* 115 (Leiden)

Mørkholm, O., "The Speech of Agelaus at Naupactus, 217 B.C.," *Class. & Med.* 28 (1970), pp. 240–253

Mørkholm, O., "The Speech of Agelaus Again," *Chiron* 4 (1974), pp. 127–132

Müller, S., "Philip II," in J. Roisman and Ian Worthington (eds.), *A Companion to Ancient Macedonia* (Malden: 2010), pp. 166–185

Nachtergael, G., *Les Galates en Grèce et les Sôtéria de Delphes* (Brussels: 1977)

Nicholson, E., "Polybius, the Laws of War, and Philip V of Macedon," *Historia* 67 (2018a), pp. 434–453

Nicholson, E., "Philip V of Macedon, 'Eromenos' of the Greeks': A Note and Reassessment," *Hermes* 146 (2018b), pp. 241–255

Nogueira Borell, A., "L'armée macédonienne avant Philippi II," *Ancient Macedonia* 7 (Institute for Balkan Studies, Thessaloniki: 2007), pp. 97–111

O'Neil, J.L., "A Re-Examination of the Chremonidean War," in P. McKechnie and P. Guillaume (eds.), *Ptolemy II Philadelphus and His World* (Leiden: 2008), pp. 65–89

Palagia, O., "Hellenistic Art," in R. Lane Fox (ed.), *Brill's Companion to Ancient Macedon* (Leiden: 2011), pp. 477–493

Papazoglou, F., *The Central Balkan Tribes in Pre-Roman Times* (Amsterdam: 1978)

Papazoglou, F., "Quelques aspects de l'historie de la province de Macédoine," in H. Temporini (ed.), *Aufstieg und Niedergang der Romischen Welt* 2.7.1 (Berlin: 1979), pp. 302–369

Papazoglou, F., "Sur l'Organisation de la Macédoine des Antigonides," *Ancient Macedonia* 3 (Institute for Balkan Studies, Thessaloniki: 1983), pp. 195–210

Papazoglou, F., *Villes de Macédoine à l'époque romaine* (Paris: 1988)

Paspalas, S.A., "Classical Art," in R. Lane Fox (ed.), *Brill's Companion to Ancient Macedon* (Leiden: 2011), pp. 179–207

Pedech, P., *La méthode historique de Polybe* (Paris: 1964)

Pelling, C., *Plutarch and History* (London: 2002)

Perrin-Saminadayar, É., "Romains à Athènes (IIe et Ier siècles av. J.-C.): Entre Acculturation et Malentendu Culturel," in A. Gangloff (ed.), *Médiateurs Culturels et Politiques l'Empire Romain* (Paris: 2011), pp. 123–139

Petzold, K.E., "Die Freiheit der Griechen und die Politik der *nova sapientia*," *Historia* 48 (1999), pp. 61–93

Pfeilschifter, R., *Titus Quinctius Flamininus: Untersuchungen zue römischen Griechenlandpolitik* (Göttingen: 2005)

Pouilloux, J. and N.M. Verdélis, "Deux Inscriptions de Démétrias," *BCH* 74 (1950), pp. 33–47

Psoma, S., "The Kingdom of Macedonia and the Chalcidic League," in R. Lane Fox (ed.), *Brill's Companion to Ancient Macedon* (Leiden: 2011), pp. 113–135

Pugliese, A., "The Literary Tradition on King Perseus and the End of the Macedonian Kingdom: Between History and Propaganda," *Ancient World* 45 (2014), pp. 146–173

Rawlings, L., *The Ancient Greeks at War* (Manchester: 2007)

Reiter, R., *Aemilius Paullus: Conqueror of Greece* (London: 1988)

Rhodes, P.J. and R. Osborne (eds.), *Greek Historical Inscriptions, 404–323 BC* (Oxford: 2003)

Rich, J.W., "Roman Aims in the First Macedonian War," *PCPS* 30 (1984), pp. 126–180

Roisman, J., "Royal Power, Law and Justice in Ancient Macedonia," *AHB* 26 (2012), pp. 131–148

Roisman, J., "Opposition to Macedonian Kings: Riots for Rewards and Verbal Protests," in T. Howe, E.E. Garvin, and G. Wrightson (eds.), *Greece, Macedon, and Persia: Studies in Social, Political, and Military History in Honour of Waldemar Heckel* (Philadelphia: 2015), pp. 77–86

Roisman, J., *Alexander's Veterans and the Early Wars of the Successors* (Austin: 2012)

Roisman, J. and Ian Worthington (eds.), *A Companion to Ancient Macedonia* (Malden: 2010)

Rosenstein, N.S., *Rome and the Mediterranean, 290–146 BC: The Imperial Republic* (Edinburgh: 2012)

Russell, D.A., *Plutarch* (London: 1973)

Saatsoglou–Paliadeli, C., "The Arts at Vergina-Aegae, The Cradle of the Macedonian Kingdom," in R. Lane Fox (ed.), *Brill's Companion to Ancient Macedon* (Leiden: 2011), pp. 271–295

Sacks, K., *Polybius on the Writing of History* (Berkeley and Los Angeles: 1981)

Sacks, K., *Diodorus Siculus and the First Century* (Princeton: 1990)

Sacks, K., "Diodorus and His Sources: Conformity and Creativity," in S. Hornblower (ed.), *Greek Historiography* (Oxford: 1994), pp. 213–232

Sawada, N., "Macedonian Social Customs," in J. Roisman and Ian Worthington (eds.), *A Companion to Ancient Macedonia* (Malden: 2010), pp. 392–408

Scherberich, K., *Koinè symmachia. Untersuchungen zum Hellenbund Antigonos III Doson und Philipps V* (Stuttgart: 2009)

Schleussner, B., "Zur Frage der geheimen pergamenisch-makedonischen Kontakte im 3. Makedonischen Krieg," *Historia* 22 (1973), pp. 119–123

Scholten, J.B., *The Politics of Plunder: The Aetolians and Their Koinon in the Early Hellenistic Era, 279–219 B.C.* (Berkeley and Los Angeles: 2000)

Scholten, J.B., "Macedon and the Mainland, 280–221," in A. Erskine (ed.), *A Companion to the Hellenistic World* (Malden: 2003), pp. 134–158

Scuderi, R., "Filippo V e Perseo nei frammenti diodorei," in C. Bearzot and F. Landucci (eds.), *Diodore e l'altra Grecia: Macedonia, Occidente, Ellenismo nella "Biblioteca storica"* (Milan: 2004), pp. 385–405

Scullard, H.H., "Carthage and Rome," in F.W. Walbank, A.E. Astin, M.W. Frederiksen, and R.M. Ogilvie (eds.), *Cambridge Ancient History*[2] 7.2 (Cambridge: 1989), pp. 537–569

Sekunda, N.V., "The Sarissa," *Acta Universitatis Lodziensis, Folia Archaeologica* 23 (2001), pp. 13–41

Sekunda, N.V. "The Macedonian Army," in J. Roisman and Ian Worthington (eds.), *A Companion to Ancient Macedonia* (Malden: 2010), pp. 446–471

Sekunda, N.V., *The Antigonid Army* (Gdansk: 2013)

Sekunda, N.V. and P. Dennis, *The Macedonian Army after Alexander 323–168 BC* (Oxford: 2012)

Shear, T.L., Jr., "The Athenian Agora: Excavations of 1971," *Hesperia* 42 (1973), pp. 121–179

Sherk, R.K., *Roman Documents from the Greek East: Senatus Consulta and Epistulae to the Age of Augustus* (Baltimore: 1969)

Sherk, R.K., *Rome and the Greek East to the Death of Augustus* (Cambridge: 1984)

Sherwin-White, A.N., *Roman Foreign Policy in the East, 168 B.C. to A.D. 1* (Norman: 1984)

Sivignon, M., "The Geographical Setting of Macedonia," in M.B. Sakellariou (ed.), *Macedonia, 4000 Years of Greek History and Civilization* (Athens: 1983), pp. 12–26

Suk Fong Jim, T., "Private Participation in Ruler Cult: Dedications to Philip Soter and Other Hellenistic Kings," *CQ* 67 (2017), pp. 429–443

Tarn, W.W., *Antigonos Gonatas* (Oxford: 1913)

Tarn, W.W., "Philip V and Phthia," *CQ* 18 (1924), pp. 17–23

Tarn, W.W. and G.T. Griffith, *Hellenistic Civilisation*³ (London: 1952)

Taylor, M.J., "The Battle Scene on Amelius Paullus' Pydna Monument: A Reevaluation," *Hesperia* 85 (2016), pp. 559–576

Taylor, R., *The Macedonian Phalanx*: *Equipment, Organization and Tactics from Philip and Alexander to the Roman Conquest* (Barnsley: 2020)

Thomas, C.G., "The Physical Kingdom," in J. Roisman and Ian Worthington (eds.), *A Companion to Ancient Macedonia* (Malden: 2010), pp. 65–80

Touratsoglou, J., "Art in the Hellenistic Period," in M.B. Sakellariou (ed.), *Macedonia: 4000 Years of Greek History and Civilization* (Athens: 1983), pp. 170–191

Toye, D., Porphyry, *BNJ* 260 (Leiden)

Twyman, B.L., "Philip V, Antiochus the Great, the Celts, and Rome," *Ancient Macedonia* 4 (Institute for Balkan Studies, Thessaloniki: 1986), pp. 667–672

Twyman, B.L., "Roman Frontier Strategy and the Destruction of the Antigonid Monarchy," *Ancient Macedonia* 5 (Institute for Balkan Studies, Thessaloniki: 1993), pp. 1649–1656

Vanderspoel, J., "Provincia Macedonia," in J. Roisman and Ian Worthington (eds.), *A Companion to Ancient Macedonia* (Malden: 2010), pp. 251–275

Vanderspoel, J., "Rome's Apparent Disinterest in Macedonia 168–148 BCE," in T. Howe, E.E. Garvin, and G. Wrightson (eds.), *Greece, Macedon, and Persia: Studies in Social, Political, and Military History in Honour of Waldemar Heckel* (Philadelphia: 2015), pp. 198–206

Vokotopoulou, J., A. Despinis, D. Misailidou, and M. Tiverios, *Sindos: Katalogos tes ektheses* (Thessaloniki: 1985)

Walbank, F.W., "*Philippos Tragoidoumenos*: A Polybian Experiment," *JHS* 58 (1938), pp. 55–68

Walbank, F.W., *Philip V of Macedon* (Cambridge: 1940)

Walbank, F.W., "A Note on the Embassy of Q. Marcius Philippus," *JRS* 31 (1941), pp. 82–93

Walbank, F.W., *A Historical Commentary on Polybius* 1–3 (Oxford: 1957, 1967, 1979)

Walbank, F.W., "Polybius and Rome's Eastern Policy," *JRS* 53 (1963), pp. 1–13

Walbank, F.W., "Polybius and Macedonia," *Ancient Macedonia* 1 (Institute for Balkan Studies, Thessaloniki: 1970), pp. 91–106

Walbank, F.W., *Polybius* (Berkeley and Los Angeles: 1972)

Walbank, F.W., "The Causes of the Third Macedonian War: Some Recent Views," *Ancient Macedonia* 2 (Institute for Balkan Studies, Thessaloniki: 1977), pp. 81–94.

Walbank, F.W., "Sea-Power and the Antigonids," in W.L. Adams and E.N. Borza (eds.), *Philip II, Alexander the Great, and the Macedonian Heritage* (Washington: 1982), pp. 213–236

Walbank, F.W., "H ton olon elpis' and the Antigonids," in *Ancient Macedonia* 3 (Institute for Balkan Studies, Thessaloniki: 1983), pp. 1721–1730

Walbank, F.W., "Macedonia and the Greek Leagues," in F.W. Walbank, A.E. Astin, M.W. Frederiksen, and R.M. Ogilvie (eds.), *Cambridge Ancient History*[2] 7.1 (Cambridge: 1984a), pp. 446–481

Walbank, F.W., "Monarchies and Monarchic Ideas," in F.W. Walbank, A.E. Astin, M.W. Frederiksen, and R.M. Ogilvie (eds.), *Cambridge Ancient History*[2] 7.1 (Cambridge: 1984b), pp. 62–100

Walbank, F.W., "Macedonia and Greece," in F.W. Walbank, A.E. Astin, M.W. Frederiksen, and R.M. Ogilvie (eds.), *Cambridge Ancient History*[2] 7.1 (Cambridge: 1984c), pp. 221–256

Walbank, F.W., *Selected Papers: Studies in Greek and Roman History and Historiography* (Cambridge: 1985)

Walbank, F.W., "Supernatural Paraphernalia in Polybius' *Histories*," in Ian Worthington (ed.), *Ventures into Greek History. Essays in Honour of N.G.L. Hammond* (Oxford: 1994), pp. 28–42.

Walbank, F.W., "Hellenes and Achaeans: 'Greek Nationality' Revisited," in P. Flensted-Jensen (ed.), *Further Studies in the Ancient Greek Polis* (Stuttgart: 2000), pp. 19–33

Walbank, F.W., *Polybius, Rome and the Hellenistic World: Essays and Reflections* (Cambridge: 2002)

Walsh, J.J., "The Disorders of the 170s B.C. and Roman Intervention in the Class Struggle in Greece," *CQ* 50 (2000), pp. 300–303

Walsh, P.G., *Livy: His Historical Aims and Methods* (Cambridge: 1961)

Warrior, V.M., "Livy, Book 42: Structure and Chronology," *AJAH* 6 (1981) [1983], pp. 1–50

Warrior, V.M., *The Initiation of the Second Macedonian War* (Wiesbaden: 1996)

Waterfield, R., *Dividing the Spoils: The War for Alexander the Great's Empire* (Oxford: 2011)

Waterfield, R., *Taken at the Flood: The Roman Conquest of Greece* (New York: 2014)

Waterfield, R., *The Making of a King: Antigonus Gonatas of Macedon and the Greeks* (Chicago: 2021)

Welles, C.B., "New Texts from the Chancery of Philip V of Macedon and the Problem of the 'Diagramma,'" *AJA* 42 (1938), pp. 245–260

Werner, R., "Quellenkritische Bemerkungen zu den Ursachen des Perseukrieges," *Grazer Beiträge* 6 (1977), pp. 149–216

Wheatley, P. and C. Dunn, *Demetrius the Besieger* (New York: 2020)

Wilkes, J., *The Illyrians* (Oxford: 1995)

Will, E., "The Succession to Alexander," in F.W. Walbank, A.E. Astin, M.W. Frederiksen, and R.M. Ogilvie (eds.), *Cambridge Ancient History*[2] 7.1 (Cambridge: 1984a), pp. 23–61

Will, E., "The Formation of the Hellenistic Kingdoms," in F.W. Walbank, A.E. Astin, M.W. Frederiksen, and R.M. Ogilvie (eds.), *Cambridge Ancient History*[2] 7.1 (Cambridge: 1984b), pp. 101–117

Wiseman, D.J., "Hoplite Warfare," in J. Hackett (ed.), *Warfare in the Ancient World* (New York: 1989), pp. 54–81

Witt, R., "The Egyptian Cults in Ancient Macedonia," *Ancient Macedonia* 1 (Institute for Balkan Studies, Thessaloniki: 1970), pp. 324–333

Worthington, Ian, *Philip II of Macedonia* (New Haven and London: 2008)

Worthington, Ian, *By the Spear: Philip II, Alexander the Great, and the Rise and Fall of the Macedonian Empire* (New York: 2014)

Worthington, Ian, *Ptolemy I: King and Pharaoh of Egypt* (New York: 2016a)

Worthington, Ian, "Ptolemy I as *Soter*: The Silence of Epigraphy and the Case for Egypt," *ZPE* 198 (2016b), pp. 128–130

Worthington, Ian, *Athens after Empire: A History from Alexander the Great to the Emperor Hadrian* (New York: 2021a)

Worthington, Ian, "The Date of the Athenian-Roman *Foedus*," *Klio* 103 (2021b), pp. 90–96

Xydopoulos, I.K., "Upper Macedonia," in M. Tiverios, P. Nigdelis, and P. Adam-Veleni (eds.), *Threpteria: Studies on Ancient Macedonia* (Thessaloniki: 2012), pp. 520–539

Yardley, J.C., *Justin and Trogus: A Study of the Language of Justin's Epitome of Trogus* (Toronto: 2003)

Index